MW01705489

Contradictory Impulses

Edited by Greg Donaghy
and Patricia E. Roy

Contradictory Impulses
Canada and Japan in the Twentieth Century

UBCPress · Vancouver · Toronto

© UBC Press 2008

All rights reserved. No part of this publication may be reproduced, stored in a retrieval system, or transmitted, in any form or by any means, without prior written permission of the publisher, or, in Canada, in the case of photocopying or other reprographic copying, a licence from Access Copyright (Canadian Copyright Licensing Agency), www.accesscopyright.ca.

17 16 15 14 13 12 11 10 09 08 5 4 3 2 1

Printed in Canada on ancient-forest-free paper (100% post-consumer recycled) that is processed chlorine- and acid-free, with vegetable-based inks.

Library and Archives Canada Cataloguing in Publication

Contradictory impulses: Canada and Japan in the twentieth century / edited by Greg Donaghy and Patricia E. Roy.

Includes bibliographical references and index.
ISBN 978-0-7748-1443-0 (bound); ISBN 978-0-7748-1444-7 (pbk.)

1. Canada – Foreign relations – Japan. 2. Japan – Foreign relations – Canada. I. Donaghy, Greg. II. Roy, Patricia, 1939-

FC251.J3C66 2008 327.71052 C2008-900647-X

Canada

UBC Press gratefully acknowledges the financial support for our publishing program of the Government of Canada through the Book Publishing Industry Development Program (BPIDP), and of the Canada Council for the Arts, and the British Columbia Arts Council.

This book has been published with the help of a grant from the Canadian Federation for the Humanities and Social Sciences, through the Aid to Scholarly Publications Programme, using funds provided by the Social Sciences and Humanities Research Council of Canada.

UBC Press
The University of British Columbia
2029 West Mall
Vancouver, BC V6T 1Z2
604-822-5959 / Fax 604-822-6083
www.ubcpress.ca

For Michael and Maureen Donaghy

Contents

Figures and Tables

Figures

Tables

Acknowledgments

This book was made possible through the active support of a number of individuals and organizations. The Department of Foreign Affairs and International Trade and the University of Victoria encouraged the editors to pursue this project from the start. Robert Desjardins, former director of the Japan division; Victoria Jull, Japan desk officer; Jean Labrie, head of the department's Canadian Studies programme; and his colleague, Caroline Laplante, generously provided the funding that made it possible for the contributors to share their research in a conference in September 2004 marking the seventy-fifth anniversary of Canada-Japan diplomatic relations. Additional funding was provided by the University of Victoria and the Canadian Committee for the History of the Second World War.

Other Canadians with a profound interest in Canada-Japan relations were also very helpful. Joe Kess, who recently retired from the Centre for Asian Studies at the University of Victoria after a long and distinguished career, graciously allowed us to combine our conference with his own gathering of the Japan Studies Association of Canada. His assistant, Stella Chan, cheerfully and efficiently handled the extra administrative burden that our presence generated. The success of our sessions was in no small measure due to the lively and challenging role played by our five chairs: Midge Ayukawa, Donald W. Campbell, Stephen Koerner, Anne Park Shannon, and Fr. Mako Watanabe. We thank them wholeheartedly.

Gratefully, we would also like to acknowledge the help and encouragement of Roger Bélanger, Richard Bingham, John Clearwater, Julia Gualtieri, Mary Halloran, Stephen Heeney, John Hilliker, Norman Hillmer, Bruce Muirhead, and Ryan Touhey.

Last, but not least, we must thank our editors – Emily Andrew and Camilla Blakely – and their associates at UBC Press for their care and attention to the manuscript.

Contradictory Impulses

Introduction

Greg Donaghy and Patricia E. Roy

For most of the past two decades, Japan has been one of Canada's most important economic and political partners. In 2004, it was Canada's second most important export market and the fourth greatest source of imports.[1] Japanese investments in Canada total over $10.5 billion, ranking Japan fifth among foreign investors, and it is the ninth most important destination for Canadian investment abroad.[2] Politically, Canadian and Japanese leaders are closely allied through shared membership in the G8, while Canada's diplomatic presence in Japan is its third largest in Asia.

Despite the importance of this trans-Pacific relationship, scholars in neither country have yet developed an accessible overview of Canada-Japan relations. Instead, comfortably confined within their own areas of specialization, students of the relationship have tended to work in relative isolation on narrow topics within limited time periods.[3] Thus, there is an extensive literature on Canadian Protestant but not Catholic missionaries in Japan; on Japanese immigration and the treatment of Japanese Canadians during the Second World War, but little on political-security relations from 1914 to 1939. Similarly, there are scholarly debates on the unhappy career of Herbert Norman, the alleged communist-turned-Canadian-diplomat, but almost no archivally based work on relations since 1945. The narrow focus of the historiography often obscures enduring and broad themes in the Canada-Japan relationship, thus reinforcing the tendency of foreign policy scholars to emphasize Canada's relations with the Atlantic world.[4] This book attempts to restore some balance to the literature on Canada's place in the world and contends that Canadians and their governments have long had a world view that includes Asia, the Pacific, and Japan. Though the individual authors within this volume may sometimes differ, together their contributions trace the evolution of an important bilateral relationship that, while often characterized by contradiction and uncertainty, has matured in fits and starts over the past century.

Canadians have always been conscious and proud of their status as a Pacific nation, but their early efforts to develop a role in that region were hindered by the contradictory impulses shaping their approach. For more than half a century, racist restrictions curtailed immigration from Japan, even as Canadian traders, diplomats, and missionaries manoeuvred for access to the fabled wealth (measured in dollars or souls) of the Orient. Until the expiry of the Anglo-Japanese alliance in 1921, Canadians, who feted the Japanese as the "British of Asia," relied on Japan to protect their western coast, while simultaneously fearing Tokyo's imperial ambitions.

Though racial antipathy often characterized early Canadian attitudes towards the Japanese, Canada's relations with Japan in the late nineteenth and early twentieth centuries were more complex and warmer than is commonly acknowledged. Many Canadians admired the Empire of the Rising Sun for its rapid and orderly drive towards modernization and cheered heartily when the Anglo-Japanese treaty of 1902 formally allied Japan and the British Empire, of which Canada was then a part. The *Ottawa Evening Journal* praised the new alliance as "an extraordinary mark in history," while Prime Minister Wilfrid Laurier described it as "one of the happy events of this century."[5]

As Laurier acknowledged implicitly, Canada's relations with Japan were already constrained by the influences of its two closest and much more powerful allies, Britain and the United States. The Asian preoccupations of these major powers, particularly China's expanding role throughout the Pacific, form much of the backdrop for the evolution of the Canada-Japan relationship during the twentieth century. Even so, what Canada lacked in military and economic strength could be offset to some extent by "soft power." In defining this concept, the American political scientist Joseph Nye states that countries can sometimes achieve their foreign policy objectives "through attraction rather than through coercion,"[6] by projecting their values abroad to cultivate relations with foreign civil society "so that they want what you want."[7] Protestant and Catholic missionary activities, underwritten financially and spiritually by a youthful Canada searching for a way to make its mark on the world, were an exercise in "soft power" par excellence.

There were undoubted differences in emphasis between English-speaking Protestant missionaries, rooted in Ontario, and French-speaking Catholic missionaries, drawn largely from Quebec. Protestants were quicker to address Japanese social problems than Catholics, who placed greater emphasis on spiritual objectives. There were chronological distinctions too: Protestant missionaries flourished before 1941, while Catholics, who started slightly later, continued to arrive in strength through the 1950s. They were geographically distinct as well, with Protestant missions cutting a swath through central Japan, while their Catholic competitors clustered close to the major cities along the coast (see Figure 1.3).

The similarities, however, were far more striking. Both sets of missionaries were starry-eyed at the prospect of converting the Japanese masses and saving a "million souls for Christ." Neither made many converts, though both made other contributions to Japan in the fields of education (especially of girls and women), social work, medical care, and scholarship. More important, priests and ministers alike participated vigorously in discussions at home on the meaning of social and political developments in Japan, and on bilateral relations, frequently becoming influential, if sometimes misguided, interpreters of Japan to Canadians.

Canada's imperial links played an important role in shaping early encounters between Canadian and Japanese citizens. The Japanese sponsor of a shady scheme to land undocumented Japanese immigrants along the British Columbia coast in 1906 escaped serious penalty for violating Canadian customs and immigration laws partly because of Japan's close ties with imperial Britain. Yet, relations with Japan were increasingly complicated by Canada's growing attachment to the emerging American empire. As British Columbians' antipathy to the Japanese rose with an influx of immigrants in 1907, they borrowed an American idea and formed an Asiatic Exclusion League. Its activities helped spark Vancouver's anti-Asian riot of 1907, which led to tighter restrictions on immigration from Japan. Those restrictions did not end opposition to Japanese immigration in British Columbia, but they did cause lingering resentment in Japan.

That riot helped shape official attitudes towards Japan and drew attention to Canada's place in the Pacific. By the early 1920s, Canada's military viewed Imperial Japan with a new sense of foreboding, a sentiment that reinforced racial stereotypes and contradicted the more positive images of Japan promoted by missionaries. As Canada's small professional military became increasingly sophisticated, it abandoned its farcical notions of a Japanese invasion in favour of a realistic analysis that stressed the dangers to Canada of unbridled competition between the United States and Japan in the Pacific. Then, as now, Washington feared that a weak Canada threatened its own borders, and Canadian military leaders insisted that if Canadians could not (or would not) defend their shores, Americans would. This was a compelling argument, and when Mackenzie King's government authorized a modest expansion of the navy in the late 1920s, it was acting more in response to US stimuli than to any fear of the Japanese.

Even as some Canadians viewed Japan and the Pacific as a source of danger, Canada was still drawn towards Japan. Like many Canadians, Prime Minister Laurier was inspired by what one historian of the early economic relationship has called "the myth of the Japan market."[8] He sent a trade commissioner on a reconnaissance mission to Japan in 1897 and established a commercial agency in Yokohama in 1904.[9] Trade with Japan grew slowly – over the next decade, total trade averaged less than $2.5 million annually,

Table I.1

Canadian trade with Japan, 1870-1929 (Cdn$)

Year	Exports to Japan	Imports from Japan
1870	1,000	311,000
1880	26,891	542,972
1890	26,825	1,258,763
1900	110,735	1,751,415
1910	659,118	1,673,542
1920	7,732,514	13,637,287
1929	42,100,000	12,921,000

Source: Klaus H. Pringsheim, *Neighbors across the Pacific: The Development of Economic and Political Relations between Canada and Japan* (Westport, CT: Greenwood, 1983), 24.

with the balance consistently in Japan's favour (see Table I.1). In exchange for pottery, silk, toys, and tea, Japan's main exports across the Pacific, Canada shipped salt fish and the occasional boatload of coal and lumber.[10]

Prime Minister W.L. Mackenzie King was also attracted to Japan, encouraged in part by the rapid shift in the early 1920s in the terms of trade. Japan's poor crops in 1921-23 and the lumber required to rebuild after the Kanto earthquake of 1923 boosted sales of Canadian wheat, flour, and lumber. Japan's industrial expansion during the 1920s added a new market for Canadian metals. "It is true," boasted Mackenzie King in 1928, "that our trade with the Orient today is greater than was the trade of Canada with the United Kingdom at the time the government of Sir Wilfrid Laurier came into office."[11] The following year, Canada opened its third overseas diplomatic legation in Tokyo, in a fine neo-colonial building built by the first minister, Liberal Party bagman and Montreal financier, Sir Herbert Marler. King's motives were complex and contradictory; in addition to promoting trade, the new mission was intended to administer the regulations designed to curtail Japanese immigration and demonstrate Ottawa's growing diplomatic autonomy.

The contradictions defining the relationship intensified in the 1930s when Japan's military leaders seized Manchuria, and then parts of China, their dangerous adventures fuelled by copper, nickel, and other vital minerals exported from Canada. In many parts of Canada, these tensions sparked a long and public debate over the nature and value of the country's ties with Tokyo. Often uncertain about how to respond to these pressures, Ottawa looked timidly to London and Washington for guidance.

This preoccupation with American and British policy in Asia shaped Canadian defence policy in the Far East in the late 1930s and into the Second World War. The government's emphasis on home defence after the Japanese attacks on the US base at Pearl Harbor in December 1941 reflected this established policy while meeting western Canada's demands for protection. Domestic considerations also influenced the government's unfortunate decision to remove Japanese Canadians from the West Coast. Though support for this policy was widespread, it was by no means universal, a point explored in Greg Robinson's pioneering examination of the Japanese-Canadian experience in Quebec. Many Quebecers shed their pre-war anti-Japanese prejudices and graciously made room for the small Japanese-Canadian community that developed in wartime Montreal.

The war in the Pacific was not a Canadian priority. Though Canadian forces joined the Americans in the assault on the Aleutians in 1943, Mackenzie King's government resisted the extravagant demands of its military advisors to become more deeply involved in the final phase of the war against Japan. It soon became clear that the consolidation of US power in Asia left little room for Canadian initiative. US unilateralism, the bitterness that accompanied the removal of Japanese Canadians from the West Coast, and the mistreatment of Canadian prisoners of war ended Canada's ambivalent flirtation with Japan for almost a generation.

The United States looms large in Canada's postwar relationship with Japan. As Washington tightened its Cold War hold on Asia, L.B. "Mike" Pearson, deputy minister and then minister of external affairs, sought to minimize potential disagreements with Canada's closest ally. Pearson largely dismissed the concerns of Canada's top Japanese specialist, the controversial diplomat Herbert Norman, about Allied occupation policy and the 1951 Japanese peace treaty and lined up solidly behind the United States. As a result, Canada increasingly confined its postwar interests in Japan to concrete issues such as fisheries and trade. Over the next two decades, such parochial interests defined bilateral relations, which expanded slowly and fitfully. The conclusion of a limited trade agreement in 1954 and the creation of the Canada-Japan Ministerial Committee in 1961 – the two highlights of the period – underscored how slight the relationship remained.

Nevertheless, by the early 1960s, relations were changing again, as Ottawa faced growing pressure to liberalize Canada's restrictive immigration requirements and remove the colour bar. The demand for action was partly driven by the growing domestic and international revulsion against racism that followed Nazi Germany's defeat in 1945. The confrontation with the totalitarian Soviet Union placed a further premium on democratic human rights. Ottawa's motives were also practical. During the early stages of the Cold War, Canada was reluctant to do anything that might encourage Japan to turn against the West. In addition, Japanese Canadians became skilled political operatives and generated considerable public support for their cause, a campaign that was undoubtedly helped by Japan's rising economic fortunes.

The removal of racial immigration restrictions clearly eliminated a major bilateral irritant. At the same time, the advent of cheap jet travel in the

1960s made it easier than ever for inhabitants of the two countries to visit each other. Before 1941, few Canadians and even fewer Japanese could afford the time or the money for trans-Pacific tourism, but that changed during the 1960s. While only slightly more than 5,000 Canadians visited Japan in 1960, by the end of the decade their number had increased to almost 17,000 annually. In the two decades after the war, the low value of the yen and currency restrictions made overseas vacations almost impossible for Japanese. With an improving economy, Japan eased currency travel restrictions in 1964, making overseas travel easier for its citizens. Though only 400 or so Japanese visited Canada in 1960, the numbers soared in the latter half of the decade. Expo '67 drew much attention and almost 19,000 Japanese tourists to Canada.[12]

Ottawa and Tokyo acknowledged the importance of tourism as a source for closer relations, and it figured in the Framework for Economic Cooperation they signed in 1976. A Canadian government travel agency worked hard in Japan to convince potential tourists that Canada was more than the Rocky Mountains, a popular image in school geography texts and travel brochures.[13] However, economic realities, not advertising, were more responsible for increased travel to Canada. After Japan agreed in 1985 to allow the yen to rise in value to reduce its trade surplus, Japanese tourism soared. By 1992, the Canadian dollar, which cost 213 yen in 1985, was worth only 104 yen.[14] Moreover, to reduce its surplus, the Japanese government encouraged its citizens to travel abroad by easing restrictions on school trips, making passports more accessible, increasing the duty-free allowance, and offering tax concessions for business travel. Dealing specifically with Canada, Tokyo introduced a Two Way Tourism Program in 1991, whose goal was to see two million visits across the Pacific per year with 1.5 million arriving from Japan and half a million Canadians going there.[15] Though the collapse of the Japanese "bubble economy" and a low Canadian dollar made this an impossible target, the Canada-Japan Tourist Conference still called for "aggressive efforts" to send 200,000 Canadian visitors to Japan and 800,000 Japanese to Canada in 2004. For Japanese tourists, the Rockies and nearby Calgary and Vancouver remained the most popular destinations, followed by Niagara Falls and Toronto.[16] Despite the legendary fame of Anne of Green Gables, whose story figured in translation on the Japanese school curriculum, only 13,600 of the 391,000 Japanese who visited Canada in 2004 ventured as far east as Prince Edward Island, Anne's home. That year, 161,000 Canadians went to Japan.[17]

Though there is now more contact than ever before between the two countries, just how much Canada's relationship with Japan has changed since the mid-1960s remains unclear. This is the subject of vigorous debate in the final chapters of this volume. According to Carin Holroyd, the answer is, not much. While British Columbians (and other Canadians) welcomed

Japanese investments in the 1960s that they would have denounced as treasonous just a few decades earlier, Holroyd argues that Canadians remained uninterested in Japan and reluctant to exploit the relationship's potential. As a result, Japanese investors were able to maintain a low profile as they purchased an important stake in Canada's natural resource industries before moving into the manufacturing sector in the 1970s. Dangling promises of future investments, Japanese investors played local, regional, and provincial interests in Canada against each another. These astute tactics, combined with Canada's unhealthy preoccupation with the American market, inhibited Canadian efforts to craft a strategic response to Japanese investment and reinforced Canada's traditional dependence on the resource trade. The result, Holroyd concludes, is a partnership of diminishing returns as Tokyo seeks out new partners in other countries that are more interested in a developed relationship.

Others reject these dismal conclusions and argue, with varying degrees of forcefulness, that Canadians have indeed come to recognize Japan's importance. Greg Donaghy contends that Prime Minister Pierre Trudeau, in his Japan initiative, was anxious to interest Tokyo in a deeper and more political relationship. Unhappy with the emphasis that Canada's postwar foreign policy had placed on relations with North Atlantic countries and the United States, Trudeau embraced Japan as a possible counterweight. But contradictory impulses, centred on the United States, were at work. While the prime minister's initiative was welcomed in Tokyo, where policy makers were also anxious to seek new diplomatic partners, the bureaucratic mavens in Ottawa, who had a profound stake in the existing order, resisted it. Without a sustained government-wide effort to alter the postwar pattern of Canadian commerce, it proved impossible to wean Canadian exporters from the vast and familiar market of the United States.

Despite their different assessments of Canadian awareness of Japan, Donaghy and Holroyd agree that Canada's recent efforts to engage Japan have been overwhelmed by the contradictory attractions of its great-power partner, the United States. Political scientist John Kirton, in contrast, finds a much different and more constructive role for the United States in contemporary Canada-Japan relations. In his view, the process started by Trudeau was revived under Conservative Prime Minister Brian Mulroney in the 1980s as both Canada and Japan, by pursuing closer relations with Washington, created a dynamic "North Pacific triangle" centred on the United States. The economic and political challenge represented by a resurgent post-Cold War United States drew its two partners more closely together than ever before. This rapprochement was partly based on the deepening trade and financial relationship that developed as Canada and Japan weathered the forces of globalization and trade liberalization in the late 1980s and 1990s. More important, closer bilateral relations were forged by a new set of international linkages – the G8, the Group of 20, and the Association of Southeast Asian Nations (ASEAN) – aided by the willingness of political leaders in both Canada and Japan to recognize the growing importance of the bilateral relationship. In short, Kirton contends, systemic, summit-level forces compelled Canada and Japan to begin to deal with each other in new, more profound ways as the twentieth century ended.

Kirton, however, is almost alone among Canadian observers in his uncritical description of a robust contemporary Canada-Japan partnership.[18] The Canada-Japan Forum, a consultative non-governmental organization, recently echoed the statement made in January 2005 by the prime ministers of the two nations, that "co-operation has yet to reach its full potential," pointing to a "lack of attention on both sides."[19] Certainly, Prime Minister Stephen Harper's decision in January 2007 to close two consular posts – in Osaka and Fukuoka – while his government searches for a more active and global diplomacy centred on closer relations with the United States, strongly suggests that the old contradictory impulses continue to shape Canada-Japan relations. Indeed, the persistence of these contradictory impulses was neatly captured in the architecture of Canada's new embassy in Tokyo. The gleaming postmodern structure that architect Raymond Moriyama erected in the 1990s contrasts favourably with the derivative architecture of Canada's first mission in Tokyo, the diplomatic enclave built by Marler in the 1930s. His neo-colonialism has been replaced with a mature Canadian sensibility that is reflected in the new embassy's embrace of Japanese influences, its generous display of Canadian art, and its emphasis on cultural diplomacy. At the same time, the new embassy's design reflects some historic themes. Its fusion of Canadian and Japanese elements, representing the deepening and broadening of bilateral relations, is overwhelmed by its commercial elements, which evoke the same haunting myth of vast Oriental riches that attracted Canadian missionaries and traders a century ago.

Canada's relations with Japan have changed profoundly over the past century, though probably not as much as its partisans might wish. Always a Pacific presence, Canada's early efforts to discover Japan were complicated by the contradictory impulses that shaped its view of Tokyo. The aspirations of missionaries and traders were burdened with harmful restrictions on Japanese immigration and well-founded apprehensions about the diplomatic and military challenges of Asia. These tentative Canadian forays into Japan ended with the outbreak of the Pacific war in 1941, a conflict that cast a long shadow over bilateral relations, which did not begin to recover until the mid-1970s. Canada has since tried to engage Japan with a modest amount of success, but has too frequently been drawn aside by echoes of the historic impulse that continues to pull Canada and Canadians southward. Even so, as the closing essays in this volume demonstrate, the two countries' political, economic, and diplomatic interests are more closely aligned and entwined in a web of reinforcing cultural and social ties than ever before, raising the prospect of closer relations yet to come.

Notes

1 Global Trade Information Services World Trade Atlas, Canada Edition, Trade data, accessed 2 September 2005.

2 Investment data retrieved from http://www.dfait-maeci.gc.ca/eet/cimt/2004/CIIP04-en.asp, accessed 2 September 2005.

3 The existing literature on the relationship is discussed extensively in the "Suggested Reading" section at the end of this book.

4 Despite the obvious importance of the Asia-Pacific region, especially since the mid-1970s, many Canadian historians still overlook it. See, for example, Norman Hillmer and J.L. Granatstein, *Empire to Umpire: Canada and the World to the 1990s* (Toronto: Irwin Publishing, 2000). See also the 600-page collection edited by Patrick James, Nelson Michaud, and Mark J. O'Reilly, *Handbook of Canadian Foreign Policy* (Lanham, MD: Lexington Books, 2006), which contains essays on Europe, the United States, the Middle East, Latin America, and la francophonie, but nothing on Asia.

5 "Britain and Japan," *Ottawa Evening Journal,* 15 February 1902; Laurier quoted in the minutes of the 111th meeting of the Committee of Imperial Defence, Committee of Imperial Defence Records, Minutes and Memoranda, 26 May 1911, CAB38/18, National Archives at Kew.

6 Joseph S. Nye Jr., *The Paradox of American Power* (New York: Oxford University Press, 2002), 9.

7 Joseph Nye, "Soft Power: The Means to Success in World Politics," Address to the Carnegie Council Books for Breakfast Program, 13 April 2004, http://www.cceia.org/resources/transcripts/4466.html, accessed 7 July 2006.

8 Robert J. Gowen, "Canada and the Myth of the Japanese Market, 1896-1911," *Pacific Historical Review* 39, 1 (1970): 63-83.

9 The chequered history of the trade commission in Japan is traced briefly in O. Mary Hill, *Canada's Salesman to the World: The Department of Trade and Commerce* (Montréal and Kingston: McGill-Queen's University Press, 1977), *passim.*

10 Patricia Roy, "Has Canada Made a Difference? North Pacific Connections: Canada, China, and Japan," in *Making a Difference? Canada's Foreign Policy in a Changing World Order,* ed. John English and Norman Hillmer (Toronto: Lester Publishing, 1992), 131; Klaus H. Pringsheim, *Neighbors across the Pacific: The Development of Economic and Political Relations between Canada and Japan* (Westport, CT: Greenwood, 1983), 22.

11 Walter A. Riddell, ed., *Documents on Canadian Foreign Policy, 1917-1939* (Toronto, 1962), 281.

12 These statistics are drawn from Pringsheim, Neighbors across the Pacific, 213.

13 Tom Waldichuk, "Japanese Travel Brochure Images of Canada and the Promotion of Japanese Tourism in Canada," in *Why Japan Matters!* ed. Joseph F. Kess and Helen Lansdowne, 218-26 (Victoria: Centre for Asia-Pacific Initiatives, 2005).

14 Martin Thornell and Klaus H. Pringsheim, *Japanese Travel to Canada* (Ottawa: Canada-Japan Trade Council, 1993).

15 Canadian Tourism Commission. *Japan: Canadian Highlights Report: Pleasure Travel Markets to North America* (Ottawa: Coopers and Lybrand for Canadian Tourism Commission, 1996).

16 Waldichuk, "Japanese Travel Images," 223.

17 *Economic Impact: Tourism 2004: Final Report* (Charlottetown: Tourism PEI, 2005), 35. http://www.gov.pe.ca/photos/original/tourism_ecimp04.pdf, accessed 16 June 2006; Canadian Tourism Stats and Figures, 2004, http://www.CanadaTourism.com, posted 23 January 2006, accessed 15 June 2006.

18 Kirton's critics are legion and are identified in the "Suggested Reading" section at the end of this book.

19 Canada-Japan Forum, *Report of the Canada-Japan Forum 2003-2006* (June 2006), http://www.mofa.go.jp/region/n-america/canada/report0606.pdf.

1

Soul Searchers and Soft Power: The Canadian Protestant Missionary Movement in Japan, 1873-1951

Hamish Ion

> No nation with a nationalistic background and with a long history of militarism can ever become a peacemaker until it becomes Christian through and through. We hear talk to-day about Japan becoming a second Sweden – a peace-loving democracy – but it can become that only if it becomes Christian.
>
> A.R. "Alf" Stone, United Church of Canada missionary, 20 August 1946[1]

Wind and steam brought Commodore Matthew Perry and the black ships of the United States Navy to Japan in 1853 to open the country to Western intercourse. The Sheffield steel guns of the Royal Navy and the presence of British and French garrisons in Yokohama until 1875 guaranteed Western access to the treaty ports of Japan before and after the Meiji Restoration of 1868.[2] As part of the British Empire, which had extensive interests in Pacific affairs, Canadians were delighted to join the Great Powers in their discovery of Japan and to become a vital link in the all-red route that joined Britain to Asia and challenged the American hold over trans-Pacific trade. From 1891 until the start of the Pacific War in 1941, Canadian Pacific (CP) White Empress liners carried mail, cargo, and tourists from Vancouver to the magical Far East. In return, they brought Asian immigrants and exotic fabrics that high speed "silk trains" rushed to the fashion bazaars of Montreal, London, and Paris. While CP posters might have exaggerated the world of enchantment waiting in Asia, a mere twenty-one days from Europe, they captured the novel sense of grand adventure that accompanied the development of this link across the Pacific.[3]

From the beginning, then, the activities and interests of the major Pacific powers have shaped Canada's relations with Japan. But another competing theme has also animated bilateral relations for much of the past century.

Figure 1.1 "Empress of Japan." The allure of the Far East is reflected in this poster advertising the Canadian Pacific's service to the Pacific. *Courtesy of Canadian Pacific Railway Archives, A6207.*

Though Canada has never been able to marshal the military assets or economic might of the larger powers, Canadians have sought to exert an influence in Japan through other means, using what the contemporary American international relations theorist, Joseph Nye, refers to as "soft power." In Nye's view, states can often achieve their foreign policy goals more effectively "through attraction rather than coercion," through a network of coalitions that extend beyond traditional state-to-state relationships to embrace academics, non-governmental organizations, business people, and other members of civil society.[4] In this book, Masako Iino's concluding reflections on the projection of Canadian values through Canadian Studies in Japan and Marie-Josée Therrien's chapter on the cultural exchanges involved in building Canada's missions in Tokyo are classic examples. Canada's use of soft power might even include its growing capacity to build a values-based partnership with Japan within the G7/8, as described in this volume by John Kirton. But the concept of soft power can be applied more broadly, helping us understand the impact and significance of Canadian missionary activities in Japan, beginning in the last century.

Christianity, the religion of most Canadians at least until the latter part of the twentieth century, is a soft power, and it was part of an arsenal of governmental, parliamentary, legal, cultural, and sporting institutions that projected the "civilizing" mission of Canada. The major denominations of Canadian missionaries in Japan – Methodists[5] (after 1925, United Church of Canada), Anglicans[6], and Roman Catholics – used soft power and moral suasion rather than military force or economic power in their attempts to convince Japanese of the benefits of a Canadian style of Western civilization. The establishment of overseas missions soon after Confederation was an early sign that Canadians believed that Canada could play an international role.[7] This chapter and the following one on Catholic missionaries deal with this trans-Pacific religious endeavour, a symbol of the desire of Canadian Christians to share their religious ideas and so improve the physical and spiritual well-being of the Japanese people.

Canadian missionaries engaged in evangelistic work and built churches; they also erected schools, created social welfare centres, and conducted specialized medical work. In doing so, they and their constituents at home learned much about Japan and the Japanese. More than other connections, the missionary movement laid a broadly based foundation of goodwill between the two countries at the person-to-person level long before the two nations established diplomatic relations. The importance of these linkages is reflected in the enormous canon of primary and secondary literature in English and Japanese on Canadian missionaries.[8]

Through reports published in church magazines and journals, and letters to Sunday school classes, the missionaries served as respected interpreters of Japan to the Christian community in Canada. Unfortunately, they did not always distinguish between their genuine sympathy and affection for Japanese people and the motives of Japan's political and military leaders in handling the East Asian crisis and the war in China. In Canada, this difficulty eroded the missionaries' position. In Japan, with the rise of *tenno*-centred (emperor-centred) militarism, missionaries failed to inculcate western democratic values, were isolated from Japanese Christianity, and were forced to leave the country in 1940. After the Second World War, with the development of greater intergovernmental and economic ties and the increased secularization of Canada, missionaries became less prominent in explaining Japan to Canada and in transmitting Western values to Japan. Their successors are the many Canadians who have gone to rural Japan with the Japan Exchange and Teaching (JET) Programme.

Missionaries and the Rhythm of Their Lives

Even though many missionaries spent their whole working lives in Japan, they remained Canadian in their lifestyle, habits, and outlook. Missionaries were drawn from Anglo-Canadian families largely from rural Ontario; a smaller number were from Quebec, the Maritimes, or Manitoba. All of them saw overseas missionary work as a means of gaining freedom from the penury of the farm and securing upward mobility for themselves and their families. Ernest Bott, a United Church missionary, who did outstanding relief work during the Allied occupation of Japan, exemplified this trend. Bott belonged to a generation of small-town Ontarians who had served in the First World War or had family members who had done so. Christian service overseas enabled them to exercise their deep compassion and sympathy for the less fortunate, which had been engendered by the horrors of war.

For single women, missionary work in Japan provided an opportunity to exchange the prison of marriage or the torment of rural school teaching for a fulfilling life teaching under more favourable conditions and serving the church amidst exotic surroundings. Undoubtedly, this was why educational work attracted so many Canadian women, who formed the majority of Canadian missionaries at the beginning of the twentieth century, and why they founded so many schools. In 1884, Martha Cartmell founded the Tōyō Eiwa Jo Gakkō in Toriizaka, Tokyo; Mary Cunningham from Halifax founded the Shizuoka Eiwa Jo Gakkō in 1889; and Agnes Wintemute established the Yamanshi Eiwa Jo Gakkō in the same year in Kofu.[9] These schools, created to provide Christian education for girls, continue to thrive. Canadian Methodists also participated in the formation, in 1918, of the Tokyo Woman's Christian College, which was formed by several Protestant denominations (Tokyo Joshi Daigaku), with Nitobe Inazō as its first principal. The Canadian Anglican Loretta Shaw[10] was a long-time teacher at the Poole Memorial School for girls in Osaka. Mary Chappell, who was born in Japan, taught for many years at the prestigious Tsuda Juku Daigaku in Tokyo, while her twin sister, Constance Chappell, a United Church of Canada missionary, taught at Tokyo Woman's Christian College. These are only examples of a host of Canadian women who contributed to the education of Japanese Christian women.

Canadian missionary work was often a family affair, with two generations of the same family, fathers and daughters or sons, successively serving in the mission field.[11] Similarly, certain universities were identified with missionary work, especially the University of Toronto with its various denominational universities and colleges: Victoria (Methodist, United Church), Trinity (High Anglican), and Wycliffe (Low Anglican). Of much less importance were Mount Allison in Sackville, New Brunswick, and Queen's University in Kingston, Ontario, which were identified with the Methodist and Presbyterian churches respectively. Many of the scions of missionary families who returned home (dubbed the "mish kids,") played significant roles in academia, government service, or the church in Canada: the Normans of Nagano, the Powles of Takata, the Watts of Nagoya, and the Armstrongs of Nishinomiya. Until recently, Queen's University, for instance, had a Watts as principal, and a Powles and a Norman on its staff. Several children from these families, including Herbert Norman, whose career in postwar Japan is the subject of Chapter 7, provided Canada's growing diplomatic service with Asian expertise.[12]

While these missionaries were Canadian, they did not live in a linear state with Canada and Japan at either end; many, in fact, lived in a triangular context involving Britain, Canada, and Japan.[13] Some missionaries, like the pioneer George Cochran, were born outside of Canada, in his case in Ulster. Some Canadian Anglicans went to Japan under the auspices of the British Society for the Propagation of the Gospel in Foreign Lands (SPG), as did Alexander Croft Shaw in 1873 and, later, William Gemmill, another Trinity graduate, who worked for the SPG until 1925. While he was headmaster of Trinity College School in Port Hope, Ontario, Arthur Lloyd influenced a number of young Canadians including Stephen Cartwright, who became a missionary first in Japan and then to Japanese within the Korean Anglican Church. Arthur Lea, a Wycliffe graduate, did much as a missionary in Gifu to develop a pioneering school for the blind in the 1890s before becoming the bishop of Kyūshū, an Anglican diocese supported by the British Church Missionary Society (CMS). His daughter, Leonora Lea, a long-time educational missionary in Kobe diocese, lived safely there through the Second World War with the help of Bishop Yashiro Hinsuke. Horace Watts, an Englishman serving in the Canadian Anglican mission, went to Canada after leaving Japan in 1940 and became a leading figure in the Canadian Anglican missionary society. The missionaries showed their connection to the British Empire, in which Canada constituted the hope for the future, in a myriad of ways. Robert Emberson in Shizuoka waved a flag to show his joy at the victory of Britain's Asian ally in the Russo-Japanese War in 1905; Gwen Norman, a young missionary wife in Nagano, worried about the abdication crisis of Edward VIII in 1936.

Despite the close British connection, some Canadian missionaries worked for American missionary bodies. The Methodists, together with the missions of the American Methodist Episcopal Church North and South, supported the Japan Methodist Church formed by the union of the three Japan missions in 1907 (and, after 1941, the amalgamated Protestant denomination, the *Nihon Kirisutokyōdan* or Japan Christian Church.) Benjamin Chappell, a Maritimer, joined the Methodist Episcopal North mission. John Dunlop, a Queen's graduate, became an American Presbyterian missionary after originally going to Japan as a member of Charles S. Eby's quasi-independent Self-Support Band in 1888. From 1907, after the creation of the Japan Methodist Church, Canadian Methodist men joined the American Methodist Episcopal South in concentrating their educational efforts in the Kwansei Gakuin, a higher school for boys in Nishinomiya, near Osaka. This school attained university status in 1934.

For most Canadian missionaries, life followed the characteristic rhythm established by the mission schools. The schools kept at bay the alien Japanese society outside the mission compound gates. Where they were in control, women missionaries could pursue a familiar teaching career without the added stress and unexpected challenges that they might encounter at a Japanese school under a Japanese headmaster. The school year also allowed for long summers away from the fetid heat of the coastal cities in the sylvan cool of hill stations at Karuizawa or Lake Nojiri, where missionaries could hold annual conferences and seek fellowship among their own kind with the Japanese kept at arms' length. Unfortunately, this life often separated missionaries from the mainstream of Japanese education and tended to isolate them from the changing currents in Japanese thought and society.

Canadian Anglicans shared the enthusiasm of the Methodists for summers at the hill stations but had a different approach to mission work. The Anglicans eschewed the building of mission schools beyond the ubiquitous kindergarten in favour of pastoral work. At the behest of the Anglican bishop of South Tokyo, Edward Bickersteth, the Canadian Anglican Church began sending missionaries to Japan in 1889.[14] John Waller, a Trinity graduate, served as a parish priest in Nagano from 1892 until his retirement from active work in the mid-1930s and only left that city after his internment in 1941.[15] His Wycliffe counterpart, James Cooper Robinson, went to Japan in 1889 and worked long years in Nagoya. In 1912, Heber J. Hamilton, also from Wycliffe, was named bishop of the diocese of Mid-Japan, which stretched across central Honshū from Nagoya to Niigata on the Japan Sea side including Nagano with its alpine reaches as well as the snow country around Takata. It became the missionary responsibility of the Canadian

Anglican Church, and a steady stream of Canadian Anglicans, men and women, served in it until the beginning of the Pacific War.

Canadian missionaries were also among the pioneers in Japanese studies. Robert Cornell Armstrong wrote on Japanese Confucianism and Buddhism,[16] Harper Coates co-authored a significant study of Hōnen,[17] Egerton Ryerson explored the wonders of *netsuke* (ivory carvings),[18] Ronald Shaw translated Buddhist writing,[19] Howard Norman translated some of Akutagawa Ryūnosuke's stories[20] and was interested in Uchimura Kanzō. Arthur Lloyd, a British Anglican priest with connections to Canada and a Canadian wife, was a pioneer in the study of Japanese Buddhism.[21] George Cochran served on the committee that translated the Old Testament into Japanese.

Canadian Missionaries in Meiji Japan

The Canadian missionary adventure in Japan began on 30 June 1873, when the pioneer Canadian Wesleyan Methodist missionaries, George Cochran and Davidson McDonald and their families, arrived in Yokohama after the Japanese government removed the proscription edicts against Christianity from public view. Although Christianity remained a proscribed religion until 1889, the missionary movement took the removal of the edicts as the signal to begin active and open propagation of the Christian Gospel to the Japanese.

Evangelizing the Japanese was the primary goal of Canadian missionaries. The most outstanding and most controversial of the early Canadian Methodist evangelists was Charles S. Eby, who arrived in Japan in 1876. Eby extended Methodist work to Kofu and Yamanashi prefecture, but his enthusiasm often exceeded the resources of the Mission Board at home. As part of his plans for the immediate Christianization of Japan and to allow Methodists to push beyond the confines of the earlier Tokyo-Shizuoka-Kofu triangle into central Honshū, he formed the so-called Self-Support Band. The Band's lay missionaries were to support themselves by teaching English in Japanese schools, but without support from the Mission Board the Band was short-lived. Undaunted, in the 1890s, Eby built a very large church, the Central Tabernacle Church in Ginza, Tokyo.

For many years, the church was a financial albatross for the Canadian Methodist mission, but in its congregation were a number of influential and wealthy, philanthropic Japanese, especially Kobayashi Yatarō, a multi-millionaire who had married into a family that had made its fortune through the sale of Lion Brand dental and other hygienic products. His generosity not only helped the Methodists maintain the Tabernacle but also assisted them in their social welfare and relief work in the slums of Tokyo.

Early Japanese Protestants assumed that Christianity was the basis of Western civilization and that Japan must become a Christian nation if it wished to adopt Western technology successfully. Further, many early Christian

Figure 1.2 Missionary Charles Eby built the large Canadian Methodist Central Tabernacle in Ginza, Tokyo, circa 1894. Although the congregation included a number of wealthy and influential Japanese parishioners, the church was an ongoing financial burden for the Canadian Methodist mission. *From the collection of Hamish Ion.*

ex-samurai believed that Christianity could be grafted on to a Japanese Confucian or even *bushidō* root to create a new perfected moral code for Japan. The majority of ordinary Japanese, however, subscribed to the popular religions of Buddhism and Shinto, which thrived during the late nineteenth century while Confucianism was eclipsed. Thus, a connection between Christianity and Confucianism had neither a long-term nor a deep resonance in Japanese society. The desire to acquire new knowledge to equip themselves better for changing times remained the most common motive for most converts.

Protestant missions experienced some growth in the early Meiji period. Convert bands coalesced around missionaries or Western lay Christians teaching in new schools of Western studies in the treaty ports, and in provincial towns and cities. Missionaries or lay Christians formed Protestant bands in Shizuoka, Hirosaki, Niigata, Osaka, Kumamoto, and Sapporo, as well as in the Tokyo areas of Tsukiji, Shiba, and Koishikawa (see Figure 1.3). These bands developed along skeins of contact, friendship, family relations, and,

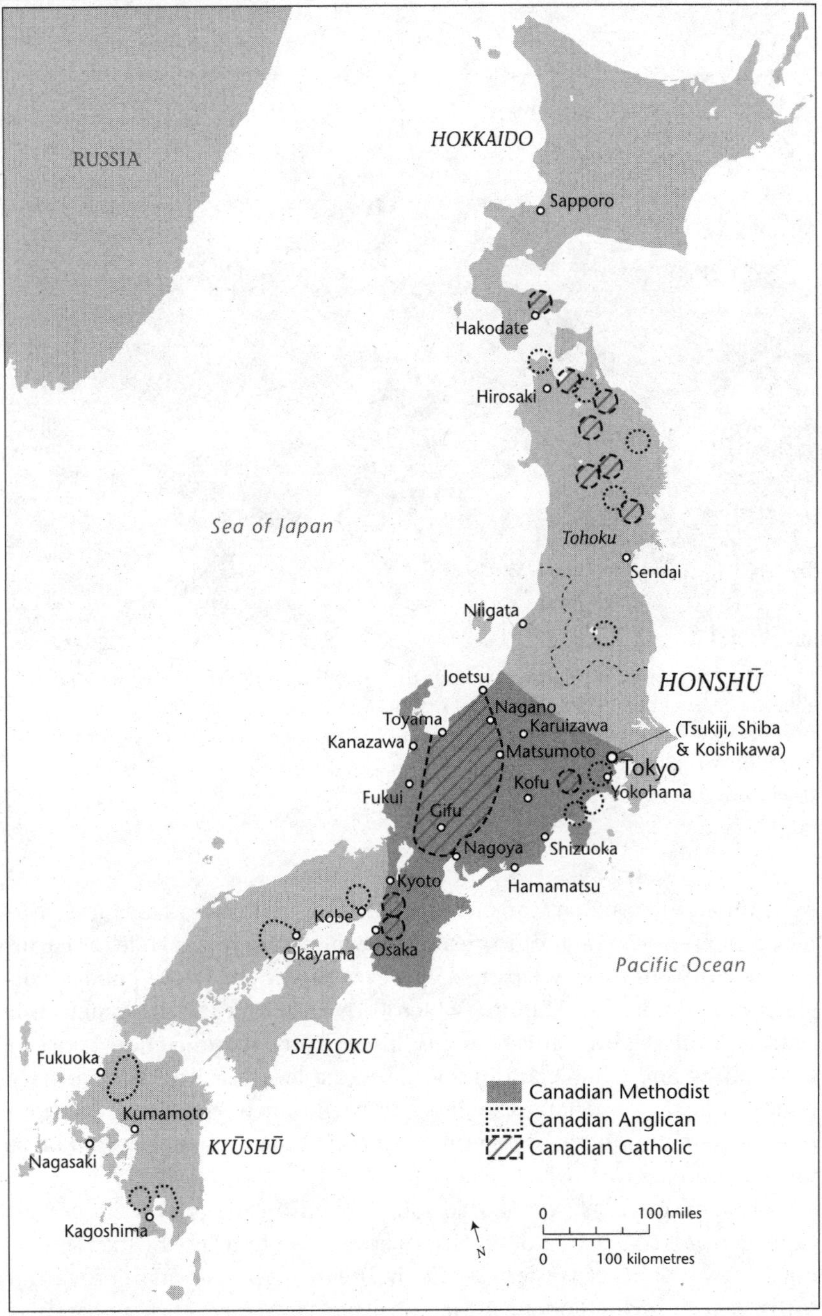

Figure 1.3 Map of Canadian missionary territories in Japan

in rural areas, family influence and economic power. A large percentage of the initial converts were ex-samurai attracted to Protestantism through the educational work of missionaries and the influence of such prominent intellectuals and educators as Nakamura or Tsuda Sen, an agricultural expert and early American Methodist Episcopalian convert.

Personal loyalty to an outstanding leader, Japanese or missionary, provided a common pattern of conversion. Canadian Methodists formed two of these important Christian groups among students at Japanese schools of Western learning, the Shizuhataya in Shizuoka and the Dōjinsha in Koishikawa, where McDonald and Cochran respectively taught.[22] In 1874, the Shizuoka Band, one of the earliest Christian groups in the interior of Japan, made up largely of ex-samurai adherents of the former Tokugawa Shogun, formed around McDonald. Shizuoka became a stronghold of Canadian missionary work and the source of many of the first pastors in the Japan Methodist Church. A second Shizuoka Christian Band was formed in 1885-86 around Francis Cassidy and Hiraiwa Yoshiyasu.[23] Among this second Shizuoka Band was Yamaji Aizan, a thinker of national significance and one of the first historians of Japanese Protestantism. In December 1874, George Cochran baptized Nakamura Masanao (Keiū), the founder of the Dōjinsha school, a nationally important intellectual, and a leading advocate of Japan's acceptance of Christianity.[24] While teaching at the Dōjinsha, Cochran formed the Koishikawa Christian Band around Nakamura, and among its members was Hiraiwa Yoshiyasu, who became the leading Japanese pastor in the Canadian Methodist mission.

Hostile government attitudes towards Christianity, however, impeded Protestant growth. Following the Meiji Restoration in 1868, the new government responded to the perceived Christian threat by using autochthonous quasi-religious rituals to reinforce its power and legitimize the modern Japanese monarchy by linking it with a mythical past. Resistance to Christianity was also reinforced by the prestige of the intellectual tradition that was intimately connected with established religion and through arguments for the defence of the fatherland and of Japanese religion. Nationalist thinkers advanced various anti-Christian arguments with strong xenophobic undertones or spy conspiracy theories to justify its prohibition. Moreover, from the late 1870s, opponents used the new Darwinian idea of evolution imported from the West to attack Christianity. During the late 1880s, Buddhist scholars, sometimes with government support, began asserting that their theology was superior to that of Christians. Not surprisingly, in this context, Canadian missionaries made relatively few converts (apostates, who renounced Christianity, were more numerous and perhaps more influential in Japanese society than the Christians); paradoxically, the negative cultural implications of Christianity for Japan significantly affected its political, social, and religious development. In response to the perceived threat of Christianity to their culture, the Japanese made a concerted effort to restore, rejuvenate, or reinvent their own political, social, and religious forms from the mid-nineteenth century onwards.[25]

In 1889, the Meiji Constitution guaranteed religious freedom without defining its meaning. This was especially true in terms of church-state relations at the governmental and bureaucratic levels, but also applied to questions surrounding the relationship between Japanese nationalism and patriotism and Christian faith at the personal level. To the government, religious freedom meant that religion was to serve the interests of the state, and the government was prepared to ensure that religious freedom did not compromise those interests, particularly in education.

Always sensitive to swings in public opinion, the advance of the Christian movement slowed in the mid-1890s owing to Japanese outrage at the Triple Intervention of 1895 in which Russia, Germany, and France opposed many of the concessions that Japan had obtained from China in the Treaty of Shimonoseki ending the Sino-Japanese War of 1894-95. Further, Japan was irritated at Britain's reluctance to revise the 1858 Treaty of Yedo with its extraterritorial clauses that restricted Japanese sovereignty. In 1899, the Tokyo government, eager to prevent foreign religious influence on male education at the primary and secondary level, prohibited the teaching of religious subjects in all schools seeking the official accreditation on which their survival depended. Because they could not teach religious subjects, Canadian Methodists transferred control of the Tōyō Eiwa Gakkō, their boys' school, to Ebara Soroku, a Japanese Christian, rather than continue it as a mission school. These government regulations did not apply to female education, so the Canadian Methodists were able to continue their three girls' schools as mission schools.

Unlike Buddhists, who suffered no conflict between their religion and their Japanese identity, Japanese Christians found it exceedingly difficult to overcome the doubts that non-Christian Japanese and the Japanese government had about their loyalty to Japan, and even their "Japaneseness." In order to assert their Japaneseness, by the end of the Meiji era in 1912, some Japanese Christians were suggesting the creation of a Japanese Christianity (*Nipponteki Kirisutokyō*) that would be free of any Western influence and completely distinct from the Christianity propagated by Western missionaries. Yet, even before this radical solution was suggested, the mainstream Japanese Christian movement, in its desire to be identified with nationalism, had become – especially in the wake of the Russo-Japanese War of 1905 – an ardent supporter of Japan's expansionism and imperialism overseas. By supporting Japanese imperial and military ambitions in continental East Asia, Japanese Christians could dramatically demonstrate their loyalty to Japan.

The Calm and the Storm

Japan's victory over Russia in 1905 catapulted Japan into the ranks of the world's great powers. The Treaty of Portsmouth, which ended the conflict, also marked a watershed in Japan's political and social development by stimulating irresistible calls for political reform, ultimately leading to the establishment of responsible government in 1918 and universal male suffrage in 1925. In response to the dangers posed by political liberalization, the ruling elite strove to buttress its hold on power by developing the *tennosei* (emperor worship) ideology that underpinned state Shinto, by enacting repressive legislation against trade unions and socialists, and by providing sweeping powers to the gendarmerie. After 1905, Japan also underwent rapid urbanization and industrialization, especially during the boom years of the First World War, when Tokyo and Osaka developed into modern cities with all the conveniences of the early twentieth century and its attendant problems of widespread slums, poverty, prostitution, and labour unrest.

Canadian missionaries responded to the new conditions by developing new specialized forms of missionary work that focussed on welfare work in the slums of east Tokyo. In the 1920s and 1930s, for instance, the social work of Annie Allen and Ernest Bott among the poor, and of Percy Price and Kobayashi Yatarō in forming the Airindan, which ran night school classes for labourers and elementary school classes for impoverished children in Tokyo, helped draw the attention of Japanese authorities to a hitherto neglected area of social welfare. Likewise, the establishment of a sanatorium by Canadian Anglican missionaries in rural Nagano prefecture helped demonstrate the need for proper facilities for tuberculosis sufferers. Caroline Macdonald, a Canadian Presbyterian, went to Japan at the turn of the century under the auspices of the YWCA, and became known as the White Angel of Tokyo for her work among prisoners and her advocacy for prison reform. Emma R. Kaufman, her contemporary, also made a significant contribution to the YWCA.

In the years immediately following the Edinburgh Missionary Conference in 1910, missionaries continued to help organize major national evangelistic campaigns. Through the 1920s and early 1930s, Dan Norman mounted extensive campaigns in the farming communities of Nagano, while Bishop Hamilton was an animated street preacher. This soon changed. After the formation in 1922 of the National Council of Churches (NCC), which came to include most Protestant denominations and Christian schools, social institutions, the YMCA, the YWCA, and the Woman's Christian Temperance Union (WCTU), the emphasis shifted from denominational to ecumenical work. Though its actual power over individual denominations was limited to moral persuasion, the NCC came to play an increasingly important role in coordinating the cooperative endeavours of the Protestant movement. It took the lead in 1928, for instance, in promoting the major evangelistic campaigns headlined by the charismatic Kagawa Toyohiko (the most internationally famous Japanese save for an occasional military officer and the emperor until the advent of Yoko Ono) under the banner of the Kingdom of God movement. The NCC also came to represent the Protestant movement in its dealings with the Japanese government. Therein lay the rub. By the 1930s, missionaries had increasingly turned over direct evangelistic work to Japanese Christians and, consequently, were becoming isolated in their educational and specialized social work from ordinary Christians at the parish level.

The growing East Asian crisis following Japan's occupation of Manchuria in 1931 meant that the NCC and Japanese Christian movement were increasingly unable to resist government pressure to conform to its policies and perceived wishes in regard to Christian attendance at state Shintō ceremonies. After the beginning of the Second Sino-Japanese War in July 1937, Christian opposition to the conflict was extremely rare. In part, this stemmed from fear, as the thought-control police (*tōkkō kempetai*), after oppressing heterodox Japanese new religions, turned their attention (largely because they needed employment) to the persecution of millenarian Christian groups like the Nippon Seikokai (NSKK) and Salvation Army with clear foreign connections. Genuine feelings of patriotism and national sentiment, coupled with their desire to free the Japanese and other East Asian Christian movements from Western influence and missionary control, led Japanese Christian leaders to participate in the spiritual mobilization campaign in 1937. In addition, they barely protested the removal of Western missionaries from Christian schools and enthusiastically supported the government initiative to amalgamate all Protestant denominations into one Protestant church, the *Nihon Kirisutokyōdan* (known as the Kyōdan for short), in 1941.

Among the major Protestant denominations, only an Anglican rump of the NSKK led by Bishop Sasaki Shinji, who had succeeded Hamilton as bishop of Mid-Japan, and Bishop Yashiro Hinsuke of Kobe refused to join the Kyōdan. While remaining patriotic and nationalistic, their belief that the episcopal system of the NSKK represented a better form of religious organization than the one offered by the Kyōdan inspired them to risk imprisonment for their religious beliefs. Worried that their continued presence might endanger their Japanese Christian friends in the pervasive anti-British atmosphere, most Canadian missionaries, regardless of denomination, left Japan by the end of 1940. Yet, some were hurt and disappointed by the failure of most Japanese Christian leaders to stand up against their government's religious policies and defend the foreign missionaries with whom they had worked closely for over fifty years. Canadian Anglicans, in particular, felt let down by Bishop Sasaki because their past loyalty to him made them expect he would support them.

When war came in 1941, the Japanese government interned most of the remaining Canadian missionaries at the Canadian Academy in Kobe or the

Sumire internment camp in Tokyo until 1942, when they were repatriated on the exchange ship *Gripsholm*. They were well treated and left before living conditions in Japan dramatically deteriorated.[26] Among the handful that escaped internment were Ernest Bott and his wife, who were allowed to live quietly in their own home before being evacuated, probably protected by Welfare Ministry officials who recognized their work in the east Tokyo slums. Two former missionaries remained through the war: Margaret Armstrong, who had taken out Japanese citizenship and lived quietly in Toyama, and Agnes Wintemute (Mrs. Harper Coates), who died in unhappy circumstances in early 1945.

During the war, many former missionaries who had returned to Canada became deeply concerned about the plight of Japanese Canadians, who were forcibly removed from the West Coast. Among the most active was Percy Powles, a Canadian Anglican clergyman, late of Takata. With his family, as Greg Robinson's essay later in this volume notes, he did much to help ease the difficulties of Nisei (the first generation born in Canada) relocated to Montreal. Constance Chappell, a teacher at the Tokyo Woman's Christian College, was another outspoken critic of the treatment of Japanese Canadians. Other former missionaries, such as Howard Norman, who became a civilian instructor at the Canadian Army Japanese Language School (S-20) in Vancouver, where he was commanded by a former missionary colleague, Arthur McKenzie, also helped Japanese Canadians as much as they could.[27] Indeed, the realization that their fellow Canadians were mistreating Japanese Canadians coloured missionary attitudes towards Christians in metropolitan Japan and reinforced the prevalent missionary view that the Japanese Christian leadership was blameless of any wrong during the war.

Bott, in particular, was deeply influenced both by the Canadian government's decision to deport Japanese Canadians back to Japan after the war and the means it used to convince them to accept "repatriation." In early August 1945, he speculated that Ottawa's repatriation policy would be the most serious concern in postwar relations with Japan and was appalled that the Canadian churches were unwilling or unable to prevent the projected deportation of Canadian-born Japanese. Bott presciently insisted that "every Canadian Japanese who goes to Japan after the war will be a living demonstration of the fact that Canada is neither Christian nor democratic and that Canada's signature on the United Nations Charter guaranteeing justice for minorities is a hollow mockery."[28] Deeply ashamed at their government's treatment of its Japanese-Canadian residents, missionaries like Bott were inclined to see the Japanese as victims rather than aggressors.

Even before the end of the war, missionaries favoured a generous political settlement. In July 1945, Howard Outerbridge, who had taught for many years at Kwansei Gakuin University, expressed a representative opinion when he said that the Allies would be very stupid if they did not find a "way of turning the Emperor with his great prestige and influence into an asset, instead of hanging him, when everyone knows that he has been the reluctant tool of the revisionists, and thus turning everyone in Japan – liberal and reactionary alike – into our implacable foes."[29] Modern scholarship might suggest that the Emperor was less of a reluctant tool than Outerbridge thought.[30] Nevertheless, Outerbridge correctly saw that the Emperor did and could wield considerable influence. Recalling the role of the Meiji Emperor in giving Japan a constitution in 1889, Outerbridge believed that the Showa Emperor could perform a similar service. While virtually every missionary agreed with the need for political change in postwar Japan, they were mainly concerned with easing the suffering of the Japanese, which had been caused by chronic food shortages and massive wartime destruction of property.

Reconciliation

What stands out about Canadian missionaries during the Allied occupation of Japan was a generosity of spirit, a deep compassion, and a genuine concern for the welfare of ordinary Japanese folk, Christian and non-Christian alike. This was particularly evident in the work undertaken by Bott in conjunction with Licensed Agencies for Relief in Asia (LARA) to help ordinary Japanese cope with hardship during the first terrible years of the occupation. LARA was the only agency through which Supreme Commander Allied Powers (SCAP) allowed North American religious organizations to send relief supplies on a large scale to Japan. While it is fashionable to question the achievements of the occupation and to highlight its seamier side,[31] the unstinting efforts of Bott and LARA are reminders of the positive and generous element that was also at work. Sybil Courtice, who returned to occupied Japan to help rebuild the Tōyō Eiwa Jo Gakkō, the Canadian Methodist school for girls in Tokyo, or Percy Powles, the long-serving Canadian Anglican missionary in Takata, who came back in 1948 to serve as assistant bishop of the diocese of Mid-Japan, illustrate the same generosity of spirit.

The housing and food supply crisis in Japan during the early years of the occupation made it difficult for missionaries to return. Occupation authorities underlined this by not permitting the direct shipment of food to non-Japanese with no official connection with occupation authorities.[32] This scotched any idea that missionaries might be able to return if they provided their own food, though Bott was eventually allowed to return to help in Japan.[33] The sheer extent of the terrible destruction deeply affected Bott.[34] Nevertheless, he found himself warmly received by Japanese Christians. He admired the fact that they never complained, though many had lost virtually everything. Leading Japanese Christians also appeared eager to have the missionaries return. Tomita Mitsurō, a prominent figure in the Kyōdan, made this clear. After explaining that Japan's treatment of Korea had inspired the violently hostile attitude of Koreans to Japan and that Japan's victories over China and Russia in 1895 and 1905 had proved calamitous for Japan, Tomita told Bott that "the defeat has brought about a fundamental change of outlook which promises well for co-operation between the Churches of North America and the Church in Japan."[35] Missionaries accepted this *volte-face* at face value.

Conditions remained appalling throughout Japan. In late July 1946, after travelling extensively in northern and central Honshū, Bott noted that the destruction and dislocation of churches and congregations was beyond imagining and that reconstruction would be slow and expensive.[36] Worsening food shortages overshadowed all other problems. He stressed that the LARA relief program was very much needed, and, despite being too small (it was still thousands of tons a month) to make much difference overall, it remained a valuable expression of goodwill towards the Japanese on the part of the people of North America.[37] By 1947, Bott reported that he or one of the other two LARA representatives had visited every prefecture, had met their leading social workers, and had explained the spirit in which the relief supplies were sent and the agencies that had sent them.[38] Another United Church missionary, Alf Stone, underlined the importance of LARA in February 1947 when he noted that the practical work of "LARA (of which Church World Service is the biggest contributor) is doing more to atone for the atomic bomb, and build up good-will in this country, than all the *talk* [by Western commentators]."[39] Like many missionaries, Stone felt a deep sense of guilt about the use of the atomic bomb, and the need for atonement obviously influenced missionary motives in wanting to help the Japanese.

That postwar Canadian missionaries should act as Bott did should not be considered remarkable. Almost without exception, Canadian Protestant missionaries had responded warmly and generously to Japan since their extraordinary adventure began in 1874. With a commitment fired by their Christian faith, the Cochrans, the McDonalds, the Cooper Robinsons, the Hamiltons, and the Powles, together with hundreds of other Canadian missionaries and their supporters at home, journeyed west across the Pacific because they felt that Canada had something worthwhile of a religious kind to share with peoples beyond its borders. In many respects, this movement was the East Asian harbinger of the "soft power" that Lloyd Axworthy would trumpet during his tenure as Canada's minister of foreign affairs in the 1990s. Though budget cuts and a decline in Canada's global standing drove Axworthy to "soft power," missionaries embraced person-to-person "diplomacy" from the start. Though the effort resulted in few conversions, it left a lasting legacy of goodwill towards Canadians and a favourable image of

Canada as a tranquil land of Rockies, prairies, and lakes. How this translates into trade statistics and political influence is impossible to determine, but it surely helps persuade many Japanese parents to send their children to Canadian schools and universities. Today, of course, these temporary immigrants no longer come in White Empress liners, but in Air Canada planes, which carry back young secular English instructors to teach in the schools of provincial Japan, where missionaries once taught from faded Ontario primers. On both sides of the Pacific, the educational mission that was so fundamental to the Protestant missionary enterprise continues to provide the context for new person-to-person bridges.

Notes

1 A.R. Stone to Bell, 20 August 1946, box 6, file 144, United Church of Canada Archives: Board Foreign Missions Japan (hereafter UCC: BFMJ).

2 See Yokohama Taigaikankeishi Kenkyūka/Yokohama Kaikō Shiryōkan hen, *Yokohama Eibu Chūten Gun to Gaikokujin Kyoryūchi* (Tokyo: Tokyo Dō Shuppan, 1999).

3 See Yokohama Kaikō Shiryōkan hen, *Yokohama and Bankuba: Taiheiyō o koete* (Yokohama: Yokohama Kaikō Shiryōkan, 2005). An 1891 poster advertised Yokohama to London in twenty-one days (p. 8; see also poster on p. 11). In 1891, the Empress of India could carry 120 passengers; in 1922, the Empress of Canada could carry up to 488 passengers. In 1920-21, the White Empress liners carried 35,555 passengers across the Pacific, most of whom were Asian immigrants entering Canada or returning home for visits or permanent residence.

4 Joseph S. Nye Jr., *The Paradox of American Power* (New York: Oxford University Press, 2002), 9. See also Greg Donaghy, "All God's Children: Lloyd Axworthy, Human Security and Canadian Foreign Policy, 1996-2000," *Canadian Foreign Policy* 10, 2 (2003): 43.

5 Although dated, Kuranaga Takashi, *Kanada Mesojisuto dendō shi* (Tokyo: Kanada Gōdō Kyōkai senkyōshika, 1937) remains a highly useful fact-filled history of the pre-war Canadian Methodist mission.

6 There is no individual history of the Canadian Anglican mission, although it is well represented in the standard history of the Nippon Seikokai, Nippon Seikokai rekishi henshu iinkai hen, *Nippon Seikokai hyakunen shi* (Tokyo: Nippon Seikokai kyōmuin bunsho kyoku, 1959).

7 Canadian Confederation had inspired Methodist churches to embark upon a spiritual union in order to create a truly national Methodist Church in the new Canada. Marilyn Färdig Whitely in her investigation of the Woman's Missionary Society of the Methodist Church in Canada stressed that "the Methodist Church saw itself as the most Canadian of denominations, with a special role to play in building the nation." See "Open-Winged Piety: Reflex Influence and the Woman's Methodist Society of the Methodist Church in Canada," in *The Foreign Missionary Enterprise at Home: Explorations in North American Cultural History*, ed. Daniel H. Bays and Grant Wacker (Tuscaloosa: The University of Alabama Press, 2003), 123-33. In 1872, at the annual meeting of the Wesleyan Methodist Missionary Society, a definite nationalistic feeling among Methodists held that "the day of small things, as regards the Dominion, was past and the same was true of our Mission work," and that "we have a glorious future before us in this great country." Wesleyan Missionary Notices 17 (November 1872), 258. The outcome of this meeting was the decision to commence that church's first overseas mission in Japan.

8 For a detailed history of the Canadian Protestant missionary endeavour in Japan, Korea, and Taiwan between 1872 and 1945, see A. Hamish Ion, *The Cross and the Rising Sun: The Canadian Protestant Missionary Movement in the Japanese Empire 1872-1931* (Waterloo: Wilfrid Laurier University Press, 1990); and *The Cross in the Dark Valley: The Canadian Protestant Missionary Movement in the Japanese Empire, 1931-1945* (Waterloo: Wilfrid Laurier Univer-

sity Press, 1999). A short survey can be found in A. Hamish Ion, "Ambassadors of the Cross: Canadian Missionaries in Japan," in *Canada and Japan in the Twentieth Century*, ed. John Schultz and Kimitada Miwa (Toronto: Oxford University Press, 1991), 29-47. Also of interest is the detailed church-sponsored study of the first century of United Church of Canada work in Japan: G.R.P. Norman and W.H.H. Norman, *One Hundred Years in Japan, 1873-1973*, 2 vols. (Toronto: Division of World Out-Reach, United Church of Canada, 1981). An interesting study of Canadian Methodist women missionaries is Rosemary B. Gagan, *A Sensitive Independence: Canadian Methodist Women Missionaries in Canada and the Orient, 1881-1925* (Montreal: McGill-Queen's University Press, 1992); an important biography of the most famous YWCA worker in early twentieth century Japan is Margaret Prang, *A Heart at Leisure from Itself: Caroline Macdonald of Japan* (Vancouver: UBC Press, 1995). For the Canadian Roman Catholic missionary movement, see Richard Leclerc, *Des Lys à l'Ombre du Mont Fuji: Histoire de la présence de l'Amérique française au Japan* (Sillery: Éditions du Bois-de-Coulogne, 1995). For a valuable account of Canadian Roman Catholic priests interned in Kyūshū during the Pacific War, see Samuel Lapalme-Remis, "Enemy Nationals: The St.-Sulpice Mission in Fukuoka 1933-45" (MA thesis, Sheffield University, 2003).

9 For the detailed history of these three schools, see Shizuoka Eiwa Jo Gakuin hechijūnen shi hensan iinkai, *Shizuoka Eiwa Jo Gakuin hachijūnen shi* (Shizuoka: Shizuoka Eiwa Jo Gakuin, 1971); Tōyō Eiwa Jo Gakuin hyakunen shi henshan jitsukū iinkai, *Tōyō Eiwa Jo Gakuin hyakunen shi* (Tokyo: Tōyō Eiwa Jo Gakuin, 1984); Yamanashi Eiwa Jo Gakuin hensan iinkai, *Yamanashi Eiwa Jo Gakuin hachijūnen shi* (Kofu: Yamanashi Eiwa Jo Gakuin, 1970).

10 Loretta Shaw wrote a perceptive book on changing Japan after the First World War, *Japan in Transition* (London: Church Missionary Society, 1922).

11 For instance, the Anglicans included Alexander C. Shaw and his son Ronald D.M. Shaw, Percy Powles and Cyril Powles, and Arthur Lea and his daughter, Leonora Lea; the Methodists included Dan Norman and Howard Norman, Robert D. McKenzie and Arthur P. McKenzie, and Benjamin Chappell and Constance Chappell (Constance's twin, Mary, taught in Japan but was not a missionary).

12 John Hilliker, *Canada's Department of External Affairs*, vol. 1: *The Early Years, 1909-1946* (Montreal and Kingston: McGill-Queen's University Press, 1990), 190-92.

13 Howard Norman, the older brother of E.H. Norman, the diplomat, intimated that this was the case in a private conversation with the author.

14 Hamish Ion, "The Archdeacon and the Bishop: Alexander Croft Shaw, Edward Bickersteth, and Meiji Japan," in *Britain & Japan: Biographical Portraits*, vol. 3, ed. J.E. Hoare (Richmond, England: Japan Library, 1999), 108-20.

15 Nippon Seikokai rekishi henshū iinkai, *Akashi bitotachi: Nippon Seikokai jinbutsu shi* (Tokyo: Nippon Seikokai shuppan jigyobu, 1975), 73-75.

16 See, for instance, Robert Cornell Armstrong, *Just before the Dawn: The Life and Work of Ninomiya Sontoku* (New York: Macmillan, 1912).

17 Harper H. Coates and Ryugaku Ishizuka, *Honen, the Buddhist Saint: His Life and Teachings* (Kyoto: Chionin, 1925).

18 Egerton Ryerson, *The Netsuke of Japan* (London: G. Bell, 1958).

19 R.D.M. Shaw, *The Embossed Tea Kettle*, trans. Hakuin Zenji (London: Michael Joseph, 1961).

20 W.H.H. Norman, trans., *Hell Screen ("Jigoku Hen") and Other Stories by Ryunosuke Akutagawa* (Tokyo: The Hokuseido Press, 1948).

21 See, for instance, Arthur Lloyd, *The Wheat among the Tares: Studies of Buddhism in Japan* (London: Macmillan, 1908).

22 For a more detailed account of this, see A. Hamish Ion, "Shizuoka Christians and Tokyo Evangelism in the early 1870s," *Meiji Gakuin Kirisutokyō Kenkyūjo Kiyō* 37 (2005): 251-97.

23 For Hiraiwa, see Kuranaga Takeshi, *Hiraiwa Yoshiyasu den* (Tokyo: Kanada Gōdō Kyōkai senkyōshikai, 1937).

24 Takahashi Masao, *Nakamura Keiū* (Tokyo: Yoshikawa Kōbunkan, 1967), 132. Nakamura was the translator of John Stuart Mill's *On Liberty* and Samuel Smiles' *Self-Help*, and he was a member of the influential Meirokusha, the learned society, which included among its members Fukuzawa Yukichi, Mori Arinori, Nishi Amane, and many other leading Japanese specialists in Western studies.

25 For a brief overview of the Protestant movement in Japan, see A. Hamish Ion, "Japan," in *The Encyclopedia of Protestantism*, ed. Hans J. Hillerbrand (New York and London: Routledge, 2004), 972-75. For a valuable recent collection of papers on Japanese Christianity, including its history, see Mark R. Mullins, ed., *Handbook of Christianity in Japan* (Leiden: Brill, 2003).
26 Ion, *The Cross in the Dark Valley*, 312-13.
27 For a brief summation of McKenzie's military career in the Second World War, see McKenzie to Arnup, 18 June 1946, box 6, file 147, UCC: BFMJ.
28 Bott to Armstrong, 5 August 1945, box 6, file 142, UCC: BFMJ. See also Armstrong to Bott, 16 May 1946, box 5, file 144, in which Armstrong informed Bott that the Board of Overseas Mission was protesting formally the expulsion of Canadian citizens of Japanese ancestry.
29 Outerbridge to Armstrong, 4 July 1945, box 6, file 142, UCC: BFMJ.
30 For a recent critical study of the Japanese Emperor, see Herbert P. Bix, *Hirohito and the Making of Modern Japan* (New York: Harper Collins Publishers, 2000).
31 See, for instance, Yuki Tanaka, *Japan's Comfort Women: Sexual Slavery and Prostitution during World War II and the US Occupation* (London and New York: Routledge, 2002); and John W. Dower, *Embracing Defeat: Japan in the Wake of World War II* (New York: W.W. Norton, 1999).
32 Bott to Taylor, 24 April 1946, box 6, file 144, UCC: BFMJ.
33 Between 1946 and 1950, some twenty-four pre-war United Church missionaries returned to Japan. See Norman, *One Hundred Years in Japan,* vol. 2, 430.
34 Bott to Bell, 22 April 1946, box 6, file 144, UCC: BFMJ. The devastation of Japan and the chronic food shortages are vividly described in Dower, Embracing Defeat, especially 33-120.
35 Bott to Bell, 22 April 1946, box 6, file 144, UCC: BFMJ.
36 Bott to Courtice and Armstrong, 22 July 1946, box 6, file 144, UCC: BFMJ.
37 Bott to Birkel, 7 July 1946, box 6, file 144, UCC: BFMJ.
38 Bott to Arnup, 8 July 1947, box 5, file 157, UCC: BFMJ.
39 Stone to Arnup, 15 February 1947, box 6, file 153, UCC: BFMJ.

2
God's Envoys: Canadian Catholic Missionaries in Japan, 1898-2000

Richard Leclerc

The Canadian missionary enterprise in Japan was not confined to the Protestant movements described in the previous chapter. Not surprisingly, given the religious composition of Canada in the first half of the twentieth century, Canadian Roman Catholics also sent missionaries to Japan. Whereas the Protestant missionaries were mainly anglophones with roots in rural Ontario, most of the Roman Catholics were francophones from Quebec. Yet, there were more similarities than differences between the two endeavours. Both had proselytization as their main goal, and both enjoyed only limited success in this field. Even so, the Japanese often welcomed the missionaries as bearers of Western learning, and the educational and social services used by the missions to attract potential converts effectively introduced many Japanese to Canada. But for Catholics, like Protestants, relations with the Japanese state were not always harmonious, especially during the series of crises that preceded the outbreak of the Pacific War. Despite a brief spurt in activity in the immediate postwar years, the Protestant and Catholic missionary presences faded in the latter half of the twentieth century. Nevertheless, in their heyday, both were powerful illustrations of Canadian "soft power" abroad.

For more than a century, the Roman Catholic Church in Canada was profoundly marked by the call of the missions. Japan was especially alluring. In October 1898, Sister Hélène Paradis, with a handful of associates from France, founded the mission of the Franciscaines Missionnaires de Marie in Kumamoto. Over the next century, nearly one thousand Canadian Catholic churchmen and churchwomen spread out across Japan and laid solid foundations for their work in the main cities of Honshū and Kyūshū, establishing twenty-eight separate missions and contributing to the operations of seven international communities (see Table 2.1).[1] This chapter represents a preliminary effort to trace the evolution of Canada's Catholic missions in Japan from 1898 to the late twentieth century, when they declined sharply following the liberalizing reforms of Vatican II and the

Table 2.1

Catholic religious communities in Japan with Canadian members

Communities and countries of origin	Foundation	Canadian presence
Women		
Sœurs de l'Enfant-Jésus de Chauffailles (France)	1877	1928-1980
Sœurs de Saint-Paul de Chartres (France)	1878	1935-2001
Franciscaines Missionnaires de Marie (France)	1898	1898-2005
Religieuses du Sacré-Cœur de Jésus (France)	1908	1932-1985
Sœurs Missionnaires de l'Immaculée-Conception (Québec)	1926	1926-
Congrégation Romaine de Saint-Dominique (France)	1931	1931-1969
Sœurs des Saints Noms de Jésus et de Marie (Québec)	1931	1931-1940 1979-2003
Congrégation de Notre-Dame (Québec)	1932	1932-
Sœurs Missionnaires du Christ-Roi (Québec)	1933	1933-
Sœurs Adoratrices du Précieux-Sang (Québec)	1934	1934-1989
Sœurs de l'Assomption de la Sainte-Vierge (Québec)	1934	1934-
Sœurs de Sainte-Anne (Québec)	1934	1934-1943
Sœurs Auxiliatrices (France)	1935	1951-2003
Sœurs de Notre-Dame de Charité du Bon-Pasteur (Québec)	1935	1935-
Ursulines de l'Union Canadienne (Québec)	1936	1936-
Clarisses (Québec)	1947	1947-
Sœurs de la Présentation de Marie (Québec)	1948	1948-
Sœurs Missionnaires de Notre-Dame des Anges (Québec)	1949	1949-
Rédemptoristines (Québec)	1950	1950-1997
Petites Filles de Saint-Joseph (Québec)	1951	1951-1957
Grey Sisters of the Immaculate Conception (Ontario)	1952	1952-1958
Sœurs de la Charité de Québec (Québec)	1953	1953-
Our Lady's Missionaries (Ontario)	1956	1956-1973
Sœurs de la Charité d'Ottawa (Ontario)	1960	1960-
Men		
Jésuites (Italy)	1549	1951-
Franciscains (Québec)	1593	1907-
Dominicains (Québec)	1928	1928-
Frères des Écoles Chrétiennes (Québec)	1932	1932
Prêtres de Saint-Sulpice (Québec)	1933	1933-
Clercs de Saint-Viateur (Québec)	1948	1948-
Redemptorists (Ontario)	1948	1948-1982
Rédemptoristes (Québec)	1948	1948-
Scarboro Foreign Mission Society (Ontario)	1948	1948-
Société des Missions-Étrangères (Québec)	1948	1948-
Frères de l'Instruction Chrétienne (Québec)	1951	1951-

Sources: Archives of the religious communities.

secularization of Quebec in the 1960s. Although largely ignored in the historical literature on Canadian missionaries, an especially striking omission given the attention devoted to Protestant efforts in Japan, Catholic missionaries made a modest but real contribution to the development of Japan and the perception of Canada in that country. They were particularly active after 1945, and though no more successful than their Protestant counterparts in converting the Japanese, they too left behind a legacy of educational and social institutions.

Early Mission Activities, 1898-1937

For almost a decade, a small number of nuns like Paradis, working alone for the most part, were the only representatives of the Canadian Catholic Church in Japan. This situation changed in 1907, when Fr. Maurice Bertin, a French priest who had ministered in Quebec, and Fr. Wenceslaus Kinold established a mission in Sapporo, Hokkaido, under the German Franciscans. In view of the size of the apostolate, the pioneers soon recruited assistants, including Fr. Pierre Gauthier and Brother Gabriel Godbout.[2] In 1921, after operating under German auspices, the French-Canadian Franciscans achieved a long-sought objective when the Holy See asked them to evangelize the Diocese of Nagasaki and they acquired their own apostolic region.

Once French-Canadian missionaries controlled their own work, they concentrated more on apostolic outreach and less on the non-apostolic or social work elements of missionary activities favoured by the Europeans. Their main focus was the island of Kyūshū, the birthplace of Japanese Catholicism, Hokkaido, and the regions of Tōhoku and Kanto. On 9 July 1921, Rome also entrusted the Franciscans with the mission of Kagoshima. On the eve of the Second World War, the Franciscans moved to the new apostolic prefecture of Urawa, north of Tokyo.

In the northern part of Japan, covering an area of almost 50,000 square kilometres, the Diocese of Hakodate, divided between the islands of Hokkaido and Honshū, had just under five million inhabitants in 1933, of whom only 3,156 claimed to be Catholic, although European missionaries had worked there since 1891. Overwhelmed by a series of local crises, particularly the numerous fires that eventually wiped out their mission, the priests of the Société des Missions Étrangères de Paris abandoned the region in 1927 to the Dominicans, who were seeking a district of their own. In August 1931, Fr. André Dumas, a member of the order's French-Canadian province, took over the diocese, where he remained until 1936. The vigour and vitality of the religious communities from Quebec transformed this diocese of seventeen parishes and five missionary posts into a focal point of church activity in Japan.[3] However, like most dioceses in Japan, Hakodate suffered from a shortage of missionaries, forcing the Dominicans to appeal to French-Canadian nuns for assistance. In due course, the Soeurs Missionnaires de

Figure 2.1 Students from a Christian Brothers parish school in Hakodate, circa 1935. *Courtesy of Frères des Écoles Chrétiennes, Quebec.*

l'Immaculée-Conception (1930), the Congrégation Romaine de Saint-Dominique (1931), the Congrégation de Notre-Dame (1932), the Congrégation de Notre-Dame de Charité du Bon-Pasteur (1935), and the Ursulines de l'Union Canadienne (1936) established missions in Japan.

To heighten the Church's influence in the more populous south, the seat of the diocese was moved to the centrally located city of Sendai, Miyagi, in the diocese of the same name on the main Japanese island of Honshū.[4] There, on 29 June 1936, amidst great pomp and with a banquet for two hundred people, members of the episcopate and representatives of the local religious communities and the municipal government, as well as the Catholic population, poured into the Sendai cathedral for the consecration of the new prelate, Monsignor Marie-Joseph Lemieux. At the youthful age of thirty-four, Lemieux became one of the few bishops of Canadian origin to serve in Japan.[5]

A second venture for the Canadian Catholic church was in the apostolic prefecture of Kagoshima. Formed from the Diocese of Nagasaki and raised to an apostolic prefecture in March 1927, Kagoshima covered over four thousand square kilometres and served the 4,735 Catholics in a total population of slightly over 2,000,000. It became a bastion of Catholicism, with relatively large numbers of conversions compared to the Diocese of Hakodate. This difference is largely explained by the presence in Nagasaki of European missionaries, who had been active since the sixteenth century, creating a solid community of believers (see Figure 1.3, p. 18).[6]

Canadian missionaries began to work in Kagoshima Prefecture in December 1926, when Florentine Dansereau, Lucienne Gagnon, and Agnès Lavallée, of the Soeurs Missionnaires de l'Immaculée-Conception, landed in Naze in response to an urgent appeal from Franciscan priests from Quebec who wanted to expand the high school for girls they had established there in April 1923. Many hopes were vested in this new school, built at the city's request on lands ceded to the nuns.[7] This was the first mandate conferred in Japan upon a community of French-Canadian women. When new nuns arrived, they extended their teaching activities to Kagoshima, before moving to Kōriyama in Fukushima at the request of the Dominicans. In addition to their regular teaching duties, the nuns gave lessons in home economics, foreign languages, and music.

Male religious communities also actively pursued educational work. Anxious to create an indigenous clergy, the Holy See conferred a mission area to the Sulpicians of Montréal. The Bishop of Fukuoka, Monsignor Albert Breton, a member of the Missions Étrangères de Paris, thought that the Sulpicians, renowned for training aspirants to the priesthood, would be the best community to meet the challenge. Consequently, Roméo Neveu, the provincial superior in Quebec, asked one of his pastors, Paul-Émile Léger, to establish a centre to train Japanese priests. In September 1933, Léger, Charles Prévost, his assistant, and forty-four members of religious communities already established in Japan embarked on the *Empress of Asia* en route to Yokohama. With a combination of joy and sadness, their sense of possibly permanent separation from loved ones was offset by the hope of being able to spread the faith in a pagan land. Their departure was all the more poignant since Japan had a reputation among French Canadians as a land of unparalleled exoticism and mystery – an impression that missionary propaganda magnified. It is hardly surprising that for the people close to them, their departure to the ends of the earth was fraught with anxiety.

After a welcome by the Bishop of Fukuoka on 7 October, the Sulpicians immediately set to work. Léger, who spent his first few months learning Japanese, was appointed parish priest of the cathedral of Fukuoka in May 1934. The opening of the seminary, however, was delayed for four years by a lack of resources and will on the part of a prelate who expected the Compagnie des Prêtres de Saint-Sulpice to provide all the necessary funding. After drawn-out discussions, Breton and the superiors of the religious institute finally agreed on funding for the new seminary, which welcomed its first ten students in April 1938.[8] Despite a substandard building, the Sulpicians, under Léger's direction, taught basic Latin, philosophy, and theology to young men eager to learn the foundations of Catholicism. The next

Figure 2.2 A secretarial class at the Omuta Commercial School, 1941.
Courtesy of Soeurs de Sainte-Anne, Lachine, Quebec.

year, the seminary moved to a more suitable building, formerly the convent of the Soeurs de Sainte-Anne, who had established a small mission in 1934.

Like many Western missionaries, Breton hoped to expand his flock by spreading the Gospel through education, and he called on the Soeurs de Sainte-Anne for help. In 1936, the eight members of the mission opened a nursery school for approximately seventy children in the Ohori district of Fukuoka. The success of this institution encouraged the nuns to open a commercial school for girls in Omuta, Fukuoka, in 1938. The nuns, supported by Japanese lay teachers, taught the rudiments of secretarial work, as well as English and French. These courses quickly became popular, since local Japanese businesses needed to replace men conscripted to fight in the escalating conflict with China.

Crisis and Conflict, 1937-45

Like their Protestant counterparts, most French-Canadian missionaries in the 1930s initially saw no danger for themselves or their country in Japan's aggression towards China. Indeed, they considered themselves Catholics first and Canadians second, whose primary loyalty was to Rome not Ottawa. Moreover, Catholics saw their faith as the most solid bulwark against the worldwide spread of communism, and many hoped that Japan would be the Asian stronghold that would repulse the atheistic ideas of Soviet Russia.

Thus, they justified the Imperial Army's invasion of China in 1937 as a way of neutralizing the forces of the Chinese communist revolutionary, Mao Zedong.[9]

Growing Japanese militarism, however, soon impeded missionary work. The army's successes in Manchuria and China boosted the confidence of Japan's ultra-nationalists, who launched a virulent campaign in the mid-1930s aimed at reducing the appeal of Western faiths, Catholicism included. Shintoism, a state-sponsored religion that emphasized patriotic sentiment and respect for one's ancestors, was clearly at odds with Catholic values. To the great annoyance of right-wing elites eager to avoid ideological divisions on the eve of war, Catholic doctrine represented a threat to the harmony and unity of the Japanese people. Heavy police surveillance imposed on the Prefecture of Kagoshima, where the Sino-Japanese conflict transformed the island of Kyūshū into a strategic shipping base, prompted Canadian Catholic missionaries to suspend their work there in 1936, when they reluctantly withdrew to Kanto and Tōhoku. However, at Tōhoku, as historian John Meehan notes, they also encountered similar police harassment.[10]

Mounting diplomatic tension between Japan and Great Britain also profoundly affected the missionaries' daily lives. As Canadian subjects of His Britannic Majesty, they were involuntary representatives of British imperialism, which had humiliated Asians since the mid-1800s, and were prime targets for retaliation. Moreover, Japanese military and political circles suspected that the missionaries might be a danger to national security since Canadians would undoubtedly support the British in any conflict with Japan. Following reprisals against missionaries in areas of China under Japanese control, the Canadian government in October 1940 urged its nationals to leave the Japanese Empire.[11] This plea had little effect. By November 1940, only fifty-two Canadians, mostly Protestant missionaries and civilians, had decided to return home, leaving quietly so as not to arouse Japanese suspicions.[12] One hundred and seventy-seven Canadians, including 108 Catholic missionaries, ignored Ottawa's appeal.[13] Edgar D'Arcy McGreer, Canada's chargé d'affaires in Tokyo, reported "that if the Japanese do not force them to leave, the majority would prefer to remain even after hostilities break out."[14] McGreer's opinion was borne out as the missionaries claimed that the Holy See was the only body with any authority over their destiny. As God's envoys abroad, missionaries were expected to abjure their patriotic loyalties to devote themselves to the propagation of the faith and to refrain from comments that might undermine the Church's credibility in Japan.[15] Maintaining their independence from secular authorities, they hoped, would spare them from the effects of any political conflict. This can be clearly seen in a letter Fr. Jean-Marie Dionne wrote to his Dominican superior, Fr. Pie-Marie Gaudrault, early in 1941:

> Apostolic Delegate this morning approved without reserve our firm determination to remain in Japan, even if the international situation comes to the worst.
> (a) As an example of our fidelity to the tradition of the Catholic Church;
> (b) Because situation of the Catholic Church here seems to have ameliorated vis-à-vis the Government with transfer of administration of Catholic Missions to Japanese and impending approbation of statutes of Catholic Church.[16]

Like their Protestant counterparts, the missionaries who remained had to conform to the Religious Organizations Law that the Diet (Japan's parliament) passed in April 1939 in an effort to unite the nation and reduce foreign domination. Under this legislation, which took effect in April 1940, all religious organizations had to be controlled by Japanese citizens. In response, foreign missionary communities transferred property and leadership positions to their indigenous clergy. Despite the resulting tension, most Canadians were not subject to serious reprisals.[17] Still, one Canadian missionary was accused of espionage. In November 1940, a Sulpician, Gaston Aubry, was detained on Kyūshū for allegedly having transmitted strategic information to the enemy. When no incriminating evidence was found, he was freed after a few days of interrogation.[18]

The Japanese attack on Pearl Harbor in December 1941 marked the start of an especially difficult period for the missionaries. Within hours, Canada declared war on Japan, prompting Japanese authorities to order the missionaries confined to their residences.[19] After lengthy negotiations between Japan and the United States, 416 foreigners, including 7 French-Canadian missionaries, embarked on the *Asama Maru* in Yokohama on 25 June 1942 and headed for the port of Lourenço Marques in Portuguese East Africa, where they boarded the *Gripsholm,* bound for New York.[20] Though a second exchange was arranged in October 1943, about 60 Canadian missionaries, mostly Catholic, remained in Japan throughout the war.[21]

Probably the most remarkable and painful event of the war for the Canadian missionaries was experienced by the seven Soeurs de l'Enfant-Jésus de Chauffailles imprisoned in Nagasaki. On the sunny morning of 9 August 1945, the drone of powerful engines rent the brittle silence of the Japanese skies. Thoroughly habituated to the criss-crossing of American bombers, the nuns paid little attention to the lone plane – a plane, though, which was about to end the war. A few minutes later, a brilliant flash of light and intense heat ripped through the skies. The second atomic bomb to devastate Japan in three days had exploded near the mission. The city was terror-stricken. A direct hit on the heartland of Japanese Catholicism, the explosion in the Urakami district killed 10,000 believers or 10 percent of Japanese

Catholics.[22] Fortunately, the nuns' internment camp was located about 6.5 kilometres from ground zero.

Postwar Prophets, 1945-2000

Although the conflict ended shortly after the bombing of Nagasaki, the task of rebuilding was obviously daunting: "50 churches, 25 convents, 30 clinics and miscellaneous institutions had been destroyed," reported the *Bulletin de l'Union missionnaire du Clergé* in June 1947, "as well as more than half the schools in the major cities."[23] In Sendai, the main religious buildings, the cathedral, the bishop's palace, and the schools had suffered a similar fate. Moreover, years of heavy military activity and American air raids had destroyed much of the country's infrastructure. Shortages of food, clothing, and fuel, and currency restrictions further complicated the missionaries' task. Nonetheless, the postwar period signalled the beginning of the most exciting era in the Catholic evangelization of Japan.

Once the immediate problems of supplying food and other supplies had been resolved, occupation authorities were eager to eliminate militarist currents in Japan, and they supported an influx of missionaries to contribute to the emergence of a more pacifist, Westernized society. They removed legal obstacles to the Church's activities and returned church buildings that had been requisitioned during the war to their former owners. Never had Catholicism enjoyed such favourable conditions. Postwar Japan became a special focus of the Holy See and soon attracted more Canadian missionaries than any other country in Asia.[24] Ecclesiastical circles looked forward to happier times for Japanese Catholicism and a phenomenal growth in the number of believers. In a country disillusioned with religious patriotism, the message conveyed by the Catholic Church seemed more in tune with the peaceful ambitions of the emerging society. Convinced that Christian ardour would soon sweep the land, most of the missionaries who had been repatriated during the war returned to Japan to resume their work, and others followed. In response to a papal appeal, fifteen Canadian Catholic communities established Japanese outposts between 1947 and 1960. Armed with knowledge gained before the war, they concentrated on education, social work, and parish activities. However, the Church never grew as much as expected; many Japanese adopted Catholicism only as a temporary refuge in hard times. Once they recovered their confidence, they had less need for the Church's spiritual support, although they often remained attached to its educational facilities, which were seen to reflect Japan's desire for excellence and high performance.

Educational Endeavours

Given the postwar emphasis on education, French-Canadian nuns, who dominated Quebec's school system, quickly became the pillars of the Church's apostolic work and arrived in large numbers in postwar Japan. Several orders of sisters – the Clarisses (1947), Rédemptoristines (1950), and Petites Filles de Saint-Joseph (1951) – arrived in Japan, bursting with hope for the future. The Soeurs Missionnaires de l'Immaculée-Conception also returned after the war. They provided a complete education in their Xaverio schools in Aizu-Wakamatsu, Fukushima, opened in April 1949, and a school in Kōriyama, founded in 1958. The Soeurs de la Présentation de Marie (1948) and Soeurs de la Charité de Québec (1953) also put their teaching skills to work restoring the Catholic school system. For their part, the Soeurs Missionnaires de Notre-Dame des Anges (1949) and Soeurs de la Charité d'Ottawa (1960) focused on social work. Two groups of nuns from Ontario, the Grey Sisters of the Immaculate Conception, who remained in Japan from 1952 to 1958, and Our Lady's Missionaries, who stayed from 1956 to 1973, were active too. Other communities, such as the Soeurs de la Présentation de Marie, responded enthusiastically to the Vatican's appeal to entrench Catholicism in Japan. The founders of their mission arrived on 6 June 1948, and after learning the language, opened a college in Himeji. Further north, the Ursulines de l'Union Canadienne devoted themselves to the people of the Tōhoku region. Starting in 1948, they taught kindergarten, primary, and secondary school in the cities of Hachinohe and Sendai. Without detracting from the efforts of other groups, the educational work done by Caritas was one of the high points of Québécois activity in Japan. This institution of the Soeurs de la Charité de Québec, located in Kanagawa Prefecture, took in more than 2,000 girls at various educational levels. Renowned for its English and French language courses, the school attracted students who wanted an international-level education that would prepare them for further studies at the most competitive Japanese and foreign universities. In 1953, the Soeurs de la Charité gave Sister Rita Deschênes the task of setting up a mission in Tokyo that would instill Christian values through education. Rose-Anna Baillargeon and Gloria Beaulieu came with her to assist in the work. Feeling more comfortable in their adopted land by April 1955, they founded the Wakabayashi Home, which housed female students, and later added a novitiate and sewing room. Six years later, building on these early successes, the community built a secondary school in Kawasaki, Kanagawa, that gradually expanded to include a kindergarten in 1962, a primary school in 1963, and a post-secondary college in 1966. For the next twenty-five years, Deschênes presided over Caritas Junior College, an effort that Emperor Showa acknowledged with an award for her contribution to Japanese society in April 1986. A similar honour was given to Sister Henriette Cantin, director of the colleges of Aomori, Aomori, and Urawa, Saitama, of the Soeurs de l'Assomption de la Sainte-Vierge.[25]

The postwar emphasis on educational work meant that fewer male religious left Canada for postwar Japan. Even so, many orders were still active. In 1948 alone, for example, the Clercs de Saint-Viateur, as well as anglophone and francophone Redemptorists, and priests from the Scarboro Foreign Missions and the Société des Missions-Étrangères du Québec settled in Japan to found schools. The Frères de l'Instruction Chrétienne, who followed in 1951, also operated Sayuri kindergarten in Yokohama (1953) and the Seiko secondary schools in Yokohama (1958) and Shizuoka (1969). The Frères des Écoles Chrétiennes, who had been active in East Asia since the nineteenth century, established La Salle school in Kagoshima in 1950. Its founder, Marcel Petit, who directed the community's schools and acted as regional superior for nearly two decades, was rewarded by Emperor Showa for his devotion to Japan.

Although Canadian Catholic educators did not found a university themselves, they actively contributed to Japanese academic life. As early as 1928, the Dominicans were asked, because of their French origins, to teach their mother tongue at the Tōhoku University in Sendai. After the war, the prestigious Kyoto University began to introduce students to the systematic study of Western thought. It asked Fr. Vincent-Marie Pouliot, who had founded the Saint Thomas Aquinas Institute in 1945, a Dominican centre specializing in the study of medieval philosophy, to lecture in July 1947. His courses covering the work of Aquinas attracted a hundred students, of whom only five were Catholics.[26] Pouliot, who taught at Kyoto until 1967, also helped to establish a chair in medieval philosophy in Kyoto University's Department of Philosophy and supervised the translation into Japanese of the works of St. Thomas Aquinas.[27] This huge project enjoyed the financial support of the Japanese Ministry of Education.

Other Japanese universities also took advantage of the talents of Canadian missionaries. In 1950, for instance, Kyūshū University in Fukuoka invited Philippe Deslauriers to teach mediaeval philosophy. When he left after five years, Louis Béliveau carried on the work until 1976. From 1956 to 1958, Paul Trahan distinguished himself as the first foreigner to teach basic Latin in Japanese at the Hirosaki University in Aomori. Between 1963 and 1974, he taught ethics, family psychology, and human relations at the Ursulines' colleges in Sendai.[28] Similarly, Canadian Jesuits helped staff their order's Sophia University in Tokyo. In addition to teaching French from 1951 to 1993, Conrad Fortin founded the Canadian Center, wrote about Canada for the Japanese public, and organized trips to Quebec to help his students better understand the realities of his homeland.

Although the education provided in Catholic schools was primarily intended to prepare young people to do well in Japanese society, it also familiarized students with the outside world by encouraging foreign contacts and the study of foreign cultures and languages. Schools administered by Canadians emphasized the linguistic realities of Canada, and even though English was enormously popular, French had its place, especially among female students interested in the culture of Molière. To serve the needs of foreign-born children residing in Japan and of Japanese children who had lived abroad and needed to ease their way back into the Japanese school system, the Frères de l'Instruction Chrétienne established the highly regarded Saint Mary's International School in Tokyo in 1954. With a total of some seventy nationalities, dominated by students from the United States, this school was a multicultural mosaic.[29]

Canadian Catholic missionaries generally agree that it was in the field of education that they made their mark on the Japanese church and society. The missionaries' educational work reached only a small number of people, but due to the elitist nature of Japanese society and its pro-Western orientation after 1945, prominent economic, political, and religious leaders spent at least some of their youth in these schools. Although the first Catholic educational institutions were established in the Meiji era, their reputation in Japanese society reached its apogee in the 1950s. The Japanese were impressed by their emphasis on the education of the whole person. The schools had particularly good resources, and in view of the conditions prevailing in postwar Japan and the popular desire to rebuild the country as soon as possible, they were well positioned to contribute meaningfully to Japan's postwar reconstruction.

Working in Japanese Society

With the painful shortage of resources in Japan after the war, it is hardly surprising that the Church's supplementary work in health care and assistance for the needy was especially welcome. Foreign missionaries, Canadian Catholics among them, helped to introduce modern Western social work practices to Japan and demonstrated that the government, which had limited its efforts to redistributing wealth before the war, must help look after society's poor. In time, the Japanese government supported some of this work financially or took it over completely.

The activities of the Redemptorists from Toronto and the Sisters of the Visitation are among the most important examples of this type of missionary endeavour. In 1949, the two orders purchased the buildings of an old Japanese military camp, where the Redemptorists opened a monastery and a hospital.[30] Similarly, in Sendai, the Soeurs de la Congrégation Romaine de Saint-Dominique ran an orphanage for many years that cared for abandoned children born of fleeting relationships between Japanese women and American soldiers. With the support of the public authorities, this home cared for young children whom virtually everyone preferred to forget. The

Frères des Écoles Chrétiennes also ran an orphanage in Sendai supported by the local authorities.

The Soeurs Missionnaires du Christ-Roi cared for dozens of abandoned children and war orphans in the Orphanage of Saint Joseph in Minami-Sakurai, Saitama. In order to create a family spirit in the orphanage, the founders, Sisters Julia Godin and Antoinette Fournier, divided their young charges into small groups. Under the supervision of a nun, acting as their mother, the children had individual facilities reserved for them. This model so impressed the Japanese government that it was extended to orphanages throughout the country. At the request of the Bishop of Yokohama, Godin also helped with the reconstruction of the Hospital of the Resurrection in Koyama, Shizuoka, and travelled across the United States to raise money to renovate the war-damaged building.

Some members of the community, especially Sister Lucienne Jacques, played an active part in renewing Japanese medicine. She revolutionized the treatment of leprosy and tuberculosis by importing medicines that helped eradicate these illnesses in Japan. The method used to treat tuberculosis at the Hospital of Christ the King in Nishinomiya, Hyogo, was so successful that it was adopted widely in Japan. The Soeurs Missionnaires du Christ-Roi undertook a number of similar initiatives in the 1960s. They built Saint Mary's General Hospital on grounds adjacent to the Koyama leprosarium. Further south, on the island of Amami, Kagoshima, Sister Georgette Couture established a centre for the mentally handicapped in 1965 that she operated for many years. The Société des Missions-Étrangères du Québec, which settled in the Aomori area, founded parishes, kindergartens, homes for the handicapped, homes for the aged, and a leprosarium to meet the desperate need in the immediate postwar years to treat that disease.[31] The distinctive contribution of the Société des Missions-Étrangères were credit unions that helped peasants avoid the usurers, who flourished just after the war. The priests of the Scarboro Foreign Mission Society, the most active English-Canadian Catholic community in postwar Japan, also established credit unions in the communities in which they resided.[32]

By the 1970s, the missionaries of the Société des Missions-Étrangères had spread out into the cities of Kawasaki, Sendai, and Tokyo, where increasingly they helped the Japanese Church deal with the people left behind by the postwar economic miracle. Catholic charities were especially concerned with poor and foreign workers – symptoms of social problems that were often overlooked. Alone on the streets, the marginalized had little success in gaining the attention of a society preoccupied with economic growth. As part of this work, Robert Vallée, a graduate of the School of Social Service at Université Laval, established a day school for severely handicapped children in Hirosaki, Aomori, in 1968, and five years later, a home for the handicapped elderly. Charles-Aimé Bolduc, who succeeded him in 1980, continued in his footsteps, creating a daycare centre in 1981 that allowed healthy children to mingle with the slightly handicapped and, in 1985, a day centre for severely handicapped young adults.

Proselytizing the Faithful

Despite the failure to make many converts, proselytizing remained, after the war as before, the main reason for the presence of Canadian missionaries in Japan. The postwar Catholic Church, with the help of Canadian missionaries, pursued a number of different strategies to spread the Gospel. For instance, to accommodate traditional Asian modes of prayer, the Clarisses and Rédemptoristines sisters established contemplative prayer houses. With the support of the abbess of the prayer house in Salaberry-de-Valleyfield, Paul-Émile Léger, and Monsignor Alfred Langlois, the Clarisses founded a mission in Tokyo with four nuns in August 1947. Having settled first in Kamakura, Kanagawa, in June 1950, the Rédemptoristines also devoted themselves to quiet prayer. Seven years later, they added a monastic house in Nagasaki and, in March 1964, a third prayer house in Kami-Suwa, Nagano.

To meet the needs of the Japanese Church, which had a shortage of priests, and to provide the faithful with a regular presence, three Rédemptoristes moved to Kamakura in 1948 and created six parishes: Kamakura; Tokyo; Ofuna, Kanagawa; Nagasaki; Okaya, Nagano; and Kami-Suwa. The community was active in education, cultural activities, and social work, but, at the behest of the bishops, concentrated on parish and related work, especially religious ceremonies and Bible instruction.

Other missionaries adapted the ideas of the Association catholique de la jeunesse canadienne-française to inculcate Catholicism in the schools. The Franciscans first employed this approach in the Kagoshima area in the 1920s, using popular activities to steer young people towards the faith. More than ever after the war, the Church feared that, in a country where nationalist ideals had been crushed decisively, youth might be vulnerable to communism. It therefore tried to steer disoriented youth towards the Gospel, establishing the Young Catholic Workers along the lines of the French-Canadian model. Since there were so few Catholics, the movement also welcomed non-Christian workers. This organization devoted itself to promoting Christian values in a world under assault from communism and materialism. Through such traditional proselytising methods as the publication of a newspaper and regular social activities, the Young Catholic Workers tried to convince young people, who might otherwise be attracted to materialism, to embrace its social agenda, which fought against a host of urban ills, including poverty, prostitution, and drug use. By 1957, the Young Catholic Workers had a presence in Japan's main industrial regions and were converting about 300 young workers per year.[33] Nevertheless, the movement remained small and without much influence.

Motivated by a similar desire to provide spiritual guidance to the faithful young and potential converts, other missionaries built residences to house college students from rural villages. The Students Home of Shinjuku, Tokyo, founded in 1954 by Fr. Bertrand Derouin, is one example. Its ultimate objective was to propagate the Word of God while enabling Catholic students to experience a Christian environment, despite the anonymity of the large capital. Like those established in other university towns such as Hirosaki and Sendai, these residences provided places for young students to meet and improve their spiritual lives. In 1966, the dynamic trio of Fathers Arthur Beaulieu, Louis-Roland Nolet, and Robert Richard took over responsibility for the Students Home and perpetuated the spirit instilled by Derouin by continuing the apostolic and academic activities aimed at enriching the students' lives.

Conclusion

Canadian Catholic missionaries in Japan frequently went well beyond the strict limits of parish work and related duties to embrace a variety of activities. Through social and educational work, they sought to appeal to a society that remained distrustful of foreigners. Like their Protestant and English-speaking counterparts, these French-Canadian Catholics recognized that social and educational work let them reach out to Japanese families, where parish work had frequently failed. Thus, almost every parish had at least one kindergarten class, where Christian values could be inculcated in the very young. Unlike the Protestant missionaries, the Canadian Catholics did not establish any universities, but individuals taught Western languages, history, and philosophy in Japanese universities, and their academic high schools gave them entrée to the Japanese elite. While only a small portion of the population took an interest in Catholicism as a faith, corollary activities were often an unqualified success. Whether in the fields of education or social work, these missionaries made a modest but productive contribution to Japan, especially in the decade after 1945. The Emperor honoured their work, but it was rarely appreciated in Canada. However, as this chapter has demonstrated, these religious workers were effective ambassadors for the values of their homeland and helped sustain vital social and educational activities, especially in the two postwar decades, as they supported Japan's reconstruction efforts in the largest missionary campaign that Canadian Catholics ever mounted in a single country.

Notes

1 This text is mainly the product of interviews with members of religious communities established in Japan since the nineteenth century.

2 Jean Hamelin, "Les missions extérieures," in *Les Franciscains au Canada 1890-1990*, ed. Jean Hamelin (Sillery, QC: Septentrion, 1990), 126-27.
3 Paul-Henri Girard, *Dominicains canadiens au Japon, 1928-1978* (n.p., 1978), 5.
4 Oeuvre pontificale de la propagation de la Foi, *Guide des missions catholiques, Tome III* (Paris: Oeuvre pontificale de la propagation de la Foi, 1936), 88-89.
5 "Le sacre d'un évêque canadien au Japon," *Bulletin de l'Union missionnaire du Clergé* 3, 12 (1936): 403.
6 Oeuvre pontificale de la propagation de la Foi, *Guide des missions catholiques, Tome III*, 88-89. Canadian Catholic missionary posts not included on the map were in Aomori, Chino, Fukushima, Himeji, Kamakura, Kawazaki, Kochi, Saito, Utsunomiya, and Yamagata.
7 Instituts missionnaires canadiens, *La Semaine missionnaire de Joliette, 4 au 10 juillet 1927* (Quebec: Charrier and Dugal, 1928), 201.
8 Alcide Laplante, "Deux pages d'histoire sulpicienne au Japon," *Messages* 22, 1 (1973): 71.
9 Jean-Charles Beaudin, *Autour du monde, Rêves et réalités d'un voyage* (Montreal: Beauchemin, 1944), 227-86.
10 See Chapter 5 of this volume, and John D. Meehan, *The Dominion and the Rising Sun: Canada Encounters Japan, 1929-1941* (Vancouver: UBC Press, 2004), 110.
11 Chargé d'affaires in Japan to the Secretary of State for External Affairs (hereafter SSEA), Telegram 102, 14 October 1940, and SSEA to the Chargé d'affaires in Japan, Telegram 86, 25 October 1940, reprinted in David R. Murray, ed., *Documents on Canadian External Relations* (hereafter *DCER*), vol. 8: *1939-1941*, part 2 (Ottawa: Queen's Printer, 1976), 1143, 1146.
12 Chargé d'affaires in Japan to SSEA, Telegram 126, 1 November 1940, reprinted in Murray, *DCER*, vol. 8: *1939-1941*, part 2: 1146-47.
13 Chargé d'affaires in Japan to SSEA, Telegram 15, 6 February 1941, reprinted in Murray, DCER, vol. 8: *1939-1941*, part 2: 1148.
14 Chargé d'affaires in Japan to SSEA, Telegram 113, 23 October 1940, reprinted in Murray, DCER, vol. 8: *1939-1941*, part 2: 1144.
15 Conseil national de l'Union missionnaire du Clergé, *Actes du Premier congrès national de l'Union missionnaire du Clergé au Canada* (Quebec: Conseil national de l'Union missionnaire du Clergé, 1943), 50.
16 Chargé d'affaires in Japan to SSEA, Telegram 29, 26 February 1941, in Murray, *DCER*, vol. 8: *1939-1941*, part 2: 1152-53 (letter written in French and then translated into English).
17 Chargé d'affaires in Japan to SSEA, Despatch 11, 22 January 1941, reprinted in Murray, *DCER*, vol. 8: *1939-1941*, part 2: 1,147.
18 Samuel Lapalme-Remis, "Enemy Nationals: The St-Sulpice Mission in Fukuoka: 1933-45" (MA thesis, Sheffield University, 2003).
19 "Proclamation," *The Canada Gazette*, 8 December 1941, vol. 100: no. 75.
20 On the exchange of civilian internees, see "Exchange Ship Leaves Japan," *New York Times*, 26 June 1942, 9; "Nomura and 1,096 Sail on Gripsholm," *New York Times*, 19 June 1942, 5; "Gripsholm Starting for New York Today," *New York Times*, 28 July 1942, 6; "Gripsholm Brings 1,500 from Orient," *New York Times*, 26 August 1942, 7; "Tous heureux de revoir le Canada," *La Presse*, 27 August 1942, 3; "Émotion délirante à l'arrivée de 217 rapatriés du Japon," *La Presse*, 2 December 1943, 3, 17.
21 SSEA to Ray Atherton, US Ambassador to Canada, Despatch 261, 6 March 1946, reprinted in Donald Page, *DCER*, vol. 12: *1946* (Ottawa: Minister of Supply and Services, 1977), 351-52.
22 Jean-Marie Dionne, "Espérances catholiques au Japon," *Bulletin de l'Union missionnaire du Clergé* 9, 2 (June 1947): 78.
23 Ibid.
24 "Où sont nos missionnaires canadiens," *Bulletin de l'Union missionnaire du Clergé* 10, 8 (October-December 1950): 439-40.
25 Henriette Cantin, *Allez enseigner toutes les nations* (Nicolet, QC: Éditions S.A.S.V, 1987).
26 Vincent-Marie Pouliot, "À l'Université impériale de Kyoto," *Bulletin de l'Union missionnaire du Clergé* 9, 7 (September 1948): 351.
27 Vincent-Marie Pouliot, ed., *Sancti Thomae Aquinatis Opusculum De ente et essentia* (Kyoto: Apud Institutum Sancti Thomae Aquinatis, 1955).

28 Armed with his missionary experience in the Tōhoku region, Paul Trahan served as an advisor of the Apostolic Nuncio in Japan from 1973 to 1976 on questions related to communication problems between the Japanese and foreign Catholic churchmen living in the archipelago. In 1977, he launched a new career with the Government of Quebec, serving as its delegate in Tokyo from 1979 to 1982. Under the terms of his mandate, Trahan lent new impetus to the cultural, academic, and political relations between Japan and Quebec. In his view, healthy interpersonal relationships were more important than trade. He retired in June 2000 from Quebec's Ministère des Relations internationales and died in January 2006.

29 Albert Tassé, *Les Frères de l'Instruction Chrétienne au Japon, Une épopée mennaisienne* (Saint-Romuald, QC: Éditions Etchemin, 1986), 117.

30 James Fuller, "Up to now ... C.S.S.R. history in Japan," *Madonna Magazine* 31, 4 (April 1958): 11-13.

31 Seiji Sugo, *Nihon senkyou 50 nen, karashidane = 50 ans de mission au Japon, merci* (Aomori, Japan: Comité des célébrations de la Société des Missions-Étrangères du Québec au Japon, 1998).

32 Mark Hathaway and Gerald Curry, "Expressing Solidarity, Scarboro Missions' Commitment to Justice and Peace," *Scarboro Missions* 76, 2 (February 1995): 4. The Scarboro Foreign Mission Society priests settled in Tokyo in 1948 and then in Nagasaki, where one of their first tasks in 1950 was to reconstruct a church destroyed by the atomic bomb. In their first years in Japan, they worked on developing parishes and doing pastoral work.

33 Hideo Inohara, "La J.O.C au Japon," *Messages de l'Union missionnaire du Clergé* 14, 4 (October-December 1957): 174.

3

Transitional Relations: Japanese Immigration and the *Suian Maru* Affair, 1900-11

David Sulz

Despite the so-called Westernization of Japan that marked the shift from the Tokugawa to the Meiji era in 1868, Japan was sometimes ambivalent about Western ideas (as Canadian missionaries discovered) and often doubtful about the West itself. These doubts were reflected in the Japanese government's uncertain attitude towards emigration. There were good reasons for Tokyo to encourage emigration to Western nations like Canada in the late nineteenth and early twentieth centuries: improved access to new technologies and natural resources, economic opportunities for its citizens, remittance income, and increased traffic for Japanese shipping. Several factors, however, made the promotion of emigration less desirable, notably the frequent need for conscript soldiers and the increasingly hostile reception immigrants received abroad. Thus, Japan occasionally banned emigration altogether, as it did during the period of the Russo-Japanese war from 1904-5. Nevertheless, Japan retained an active interest in its citizens abroad and maintained a consulate in Vancouver, where the province increasingly tried to make Japanese immigrants' presence illegal.

In the black of night on 19 October 1906, the Japanese schooner *Suian Maru* anchored in Beecher Bay near Victoria, where four boatloads of illegal Japanese immigrants slipped ashore with the intention of crossing Vancouver Island on their way to Oikawa Jinsaburo's colony on Lion and Don Islands in the Fraser River near Steveston. The plot was quickly discovered by Canadian authorities, and investigations revealed that Oikawa, a respected businessman and proven immigrant smuggler, had smuggled these farmers out of Japan without official sanction or passports and landed them secretly in Canada, thereby breaking the customs, immigration, and quarantine laws of two countries. British Columbia was not a welcoming place for any Asian immigrants, let alone illegal ones tramping through the countryside wearing the military uniforms of an increasingly imperialistic Japan. The local newspapers extensively covered the mysterious incident for several weeks until, perhaps surprisingly, the Japanese were given passports and permission to stay after paying their fines.

The arrival in Canada of the *Suian Maru* with its hold full of undocumented immigrants in 1906 illustrates some of the ambiguities in the early, transitional relationship between Japan and Canada, when attitudes regarding migration were not fully formed in either country. Asian immigration to Canada, and particularly British Columbia, was already a great source of concern by 1906, but attitudes were still somewhat flexible and depended on specific circumstances. Thus, the group of illegal immigrants aboard the *Suian Maru*, whom the broader historical record suggests should not have been welcome, became a subject of media fascination and popular curiosity, but did not generate much public hostility or cause a serious diplomatic row. Within the year, however, that apparent public and official indifference had changed to grave concern on the Canadian side as a major influx of Japanese immigrants so stimulated the existing hostility to immigrant Asian labour that a riot broke out in Vancouver. The result was the 1908 Lemieux-Hayashi, or Gentlemen's, Agreement under which Canada and Japan agreed to impose strict limits on Japanese immigration to Canada.

This chapter explores this relatively unknown incident in the history of Japan-Canada relations. It proposes that the *Suian Maru* arrived when many factors were coincidentally (and temporarily) in the passengers' favour: there were no legal mechanisms to disallow their entry (e.g., no exclusionary legislation or passport requirements); Canada's diplomatic status within the British Empire dictated its obligations under the Anglo-Japanese alliance; official Japan's attitude towards emigration was ambivalent; and there was no public outcry in British Columbia. This specific context allowed Oikawa Jinsaburo's friend, Saburo Yoshie, to use his position in the Japanese consulate and his connections with a labour contracting company to negotiate permission for the immigrants to stay in Canada.[1] Finally, this chapter places the *Suian Maru* incident in the context of evolving Canadian and Japanese policies towards Japanese immigration before 1914.

Japanese immigration to Canada is usually dated to 1877 and the isolated arrival of Manzo Nagano two and a half decades after Japan's "reopening" to the world following two centuries of isolation and strict sanctions against citizens' leaving the country. As Japan gradually eased restrictions on emigration, it tried to control migration through internal restrictions as well as by establishing consulates abroad (such as in Vancouver in 1889). The first Japanese immigrants to Canada congregated in British Columbia, and census numbers show too few to record in 1891, 5,000 by 1901, and about 10,000 by 1911.[2]

In contrast to the much more numerous Chinese immigrants, the Japanese were at first mostly ignored if not respected as part of a rapidly industrializing and Westernizing nation. As Imperial Japan grew in power and white British Columbians came to perceive a mass influx of extremely capable and competitive Japanese immigrants, tensions arose. White British Columbians used various methods to limit Japanese immigration and restrict the employment opportunities open to new arrivals. Legislation and disfranchisement in 1895, for instance, effectively excluded them from certain professions and from participation in political activities. The responses may seem severe given the low census figures, but the years and months between censuses were characterized by wildly fluctuating numbers. For example, in just three months in 1900, over 7,000 Japanese arrived in British Columbia. Even though many of those were in transit to the United States or Mexico, or were earlier immigrants returning from visits to Japan, the apparent influx prompted outrage in the province. In response, the Japanese minister of foreign affairs, Viscount Aoki, accepted Consul S. Shimizu's advice and severely limited emigration.[3] After Japan's victory in the Russo-Japanese War in 1905, immigration gradually resumed until a large influx in 1907 sparked a riot in Vancouver and the subsequent Gentlemen's Agreement of 1908, which limited immigration through the First World War, when Japan's status as ally and defender of the Pacific coast eased tensions temporarily.

The *Suian Maru's* arrival in October 1906 was not the first or largest influx of Japanese. Rather, its interest lies in the mysterious nature of its arrival, the negotiating challenge it posed to both Canadian and Japanese authorities for its irregular departure and entry at a time of potentially great racial tension, and the importance of the descendants of its passengers in the Japanese-Canadian community. From its arrival on 21 October 1906 until all was apparently resolved on 9 November 1906, Victoria's *Daily Colonist* and *Daily Times* gave it extensive and almost daily coverage.[4] At first, the incident was portrayed as a "bold attempt to elude the officials" by surreptitiously leaving Japan and entering Canada without passports. Some headlines were provocative (e.g., "Jap Coolies Land and Are Arrested," "Small Army of Japs Captured," "Jap Was Wily Schemer"), but the articles reflected more curiosity than outrage as details emerged of "one of the most mysterious things that ever happened [on our coast]." This is not to say that the newspapers warmly welcomed the *Suian Maru* immigrants. Readers were assured that laws would be upheld and penalties enforced. Furthermore, the editorial language underlined the prevailing racist attitude with a liberal sprinkling of expressions like "Jap," "coolie," "little brown men," and "little soldiers."

The first article on the incident related how Dr. A.T. Watt, dominion quarantine officer, boarded the *Suian Maru* on 20 October 1906. The captain maintained the ship was merely a fishing vessel blown off course until Watt confronted him with evidence of insufficient and unused fishing gear as well as much unclaimed baggage. After an unsuccessful attempt to bribe

Watt, the captain admitted that the ship had been chartered in Japan to land illegal immigrants on Vancouver Island, though he remained cagey about the actual number that had gone ashore. The *Colonist* reporter was confused by the illegal landing, since under Canadian law "any Japanese may land who is in a healthy condition and has the necessary passport with which every Japanese immigrant who leaves home regularly is armed."

Over the next few days, in what reads like a mystery novel with many twists, turns, theories, false leads, and surprises, the details gradually came to light in the fulsome newspaper coverage that captured the imagination of readers in Victoria and Vancouver. With every apprehension of a wandering immigrant, the total number increased – from twenty-two to thirty-seven to sixty-five to the final eighty-two. As well, their identities changed almost daily. One report said that the provincial police in Victoria received a message from Sidney that "an army of Japanese was marching down upon the quiet little town," although the informant declined to round them up because of "the record of these little soldiers in the war with Russia." The next day, the press explained that the Japanese lacked passports and had only endured uncomfortable travel aboard the *Suian Maru* because they were deserters from the Japanese army. Finally, the press characterized them as victims of one Oikawa Jinsaburo, who had duped them into believing that "Japanese were debarred from entering Canada" and then charged exorbitant fares, extracted promises to "pay further monthly instalments on arrival," and sold surplus uniforms, biscuits, and blankets to them for "ten and twenty times [the] price."

Although Oikawa Jinsaburo was quite quickly identified as the owner of the vessel, his character and motives were less than clear. First reports suggested he was starting a smuggling operation and planned to bring "natives of the Orient in large numbers without complying with the ordinary regulations." Indeed, Yoshie, described as "chancellor of the Japanese consulate at Vancouver," reportedly said Oikawa had been living on an island near New Westminster in the Fraser River and had brought the contract labourers to work in his cannery and saltery. Yoshie also informed the newspapers that police in Japan had foiled Oikawa's similar attempt to charter a schooner, the *Dainomaru*, a few years earlier. In the end, however, the press reported that Oikawa owned property on the mainland and enjoyed "good standing among his fellow countrymen."

When they did not have hard news, the press speculated about the actions to be taken against the *Suian Maru*. John C. Newbury, the collector of customs and first official to act, fined Oikawa $800 for "having landed passengers at a place that is not a port of entry." In addition, the press was confident that if the immigration and quarantine departments were unable to punish him, Oikawa would "certainly have to face prosecution on account of the expedition if he returns to Japan." The passengers themselves were reported to be in despair as they faced imprisonment in Japan for leaving home under false pretences and without passports. One passenger later recalled how Yoshie, a representative of the Japanese consul, warned that "they are talking about sending you back to Japan," while a descendant claimed that in "normal times, these people would have been deported to Japan."[5]

After 27 October, with the last of the "runaways" captured and Magistrate Hall having imposed stiff fines for landing passengers not at a port of entry and for failing to notify the proper authorities, newspaper coverage of the first case of its kind to be dealt with in Victoria fell dramatically. The total fines, including the $800 from customs and $3.15 in court costs, came to $3,078.15 or $35 for each of the sixty-five passengers. Captain Nishikiori was granted time to raise money for the fines, and the passengers, except four detained for medical treatment, were given their liberty. Once the fines were paid, the *Suian Maru* was allowed to leave. In a final report, the *Victoria Daily Times* merely noted that the "*Suian Maru*'s escape and capture caused a mild sensation at the time."[6]

Despite this considerable press coverage, the few surviving official records shed little light on the negotiations for permission to land. Indeed, the official report of Dr. G.L. Milne, the medical inspector and immigration agent in Victoria, to the superintendent of immigration in Ottawa included two newspaper articles giving "a full account of their doings." As to the negotiations, he merely recorded the "valuable assistance and services of Mr. S. Yoshiye" in bringing the case to completion, that is, paying the fine for breaking quarantine, customs, and immigration laws. The Victoria provincial court records and provincial police force record book of activities refer to the event but offer no details.[7] The Japanese consulate in Vancouver simply reported to the minister of foreign affairs in Tokyo that "Mr. Yoshie was able, through a detailed explanation of why they had entered the country illegally, to convince the authorities to exercise clemency in not prosecuting and, in fact, grant legal permission to immigrate" based on their "especially pitiable circumstances."[8] Goto Kimpei, a *Suian Maru* passenger, later recalled that "a few days later we received the wonderful news. Permission to land had come from Ottawa."[9] Although not specifically interested in the *Suian Maru* incident, a 1907 Royal Commission into the Vancouver riot investigated the Canadian Nippon Supply Company and Yoshie Saburo, both intimately involved with the *Suian Maru*. As its focus was on post-January 1907 immigration, the commission's report does not deal with the incident, though tantalizingly, it mentions the company's card catalogue, recording residence, date of employment, and job details for each individual. There are no indications that this record survives.[10]

Later historians have mentioned the incident, but added little detail. A 1921 article in the *Historical Materials of Japanese Immigration to Canada* suggests that the immigrants "neglected the formal immigration procedures" resulting in "severe measures" and court proceedings.[11] This source is unclear about whether they consciously evaded the regulations or were legitimately unaware of them. Scattered and brief accounts of the *Suian Maru* negotiations in later collections on Japanese-Canadian history add no depth. Toyo Takata reports only that "the courts proved lenient and permitted them to remain in Canada, first fining them for illegal trespass," while Roy Ito relates that Yoshie explained to Canadian authorities that each immigrant had a "great desire to work in Canada" and that being sent back to Japan would be a "tragedy."[12] In the 1970s, Japanese documentary novelist Nitta Jiro wrote an extensive account of Oikawa Jinsaburo's life entitled *Mikkousen Suian Maru* (literally, "Stowaway Ship Suian Maru.")[13] Although presented as a historical novel, it is quite accurate and has become a standard account, especially among descendants of the passengers. Nitta presents the *Suian Maru* incident from the Japanese point of view and covers Oikawa's previously foiled attempts at smuggling, the recruitment of passengers, details of the crossing and landing, and the immigrants' treatment on arrival. Nitta suggests that Oikawa and Yoshie arranged the plan well in advance: "We'll pull into port on the pretence of an emergency. Then we'll leave all the formalities and paperwork to the Consulate. If the Canadian government really is keen on Japanese workers, there should be no problem getting permission to stay. You know as well as I that most immigrants pretend to be sailors or fishermen to get into the country." Nitta explains the ultimate success of the negotiations by portraying Yoshie telling the passengers that Consul-General Morikawa Rishiro, whose duty was to care for Japanese citizens, had taken advantage of "good relations between Japan and England, the fact that Canada is in need of labourers, and that they like Japanese workers very much" to make "a special arrangement ... [to] allow you to enter the country legally." He added that "you are not criminals ... you were not really illegal immigrants despite appearances." A promise to work a minimum of one year on the railroad was part of the deal by which the Nikka Yōben Company in Vancouver lent them $37 each to cover their respective shares of Captain Nishikiori's fines for putting them ashore illegally and not having customs clear their baggage.[14]

However accurate Nitta's extensive account may be, even it glosses over what must have been complicated negotiations around the immigrants' legal status given the international, domestic Canadian, and domestic Japanese contexts surrounding their arrival. Under the Meiji government, Japan emerged as a potent imperial power and signed a treaty of commerce and navigation with the United Kingdom in 1894. That treaty granted their respective subjects "the full liberty to enter, travel, or reside in any part of the dominions and possessions of the other Contracting Party, [with] full and perfect protection for their persons and property." Canada, however, exercised an exemption and did not sign until January 1906 (with ratification in July and Parliamentary assent in January 1907).[15] Canada did consider requesting the right to exclude labourers and artisans through a clause agreed to by Japan in 1897 but opted to "adhere absolutely and without reserve" because the Japanese consul-general in Ottawa indicated that Japan "would refuse to enter into any commercial treaty which involved its admitting Canada's right to differentiate against the entry of Japanese."[16]

In 1902, Japan and the United Kingdom cemented their friendship with the formation of the Anglo-Japanese alliance. Though strengthening Japan's friendly relations with Britain and its empire, it interfered with British Columbia's attempts to limit Japanese immigration. As one immigrant recalled, "Oikawa had to contend with intense hostility to Oriental immigration" because British Columbia was not a friendly place for Asians.[17] From the late 1870s, the British Columbia legislature had attempted to limit or exclude Chinese immigrants and was partially assuaged by the federal government's imposition of a head tax on Chinese immigrants (there were insufficient Japanese immigrants to arouse any concern until the 1890s). Beginning in 1900, the legislature almost annually passed laws to halt Asian immigration, which the federal government just as regularly disallowed. The most recent of these, "An Act to regulate Immigration into British Columbia," had been passed in April 1905 and disallowed that October. Disallowance did not mean the federal government opposed anti-Asian legislation per se (it would have preferred not to aggravate British Columbians), but it had "to weigh Japan's position in the international world and her relationship with the British Empire," especially after Canada officially became a party to the Anglo-Japanese treaties.[18] Whether these treaties and reciprocal rights of travel and residence were granted automatically or had to be invoked on behalf of immigrants is another matter, especially when the *Suian Maru* migrants left without permission and had no passports to prove themselves Japanese citizens.

Newspaper articles about the *Suian Maru* expressed surprise at the attempt to evade customs and immigration regulations because any healthy Japanese with "the necessary passport" could enter. The *Colonist* noted: "If they are deported, as they fear they will be, imprisonment stares them in the face, for they left home by false pretences, as it were, signing the records of the Kencho on being permitted to engage in deep-sea fishing for six months. None have passports, and it is a crime under the Japanese laws to leave for foreign countries without passports."[19] In fact, the *Suian Maru*'s arrival was governed by Canada's Immigration Act of 1906, which stipulated that permission to leave a vessel depended upon such requirements as a clean bill of health, possibly a prescribed amount of money, and not being included in certain classes of "undesirables." However, it did not refer to passports.[20]

The press did not pursue the passport matter, but Canadian immigration officials did. A few weeks after the *Suian Maru* incident, W.D. Scott, federal superintendent of immigration, reminded local immigration agents, including Dr. Milne in Victoria, that "you shall not permit any Japanese to land in Canada who are not in possession of a passport."[21] In May 1907, however, two Japanese "stowaways" without passports successfully contested a deportation order because no proclamation had been made under Section 30 of the Immigration Act regarding passports.[22] Later in 1907, Prime Minister Wilfrid Laurier sought a cabinet order "prohibiting the landing in Canada of Japanese immigrants, other than those who come from Japan direct, bearing passports," but handwritten notes on the request show that the "recommendation was not acted upon as we have rec'd no O[rder]-in-C[ouncil]."[23] The next month, shortly after the anti-Asian riot in Vancouver, newspapers reported that "Japs May Have to Secure Passports," but acknowledged that an "understanding with Japan would be necessary to enforce such an order" since it interfered with the treaty.[24]

Although Japan's Meiji era is often characterized by internationalization and wholesale Westernization, the influence of a centuries-long Tokugawa-era policy of seclusion, which disallowed foreign travel and forbade overseas Japanese from returning home, was slow to change.[25] At the time of the *Suian Maru*'s adventure, prospective emigrants applied for a passport to the foreign office with a certified copy of the "register record" and the name of a "bondsman" who would personally guarantee that the migrant complied with all requirements. The foreign office and the local police conducted extensive investigations before granting a passport.[26] By leaving without passports, the *Suian Maru* passengers circumvented this system, but was that really important?

It seems the consul in Vancouver could vouch for an immigrant or grant a passport on arrival. The 1904 and 1908 "Record of Japanese and East Asians Entering British Columbia" has a column headed "why passed" with variations on "certified by Jap Consul."[27] Indeed, Nitta's version of the *Suian Maru* story has Yoshie Saburo of the consulate informing the passengers that "we will go into Victoria to get your pictures taken and by this time tomorrow, you will each have a legal passport."[28] In other words, passports could be issued after landing if the immigrants suited the consulate's goals or, at least, did not interfere with them.

As Japan became a powerful member of the imperial club, its desire to maintain "face" led to a concern that "the character of the Japanese abroad [would] be taken as an index of the character of the nation at home."[29] When, in the late 1890s, the consul general in Vancouver reported that many Japanese there were poor, destitute, chronically ill, and "spend all they have earned to indulge in drinking, gambling or other kinds of pleasure," prefectural governors were directed to suppress the departure of contract labourers, and the Vancouver consulate was charged with helping Canadian officials keep out bad examples.[30] In 1900, labour migrants to Canada or the United States were "prohibited entirely, for the time being," partly due to Canadian reactions to a huge influx of immigrants in early 1900 and possibly due to the pending Russo-Japanese war. However, "people worthy of representing a growing, imperial East Asian nation" were still allowed to emigrate.[31]

Why then, did the consulate assist the farmers and labourers aboard the *Suian Maru* despite their disregard for laws and restrictions designed to keep people like them from emigrating to Canada? Part of the answer is that the Meiji government did favour emigration overall: migrants provided traffic for shipping lines, revenue to the state through remittances and taxes, a market for exports, and access to a supply of raw and partly finished materials.[32] The willingness of the consulates to intervene on behalf of Japanese citizens was not a given. A more established Steveston resident told Jinsaburo that at times the consulates were "merely decorative [with] absolutely no power"; yet, according to the historian Ken Adachi, they sometimes "expended a great deal of energy in looking after the welfare of immigrants."[33]

Japan was constantly balancing the "risk of political repercussions and the fear of damaging commercial prospects" in its decisions to assist, restrict, or make concessions to discrimination against certain classes.[34] As Japan's stature increased, its willingness to concede lessened. In 1903, the Canadian minister of agriculture warned that "the proud and sensitive Japanese would be sure to resent any legislation specifically directed against them."[35] By 1906, Japan refused to grant the dominions the unilateral right to exclude labourers and artisans under the Anglo-Japanese alliance, and its protests were heeded because they were backed by "blood and iron."[36]

Given these conflicting responsibilities, the Japanese consul in Vancouver might have had two choices in dealing with the *Suian Maru*: create a strong precedent by refusing assistance, or somehow minimise the issue. For a time, the latter seemed unlikely given the extensive press coverage and expectations of action. Leniency was risky; if word got out that a large group had smuggled themselves out of Japan on false pretences and had been allowed to stay in Canada, Japan's emigration policy would be undermined and international relations damaged. The consul warned the foreign minister in Tokyo of the "volatile nature of the incident and the fear that the English newspapers would exaggerate the event and raise public opinion against immigrants stealing employment."[37] Yet, despite the intense interest in the *Suian Maru* and the fate of its passengers, the expected outrage did not arise. There were neither organized demonstrations nor public demands for deportation. Interest in the story died quickly after the passengers were convicted, fined, and given their liberty. This lack of public outcry despite the anti-Asian environment seems anomalous, but a closer examination of the

Suian Maru's arrival shows how the hostile environment was modified by specific circumstances.

Some secondary sources indicate that "mounting racial tensions" in British Columbia in the summer of 1906, following the arrival of yet another group of Asians (i.e., East Indians), resulted in a frenzy of newspaper articles and public meetings where the "old call for a white Canada" was renewed with vigour. Hostility was not confined to British Columbia. Toronto's *Saturday Night* magazine in September 1906 asserted that "the slant-eyed Asiatic with his yellow skin, his unmanly humility, his cheap wants, would destroy the whole equilibrium of society."[38] However, other sources suggest that "British Columbians had been relatively quiet on the Asian question" because of a sharp decline in Asian immigration due to the increase in the Chinese head tax and Japan's prohibition of "the emigration of Japanese labourers."[39] This created a shortage of cheap labour just when it was in high demand. Indeed, Gotoh Saori, the largest Japanese labour contractor in Vancouver, testified that it was becoming more difficult to secure labour in Japan,[40] and the superintendent of immigration reportedly said in September 1906 that he would place no limit on the number of immigrants because he had been "utterly unable to meet the demands for labour that pour in upon me from all parts of the west well nigh every day."[41]

Newspaper evidence from the autumn of 1906, when the *Suian Maru* arrived, further confirms the importance of these complicating factors.

Figure 3.1 A typical group of Oikawa Jinsaburo's labourers, prior to the arrival of the *Suian Maru*. Given the fashionable clothing of the group, the photograph was undoubtedly taken for a special occasion. *From the album of Mr. Saito Yaichi.*

Employers wanted Asian labour, though the local labour press warned that such workers would be "taken advantage of and compelled to work for a smaller wage."[42] After Japan's victory over Russia, there was interest in Japan and its culture: prominent ads for "Japanese fancy goods" available at J.M. Nagano & Co. and the Mikado Bazaar appeared daily in Victoria papers, and many news items and editorials were complimentary of Japanese culture, technical skill, business acumen, and international achievement. In fact, there was a marked sympathy and support for Japan in its increasingly strained relations with the United States, especially since Great Britain was proud to recognize the militarily strong Japan as an ally.[43] Given such sympathies and the concomitant lack of public outrage, the Japanese consulate could minimize the *Suian Maru* affair by explaining to the Canadian authorities why the *Suian Maru* had entered illegally and convincing them to "exercise clemency in not prosecuting, and, in fact, grant legal permission to immigrate."[44] Thus, the *Suian Maru* passengers became "not really illegal" immigrants.

Yoshie Saburo was the real key to resolving the issue. He had authority through his position in the consulate, a solution through his connections with a labour contracting company, and the twin desires of helping his personal friend Oikawa Jinsaburo and contributing to his own personal success. Nitta Jiro's historical novel rightly credits Yoshie with the official consular negotiations and names a *Nikka Yōben Kaisha* for putting up money to pay the fines, arranging work on the railway for the immigrants, and outfitting them with clothing and tools. While this company name is not referenced in the historic literature, *Suian Maru* passenger Bunji Goto referred to a *Nikka Yōtatsu Kaisha* in his diary, and it does show up several times in the *Historical Materials of Japanese Immigration to Canada* as the "C.N.S. Co." or "Canadian Nippon Supply Co." in Vancouver.[45] It turns out that this company was formed by Saori Gotoh and Yoshie in 1906, just after the *Suian Maru* arrived. Gotoh, a Japanese labour contractor for the Canadian Pacific Railway (CPR), had been unable to fulfill his obligations due to his countrymen's preference for fishing and a lack of new arrivals from Japan when he became associated with Yoshie at the Vancouver consulate.

Thus, the arrival of the *Suian Maru*'s eighty-two hard-working passengers, if not orchestrated by Oikawa, Yoshie, and Gotoh in advance, was certainly fortuitous for them. Furthermore, their arrival, by chance more than planning, happened to coincide with a temporary easing of anti-Asian sentiment in British Columbia, allowing an acceptable conclusion for all. The immigrants received permission to stay and work, Oikawa profited monetarily and in reputation, and the CNS was given labourers to fulfill its contracts, meeting the CPR's needs. At the same time, British Columbians saw the immigrants employed safely outside the Lower Mainland, where labour competition and unrest was most pronounced. Moreover, Canada fulfilled its imperial obligations under the Anglo-Japanese alliance, and Japan did not have to admit any problems with its emigration policies.

This window of opportunity did not last long after the *Suian Maru* incident. For one thing, Yoshie left the Vancouver consulate soon after, and it was unlikely that anyone else would have the personal connections and profit incentive necessary to exploit any similar incidents (although Yoshie himself was investigated and charged for "shady" immigration activities in the 1920s and 1930s).[46] More important, anti-Asian sentiment became a hot issue again in the February 1907 provincial election, and it exploded, after heavy immigration in the spring and summer, in the Vancouver riot of September 1907, which originated in a peaceful parade and public rally organized by the Asiatic Exclusion League. In the heat of the protest, a mob broke off and marched on Chinatown and Little Tokyo, causing much damage. An embarrassed Canadian government simultaneously sent the conciliatory deputy minister of labour, William Lyon Mackenzie King, to Vancouver to investigate compensation to property owners, and Rodolphe Lemieux, the minister of labour, to Tokyo to negotiate a deal limiting Japanese immigration. Mackenzie King found in favour of the Japanese property owners and established damages at just over $9,000.[47] Lemieux, for his part, was able to conclude the somewhat satisfactory Gentlemen's Agreement. Despite complex diplomatic considerations, the Japanese agreed to limit immigration to 400 annually in order to maintain good relations with Great Britain. However, many details were kept secret and informal so as to maintain Japanese honour, and British Columbians thus misunderstood the annual limit to apply to all Japanese immigrants, not just contract labourers. When the immigration statistics later showed more than 400 immigrants, the agreement was denounced as a failure and Japan accused of bad faith. The issue of Asian immigration arose again in the 1911 federal election, but the new government effectively maintained the status quo until the First World War, when Japan's worth as an ally was beyond reproach as the Japanese navy defended the west coast of Canada.[48]

To conclude, the lower-class labour immigrants of the *Suian Maru* left Japan irregularly (if not illegally) and violated several Canadian laws on arrival. The Japanese government, as represented by the Vancouver consulate, was aware of the potential damage to its credibility by failing to punish them severely for leaving Japan without permission and on false pretences. Given the lack of concern with the *Suian Maru*'s arrival, however, the consulate could support the bid of its passengers to stay and further its desire to encourage immigration to Canada, albeit quietly. The active force in the negotiations was Yoshie with his influence through his consular position, his connections to the Canadian Nippon Supply Company (and the CPR), his friendship with Oikawa Jinsaburo, and the chance to further his own success.

Nitta's simple explanation that Yoshie Saburo brokered a deal between the Canadian and Japanese authorities, allowing the *Suian Maru* passengers to stay in exchange for a year's work on the railroad, is accurate but misses the complex context surrounding the negotiations. The *Suian Maru* arrived in British Columbia when anti-Japanese sentiments, although always present, were at a low ebb due to factors such as good economic times, a lengthy period with relatively few Asian immigrants, and respect for Japan as an ally. Whether or not the story of the "pitiable" yet admirable passengers struck a chord with British Columbians, there was no organized call for their deportation. Even if there had been, Ottawa was more concerned with obligations to the empire and upholding the Anglo-Japanese alliance than provincial attitudes towards Asian immigration, so there were no legal means to refuse them entry through either passport requirements or exclusionary legislation.

Finally, the intriguing tale of the *Suian Maru* and its cargo of illegal immigrants offers a glimpse of the fate of one group of individuals who crossed the Pacific for a better life just as the political order was beginning to shift around them. The incident underlines the transitory nature of Canada-Japan relations in the first decade of the twentieth century. Though the unbounded optimism and fascination with the Orient that inspired the missionary enthusiasm recounted in the first two chapters of this volume were far from extinguished, they were increasingly overlaid with hostility and suspicion. The largely curious and administratively flexible attitudes the *Suian Maru* encountered in Vancouver were soon to become more formalized as Japanese-Canadian diplomacy responded to increased tensions over immigration with a system that left both sides unsatisfied. Against the backdrop of Ottawa's maturing role within the British Empire, as the following chapter makes clear, new geopolitical considerations would join immigration questions to render Canada's relations with Japan more complex still.

Notes

1 Saburo Yoshie's name appears in other sources as S. Yoshie, Yoshy, Yoshiye, Yoshi, and even Fred Yoshi alias Kiyoshi Suhinoto.

2 Patricia E. Roy, *A White Man's Province: British Columbia Politicians and Chinese and Japanese Immigration, 1858-1914* (Vancouver: UBC Press, 1989), xii.

3 Roy, *A White Man's Province*, 103-4; W.L. Mackenzie King, *Report of the Royal Commission Appointed to Inquire into the Methods by which Oriental Labourers have been Induced to Come to Canada* (Ottawa: King's Printer, 1908), 20. Charles J. Woodsworth reports that 10,302 Japanese landed at Canadian ports in 1900 in *Canada and the Orient* (Toronto: Macmillan, 1941), 51, using data from Canada, "Report of the Royal Commission on Chinese and Japanese Immigration," *Sessional Papers, 1902,* no. 54, 327. See also Patricia Roy, "Not All Were Welcome" in *Canada and Japan in the Twentieth Century*, ed. John Schultz and Kimitada Miwa (Don Mills: Oxford University Press, 1991), 2-16.

4 The quotations from Victoria newspapers are to be found in the following editions. *Victoria Daily Colonist*, 21 October 1906, 1; 23 October 1906, 7; 24 October 1906, 5; 25 October 1906, 3; 26 October 1906, 4; 27 October 1906, 9; 1 November 1906, 9; 8 November 1906, 9;

9 November 1906, 8. *Victoria Daily Times,* 22 October 1906, 4; 23 October 1906, 5; 23 October 1906, 4; 24 October 1906, 1; 25 October 1906, 2; 30 October 1906, 5; 7 November 1906, 10; 8 November 1906, 4. The *Vancouver Daily World, Vancouver Daily Province,* and *Daily Columbian* (New Westminster) selectively carried the Victoria coverage but made no editorial comment.

5 It is not clear who "they" were. Goto Kimpei's recollections from 1966 in Roy Ito, *Stories of My People: A Japanese Canadian Journal* (Hamilton: Roy Ito, 1994), 52. Gordon C. Nakamura, *Issei* (Toronto: NC Press, 1984), 49.

6 *Victoria Daily Times,* 8 November 1906, 9.

7 Milne to Scott, 29 October 1906, Library and Archives Canada (hereafter LAC), Canada, Immigration Branch, vol. 401, file 574351, reel C10292. The articles were: "Several Charges against Vessel," *Victoria Daily Times,* 23 October 1906, 5; and "Small Army of Japs Captured as they Descended upon Sidney Town," *Victoria Daily Times,* 24 October 1906, 1; Moritaro Nishikiyori, 30 October 1906, Victoria Provincial Court Records, vol. 3, 4 February 1904-18 July 1910, 73, British Columbia Archives (hereafter BCA); British Columbia, Provincial Police Force Record Book of Activities, 20 October 1906-30 October 1906, 288-92, BCA.

8 Japan, Ministry of Foreign Affairs, "Miscellaneous file relating to Illegal Japanese Immigrants to Foreign Countries," Public Document 805-21027, 5 November 1906, quoted in Jiro Nitta, *Phantom Immigrants,* trans. David Sulz (Shawnigan Lake, BC: Eclectica, 1998), 135-36. Originally published as *Mikkousen Suian Maru* (Tokyo: Kodansha, 1979).

9 Goto Kimpei's recollections in Ito, *Stories of My People,* 52.

10 Mackenzie King, *Report of the Royal Commission...Oriental Labourers,* 25-63.

11 Oikawa Jinsaburo to Imin Mondai [Oikawa Jinsaburo and the Immigration Problem] (October 26, 1906)," in *Kanada Doho Hatten Taikan: Zen* [Encyclopedia of the Japanese in Canada: Complete], ed. Jinshiro Nakayama (Tokyo: Japan Times, 1921), 1893, reprinted in Toshiji Sasaki and Tsuneharu Gonnami, eds., *Kanada Iminshi Shiryo* [Historical Materials of Japanese Immigration to Canada] vol. 8 (Tokyo: Fuji Shuppan, 2000), 1893.

12 Toyo Takata, *Nikkei Legacy: The Story of Japanese Canadians from Settlement to Today* (Toronto: NC Press, 1983), 67; Roy Ito, *Stories of My People,* 46.

13 English references to Nitta's work are from the translation by Sulz, *Phantom Immigrants.*

14 The quotations in this paragraph are from Sulz, *Phantom Immigrants,* 95, 133, 142 (or the Japanese original, Nitta, *Mikkousen Suian Maru,* 149, 208, 220); Buck Suzuki and Tom Oikawa, sons of two of the immigrants, also recalled their fathers saying they were allowed to stay because Canada needed labourers; Buck Suzuki interview, 26 April 1973, Oral History Collection, tape 31, side 1, Richmond City Archives.

15 "Japanese Treaty Act, 1906, Article I," and "Article XIX" in *Statutes of Canada,* ch. 50 (Ottawa: King's Printer, 1907), 349, 356.

16 "Anglo-Japanese Alliance," *Round Table* 1, 2 (February 1911): 133.

17 Ito, *Stories of My People,* 46.

18 Ken Adachi, *The Enemy That Never Was* (Toronto: McClelland and Stewart, 1976), 71.

19 *Victoria Daily Colonist,* 21 October 1906, 1; *Victoria Daily Times,* 23 October 1906, 5; *Victoria Daily Colonist,* 24 October 1906, 5.

20 Canada, Immigration Act, 1906, sections 18, 20, 26, 27, 28, 29. Undesirables were immigrants who were "feeble-minded, an idiot, or an epileptic, or who is insane ... deaf and dumb, or dumb, blind or infirm ... afflicted with a loathsome disease ... a pauper, or destitute, a professional beggar, or vagrant ... [or has been] convicted of a crime involving moral turpitude" or is in any way involved in prostitution.

21 W.D. Scott to G.L. Milne, 29 December 1906, Department of Immigration Records (hereafter DImm), vol. 331, file 330483, pt. 4, reel C10243, LAC.

22 MacDonnel and Henderson to Deputy Minister of Justice, 6 May 1907, DImm, vol. 332, file 330483, pt. 5, reel C10243, LAC. Section 30 read "The Governor in Council may, by proclamation or order, whenever he considers it necessary or expedient, prohibit the landing in Canada of any specified class of immigrants, of which due notice shall be given to the transportation companies."

23 Wilfrid Laurier to Governor General in Council, 9 August 1907, DImm, vol. 83, file 9309, reel C4750, LAC.

24 *Manitoba Free Press,* 27 September 1907, in DImm, vol. 83, file 9309, reel C4750, LAC.

25 Tokugawa nationalism (early 1600s to 1860s) used isolation and seclusion from outside influences (*sakoku*) to strengthen the nation. The Meiji tactic was to meet the outside on its own terms (*fukoku kyōhei*).

26 Mackenzie King, *Report of the Royal Commission . . . Oriental Labourers,* 17-18. This "register record" had been kept in every municipality for generations and listed births, deaths, marriages, and changes of residence so that each individual was bound up in the record of his family connections and, conversely, the family could be held accountable for the actions of its individuals. Some in Canada and the US alleged that the pre-emigration investigations were easily corrupted.

27 "Record of Japanese and East Asians Entering British Columbia," British Columbia, Provincial Secretary, Immigration Record, box 1, BCA. There are several variations: "certified by Consul," "cert by Jap Consul," "Reg. Jap Consul," "Reg. Ja Consul," "Reg Jap Consul." Given the small ledger column, there is probably nothing racist to be read into the abbreviations.

28 Sulz, *Phantom Immigrants,* 133. The Japanese original is Nitta, *Mikkousen Suian Maru,* 207-8.

29 W.M. Rice, "Report of the United States Commissioner" in Canada, *Report of the Royal Commission on Chinese and Japanese Immigration* (Ottawa: King's Printer, 1902), 413.

30 Quoted in Donald Teruo Hata, *Undesirables: Early Immigrants and the Anti-Japanese Movement in San Francisco, 1892-1893, Prelude to Exclusion* (New York: Arno Press, 1978), 69.

31 Canada, *Royal Commission on Chinese and Japanese Immigration,* 396; Mitziko Sawada, *Tokyo Life, New York Dreams* (Berkeley: University of California Press, 1996), 45.

32 Neville Bennet, "Japanese Emigration Policy 1880-1941," in *Asians in Australia: The Dynamics of Migration and Settlement,* ed. Christine Inglis et al. (St. Leonards, Australia: Allen and Unwin, 1992), 25; "Anglo-Japanese Alliance," 136.

33 Sulz, *Phantom Immigrants,* 56 (the original Japanese is Nitta, *Mikkousen Suian Maru,* 84); Adachi, *Enemy That Never Was,* 42.

34 Memorandum by Komura to Cabinet, as approved 25 September 1908, reprinted in Ian Nish, *Japanese Foreign Policy, 1869-1942: Kasumigaeseki to Miyakezaka* (London: Routledge and Kegan Paul, 1977), 281.

35 Klaus Pringsheim, *Neighbours across the Pacific: The Development of Economic and Political Relations between Canada and Japan* (Westport, CN: Greenwood Press, 1983), 11.

36 Quoted in "Anglo-Japanese Alliance," 137.

37 Japan, Ministry of Foreign Affairs, "Miscellaneous file relating to Illegal Japanese Immigrants to Foreign Countries," Public Document 805-21027, 5 November 1906, quoted in Sulz, *Phantom Immigrants,* 135 (the original Japanese is Nitta, *Mikkousen Suian Maru,* 212-14).

38 Peter Ward, *White Canada Forever* (Montreal and Kingston: McGill-Queen's University Press, 1978), 65. *Saturday Night* magazine, quoted in Augie Fleras and Jean Leonard Elliot, *Unequal Relations: An Introduction to Race and Ethnic Dynamics in Canada* (Toronto: Prentice Hall, 2003), 255.

39 Roy, *A White Man's Province,* 153, and table on 270.

40 Mackenzie King, *Royal Commission ... Oriental Labourers,* 20.

41 Clive Phillips-Wolley, "Obstacles in the Way of Labour," *Victoria Daily Colonist,* 28 October 1906, 19.

42 *Western Clarion* (Vancouver), 27 October 1906, 1.

43 *Victoria Daily Times* and *Victoria Daily Colonist,* September to December 1906. Japanese-American tensions resulted from the American protest against the Japanese in Manchuria, the killing of Japanese sealers, a Japanese banker murdered in San Francisco, Japanese immigrants being excluded from Hawaii and school children from California public schools, *Victoria Daily Colonist,* 23 October 1906, 2.

44 Japan, Ministry of Foreign Affairs, "Miscellaneous file," quoted in Sulz, *Phantom Immigrants,* 135 (the Japanese original is Nitta, *Mikkousen Suian Maru,* 212-14).

45 Bunji Goto, "Kōkai Nisshi [Diary of a Voyage]" in Kanichi Onodera, *Kanada e Watatta Tōhoku no Mura* [The Tōhoku Village that Crossed Over to Canada] (Towa, Miyagi: Self-published, 1996), 275; Tairiku Nippo Sha, ed., *Kanada Doho Hatten Shi* [History of the Japanese in Canada], vols. 1, 2, and 3 (Vancouver: Tairiku Nipposha, 1909, 1917, 1924), in

Sasaki, Kanada Iminshi Shiry [Historical Materials of Japanese Immigration to Canada], vol. 1 (Tokyo: Fuji Shuppan, 1995), 78, 128, 358.

46 For extensive details regarding the case against Yoshie Saburo, see Canada, DImm, vol. 342, file 361435, LAC.

47 Mackenzie King, *Report of the Royal Commission*, 11.

48 For a detailed description of the Vancouver riot, the Mackenzie King Commission, the Gentlemen's Agreement (or Lemieux Agreement, or Hayashi-Lemieux Agreement), and Asian immigration to BC, see Roy, *White Man's Province*, especially 184-226. Also Masako Iino, "Japan's Reaction to the Vancouver Riot of 1907," *BC Studies* 60 (Winter 1983-84): 47.

4
A Menace to the Country and the Empire: Perceptions of the Japanese Military Threat to Canada before 1931

Gregory A. Johnson and Galen Roger Perras

The series of international confrontations that followed Japan's invasion of Manchuria in September 1931 – collectively known for years as the Far Eastern Crisis of 1931-33 – prompted several nations to reassess their foreign and defence policies in the Pacific.[1] Recent scholarship has suggested that the crisis had a similarly significant impact on the Canadian military, forcing "a dramatic shift in focus" as "defence planners in Ottawa seriously considered the prospect of a full-blown Pacific war."[2] While Canadian officials began formal contingency planning for a conflict in the Pacific after 1933, the shift in focus was not as dramatic as might first appear. Indeed, Canadian authorities had expressed increasing concern over the potential military threat Japan presented to Canada long before the Japanese Imperial Army marched into Manchuria, concern that historians have largely overlooked.[3] If indeed, as John Meehan suggests in the next chapter, Canadian missionaries, traders, and diplomats viewed Japan with great promise and optimism in the period before 1931, there was at the same time a competing current of opinion that perceived Japan with hostility and mistrust.

Ostensibly, Canada's public attitude towards the Pacific and Japan during the first three decades of the twentieth century was generally indifferent and detached. Prior to the outbreak of the First World War in August 1914, concerns about conflict in the Pacific region and the defence of British Columbia were muted by several widespread notions about Canada's strategic posture: Europe was the most important and dangerous region of the world; the Anglo-Japanese alliance of 1902 protected Canada from Pacific threats; and Asian developments posed little danger as long as they created no political problems for the government in Ottawa. This apparent sang-froid continued after the war and into the 1920s and was influenced by growing anti-militarism in Canada and a belief that the peace in Asia was guaranteed by the disarmament measures adopted at the Washington Naval Conference of 1921-22.

Privately, Canadian military planners were rarely so sanguine, demonstrating a keen awareness of the international rivalries that characterized the "Far East" and Canada's place in those contests.[4] Partly influenced by sometimes crude racist stereotypes, partly by xenophobic reactions to Japanese immigrants (though, as David Sulz notes in Chapter 3, not all Canadians, even in British Columbia, opposed the entry of Japanese migrants), Canada's military and others became increasingly suspicious of Japanese aims in the region after 1907, developing some fantastic notions about Japan's potential to threaten Canada. By the early 1920s, however, these views were largely replaced by more sophisticated assessments about Canada's fate in any conflict between the Pacific's two increasingly prominent powers, the United States and Japan. These concerns, which echoed the political judgements of the government's diplomatic advisors, made it easy for Canadian officials to shift to formal planning for the defence of the Pacific coast when the international situation deteriorated after 1931.

Canadian strategic attitudes towards Japan at the turn of the century were largely conditioned by a series of complex and extensive changes in the international environment that occurred during the final quarter of the nineteenth century. In the Pacific, Japan threatened the established order thanks to its meteoric rise as a modern power following the Meiji Restoration of 1868, its convincing military victory over China in 1895, and its broad expansionist aims in Asia.[5] Tokyo's expanding reach, however, was challenged by the United States, whose purchase of Alaska and the Aleutians in 1867 heralded its arrival as a Pacific power. The acquisition of Midway Island, the Philippines, and Hawaii in 1898 confirmed Washington's Far Eastern orientation and made it clear, as Akira Iriye has pointed out, that "Japanese-American relations would now be those of rival empires."[6] Just as worrisome, long-established Anglo-American tensions were finally beginning to ease, but the process was by no means smooth and remained uncertain.[7] Nor could Canadians determine what the future might hold. The situation was further complicated in 1902 when Japan and Britain signed a treaty of alliance, to which Canada – a newly independent dominion but not yet in control of its own foreign policy – became a party. British officials were confident that this new alliance, designed to check Russian ambitions in Asia, would also restrain Japanese aggression in the Pacific, thereby reducing the possibility of a clash between the United States and Japan. This deal permitted Britain to turn its attention to Europe, where Germany's formidable navy posed a direct threat to British (and Canadian) interests.

Popular opinion in Canada tended to support Britain's interpretation of the changed global environment. Thus, in the half decade following the signing of the Anglo-Japanese alliance, the outlook in Canada was decidedly pro-Japanese. The *Ottawa Evening Journal*, for instance, praised the new alliance as "an extraordinary mark in history."[8] When Japan struck Russia with a pre-emptive blow in 1904, Ottawa was flooded with applications from individuals seeking to join the Japanese military. Newspapers carried up-to-the-minute reports on the war, while Methodist congregations in Ontario petitioned God to bring victory to the gallant Japanese. If Canadians had any doubt as to whom they should support, the *Winnipeg Free Press* declared, they should consider that Japan's navy "is the child of Great Britain," its ships British-built and its crews British-trained.[9] And when Admiral Heihachiro Togo's forces destroyed the Russian fleet in 1905, Vancouver's mayor joined the two thousand cheering Japanese immigrants who had gathered at the Powell Street grounds to celebrate the victory while the city band struck up a salute. Two years later, Prince Fushimi, the emperor's cousin, was welcomed to Vancouver by the mayor, fifteen thousand onlookers, and an enthusiastic press as the symbol of an enlightened and progressive world power.[10]

Despite such strong public support for Japan, there was a perceptible undercurrent of apprehension over the new Asian power in the Pacific. A small Fraser Valley newspaper captured something of that unease when it commented a few months after the outbreak of the Russo-Japanese war that "yesterday, Japan meant the daintiest musical comedy with teagarden and doll house ... Today Japan means the meeting of east and west, the swift shrewd opponent of the great slave power [Russia] in Asia. Japan is a new unfathomed force with a future hard to read."[11]

These concerns were soon amplified by two developments that exposed Canada directly to the consequences of the shifting distribution of world power. First, Britain decided in 1904 to scale down its military commitments in the western hemisphere so that it could concentrate on European affairs – part of the reforms instituted by Admiral of the Fleet Sir John Fisher, who justified the policy on the grounds that war between the United States and Britain was improbable.[12] The cuts were dramatic. British authorities withdrew troops from Canada, abolished the North American and West Indies squadrons, and withdrew from the Royal Navy's bases at Halifax and Esquimalt on Vancouver Island. Under strong pressure from Ontario to contribute more to imperial defence and from French-Canadians in Quebec to extend Canadian autonomy through an independent military, Laurier agreed to take charge of the Halifax and Esquimalt naval bases in 1905. The decision also defused growing pressure from Premier Richard McBride of British Columbia, who reminded a mostly indifferent prime minister that Ottawa was bound to maintain a naval base at Esquimalt under the province's terms of union with Canada. By taking on the base at Esquimalt, whose garrison was reduced from 350 troops to 79, the Canadian military was forced to confront the strategic situation in the Pacific. It did so nervously, from a tiny naval base that the Committee of Imperial Defence concluded in 1905 was easy prey to modern torpedo craft and indefensible against anything larger than a landing party from one or two cruisers.[13]

The second development to have a significant impact on Canadian thinking about potential threats from the Pacific was mounting anti-Japanese sentiment in the western United States, where the Russo-Japanese war had sparked fears of an invading "Yellow Peril." Spurred on by a hyperbolic and racist popular press, there were wild rumours of Japanese spies lurking near US military installations, of secret treaties between Japan and Mexico to support a move against the vital Panama Canal, and of clandestine troop movements in both countries.[14] For a brief time, American military authorities even contemplated war with Japan, and the Joint Army and Navy Board urged President Theodore Roosevelt to lay minefields off west coast cities. In an effort to appease enraged Californians, Roosevelt issued an executive order on 14 March 1907 that restricted Japanese immigration from Hawaii, Mexico, and Canada.[15]

As Chapter 3 points out, some Canadians initially sided with Japan, a British ally, against America in this contretemps. But the American decision to close the door to Japanese immigrants had an immediate impact on British Columbia. Within months, Japanese immigration to the province rose dramatically. In July 1907 alone, 2,324 Japanese immigrants arrived, adding to the 3,247 that had come during the previous six months. The influx, which was expected to continue, sparked rumours that British Columbia was about to be flooded with cheap labour. During the summer, the Vancouver Trades and Labour Council spearheaded a move to form an Asiatic Exclusion League modelled on similar American organizations. While the League had trouble recruiting members, it sponsored a rally in early September 1907 that led to rioting and, eventually, a bilateral agreement with Tokyo – the Gentleman's Agreement – to restrict Japanese immigration to Canada.[16]

The American-Japanese war scare and the Vancouver riot were important turning points in international relations along the Pacific Rim and in Canadian thinking about the dangers that lurked in the East. In the United States, the war scare led to formal planning for a conflict against Japan in the form of War Plan Orange.[17] In Canada too, senior military officials began to ponder the prospect of war with Japan. In August 1908, Colonel Willoughby Gwatkin, a respected British officer attached to militia headquarters in Ottawa, told his superiors that "the Japanese in British Columbia are very numerous. The great majority have served in the Japanese Army. They are in possession of arms and ammunition. In a military sense, they are organized; and they are in close touch with their own Foreign Office. Had war broken out a year or two ago between the United States and Japan, the Japanese residents in the United States would have cut the transcontinental railways, and a contingent from British Columbia, it is said, was ready to cross the frontier."[18] In a similar vein, Major Rowland Brittain of Military District 11 in British Columbia cautioned that the presence of so many Japanese immigrants and their "aggressive patriotism" made them "a menace to the Country and to the Empire." The implications were clear. "Unless all that the white man stands for is to be overwhelmed by an influx of Asiatic hordes," Major-General Percy Lake, the inspector general of the militia, informed a University of Toronto audience, Canadians "must stand ready to appeal to the arbitrament of war."[19]

Given good Anglo-Japanese military relations prior to 1914, a serious and immediate Japanese threat to Canada seemed improbable. When asked by the British in 1909 to provide more resources for imperial defence, including a Pacific fleet unit, Laurier declined, arguing that the $100 million that Canada had spent on the Canadian Pacific Railway was a far "more effective contribution" to imperial defence than any warship.[20] A 1911 study of Canada's Pacific defences by Britain's Colonial Defence Committee (CDC) reinforced this view. While Japan could attack Canada with "a military force of considerable size," such an assault would deprive Japan of the chance to seriously damage British interests in Asia and might embroil Japan in a conflict with the United States. As long as the Anglo-Japanese alliance remained operative, the CDC thought that a general Japanese offensive in the Pacific was "excluded from the category of reasonable probabilities to be provided against."[21]

However, the outbreak of world war in August 1914 exposed Canada's weak Pacific defences and forced Canadians to qualify this judgement. As sleek German surface raiders relentlessly sought vulnerable targets of opportunity, Canada's sole protection in the Pacific was HMCS *Rainbow*, a decrepit warship patently inferior to any German vessel it might encounter. Panicking, Premier McBride took matters into his own hands by purchasing two American-built submarines and warning the Conservative prime minister, Robert Borden, that if the war went badly for Britain, Japan might join the German cause and threaten the BC coast. Though McBride was badly mistaken, the war provided Japan with an opportunity to demonstrate its military reach. On 23 August, Tokyo declared war on Berlin, promptly attacked German possessions in Asia, and sent a warship to defend Vancouver against German raiders.[22] Until America's entry into the war in April 1917, Japan's navy provided much of the naval protection enjoyed by British Columbia. As C.P. Stacey later pointed out, the Anglo-Japanese alliance had "paid Canada a considerable dividend," something even McBride had to acknowledge when he thanked Japan in January 1915 for its "immense service" to his province.[23]

Japan emerged from the Great War strong and confident. While the European powers bled themselves dry on the battlefields of France and Belgium, Tokyo seized German colonies in the central Pacific and China, greatly

Figure 4.1 "Banzai!" *The Sun* (Vancouver), 19 June 1914. As cartoonist Jack Innes shows, Vancouverites cheered visiting Japanese on the eve of the First World War. During the war, Japan would defend the Canadian coast.

strengthening its position in Asia. As Lord Curzon of the British War Cabinet caustically noted in October 1917, Japan had "far from pulled her fair weight in the war," and any aid provided was "qualified at each stage by a most scrupulous regard for her own interests."[24] Thus, when Canadians nervously contemplated the postwar world across the Pacific, Japan loomed large. Indeed, in 1914 McBride had told J.D. Hazen, the minister of marine and fisheries, that "just as soon as the war ends we shall find Japan in complete control of the Pacific." If British Columbia lacked protection, "the position here would simply be most appalling." And appalling consequences seemed possible. Asked to examine British Columbia's security needs in 1918, British Major-General Louis Jackson pushed hard for a sizeable naval base in the province. Convinced that Germany would continue its quest to dominate Europe, Jackson believed that Japan would join the Germans "if she thought it to her interest."[25]

The base issue did not die easily. In May 1919, the naval war staff of the Royal Canadian Navy (RCN) lobbied to build a major facility at Vancouver as soon as possible. With the German presence eliminated from Asia, staff worried that British and Japanese interests were "now less coincident" and grimly concluded that the "problem in the Pacific may be approached from other points of view but it always leads to the same conclusion, namely, that Japan is the enemy." A second staff report in July put matters as bluntly: Japan was "the most probable enemy of the future."[26] These views fit in with the federal government's postwar defence plans. Following a decision by Prime Minister Borden in 1918, Canada envisioned building an independent navy, which would be designed on the basis of recommendations supplied by the First Sea Lord, Admiral Sir John Jellicoe. In October 1919, the head of the RCN, Admiral Charles Kingsmill, outlined Ottawa's strategic concerns for Jellicoe, raising a series of leading questions about the need to build naval facilities and land defences in British Columbia.[27]

By the time Jellicoe arrived in Canada in late 1919, he was already more or less persuaded of the RCN's view. His voyage by way of India, Australia, and New Zealand had convinced him that the British Empire's strategic centre had shifted to the Pacific and that Japan was now its greatest source of danger. The Admiralty, which roundly rebuked Jellicoe for these views, ordered him not to communicate any potentially embarrassing strategic opinions to Canadian leaders without its explicit approval. Nevertheless, when he met Mackenzie King, now head of the opposition Liberal Party, Jellicoe "spoke of Japan as the only possible menace of [the] future" and showed the skeptical Canadian a secret despatch on Japan's ambitious naval construction program.[28] Jellicoe thought Canada could opt either for a major fleet unit of battle cruisers and aircraft carriers, or a more modest coastal defence force comprised of cruisers, torpedo craft, and submarines, for which a special west coast naval base would not be necessary. Despite his comments to Mackenzie King, Jellicoe's formal report, issued in December 1919, played down the Japanese threat. He doubted the Japanese would attempt "a landing in Canada, because such action on their part would perhaps bring them into conflict with America." Instead, Canada would face limited Japanese attacks on its trade in the Pacific.[29]

Canada's militia hotly disputed that rosy conclusion in two rather fanciful reports in 1920. The first, authored by Brigadier J.H. MacBrien, worried about Germany's military revival and its potential conquest of a chaotic Russia, predicting that "we may see the North Pacific the storm centre of the world" by the close of the decade, with two powerful empires dominated by Berlin and Tokyo facing "the United States and Canada, the bulwarks of western civilization." A second assessment described Japan as boasting "a virile people, industrious and warlike," adding "it was not inconceivable that it will require force of arms to prevent its encroachment upon our shore."[30]

But Borden's tottering Union government was not convinced. Facing financial difficulties and slumping public support for the military after the Great War's immense losses, it provided the postwar RCN with just one additional cruiser and two torpedo craft to supplement its two submarines and nine other torpedo boats. Refusing to accept this defeat, the naval war staff cautioned in February 1921 that if Japan took advantage of Russia's revolutionary chaos to seize the Kamchatkan Peninsula, Japan's navy would possess bases a thousand miles closer to British Columbia. Three months later, navy planners asserted that "Japan has more than taken the place of Russia" as the leading threat to Canada in the Pacific. Though an invasion of British Columbia seemed unlikely, the navy warned that Canada would probably face naval and aerial raids during any conflict.[31]

C.F. Hamilton dismissed such assessments as unrealistic. A former militia officer and journalist whose writings on naval policy had influenced both the Laurier and Borden governments, Hamilton was working in the early 1920s as an intelligence officer for the Royal Canadian Mounted Police (RCMP), an agency whose commissioner favoured an intelligence system to investigate possible espionage among Japanese Canadians.[32] In March 1921, Hamilton composed a draft memorandum on the deteriorating strategic situation in the north Pacific that indicated a new sophistication in the way Canadians thought about their strategic situation. War between Britain and Japan appeared unlikely, but Hamilton feared that Japan, driven by "explosive and incalculable factors including overcrowding, economic distress, an inability to comprehend the West, and an intense and insular pride," was on a collision course with the United States, which was in "a curious and dangerous frame of mind" thanks to the skilful machinations of William Hearst's tabloids. While Canadians might not welcome an overwhelming American triumph over Japan, since this would inflame the United States, Canada's interests clearly lay in an American victory that would "reserve our Pacific coast for white settlement." Concerned that Japan might enjoy early success against an ill-prepared United States, Hamilton believed the Japanese military might use Canadian territory to attack American targets. If Canada could not preserve its neutrality, or if Japan invaded Alaska, the United States – thrown "into transports of rage by its defeats" – might become "an uncommonly ugly neighbour" and demand control of British Columbia. Hamilton offered two solutions: make Canada "a sufficiently powerful neutral, in appearance as well as reality, to impose respect upon both parties," or place a British intelligence gathering post in British Columbia that could preserve the appearance of neutrality while covertly passing intelligence to Washington.[33]

Loring Christie of the Department of External Affairs (DEA) was thinking about Canada's Pacific security along similar lines. A former New York attorney, Christie knew many prominent Americans (including military planners) who erroneously believed that the Anglo-Japanese alliance committed Britain (and hence Canada) to aid Japan in a war against America.[34] Thus, in June 1921, he argued that it was impossible "to renew the alliance in any form that will be 'acceptable' or 'satisfactory' to the people of the United States." Doubtful that Japan really thought Britain would support it in a war against America, Christie speculated that Tokyo viewed the alliance as a tool to ensure imperial "benevolent neutrality" if it clashed with Washington. As Canada could never be a party to any arrangement that might injure American interests, and would suffer disproportionately if Anglo-American relations ruptured, Christie insisted that Canada "must sound very loud" on matters affecting its direct vital interests. He therefore counselled Borden's successor, Arthur Meighen, to oppose the treaty's renewal at the 1921 imperial conference.[35] Meighen followed Christie's advice, incurring the pronounced enmity of Australia's redoubtable prime minister, Billy Hughes, who unabashedly lambasted the Canadian leader as the "voice of America."[36] In the end, the imperial leaders accepted US President Warren Harding's invitation to convene a conference in Washington to replace the alliance with a multinational Pacific security pact. Though many blamed Canada for this turn of events – R.G. Casey of Australia bitterly remarked that "Canada alone was for the break (owing to her United States complex)" – in fact, the Anglo-Japanese alliance collapsed because British statesmen had their own grave concerns about Japan's goals and America's attitudes.[37]

Canada's military had no influence on Meighen's decision. When the naval warfare staff assessed the alliance in April 1921, noting that Canada-Japan relations could be injured by the refusal of white British Columbians to grant equality to the Japanese, it had urged the treaty's renewal. Germany's defeat had removed the rationale for the alliance, but the pact could still limit Japanese intrigue in India and act "as an antidote against attempts at an alliance between Japan, Russia and Germany."[38] Nor could Canadian military officers block the budget slashing that came in 1922, although J. Sutherland Brown, the militia's chief planner, continued to insist on the need to defend Canada's west coast. Japan, he argued, would not forget that their three victorious wars since 1894 had led to "an increase in [national] prosperity." Though presently preoccupied with its new Chinese territories, Tokyo would sooner or later resume its offensive across the Pacific. Canada, Brown stressed, "must be prepared for raids or even occupation of our Pacific coast" even before a formal declaration of war. Thus, British Columbia had "to be strongly garrisoned" while Canada awaited instructions from the imperial general staff.[39]

Again, the government was not convinced by the military's description of the potential Japanese threat, and its response came a few weeks later with a round of deep cuts in the defence budget. Elected prime minister of a minority government in December 1921, Mackenzie King possessed little affection for things military. During a visit to Esquimalt in September 1920, he described the HMCS *Rainbow* "as a great waste of public money" and thought it "shameful" to waste money "on these military & naval fads." In 1922, his government slashed the navy's budget and mothballed the additional cruiser and submarines, a policy that James Eayrs has pointed out was "calmly, even gratefully accepted by the Canadian public."[40]

Figure 4.2 "Why Not Altogether?" *Victoria Daily Times,* 30 July 1921. Though he became famous as a journalist, Bruce Hutchison was also a cartoonist. Here, he shows how the three great powers of the Pacific met to establish a new order for the region after the end of the Anglo-Japanese Treaty in 1921. During the interwar period, Canada needed to steer carefully between the powers. *Courtesy of Robert Hutchison.*

Mackenzie King hammered the point home when he attended the imperial conference in London in 1923. Intent on centralizing control of the empire's military and foreign policies in their hands, the British pressed Canada for a contribution of resources to imperial security. Deeply suspicious of British politicians, and feeling confident after successfully denying a recent British request for Canadian military support against Turkey, Mackenzie King stood so firmly opposed to imperial pleas that the foreign secretary castigated him as "obstinate, tiresome, and stupid, nervously afraid of being turned out of his own Parliament when he gets back." But Mackenzie King's approach succeeded, and the conference's closing statement indicated that the conduct of imperial foreign policy was "necessarily subject to the actions of the Governments and Parliaments of the Empire," with each dominion responsible for its local defence.[41] While Mackenzie King promised to do his best to convince Canadians to do more to defend their nation's coasts, he told Admiralty official Leo Amery that he would not act until after the next election. In any event, as British Admiral David Beatty had admitted a few days earlier under persistent questioning from Mackenzie King, the most likely threat in the Pacific – a small fleet of a few Japanese raiding ships – would be incapable of inflicting any real damage on British Columbia.[42]

But as the 1920s progressed, Canadian military planners began to elaborate on the strategic vision of Hamilton and Christie. They grew much less concerned about the threat of a direct attack on the BC coast by Japan and increasingly worried about the real danger of being caught up in a US-Japan clash in the Pacific. Thus, in early 1924, the head of the RCN, Commodore Walter Hose, was happy to support a British effort to fly from Japan across the north Pacific to Alaska and Canada. Though keen to have the RCN identified with this well-publicized endeavour, Hose had other motives for providing a ship, the HMCS *Thiepval*, to establish supply caches in the Aleutian and Kurile island chains. Although the Aleutians had been demilitarized by the 1922 Washington Treaty, in 1923 the US Navy (USN) had surveyed the archipelago for potential naval anchorages that could be developed after the treaty had lapsed. Furthermore, a subsequent cruise by American submarines in Alaskan waters and rumours of a secret American base in the eastern Aleutians had raised Canadian concerns that America and Japan might be cheating.[43]

Hose's instructions to W.R.J. Beech, the *Thiepval*'s commander, were precise. Though HMCS *Thiepval's* primary purpose was to support the British mission, Hose espied "an opportunity which is not likely to occur again, of obtaining information of a high strategic value." Believing a parallel American aerial mission was designed "to gauge the practicability of flight from America to Japan via the Aleutian Island route and to gain experience in this matter," he wanted Beech to gather information about that flight and

Figure 4.3 Head of the Royal Canadian Navy, Commodore Walter Hose. *Library and Archives Canada, Department of National Defence Collection, PA-142594.*

an impending transpolar voyage by the USN's *Shenandoah* airship without arousing "a suspicion of espionage."[44]

Beech did as instructed. His bland coast report, no page-turning spy tale, noted an utter lack of naval or military defences in the Aleutians for a very good reason: the Americans had no facilities anywhere in the island chain, nor would there be any until Japan renounced the Washington Treaty in 1936. As for the Kuriles, that archipelago also appeared to lack a military or naval infrastructure.[45] But Beech's completed naval questionnaire was more illuminating, as it provided evidence that both the United States and Japan were active in the region. An American officer confirmed Canadian suspicions that the competing USN flight was designed "to test the air-route from US to Japan via the Aleutian and Kurile Islands, and to obtain first hand knowledge of any possible air and seaplane bases along the route." Numerous anchorages suitable for seaplane and naval bases were identified in the Aleutians, the Kuriles, and Kamchatka, and American revenue cutters regularly patrolled the Aleutians, while Japanese warships were commonly seen off Kamchatka. Though only one Japanese vessel had visited the Aleutians in 1923-24, likely to study seal herds, and no Japanese had been found in the Aleutians, Beech discovered that the Aleuts "fear and hate the Japanese, and avoid them whenever Japanese ships call at the Islands."[46]

Concerns about Canada's role in a US-Japan conflict persisted in Ottawa, a fearsome spectre to be trotted out in the struggle for bureaucratic advantage. This was the case in the summer of 1926, when the British War Office warned Ottawa of the possibility of a new Russo-Japanese conflict. By the end of July, Hose, embroiled in a desperate fight with the militia for funding, had made a pitch to Mackenzie King for more resources for his tiny service. He cited Canada's geographical position, the existence of other imperial navies, and "the probability, particularly in the case of a Pacific maritime war, of the United States being a belligerent in alliance with us." Even if Canada desired non-involvement in a US-Japan conflict, Hose believed that "strict neutrality could not be maintained without naval forces" given the dominion's extensive Pacific coastline. Inadequately defended, the BC coast would offer "temptations and opportunities to belligerents to forward their naval operations." Echoing Hamilton, Hose cautioned against allowing Canada's coastal defence to fall "entirely into the hands of the friendly neighbour" as the United States might make demands upon Canada "either during or after a war which could raise some serious difficulties between us."[47]

Hose's timing was superb. Having just won his first majority government in September 1926, Mackenzie King was in a position to act. According to historian Roger Sarty, the prime minister had long been concerned about American designs upon British Columbia, concerns dating back to his role in investigating the 1907 anti-Asian riots in Vancouver. Dismayed that so many British Columbians had looked to the United States to protect them against Japan, Mackenzie King had mused then about forming a Canadian navy to counter pro-American annexationist sentiment in the West. King noted in his diary in October 1926 that Canada's "exceptionally fortunate position of security in relation to world problems," his nation's proximity to Japan, and trade transiting the Panama Canal were added reasons "why we should not leave everything to America in way of protection of the Pacific." The prime minister instructed Hose to acquire two British destroyers and to tender orders for two more Canadian-built vessels.[48]

This modest rearmament effort barely registered in the balance of forces in the north Pacific and did nothing to ease Canada's uncomfortable place between two potential belligerents. A November 1928 Joint Service Committee (JSC) report on Pacific coast defences doubted that Japan would send its main battle fleet or much of its army against Canada, given its need to reduce the British base at Hong Kong. Still, a well executed naval and air assault could seriously damage British Columbia's coastal infrastructure. More important, the JSC pointed out, Canada's long undefended west coast constituted "a very serious weakness in the defence of the USA and one which may well give ground for complaint, leading perhaps to the occupation by them of strategic points of our territory."[49] Canada's sovereignty was clearly at risk, even though, as Meehan notes in Chapter 5, many Canadians, including the United Church, viewed Japanese power as a bulwark against Soviet-Communist expansion in Asia and the Pacific in the late 1920s.

This was not a view that Colonel Harry Crerar, one of the militia's brightest lights during the interwar period, shared. In an assessment prepared in January 1931, he noted Japan's "manifest intentions" to occupy a dominant position in the Pacific and commented presciently that war between America and Japan in the next decade was "a contingency which must be faced." Crerar feared that Canada, thanks to its geography and its close relations with the United States, would be susceptible to charges of non-neutrality by either combatant and would find itself put in a position "where armed defence of its frontiers would be the only alternative to active participation on one side or the other." Moreover, reprising the problem that had preoccupied Canadian military planners since Hamilton's 1921 memorandum, Crerar suspected that American forces would seek to employ Alaska and the Aleutians to bring air and naval power to bear against Japan. But as intervening Canadian territory might injure that effort, the United States, if the advantages to be gained were viewed as important, might deliberately violate Canadian neutrality, forcing Canada into the conflict.[50]

Crerar's report, circulated on the eve of Japan's assault on Manchuria, set the tone for Canadian military thinking about the Pacific for the remainder of the decade. The Canadian military and its uncertain civilian masters, struggling to find their strategic way in the Pacific, prepared plans to guarantee Canada's neutrality in any war between Japan and the United States as they worried more about American encroachment upon the dominion's sovereignty than any Japanese military threat. Whether this was a good use of brain power and resources remains debatable. As General Maurice Pope, one of the militia's chief interwar planners, recalled in his memoirs, General and Chief of the General Staff Andrew McNaughton had told him once in the early 1930s that Canada could avoid involvement in a US-Japan war for thirty days. Pope's response was that the time frame was more likely thirty hours, adding that if Canada could not adequately defend its neutrality against Japanese forces, the United States "would be entirely justified" in making use of Canadian territory to defend itself.[51]

Canada's appreciation of the potential military threat posed by Japan prior to 1931 was never set in stone. While some feared that Japanese military modernization and expansionism, as exemplified in the 1907 war scare, could directly threaten Canadian interests, this was a minority view for many years. Japan's alliance with Britain, Canadian admiration for a striving Japan prior to 1914, and Japan's support for the Allied cause in the First World War calmed most fears that Japan might attack British Columbia. As Japanese postwar ambitions in Asia became more problematic, however, and Japanese and American interests clashed, Canadian officials interested in the Pacific, such as C.F. Hamilton, expressed concern that Canada could be dragged into a future conflict between Japan and the United States. Rooted in an increasingly accurate analysis of Canada's precarious place in the Pacific balance of power, these concerns, which reflected the political judgement of the Department of External Affairs and the cabinet, made it easy for military staff officers to begin formal planning for the defence of British Columbia soon after Japan seized Manchuria in 1931.

Notes

1 See Christopher Thorne, "The Shanghai Crisis of 1932: The Basis of British Policy," *American Historical Review* 75 (1970): 1,616-39.

2 John D. Meehan, *The Dominion and the Rising Sun: Canada Encounters Japan, 1929-41* (Vancouver: UBC Press, 2004), 94.

3 Much of the literature tends to either ignore the perceptions of a Japanese military threat to Canada or to support the notion that such a perception developed after 1931. Examples include ibid; C.P. Stacey, *Six Years of War: The Army in Canada, Britain and the Pacific* (Ottawa: Queen's Printer, 1955); Michael G. Fry, "The Development of Canada's Relations with Japan, 1919-1947," in *Canadian Perspectives on Economic Relations with Japan*, ed. Keith A.J. Hay, 7-67 (Montreal: Institute for Research on Public Policy, 1980); Klaus H. Pringsheim, *Neighbours across the Pacific: Canadian-Japanese Relations 1870-1982* (Oakville: Mosaic Press, 1983); and John Schultz and Kimitada Miwa, eds., *Canada and Japan in the Twentieth Century* (Toronto: Oxford University Press, 1991). Some exceptions include Roger Sarty, "'There will be trouble in the North Pacific': The Defence of British Columbia in the Early Twentieth Century," *BC Studies* 61 (Spring 1984): 3-29; Patricia Roy, J.L. Granatstein, Masako Iino, and Hiroko Takamura, *Mutual Hostages: Canadians and Japanese during the Second World War* (Toronto: University of Toronto Press, 1990); and Galen Roger Perras, "Covert Canucks: Intelligence Gathering and the 1924 Voyage of HMCS Thiepval in the North Pacific Ocean," *The Journal of Strategic Studies* 28 (June 2005): 505-28.

4 The term "Far East" is used throughout this paper in the spirit of historical context and accuracy. It is not intended to be read as a Eurocentric approach to the subject at hand.

5 Akira Iriye, *Pacific Estrangement: Japanese and American Expansion, 1897-1911* (Cambridge, MA: Harvard University Press, 1972) is still one of the best studies of Japanese expansion.

6 Ibid., 54.

7 Relations would worsen again in the 1920s. See Gregory A. Johnson and David A. Lenarcic, "The Decade of Transition: The North Atlantic Triangle during the 1920s," in *The North Atlantic Triangle in a Changing World*, ed. B.J.C. McKercher and Lawrence Aronsen (Toronto: University of Toronto Press, 1996), 81-109.

8 *Ottawa Evening Journal*, 15 February 1902.

9 Captain R.G. Armstrong, "A Gunner in Manchuria: Canada Observes the Russo-Japanese War," *Canadian Defence Quarterly* 12 (Spring 1983), 37; and "The Rise of Japan's Naval Power," *Winnipeg Free Press*, 16 February 1904.

10 Patricia E. Roy, *A White Man's Province: British Columbia Politicians and Chinese and Japanese Immigrants, 1858-1914* (Vancouver: UBC Press, 1989), 181; and Asada Sadao, "The Japanese Navy and the United States," in *Pearl Harbor as History: Japanese-American Relations, 1931-1941*, ed. Dorothy Borg and Shumpei Okamoto (New York: Columbia University Press, 1973), 225-59.

11 *Chilliwack Progress*, 1 June 1904, quoted in Roy, *A White Man's Province*, 182.

12 See Arthur J. Marder, *From the Dreadnought to Scapa Flow: The Royal Navy in the Fisher Era, 1904-1919*, vol. 1: *The Road to War, 1904-1914* (London: Oxford University Press, 1961).

13 Memorandum by the Colonial Defence Committee in reference to CID letter of 4 May 1905, "Strategic Conditions of Esquimalt," 26 May 1905, Library and Archives Canada (hereafter LAC), Laurier Papers, 101371-2; *Documents on Canadian External Relations* (hereafter *DCER*), vol. 1, *1909-1919* (Ottawa: Queen's Printer, 1967), 247.

14 See Charles E. Neu, *An Uncertain Friendship: Theodore Roosevelt and Japan, 1906-1909* (Cambridge, MA: Harvard University Press, 1967).

15 *Report of the Commission on Wartime Relocation and Internment of Civilians, Personal Justice Denied* (Washington: Superintendent of Documents, 1982), 32-33. For an interesting examination of some of the wider implications of the war scare, see Ute Mehnert, "German Weltpolitik and the American Two-Front Dilemma: The 'Japanese Peril' in German-American Relations, 1904-1917," *Journal of American History* 82 (March 1996): 1452-77.

16 Roy, *A White Man's Province*, 185-226; W. Peter Ward, *White Canada Forever* (Montreal and Kingston: McGill-Queen's University Press, 1978), 53-76; Howard Sugimoto, *Japanese Immigration, the Vancouver Riots and Canadian Diplomacy* (New York: Arno Press, 1978); Masako Iino, "Japan's Reaction to the Vancouver Riot of 1907," *BC Studies* 60 (Winter 1983-84): 28-47.

17 Edward S. Miller, *War Plan Orange: The U.S. Strategy to Defeat Japan, 1897-1945* (Annapolis: Naval Institute Press, 1991), 21.

18 Gwatkin to Chief of the General Staff, 10 August 1908, Records of the Department of National Defence (hereafter RDND), Microfilm Reel C-5055, LAC.

19 Quoted in Desmond Morton, *The Canadian General: Sir William Otter* (Toronto: Hakkert, 1974), 299.

20 Lord Grey to the Earl of Crewe, 11 May 1909, Governor General's Records (hereafter GGR), vol. 14, file Jan. to June 1909, LAC; and Roger Sarty, *The Maritime Defence of Canada* (Toronto: The Canadian Institute of Strategic Studies, 1996), 18.

21 Colonial Defence Committee, no. 430M, "Canada. Scale of Attack on Pacific Coast," 12 January 1911, CAB38/17, National Archives of the United Kingdom (hereafter NAUK).

22 Sarty, *The Maritime Defence of Canada*, 46-47; and Marc Milner, *Canada's Navy: The First Century* (Toronto: University of Toronto Press, 1999), 40-42.

23 C.P. Stacey, *Canada and the Age of Conflict*, vol. 1: *1867-1921* (Toronto: University of Toronto Press, 1984), 160; and Richard McBride quoted in Patricia E. Roy, *The Oriental Question: Consolidating a White Man's Province, 1914-41* (Vancouver: UBC Press, 2003), 15.

24 Lord Curzon, "Military Co-operation of Japan in the War," 3 October 1917, War Cabinet Records, Minutes and Memoranda, CAB24/28, NAUK.

25 McBride to J.D. Hazen, 21 December 1914, Richard McBride Papers, vol. 1, folder 8, British Columbia Archives (hereafter BCA); and Major-General Louis Jackson, "Proposed Naval Base on the Canadian Pacific Coast," 15 August 1918, Kardex file 340.003 (D25), Directorate of History and Heritage, Department of National Defence (hereafter DHH).

26 Naval War Staff (hereafter NWS), "Occasional Paper No. 1: Remarks on a Canadian Naval Base in the North Pacific," 28 May 1919, RDND, reel C-8272, file HQS2732, LAC; and NWS, "Occasional Paper No. 2: Proposals for Canadian Naval Expansion," 3 July 1919, RDND, vol. 5696, file 1017-31-2, LAC.

27 Milner, *Canada's Navy*, 57-68; and Admiral C.E. Kingsmill to Admiral Sir John Jellicoe, 31 October 1919, RDND, vol. 5669, file NSS78-1-13, LAC.

28 A. Temple Patterson, *Jellicoe: A Biography* (London: Macmillan, 1969), 226-27; and W.L. Mackenzie King, diary, 3 December 1919, W.L.M. King Papers, LAC.
29 "Report of the Admiral of the Fleet Viscount Jellicoe of Scapa on Naval Mission to the Dominion of Canada (November-December 1919)," 31 December 1919, George Foster Papers, vol. 32, file Report of British Naval Mission, LAC.
30 J.H. MacBrien to the Otter Committee, "The Military Forces of Canada," early 1920, A.G.L. McNaughton Papers, vol. 109, file Otter Committee, LAC; and "Draft for Otter Committee. Canadian Military Forces. General Appreciation of the Problem of Reorganization," early 1920, A.G.L. McNaughton Papers, vol. 109, file Otter Committee, LAC. The American army worried that Japan and Germany had formed a secret alliance in December 1918; Lt. Colonel T.C. Peck to Military Attaché, the Hague; "Alleged German-Japanese Treaty," 12 August 1919, Entry M1216, War Department Records (hereafter WDR), Correspondence of the Military Intelligence Division Relating to General, Political, Economic, and Military Conditions in Japan 1918-1941, reel 1, file 2063-190, United States National Archives (hereafter USNA).
31 NWS, "Occasional Paper No. 26: Petropaulski – Its Strategical Value," 11 February 1921, RDND, vol. 5696, file 1017-31-4, LAC; and NWS, "Occasional Paper No. 31: Esquimalt – Its Future," 27 April 1921, RDND, vol. 5696, file 1017-31-4, LAC.
32 Sarty, *The Maritime Defence of Canada*, 84-85; Patricia E. Roy et al., *Mutual Hostages: Canadians and Japanese during the Second World War* (Toronto: University of Toronto, 1990), 31.
33 C.F. Hamilton memorandum, March 1921, C.F. Hamilton Papers, vol. 3, file 12, LAC.
34 In 1911, Britain had insisted that the pact must not commit either signatory to fight another power if a signatory had signed an arbitration treaty with that third power. Britain had signed such a treaty with the United States; "Agreement between Great Britain and Japan relative to eastern Asia and India," 13 July 1911, appendix to NWS, "Occasional Paper No. 28: Anglo-Japanese Relations," 1 April 1921, RDND, vol. 5696, file 1017-31-4, LAC. American plans to combat an Anglo-Japanese coalition, including Canada, are discussed in Miller, *War Plan Orange*, and Richard A. Preston, *The Defence of the Undefended Border: Planning for War in North America, 1867-1939* (Montreal and Kingston: McGill-Queen's University Press, 1977).
35 L.C. Christie, "The Anglo-Japanese Alliance: Recapitulation of Points," 1 June 1921, reprinted in *External Affairs* 18 (September 1966): 402-13. In 1888, Foreign Secretary Lord Roseberry had stated that Canada and Australia "must sound very loud" in matters directly related to their interests; H. Duncan Hall, *Commonwealth: A History of the British Commonwealth of Nations* (London: Van Nostrand Reinhold, 1975), 47.
36 Billy Hughes quoted in Peter Spartalis, *The Diplomatic Battles of Billy Hughes* (Sydney: Hale and Iremonger, 1983), 229.
37 R.G. Casey to S.M. Bruce, 12 January 1928, in W.J. Hudson and Jane North, ed., *My Dear P.M.: Casey's Letters to S.M. Bruce, 1924-1929* (Canberra: Australian Government Publication Service, 1980), 7. Canada is credited with the Alliance's demise in J. Bartlet Brebner, "Canada, the Anglo-Japanese Alliance and the Washington Conference," *Political Science Quarterly* 50 (March 1935): 45-58; and A.R.M. Lower, "Loring Christie and the Genesis of the Washington Conference of 1921-1922," *Canadian Historical Review* 47 (March 1966): 38-48. Michael G. Fry offers a useful corrective in *Illusions of Security: North Atlantic Diplomacy 1918-1922* (Toronto: University of Toronto Press, 1972).
38 NWS, "Occasional Paper No. 28: Anglo-Japanese Relations," 1 April 1921, RDND, vol. 5696, file 1017-31-4, LAC. The Admiralty had argued that hostility towards Japanese immigrants in the US and BC "might at any moment provoke a casus belli"; First Lord of the Admiralty, no. CP-2957, "Anglo-Japanese Alliance," 21 May 1921, CAB24/123, NAUK.
39 J. Sutherland Brown, "Precis of a Lecture – Japan," 3 February 1922, RDND, vol. 2643, file HQS3497, LAC. Brown's Defence Scheme No. 1, which envisaged a pre-emptive Canadian strike into America, was condemned as "a kind of creeping paralysis of the imagination" by James Eayrs. However fantastic such a war might now seem, American officers devised similar schemes; James Eayrs, *In Defence of Canada*, vol. 1: *From the Great War to the Great Depression* (Toronto: University of Toronto Press, 1964), 214-33; and J.L. Granatstein, *Canada's Army: Waging War and Keeping the Peace* (Toronto: University of Toronto Press, 2002), 167.

40 Milner, *Canada's Navy*, 60-61; Mackenzie King, diary, 27 September 1920, King Papers, LAC; and Eayrs, *In Defence of Canada*, 1:170-72.

41 Galen Roger Perras, "Parties Long Estranged: The Initiation of Australian-Canadian Diplomatic Relations, 1935-1940," in *Shaping Nations: Constitutionalism and Society in Australia and Canada*, ed. Linda Cardinal and David Headon (Ottawa: University of Ottawa Press, 2002), 137; and "Minutes and Final Report of the 1923 Imperial Conference," November 1923, Imperial Conference Records, CAB32/9, NAUK.

42 Entries for 24 and 18 October 1923, "The Private Diary of Rt. Hon. W.L. Mackenzie King, Prime Minister of Canada, on the Occasion of His Attendance at the Imperial Conference and the Imperial Economic Conference in London, England, during October and November, 1923," King Papers, LAC.

43 Hilary P. Jones to the Secretary of the Navy, "Report of Commander Fleet Base Force on Alaskan Reconnaissance," 26 March 1924, Strategic Plans Division Records, Series III, box 35, Naval Historical Center; Vincent J. Ponko Jr., "The Navy and the Aleutians before World War II: The Story of a Flirtation," *Alaska Journal* 13, 2 (Spring 1983): 128-31; Lieutenant J.D. Lawrie, "Monthly Intelligence Summary Esquimalt BC Area, No. 5," May 1923, RDND, vol. 11918, file E57-63-3, LAC; Lieutenant F. Gow, "Monthly Intelligence Summary Esquimalt BC Area, No. 9," September 1923, RDND, vol. 11918, file E57-63-3, LAC; and Gow, "Monthly Intelligence Report Esquimalt BC Area, No. 11," November 1923, RDND, vol. 11918, file E57-63-3, LAC.

44 Hastings to Gow, 9 February 1924, RDND, vol. 11924, file 1091-7-1, LAC; and Hose to Beech, 13 February 1924, RDND, vol. 3897, file NSC1034-11-3, LAC. Arctic explorer Vilhjamur Steffansson contended the *Shenandoah*'s trip was designed to reconnoitre "strategically located islands" in Canada's Arctic; Steffansson to King, 2 January 1924, Records of the Department of External Affairs (hereafter DEAR), vol. 2668, file 9058-D-40, LAC.

45 Hastings to Intelligence Officer Esquimalt, "Coast Report, Part I," 27 September 1924, RDND, vol. 11924, file 1091-7-1, LAC.

46 Beech, "Reply to Naval Questionnaire," September 1924, RDND, vol. 4043, file NCS 1076-2-2, LAC.

47 War Office to the Chief of Staff, Department of National Defence, 21st July 1926, RDND, reel C-4975, file 3367; and Commodore Walter Hose, "Naval Policy," 30 July 1926, King Papers, Memoranda & Notes, vol. 124, file 913, LAC. See also R.W.H. McKillip, "Staying on the Sleigh: Commodore Walter Hose and a Permanent Naval Policy for Canada" (MA thesis, Royal Military College of Canada, 1991).

48 Sarty, *The Maritime Defence of Canada*, 90; Mackenzie King, diary, 26 October 1926, King Papers, LAC; and Milner, *Canada's Navy*, 65-67.

49 Joint Staff Committee, "Pacific Coast of Canada," Kardex file 322.016 (D22), 22 November 1928, DHH.

50 Crerar, "Memorandum on the Re-Organization of the Non-Permanent Active Militia of Canada," 29 January 1931, Crerar Papers, vol. 11, file 958C.009 (D218), LAC.

51 Maurice A. Pope, *Soldiers and Politicians: The Memoirs of Lt.-Gen. Maurice A. Pope* (Toronto: University of Toronto Press, 1962), 91.

5
Pacific Beginnings: Canada and Japan between the Wars, 1929-41

John D. Meehan

> It is not surprising that Japan should be among the first of the nations of the world to which Canada has sent her diplomatic representatives ... As your island Empire is our nearest neighbour in the West, so we are your closest friends on the East.
>
> – Diplomatic Diary, 9 September 1929

Such was the pledge of friendship made by Herbert Marler upon his arrival at Yokohama aboard the *Empress of France* on 9 September 1929. Shortly after disembarking from the gleaming liner, Canada's first minister plenipotentiary to the Sunrise Empire assured his expectant hosts that Canada's interest in Japan went beyond its growing Pacific trade. Canada and Japan had a common mission to make the Pacific "an ocean of peace," Marler asserted, and all Canadians sincerely desired to keep their record of peaceful relations with Japan "unblemished."[1]

Marler's wish, though well intentioned, was untimely. Within the month, the stock market collapse in the United States triggered a global economic crisis that seriously undermined export markets. Both Ottawa and Tokyo responded to domestic calls for economic relief by adopting protectionist trade policies and pursuing unilateral foreign policies. With the election of R.B. Bennett's Conservatives in 1930, protectionism became the order of the day, though the new leader's rhetoric of "blasting into" foreign markets through high tariffs made little sense in economic terms. In Japan, civilian authorities faced growing threats from militarists and ultra-nationalists who promised more radical solutions to domestic woes. Tensions soon ignited in Manchuria, where long-standing rivalries between China, the Soviet Union, and Japan culminated in the latter's seizure of the region in the fall of 1931. By the time Marler left Tokyo in 1936, Japan had abandoned the League of Nations and withdrawn from the London naval conference, leading most Canadians to view it as a menace rather than an ally. Marler's hopes to the contrary, the Pacific was certainly not an ocean of peace, nor was Canada's friendship with Japan unblemished.

Yet, the interwar period, for all its turbulence, marked Canada's diplomatic debut in Asia. From the opening in 1929 of its legation at Tokyo – the third such styled office after Washington and Paris – to Canada's declaration of war against Japan in 1941, influential Canadian opinion makers and policy makers began to see their country as a Pacific as well as an Atlantic nation, a development often overlooked by Canadian historians. Analyses of internationalist groups such as the Canadian Institute of International Affairs (CIIA) and the League of Nations Society of Canada (LNSC) often neglect links between these groups and the Institute of Pacific Relations (IPR). Economic histories of the period gloss over the bitter trade war between Canada and Japan in 1935, and accounts of interwar pacifism usually overlook the national boycott and embargo campaigns that erupted after the outbreak of the Sino-Japanese conflict in 1937. Even studies of appeasement ignore Canada's response to Japanese expansion, notably Canada's increased export of strategic metals to Japan after 1937. Ritchie Ovendale is typical in jumping from Prime Minister William Lyon Mackenzie King's meeting with Adolf Hitler in July 1937 to the *Anschluss* of early 1938 without any mention of the Sino-Japanese conflict.[2]

This analysis of Canadian-Japanese relations during the interwar period examines Canada's role in Pacific appeasement by tracing its changing perceptions of Japan.[3] The opening of the Tokyo legation in many ways symbolized the initially benign view of Japan that many Canadians held. Inspired by a variety of myths, Canadian diplomats, missionaries, and traders at first saw great promise and seemingly unlimited potential in the Empire of the Sun. Within a decade, however, they saw Japan as a potential threat, though their concerns did not result in immediate action against Tokyo. While the turning point in these attitudes varied from one interest group to the next, three broad phases of this shift may be discerned: an initial optimism prior to the Manchurian crisis (or beyond in certain limited cases); a transitional period during the mid-1930s when each group, prompted by crises affecting its own interests, re-evaluated its assessment of Japanese aims; and a clear road to war, beginning with the Sino-Japanese conflict of 1937.

Pacific Promise: Myths and Challenges

In 1929, Marler's expression of friendship seemed entirely appropriate. Though no longer formally united by the Anglo-Japanese alliance, which had lapsed in 1921, Canada and Japan were still close friends, bound by a 1913 treaty of commerce and navigation and a tradition of warm bilateral relations. Goodwill towards the Asian power extended even to rural Saskatchewan, where railway towns were named after Japan's heroes of the Russo-Japanese war. The two nations had been allies during the First World

War, when Japan defended Canada's west coast from German attack, and Canadians had served under Japanese command in Siberia during the subsequent Allied intervention in the Russian civil war. These historic considerations were not unimportant for Canadian politicians formulating policies towards a country about which most of their constituents knew relatively little.[4]

Canada's attitude towards Japan during the 1920s was also conditioned by the policies of its two most important allies, the United States and Great Britain. Desiring Anglo-American harmony in the Far East, Canada was ever sensitive to Washington's growing suspicion of Japan and its exclusion from the Anglo-Japanese alliance. At the imperial conference of 1921, Prime Minister Arthur Meighen argued for the incorporation of the United States into a broader framework of Pacific security, a multilateral approach soon endorsed at the Washington conference of 1921-22. Along with nine Pacific powers, Canada agreed to an "open door" policy of equal economic opportunity in China and the resolution of Far Eastern disputes through mediation rather than force. Canada, however, remained a junior partner in this new arrangement of collective security. Though Sir Robert Borden signed one of the Washington treaties for Canada, British delegates had already endorsed it on behalf of the entire empire.[5]

Canada's diplomatic arrival in Asia occurred at a critical juncture in British imperial affairs. In 1927, buoyed by the enhanced status for dominions that they won at the 1926 imperial conference, Canada, along with Ireland and South Africa, sought expanded diplomatic representation abroad. Mackenzie King's Liberal government moved cautiously, appointing ministers (not ambassadors) to oversee legations (not embassies) in Washington, Paris, and Tokyo. If trade and proximity justified the first choice, and French-Canadian sentiment the second, then immigration, trade, and status favoured a legation in Japan. To Mackenzie King, the consummate politician, the move had widespread domestic appeal, though opposition critics feared it would be misconstrued by the "Oriental mind" as a sign of imperial disunity.[6]

The new legation would play a vital role in regulating Japanese immigration, issuing a maximum of 150 visas per year, thereby responding to the demands of West Coast exclusionists. Japan's centralized and efficient bureaucracy would adhere to this limit throughout the 1930s. Moreover, Ottawa hoped the legation would promote trade with Japan, which was now Canada's fourth largest customer, importing nearly $38 million worth of goods in 1929, with a surplus of $24 million in Canada's favour. Finally, the legation would signify to Canadians – and the world – that the dominion had come of age, taking its place at the economic and political hub of Asia. Though Marler was not Mackenzie King's first choice for minister, the Montreal notary's great personal wealth, as well as his penchant for ceremony, would ensure the promotion of Canadian prestige in the Orient.[7]

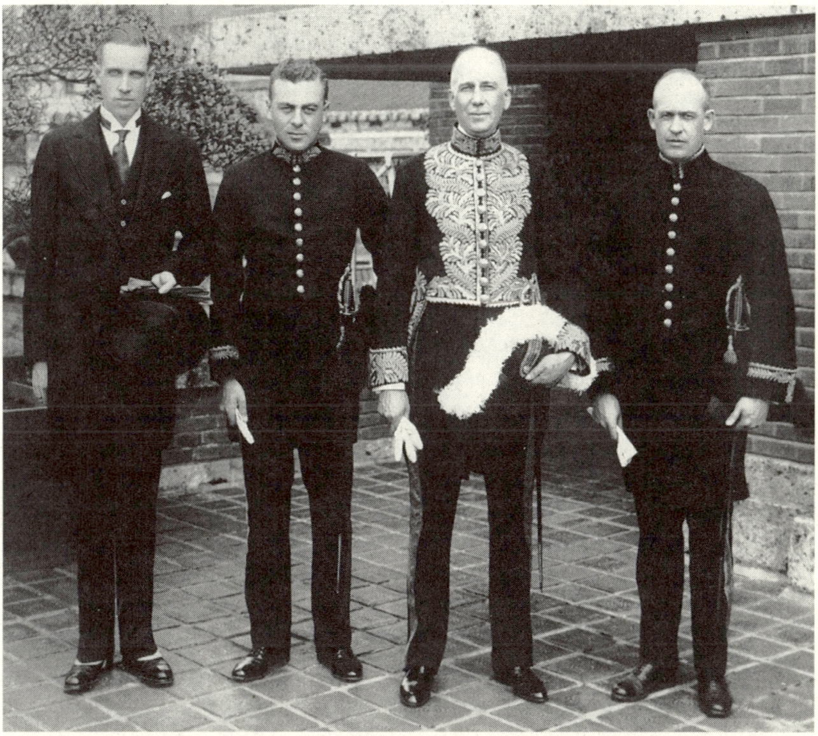

Figure 5.1 The Canadian staff of the new legation in Tokyo, 1929. Left to right: K.P. Kirkwood, H.L. Keenleyside, Herbert Marler, and J.A. Langley. *Library and Archives Canada, Ueno Makita Kogabo, PA-120407.*

Such optimism was readily evident in the Dominion Day ceremony orchestrated by Hugh Keenleyside, first secretary at the legation, in Shibuya ward, Tokyo, in 1929. In advance of Marler's arrival, Keenleyside invited scores of Canadian missionaries and traders to the minister's residence to witness the first official raising of the dominion flag in Asia. The event, which was filmed for posterity, impressed O.D. Skelton, Mackenzie King's under-secretary of state for external affairs. The pride of those assembled, despite their now silent renditions of "O Canada" and "God Save the King," is still apparent in the grainy footage of the occasion that has survived.[8]

By contrast, Japanese reaction to the initiative was subdued. Though Japan had appointed Prince Iyemasa Tokugawa as its first representative to Canada in January 1928, it was frustrated by Canada's delay of nearly a year in appointing a minister to Tokyo. British concerns over diplomatic unity as well as difficulties in Canada in arranging the exchange were to blame. By late 1928, Japan's ambassador to Washington, Katsuji Debuchi, warned that further delay might lead to embarrassment and criticism of his government in Japan. Moreover, several Japanese newspapers urged that such an exchange of ministers be conditional upon more liberal Canadian immigration policies. While the conservative *Yamato* demanded that such policies be revoked before any exchange took place, the *Kokumin* hoped the opening of relations might reverse "the anti-Japanese attitude of the Canadian people."[9]

Similar misunderstandings characterized attempts to explain Canadian autonomy. Despite Marler's publicity on the subject, confusion remained in Tokyo as to Canada's precise status within the British Empire. Legation staff did not help matters as they often relied on the good offices of the British embassy to secure meetings with Japanese officials. For his part, Marler mystified Skelton – and shocked the prime minister – when he suggested that he succeed the *British* ambassador to Japan upon the latter's retirement. Colonial mindsets clearly took longer to shed than colonial status.[10]

These reactionary attitudes helped perpetuate the varied myths about Japan and its role in East Asia that were already prevalent among many Canadians. Imperial visitors to Canada, such as Prince Takamatsu, the emperor's brother, and his charming new bride, Kikuko, were received with almost as much pomp as were members of the British monarchy in the early 1930s. Japan's use of royal diplomacy, as well as its imperial traditions, institutions, and ethos, led some to view it as the "Britain of Asia" with a similar civilizing mission. Though missionaries in Korea, notably those who documented Japanese atrocities there in 1919, told another story, many Canadian observers praised the Japanese for their civility, ethical code, and industriousness. Japan seemed a land of missionary promise, as outlined by Toyohiko Kagawa, the prominent Japanese Christian social reformer, in his crusade of "one million souls for Christ." As Hamish Ion and Richard Leclerc note in Chapters 1 and 2 of this volume, Canadian missionaries viewed such efforts as a godly alternative to Marxism and were generally sympathetic to Japan's opposition to bolshevism.[11] Amidst growing tensions in Manchuria, *New Outlook*, the journal of the United Church of Canada portrayed Japanese ambitions in a positive light: "Japan may have been warlike, but at the present we do not see any reason why she should not be one of the great factors in preserving the peace of the world. She must have room for expansion, but surely this can be arranged without any attempt at an appeal to arms."[12]

Canadian business also viewed Japan as a bulwark against communism, though it displayed a desire for profits rather than a zeal for souls. It readily appreciated the material advantages of a close association with Asia's most dynamic economy. Japan's empire seemed to provide the political order, modern infrastructure, and stable currency for trade and investment that China and other Asian nations lacked. With a population of over sixty-three million, increasing at an annual rate of about one million, Japan proper offered a vast market for raw materials. Resource-based firms, such as Alcoa

(Alcan after 1928), H.R. MacMillan Export Co., and Consolidated Mining and Smelting, responded quickly to Japan's increased demand for raw materials as its industrial sector grew and its empire expanded. Timber exports to Japan surged after the Kanto earthquake of 1923, raising the value of Canadian exports from $6.4 million in 1921 to $27 million in 1924. Canadian firms also hoped to profit from the "open door" of economic opportunity in nearby China, enshrined in the Washington agreements. Life insurance companies were similarly active: Sun Life opened an office in Japan in 1893 – the first such foreign company to do so – with Manufacturers Life following five years later. By 1930, Canadian Pacific Steamships, whose White Empress liners had plied the Pacific since 1891, had offices in Yokohama, Kobe, Shanghai, Tientsin, Hong Kong, and Manila to manage its fortnightly service from Vancouver.[13]

Canadian business interests benefited from an extensive network of trade offices under the Department of Trade and Commerce, whose reports were characteristically optimistic. Beginning with Yokohama in 1904, the department opened offices in Shanghai, Kobe, Hong Kong, Batavia, and Calcutta, eventually transferring James Langley, its trade commissioner at Kobe since 1923, to Tokyo in late 1929. His appointment was an experiment in interdepartmental cooperation: Trade and Commerce paid his salary while External Affairs covered his living expenses. His jurisdiction, according to a trade inspector's report of 1928, also included Manchuria, "given extensive Japanese influence there," though the report recommended opening a new office at Dairen, Manchuria, "within the next year or two." Japan, the report concluded, was "one of the most important territories" in the trade service and one of "the first foreign countries in which the Service should extend its operations." Marler echoed this optimism during his Western Canadian tour en route to Japan in August 1929, when he assured businesses interested in Japan that they would be welcomed by "a courteous, industrious and reliable people."[14]

During its first two years, the Tokyo legation seemed to justify such hopes, though challenges soon emerged. Cultivation of goodwill proceeded apace, as shown by Japan's cooperation in limiting emigration, Marler's entertaining of more than three thousand guests, and his plans to build at his own expense the prestigious new legation described in Chapter 13 by Marie Josée Therrien. Yet, friendship with Japan became a thorny problem in Ottawa's relations with China. A Chamber of Commerce mission in 1930, though well received in Japan, met with protests in Hong Kong calling on Canada to replace its exclusionary immigration policy with a gentlemen's agreement similar to that concluded with Japan.[15] Trade commissioners in China, echoing these concerns, were already suspicious of Marler's desire to coordinate trade with Asia, an issue that tested cooperation between the Departments of Trade and Commerce and External Affairs. Matters came to a head in early 1931, when Marler's negotiation of a major wheat sale to China was scuttled by Nanjing's inability to pay, Tokyo's wariness of the scheme, and Prime Minister Bennett's premature announcement of the deal. Chinese officials, on these and other occasions, criticized Canada for its failure to establish a legation in China.[16]

A Rude Awakening

Japan's invasion of Manchuria in September 1931 heralded the beginning of a shift in Canadian perceptions of the Sunrise Empire. The incident, immediately brought to the attention of the League of Nations by China, highlighted divisions within Canada between imperialists and those wary of communism on the one hand, and internationalists eager to defend collective security on the other. Those in the latter camp, such as the LNSC, socialist leader J.S. Woodsworth, and J.W. Dafoe, the liberal editor of the *Manitoba* (soon to be *Winnipeg*) *Free Press*, saw the imbroglio as the first major test of the League. Those in the former camp, such as Bennett's secretary of state Charles H. Cahan, business leaders, and some missionaries, were sympathetic to Japan. Such divisions were also reflected at the Tokyo legation. While Keenleyside found no justification for Japan's actions in Manchuria, Marler soon believed that Western recognition of Manchukuo, Japan's puppet state in the region after 1932, was only a matter of time.[17]

In discussing Canada's reaction to the crisis, commentators have tended to emphasize Cahan's regrettable speech at the League in December 1932, in which he questioned China's membership in the body and supported some of Japan's claims.[18] His peroration shocked many, including Skelton, who feared its apparent endorsement of Britain's softer stand on Japan might alienate Washington. Historians have portrayed the Cahan affair as an aberration in Canadian foreign policy without considering the context of his remarks or their wider domestic appeal. To Skelton's distress, the crisis suggested that Anglo-American harmony in the Far East was likely to become increasingly elusive, forcing Canada to choose between its two closest allies. Indeed, it was difficult to reconcile the non-recognition of territorial gains, as maintained by US Secretary of State Henry Stimson, with the accommodation of Japan urged by Sir John Simon, Britain's foreign secretary. This divergence, combined with poor communications, helped explain Cahan's blunder, though clearly his views resonated widely at home.[19]

In Canada, condemnation of Japan was far from universal. The press, in fact, was divided on the matter. While the *Manitoba Free Press, Toronto Star*, and *Vancouver Sun* called for decisive action at the League, the Montreal *Gazette* and Toronto *Globe* echoed British sympathies in justifying Japan's seizure of Manchuria. "There is no territory in the whole world to which Japan has as good a right to penetrate," argued the *Globe*, citing Japan's growing population and its need for markets. "Japan, like Italy, must sooner

Figure 5.2 "Yes, There's One Way He Could Be Stopped," *Vancouver Sun,* 27 February 1933. Cartoonist Les Callan illustrated the controversial view that the application of sanctions could halt the Japanese military machine. *Courtesy of Mrs. F.M. Callan.*

expand or explode." *Saturday Night,* more than any other publication, stressed the benefits of Japanese imperialism. After helping defend Canada during the Great War, it noted, Japan now offered prosperity, "order and good government" to a region threatened by Soviet communism and Chinese "disorder and rapine."[20]

Nor was there agreement in Canada on what to do about the crisis. While the *Free Press* urged sanctions, Montreal's *La Presse* recalled that the League's founders preferred moral sanctions to military intervention. The *Financial Post* predicted that League action was unlikely, since members would not go to war over Manchuria. Thus, Cahan, like Marler and others of Canada's business elite, expressed doubts that were more widespread about the very notion of collective security. As he confided just prior to his address, no one at Geneva was "prepared to give a man or a gun or a ship" to defend League principles in the Far East.[21]

With the United States and Britain – and Canadians themselves – divided over what to do about Japan, it was clear that Ottawa would eschew collective action in Asia, especially if it might lead to war. This was true of both Conservative and Liberal governments throughout the decade. When hostilities reached Shanghai in early 1932, Canadians, like most Westerners, were shocked by the threat to foreign interests there, but not to the point of advocating action against Japan. The League's adoption of Lord Lytton's report recommending non-recognition of Manchukuo led not to collective action but rather to Japan's departure from the body in February 1933. Bennett then considered joining a British arms embargo against both Japan and China but the scheme was soon abandoned due to lack of American support.

As Japan's threat to Pacific security loomed larger, however, its apologists became fewer. Canadian military planners, noting the poor state of coastal defences, increasingly envisaged the prospect of a Pacific war. In such a scenario, as British historian Arnold Toynbee soon warned, neutrality would be as useless to Canada as it had been to Belgium during the Great War. Suspicions were further aroused in April 1934, when Eiji Amau, a junior *gaimusho* (foreign ministry) official declared Japan's right to act unilaterally in East Asia. Tokyo's attempts to clarify what was widely perceived as a "Monroe doctrine" for the Far East were hardly reassuring. By early 1936, Japan had withdrawn from the London naval talks, abandoning the system that had guaranteed Pacific security since the Washington conference of 1921-22.[22]

While defenders of collective security become acutely conscious of Japan's threat to the peace of Asia on its departure from the League, others took longer to reach this conclusion. Marler, though frustrated by Ottawa's instructions to delay and downplay the move to larger premises, went ahead with opening his stately new legation in late 1933.[23] By this stage, the fiction of an independent Manchukuo, with its own flag, state apparatus, and economic planning, was nearly complete. In early 1934, it acquired an emperor – Henry Pu Yi, the last Manchu ruler of China – and diplomats in Japan, including Marler, debated whether to receive him during his upcoming visit to Tokyo. Such developments led Marler to express his sympathies more openly, explaining Japan's actions to Skelton in the following terms: "Notwithstanding my admiration in many ways for the people of Japan – and I may add to an extent my sympathy for what was bound almost unavoidably to take place in Manchukuo as expressed at great length in previous despatches – there is this factor: that the Japanese are bound most positively to their Manchukuo policy and will suffer no advice or criticism of it from anyone at all."[24]

Canadian business was equally pragmatic in dealing with Japan, though its prospects there were increasingly bleak. Pacific trade had not recovered from the global economic depression. By 1933, as shown in Table 5.1, the value of Canadian exports to Japan had plummeted to $13 million from $37.5 million in 1929 and nearly $16 million in 1931. The combination of rising protectionism after the 1932 imperial conference in Ottawa, Washington's retreat from the gold standard, and a severe depreciation of the yen in 1932 further worsened the terms of trade. Canada's share of Japan's wheat imports since 1926 had fallen from 81 percent to only 52 percent in the face of American and Australian competition. Moreover, the new trade office opened at Dairen in 1931 proved a failure when Japan seized Manchuria and restricted its trade. Despite Marler's protests, the office was closed in January 1933. Marler had advised caution due to the League's consideration of the Manchurian crisis, claiming Japan was "extremely sensitive to anything in respect to Manchuria – or to give it its new name, Manchukuo." At the Department of Trade and Commerce, Dana Wilgress, chief of its commercial intelligence service, believed Marler exaggerated the effect of closing the office, since he was overly influenced by "Japanese opinion."[25]

Table 5.1

Canadian trade with Japan, 1929-41 (Cdn$ millions)

Year	Exports to Japan	Imports from Japan	Surplus
1929	37.5	13.3	24.2
1930	23.4	10.2	13.3
1931	15.7	6.8	8.9
1932	12.0	4.6	7.4
1933	13.0	3.1	9.9
1934	16.5	4.4	12.1
1935	14.9	3.6	11.4
1936	19.8	4.3	15.5
1937	25.8	5.9	19.9
1938	20.8	4.6	16.1
1939	28.2	4.9	23.3
1940	11.4	5.9	5.5
1941	1.5	2.3	-0.8

Note: These figures are for the year ended 31 December and do not include indirect shipments.
Source: Canada, Department of Trade and Commerce, Dominion Bureau of Statistics, *Trade of Canada, 1941*, vol. 1 (Ottawa: King's Printer, 1942), 37.

Marler's efforts to maintain trade ties with Japan were ineffective amid worsening Anglo-Japanese trade relations. When an anti-British trade campaign engulfed Japan in the summer of 1933, after London imposed prohibitive tariffs on Japanese cotton entering India, the Federated Malay States, and West Africa, Marler urged Ottawa to distance itself from the move. Skelton composed a careful reply to Marler against direct representation to the Japanese government but decided not to send it. A further British tariff on Japanese imports to the West Indies and other dependencies in early 1934 caused Canada, Australia, and even the United States to distance themselves from Britain. Yet, as Keenleyside noted, confusion persisted in the Japanese press over Canadian autonomy, and most editorials failed to distinguish between British and dominion trade policies. Moreover, remarks by Japanese officials prompted some to fear Japan might strike at Britain through Canada.[26]

Matters came to a head after October 1934, when the Bennett government imposed an exchange compensation duty on Japanese imports to offset the yen's depreciation. Tokyo condemned the move as directed solely against Japan, in violation of the 1913 trade agreement, and as likely to add to Canada's already large trade surplus. The Japanese press embarked on a bitter anti-Canadian campaign and, by May 1935, Tokyo warned that reprisals might follow the arrival of its new minister to Canada, Sotomatsu Kato. Marler's plea for concessions fell on deaf ears in Ottawa. Skelton's argument that the duty was not discriminatory (as it had been applied against other countries with depreciated currencies) and that trade surpluses were normal phenomena convinced few Japanese.

Soon, even businessmen in the Japan-Canada Society were demanding "drastic action" against Ottawa, prompting legation officials to fear for their safety from mob attack. Marler, who thought that Canada had been singled out for "harsh treatment," became the target of a press campaign after Japanese officials publicly questioned his sincerity. By his own admission, no one had been "more conciliatory or more patient" with Japan than he had been, though "looking back on the past six months I sometimes think I have been too conciliatory."[27]

A full-blown trade war erupted in late July 1935 when Japan imposed a 50 percent *ad valorem* surtax on Canadian wheat, lumber, and pulp and paper, and Canada responded with a 33.3 percent surtax on all Japanese imports. Domestic divisions on the dispute immediately became apparent. While central Canadian interests, as expressed through the *Financial Post*, commended Bennett for standing up to Japan, British Columbian exporters feared the loss of three thousand jobs. The *New York Times* predicted both countries would suffer, though it attributed the dispute to Japan's drive for materials to "carry on her extensive Chinese operations." On advice from W.D. Herridge, his minister to Washington (and brother-in-law), Bennett decided to make the dispute an issue in the October general election. His public threat to suspend the 1913 trade agreement antagonized the Japanese but drew little response from Canadian voters. The victor in the election, Mackenzie King, immediately resolved the dispute by removing the surtax and limiting the future application of dumping duties. Exporters soon revived hopes of benefiting from Japanese expansion, particularly as structural changes in Japan's economy began to favour large imports of raw materials.[28]

Missionaries, increasingly the object of xenophobic outbursts, also revised their perceptions of Japan during this period. Hostility was first directed against French-Canadian Franciscans at Kagoshima and on the strategic island of Amami Oshima. Accused of espionage (with cameras ostensibly hidden in church belfries), disrespect towards Japan's state-religion of Shinto, and illicit relations with converts, some Catholic missionaries were forced off the island in 1934. Bowing to Vatican requests not to press the matter due to fear of further harassment, Marler regretted he could not do more to protect them. Protestant missions faced other challenges. By 1934, Kagawa's Kingdom of God movement had failed, its founder stricken with trachoma in the Kobe slums, and the United Church's board of missions, for the first time, was forced to institute budget cuts. In 1936, Japanese authorities, notably in Korea, began enforcing the attendance of all teachers and pupils at Shinto shrines. While many Americans and Australians refused to comply, faced with the prospect of school closures, most Canadian Anglican, United Church, and Catholic missionaries obeyed the order. Though the United Church missions board ruled this was "merely a patriotic act" and not idolatry, many Japanese, in Marler's view, began to see Christianity as a "heretical religion" opposed to the *kokutai*, or national polity. Such patriotism, as Hamish Ion notes in Chapter 1 of this volume, led Japanese Christian leaders to distance themselves from Western sponsors and align themselves more closely with national aims.[29]

The young officers' coup of 26 February 1936 sparked a sharp change in Canadian attitudes towards Japan. It was the only Far Eastern event to capture headlines across Canada that year and, despite its failure, was widely seen as the advent of fascism in Japan. In the early hours of that morning, about 1,400 young officers, inspired by ultra-nationalist ideology, seized key government posts and killed several top officials. Despite public sympathy for their aims, Emperor Hirohito rejected their demands and 15,000 soldiers of the imperial guard crushed the revolt. The Canadian press, for the first time, was united in its assessment of Japan, differing only on the *extent* to which it had become fascist. Its young rebels, even *Saturday Night* admitted, embodied the "very essence of Fascism," their German and Italian counterparts being "but poor imitations." Mackenzie King was horrified by the revolt, believing the death of moderates would lead Japan to extreme policies, such as joining Germany, Italy, and perhaps even Russia in a "terrible combination." Fearing a military dictatorship in Japan, Skelton predicted heightened concerns over Pacific defence. By year-end, Japan had concluded a pact with Germany, and Canada had doubled its naval budget to defend its vulnerable coastline.[30]

The Road to War

The Sino-Japanese conflict, which erupted after a skirmish on the Marco Polo Bridge near Beijing on 7 July 1937, marked the defining moment in Canada's relations with Japan during the 1930s. As the undeclared war progressed, most Canadians sympathized with China, although, as in the Manchurian crisis, not to the point of agreeing on sanctions against its Japanese occupier. Officially, Mackenzie King's government adopted a policy of strict neutrality (see Figure 5.3). Privately, the prime minister remained wary of what he perceived as British attempts to draw the dominions into a Pacific war. At the imperial conference of June 1937, he strongly opposed a Pacific security pact proposed by Australia and New Zealand. In October of that year, he compared British efforts to coordinate dominion views prior to a conference of Pacific powers at Brussels with Britain's previous futile attempt to enlist Canadian support for a war with Turkey in 1922. The prime minister rejected the British overture, which he received in "the most important despatch which had ever come into my hands ... with the exception possibly of the one relating to [the 1922 crisis in] Chanak."[31] Mackenzie King was equally wary of collective action at Geneva and, along with Skelton and the veteran foreign affairs advisor, Loring Christie, warned against any appearance of a British Empire bloc there. Finally, King responded to agitation for sanctions against Japan in late 1937 by depicting himself as a true pacifist, avoiding measures that might lead to war. Through its opposition to both unilateral and collective action, the Canadian government's response to Japanese aggression sheds much light on its role in Pacific appeasement.[32]

As in the Manchurian case, Canada was frustrated by Anglo-American divergence over the Far East. London's reluctance to oppose Japan was reinforced by a defence report drafted in 1934 that claimed Britain could not win a simultaneous war against Japan and Germany, and Germany posed a more immediate threat. Though relying on American leadership in the Pacific, British Prime Minister Neville Chamberlain doubted Washington's willingness to act firmly in Asia. Nine days into the Sino-Japanese conflict, US Secretary of State Cordell Hull condemned the use of force in resolving international disputes but failed to single out Japan for condemnation. President Franklin Roosevelt's subsequent call for an "international quarantine" of aggressor states was also vague, leading Chamberlain to believe it was "always best and safest to count on nothing from the Americans but words."[33]

As in 1932, Canada, like Britain and the United States, grew especially concerned when hostilities reached Shanghai in August 1937, evacuating

Figure 5.3 "See No Evil," Stewart Cameron, *Calgary Daily Herald,* 27 November 1937. Canada along with the rest of the world remained silent about the Japanese assault on China, despite its brutality. However, the war had a deep impact on popular attitudes towards Japan. *Permission by Copyright Board of Canada.*

most of its 250 nationals from the city within days. Moreover, this crisis threatened Canadian neutrality when the British ambassador to China was injured in a Japanese air attack, raising the spectre of an Anglo-Japanese conflict. Anxiously awaiting resolution of the dispute between London and Tokyo, Mackenzie King instructed Randolph Bruce, Marler's successor, to delay his departure for Japan. By this stage, however, Bruce's remarks to the Canadian press had aroused criticism. As he reportedly told the *Toronto Star* in mid-August, Japan's invasion of China was "simply an attempt to put her neighbor country into decent shape, as she has already done in Manchuria."[34]

Chastened by outraged Canadian internationalists, Bruce claimed to be misrepresented and resolved not to give any more interviews. Nonetheless, the yawning gap between Canada's professed neutrality and its actual reaction to Japanese aggression grew steadily wider. In the fall of 1937, on the eve of the Brussels conference of Washington Treaty powers, called to address the Asian crisis, Mackenzie King's government faced a barrage of criticism over its apparent complicity with Japan's war machine. According to

Table 5.2

Canadian metal exports to Japan, 1929-40 (Cdn$ thousands)

Year	Nickel	Copper	Aluminum	Lead	Zinc	Scrap iron
1929	325	44	2,014	3,279	1,430	96
1930	74	12	3,900	3,052	2,038	295
1931	111	15	2,095	1,918	698	52
1932	126	32	638	1,168	626	15
1933	93	20	783	900	744	122
1934	320	183	1,340	1,415	776	344
1935	952	21	1,590	1,400	1,129	334
1936	632	23	1,967	2,150	790	325
1937	2,050	167	1,948	3,976	1,092	674
1938	5,439	1,301	4,778	2,865	1,294	643
1939	5,578	2,155	6,506	1,555	953	626
1940	955	2,208	825	1,504	23	4

Note: Figures are rounded to the nearest $1,000 and do not include indirect shipments. Figures for 1929-39 are for the fiscal year ended 31 March. Figures for 1940 are for the calendar year ended 31 December as shipments to Japan of aluminum and zinc ended in March, nickel in July, and copper and lead in October.
Sources: Compiled from Canada, Department of Trade and Commerce, Dominion Bureau of Statistics, *Trade of Canada, 1931-41*.

Ottawa's own figures, the Japanese invasion of China had coincided with the largest gain in Canada's trade surplus with Japan since 1924. As can be seen in Table 5.2, exports of lead and scrap iron had doubled since 1936 and those of nickel more than tripled, making Canada Japan's main supplier of nickel and probably of aluminum and lead.[35]

To many, Canada seemed to be profiting from Japanese expansion, a charge later made publicly – much to Mackenzie King's outrage – by the noted China missionary, Dr. Robert McClure. Calling for decisive action at Brussels, the LNSC, the socialist Co-operative Commonwealth Federation (CCF), and the communist-front Canadian League for Peace and Democracy (CLPD) urged an economic boycott and trade embargo against Japan, inspired by similar movements in the United States and Britain. Women, farmers, labourers, students, veterans, Chinese groups, city councils, and even the Alberta legislature sent resolutions to Ottawa demanding action against Japan. Such protests failed to impress *Canadian Business*, which countered that – short of "definitely hostile relations" between Britain and Japan – "every advantage should be taken of the Japanese market."[36] When the LNSC, aided by Dafoe, tried to solicit support from banks, corporations, and the finance minister, Mackenzie King was incensed. Unlike the so-called pacifists, he was determined to avoid at all costs policies that would, in his opinion, lead to war:

> It is almost ludicrous that, of all men on earth, I should be the one to have had difficulty with the advocates of any Peace Movement. My life has been devoted to the study of that problem, and the avoidance of strife both industrial and international, and I am being made the target of the attacks of Peace Societies. Such is life! An organized attack at that. The day has been a battle throughout with the power of money and the power of the press.[37]

Mackenzie King's worries were soon put to rest. His private secretary, A.E. Pickering, exploiting divisions between radical and moderate sanctionists, persuaded the latter that hasty action might jeopardize Canada's position at Brussels. Moreover, the movement for sanctions itself, as one activist later recalled, failed to attract most Canadians, despite its mass rallies, tag days, and postcard campaigns.[38] Though London invited cooperation at the League, Mackenzie King's sensitivity on this point perhaps blinded him to Britain's own insecurity in East Asia and wariness of collective action. British officials were relieved when replies from most of the dominions, as well as the United States, indicated an unwillingness to press sanctions at Brussels. The conference itself was a dismal failure. Japan refused to attend, making the meeting resemble "Othello without Iago" (in the words of Hume Wrong, one of the Canadians present), and the US delegation appeared to have no instructions. On 12 December 1937, within days of this failure of collective security, Japanese forces entered Nanjing, where they committed horrific atrocities. Despite the veil of censorship over the city, Skelton received a brief firsthand account of the slaughter in early 1938, through a Canadian missionary in China, but left no record of a reply or follow-up with the Tokyo legation. Similarly, the Canadian press, like its counterparts elsewhere in the Western world, was more alarmed by Japan's attacks on US and British vessels in the Yangtze than by its massacre of tens, perhaps even hundreds, of thousands of Chinese.[39]

Canada eventually adopted sanctions against Japan, but not until the outbreak of war in Europe in September 1939 forged the Anglo-American consensus that had been so elusive in peacetime. With trade placed on a wartime footing, Allied coordination of metals exports, particularly of nickel, at times led to more stringent policies in Ottawa than in London or Washington. By an order-in-council of 20 September 1939, all exports of strategic metals required a permit from the Department of National Revenue, though initially only steel and scrap iron shipments were denied. Britain and the United States collaborated more closely on restricting alloy exports as the year progressed, and in early 1940, Washington allowed its commercial treaty with Japan to lapse. The Mackenzie King government, prompted by growing popular anger over Japanese attacks on missionary posts in China, and mounting concerns about Pacific defence, also acted. Ottawa ended shipments to Japan

Figure 5.4 "His Imperial Highness Presides," Argus, *Toronto Globe and Mail,* 13 January 1938. Japanese diplomats, alert to any insult to their nation, protested this cartoon in which an "insignificant and trembly figure" represented the emperor taking orders from military and naval leaders. The Department of External Affairs recognized the cause for anger but advised the chargé d'affaires in Ottawa that, although newspaper editors had a "wide measure of freedom," the Department would have a quiet talk with the *Globe*'s Ottawa representative.

of aluminum and zinc in March 1940, followed by nickel and cobalt in July, and copper and lead in October. When the embargo was extended in early 1941 to include wheat, flour, and wood pulp, foreign ministry officials in Tokyo protested that, with the near cessation of trade, a Canadian legation was no longer necessary.[40]

Wartime powers led to action in other areas. After Japan signed the tripartite pact with Germany and Italy in September 1940, Ottawa addressed rising fears in British Columbia about possible fifth column activity by registering Japanese Canadians. In response to Japan's seizure of Indochina in July 1941, Canada joined the United States and Britain in freezing Japanese assets, a largely symbolic gesture since its exports to Japan were now mainly foodstuffs paid for with US currency. On London's advice, Mackenzie King decided not to appoint a minister to Tokyo, a post left vacant since Bruce's departure in 1938, and also sent 1,975 soldiers to reinforce British troops at Hong Kong. His wariness of imperial defence notwithstanding, he privately hailed this contribution to "the battle for freedom" in Asia as "a new stage in our history." Like Britain, Canada was on the sidelines during American-Japanese talks to avert a Pacific war but, through a technicality, was the first to declare war against Japan after its attack on Pearl Harbor on 7 December 1941. Within hours, the staff of the Tokyo legation was confined to the premises until mid-1942; within months, 22,000 Japanese Canadians were uprooted from their homes and relocated to the BC interior and beyond for the remainder of the war. The friendship envisaged by Marler twelve years earlier seemed remote indeed.[41]

The story of Canada's relations with Japan between the wars is less a traditional study in bilateral relations and competing national interests than an examination of evolving perceptions among Canadians of a distant, mythical land. These shifting attitudes, on one level, reveal more about Canadians themselves in the 1930s than their erstwhile ally in the East. Largely ignorant of Japan, Canadians of all kinds happily reduced it to a useful symbol to be deployed in support of their own vision of a future and better world order. For some, its orderly empire seemed to provide a large and ever-expanding market for Canadian raw materials, offering hope of recovery amid economic depression at home. Its literate and receptive populace seemed ripe for religious conversion, leading others to believe that Japan might restore to Christianity a simplicity and harmony corrupted in the West.[42] In contrast, for Canadian internationalists and pacifists, Japan represented the threat to collective security of militarism and even fascism, as well as Ottawa's hypocrisy in responding to this danger. Such perceptions, as contradictory as they were transitory, were difficult to correct since most Canadians remained focused on Europe and few possessed first-hand knowledge of Asia.

On another level, however, Canada's relations with Imperial Japan during the 1930s have had an important and more concrete legacy. As this chapter argues, Canada's diplomatic coming of age had a Pacific dimension, which has helped define Canada's postwar relationship with Asia in several respects. The largely economic focus of Marler's early work continued for much of the postwar period, obscuring for Canadian officials in the

1950s and 1960s, as it did in the 1930s, Japan's vital political role in world affairs. Canadian interwar policy was complicated too by the ongoing domestic fears of Japanese immigration, concerns that persisted even after wartime internment.

More important, throughout the interwar period, Canada tried to follow the lead of its two great power allies – Great Britain and the United States – in dealing with Japan. Using the imperial connection to establish itself at Tokyo, Canadian diplomats relied on British influence to secure meetings with Japanese officials and protect its missionaries from harm. Dominion autonomy occurred within the context of Anglo-American harmony, as expressed in the Washington agreements. Ottawa looked first to London and Washington in formulating its response to the Manchurian crisis and its strategy for the Brussels conference. When these ends of the North Atlantic triangle were at odds – such as during Britain's ill-fated arms embargo of 1933 – Ottawa sided with Washington in the hope that London would come around. Canada's reluctance to act in advance of the great powers in a region where they had more significant interests would continue after the war.

Notes

1 Cited in "Diplomatic Diary," 9 September 1929, Kirkwood Papers, vol. 2, file 2, Library and Archives of Canada (hereafter LAC).

2 For examples, see Michael Hart, *A Trading Nation: Canadian Trade Policy from Colonialism to Globalization* (Vancouver: UBC Press, 2002); T.P. Socknat, *Witness against War: Pacifism in Canada, 1900-1945* (Toronto: University of Toronto Press, 1987); Ritchie Ovendale, "Canada, Britain, the United States and the Policy of 'Appeasement'" in *Kith and Kin: Canada, Britain and the United States from the Revolution to the Cold War*, ed. C.C. Eldridge (Cardiff: University of Wales Press, 1997), 177-203.

3 For a more detailed treatment of this question, see John D. Meehan, *The Dominion and the Rising Sun: Canada Encounters Japan, 1929-1941* (Vancouver: UBC Press, 2004).

4 Meehan, *The Dominion and the Rising Sun*, 2.

5 Departmental Memorandum on Canadian-Japanese relations, 28 August 1929, Department of External Affairs Records (hereafter DEAR), vol. 1549, file 714, LAC.

6 Canada, House of Commons, *Debates*, 30 January 1928, 29.

7 Canada, House of Commons, *Debates*, 11 June 1928, 4,161. George Stephens, another Montreal businessman, was offered the post but declined due to opposition from his wife who urged him to find work closer to home. John Hilliker, *Canada's Department of External Affairs* (Montreal and Kingston: McGill-Queen's University Press, 1990), 1:116.

8 Japan Advertiser, 2 July 1929; Keenleyside to Secretary of State for External Affairs (hereafter SSEA), 2 July 1929, and Skelton to Keenleyside, 22 July 1929, DEAR, vol. 1548, file 621, LAC. For film footage of the event, see ISN 21466, copy VI 8910-0006, LAC.

9 Massey to Skelton, 31 October 1928, DEAR, vol. 1501, file 901-B, LAC; unidentified author, memorandum entitled "Comments in the Japanese Press on the proposed exchange of Ministers between Canada and Japan," compiled by the British embassy in Tokyo and forwarded to Skelton by Geoffrey Whiskard, Dominions Office, 20 April 1928, DEAR, vol. 1501, file 901-B, LAC.

10 Hugh Keenleyside, *Hammer the Golden Day: The Memoirs of Hugh L. Keenleyside* (Toronto: McClelland and Stewart, 1981), 1:254.

11 *Montreal Daily Star,* 30 April 1931; *New Outlook* (United Church of Canada), 20 March and 1 May 1929; R. Leclerc, *Des Lys à l'Ombre du Mont Fuji* (Sillery, QC: Éditions du Bois-de-Coulogne, 1995), 53.

12 *New Outlook,* 19 September 1928.

13 *Japan Times* (Tokyo), 27 October 1930; Marler's speech, "Canada and Trade with Japan," August 1929, DEAR, vol. 795, file 472, LAC; O. Mary Hill, *Canada's Salesman to the World* (Montreal and Kingston: McGill-Queen's University Press, 1977), 310-16.

14 Hill, *Canada's Salesman to the World,* 315; Skelton to O'Hara, 24 April 1929, DEAR, vol. 1538, file 150-D, LAC; Report by A.E. Bryan to F.C.T. O'Hara, 23 February 1929, Trade and Commerce, vol. 1536, file 13908, LAC; Marler's speech, "Canada and Trade with Japan," delivered during Canadian tour, August 1929, DEAR, vol. 795, file 472, LAC.

15 Legation staff and Japanese officials worked "in closest harmony" to enforce the 1928 immigration arrangement, granting only 110 visas in 1930 and 1931. Legation annual reports for 1930 and 1931, DEAR, vol. 1538, file 150-J, LAC; Riddiford to Marler, 29 November 1930, DEAR, vol. 1539, file 178, LAC.

16 Marler to SSEA, 27 January 1931, DEAR, vol. 1565, file 285, LAC; memo entitled "Canada's Representation in the East," 9 July 1931, DEAR, vol. 796, file 480, LAC; W.L. Mackenzie King, diary, 1 July 1929, L.W.M. King Papers, LAC, MG26, J13.

17 Within a week of the Mukden incident, Keenleyside noted that "the weakness of the Japanese case arises, not from the lack of skill on the part of its expositors, but from the inherent impossibility of justifying injustice." Keenleyside to SSEA, 25 September 1931, DEAR, vol. 1606, file 786, LAC; for Marler's views, see Marler to SSEA, 7 February 1934, DEAR, vol. 1608, file 786, LAC.

18 See C. Thorne, *The Limits of Foreign Policy* (London: Macmillan, 1972); R. Veatch, *Canada and the League of Nations* (Toronto: University of Toronto Press, 1975); F.H. Soward, "Forty Years On: The Cahan Blunder Re-Examined," *BC Studies* 32 (Winter 1976-77): 126-38; D.C. Story, "Canada, the League of Nations and the Far East, 1931-3: The Cahan Incident," *International History Review* 3, 2 (April 1981): 236-55. For the full text of Cahan's speech, see Appendix 2 of R.A. MacKay and E.B. Rogers, *Canada Looks Abroad* (London: Oxford University Press, 1938), 335-40.

19 Meehan, *The Dominion and the Rising Sun,* 91.

20 *Globe* (Toronto), 21 September 1931; editorial, "Japan Represents Order," *Saturday Night,* 28 November 1931, 1.

21 *La Presse,* 14 October 1931; *Financial Post,* 21 November 1931. Cahan made the remark to Mack Eastman, then section chief at the International Labour Office's research division. See S.M. Eastman, *Canada at Geneva: An Historical Survey and Its Lessons* (Toronto: Ryerson Press, 1946), 93. To Marler, platitudes at Geneva were nothing but "a gigantic game of bluff," members not having "the faintest intention of proceeding further than the placing on the records of the League a pious desire that its wish should be respected." Marler to SSEA, 1 December 1931, DEAR, vol. 1606, file 786, LAC.

22 A.J. Toynbee, "The Next War – Europe or Asia?" *Pacific Affairs* 7, 1 (March 1934): 3-13; "T" [Lester Pearson], "Canada and the Far East," *Foreign Affairs* 13, 3 (April 1935): 393.

23 Keenleyside, *Hammer the Golden Day,* 436.

24 Marler to SSEA, 17 February 1934, DEAR, vol. 1608, file 786, LAC.

25 Dominion Bureau of Statistics, *Canada Year Book, 1932* (Ottawa: King's Printer, 1932), 404; *Canada Year Book, 1934-35* (Ottawa: King's Printer, 1935), 541; Report by J.P. Manion, 15 February 1933, DEAR, vol. 1658, file 280, LAC; Marler to Parmelee, 25 November 1932, Trade and Commerce, vol. 333, file 11780, LAC; Wilgress to Parmelee, 14 December 1932, Trade and Commerce, vol. 139, file 26128, LAC.

26 Marler to SSEA, 22 June 1933, Skelton to Marler (not sent), 27 June 1933, and Keenleyside to SSEA, 11 May 1934, all in DEAR, vol. 1667, file 536, LAC; *Montreal Gazette,* 18 June 1934.

27 Marler to SSEA, 11 May 1935, reprinted in Alex I. Inglis, ed., *Documents on Canadian External Relations* (hereafter *DCER*), vol. 5: *1931-35* (Ottawa: Information Canada, 1973), 716; Skelton to Marler, 16 May 1935, *DCER,* vol. 5: 718-19; Marler to SSEA, 20 May 1935, DCER, vol. 5: 719-20; Marler to SSEA, 1 June 1935, DCER, vol. 5: 722. More critical of Marler's role in the affair, one legation official, Kenneth Kirkwood, claimed Marler had "fallen foul" of Japanese officials after inadvertently making anti-Japanese remarks "in his moods of bad temper due to his neurotic condition" and "delirious ravings" while sick with pneumonia. Entry for 2 June 1935, "Diplomatic Journal, 1935," Kirkwood Papers, MG27 III E3, file 35-10, LAC.

28 *Financial Post,* 27 July 1935; W.A. Carrothers, "Action by Association re Japanese Trade," *Industrial Canada* 36, 8 (December 1935): 48a; *New York Times,* 21 July 1935. For more on the trade war, see Meehan, *The Dominion and the Rising Sun,* 124-29.

29 *Toronto Globe,* 25 December 1934; Marler to SSEA, 21 February 1936, DEAR, vol. 1668, file 547, LAC; United Church of Canada, Board of Foreign Missions, "The Shrine Ceremonies in Korea: A Brief Statement," n.d., MG1, vol. 2281, Public Archives of Nova Scotia (hereafter PANS); Marler to SSEA, 21 May 1936, DEAR, vol. 1668, file 547, LAC. For more on the reaction of Japanese Christians to rising nationalism, see Chapter 1 of this volume.

30 N. Ignatieff, "The Japanese and the Menace of Fascism," *Saturday Night,* 7 March 1936; King diary, 26 February 1936, King Papers, LAC; Skelton cited in G. Johnson, "Canada and the Far East," in *Canada and Japan in the Twentieth Century,* ed. J. Schultz and K. Miwa (Toronto: Oxford University Press, 1991), 117.

31 In the Chanak crisis of 1922, King declined Britain's request for military support in the Dardanelles. King diary, 19 October 1937, King Papers, LAC.

32 For more on Canada and the Sino-Japanese conflict, see J.D. Meehan, "Steering Clear of Great Britain: Canada's Debate over Collective Security in the Far Eastern Crisis of 1937," *International History Review* 25 (June 2003): 253-81.

33 I. Nish, "Japan in Britain's View of the International System, 1919-1937," in *Anglo-Japanese Alienation, 1919-1952,* ed. Ian Nish (Cambridge: Cambridge University Press, 1982), 46; Chamberlain cited in B.A. Lee, *Britain and the Sino-Japanese War, 1937-1939* (Stanford: Stanford University Press, 1973), 54.

34 Bruce also pointed out that Canada enjoyed a trade surplus with Japan, and it was up to Canadians "not to curb her markets but to help her expand and expand with her." *Toronto Star,* 12 August 1937.

35 J.S. Macdonald, Memorandum, 16 February 1938, DEAR, vol. 723, file 64, LAC; Canada, Dominion Bureau of Statistics, *Canada Year Book, 1938* (Ottawa: King's Printer, 1939), 580.

36 H. Mitchell, "Far East Trade Policy," *Canadian Business,* 10, 10 (October 1937): 91-93.

37 King diary, 29 October 1937, King Papers, LAC.

38 Pickering to Mackenzie King, 15 October 1937, DEAR, vol. 1752, file 804, LAC; Cyril Powles, interview by author, 3 September 1999.

39 Wrong to Skelton, 17 November 1937, DEAR, vol. 1753, file 804, LAC; Dandurand to King, 10 November 1937, DEAR, vol. 723, file 64, LAC; Fitch account marked "Not for Publication" in D. Carter to Skelton, 25 February 1938, DEAR, vol. 1753, file 804, LAC. For various estimates of the death toll at Nanjing, see Meehan, *The Dominion and the Rising Sun,* 225n45.

40 Mockridge to Skelton, 27 September 1939, DEAR, vol. 1749, file 652B, LAC; SSEA to Wrong, 18 October 1940, DEAR, vol. 1953, file 836Y, LAC; McGreer to SSEA, 17 April 1941, King Papers, J4 series, vol. 85, file 14, LAC.

41 King Memorandum, 27 July 1941, King Papers, J4 series, vol. 283, file 2963, LAC; Keenleyside Memorandum, 5 August 1941, King Papers, J4 series, vol. 283, file 2965, LAC; King cited in G.A. Johnson, "North Pacific Triangle? The Impact of the Far East on Canada and Its Relations with the United States and Great Britain, 1937-1948" (PhD diss., York University, 1990), 204. King signed the declaration of war the night before Congress approved Roosevelt's message, and Britain followed America's lead.

42 The Eastern form of Christianity, according to one editorial, "seems to incline towards the cross-bearing, poverty-choosing, self-denying type. May it not be that their type is revealed to us just at the time when we need it the most?" *New Outlook* (United Church of Canada), 1 May 1929.

6

Only If Necessary: Canada's War against Japan, 1941-45

Bill Rawling

When the Imperial Japanese Navy attacked Pearl Harbor on 7 December 1941, Canada declared war almost immediately, even before the United States. Canada was already engaged in the conflict against Nazi Germany and Italy, and had invoked the War Measures Act in 1939, so designating Japan an enemy required no more than cabinet's approval. Determining how to wage war against the Japanese Empire, however, was a much more complex issue. Prime Minister W.L. Mackenzie King's Liberal government, looking east to the North Atlantic and Europe, and the people of British Columbia, directly exposed to the enemy's depredations, had sharply differing views on how Canada should contribute to the Allied struggle in the Pacific. This division was further complicated by differences between the various branches of Canada's armed forces, as each framed its wartime plans with a wary eye fixed on its postwar fortunes. Though Mackenzie King was sometimes forced to accommodate British Columbians and his military advisors, he maintained his focus on Europe and ensured that Canada's contribution to the war in Asia was a modest one, reflecting Canada's small stake in the region. Over the next four years, as the war unleashed pent-up racial prejudices in Canada and altered the established international order in the Pacific, Canada's interest in Japan would grow much smaller. Indeed, by 1945, Canada's stake in Japan was perhaps smaller than it had been since the 1870s.

Although Ottawa accorded greater priority to the war in Europe, Canadian military authorities were alert to the challenges of the Pacific. As Greg Johnson and Galen Perras demonstrate in Chapter 4, the defence of Canada's west coast had figured prominently in Canadian defence planning from the 1920s, as sharp tensions emerged between Japan and the United States over China, leaving British Columbia vulnerable. Indeed, the American general and aviation advocate Billy Mitchell had warned in 1923 that, in time of war, "the Japanese could take Alaska, march down Canada's west coast, and 'we could be in for it.'"[1] Though military planners in Ottawa considered such an invasion extremely unlikely, they worried that Japan might be able to establish small stations in British Columbia or use Canadian waters to take the war to the United States. By 1936, therefore, defending Canadian neutrality had become a keystone of defence policy and was embodied in Defence Scheme No. 2. Otherwise, the United States would be justified in occupying Canadian territory in self-defence.

To ensure Canadian neutrality in the event of a Pacific war, the Department of National Defence asked the government for six destroyers, four minesweepers, twenty-three squadrons of aircraft, various coastal and anti-aircraft guns, sixty-four observation posts, six army divisions, and 200 million dollars, the latter to be spent over a period of five years.[2] Funding on this scale, just as the country was emerging from a severe economic depression, was not forthcoming, though money to improve the base at Esquimalt, near Victoria, was made available.[3] Specifically, the army sought to prepare for limited attacks by one or two enemy cruisers with 8-inch guns; or by merchantmen armed with 6-inch guns; or by torpedo boats, minelayers, or submarines carrying 4.7-inch guns; and "certain forms of attack by air or by landing-parties." Priority for coastal artillery would go to Victoria-Esquimalt since Vancouver lay in a more sheltered geographical position. Prince Rupert was also worthy of consideration, as it showed evidence of developing into "British Columbia's great northern railway terminus and sea port."[4] As for anti-aircraft defences, in 1939, guns or searchlights were allocated to Vancouver, New Westminster, and Prince Rupert.[5] The army's defence triumvirate was filled out by the infantry, whose role included defending "vulnerable points," delaying enemy landing parties until the arrival of the mobile reserve, and holding "the 'land front' of an isolated fortress against attack in force." More aggressively, the infantry was to attack hostile forces that had disembarked, while helping local police forces maintain internal security. Defence Scheme No. 3 provided district commanding officers with lists of units and their assignments on the outbreak of war; it was implemented in August 1939, with conflict in Europe looming.[6]

The situation in the Pacific remained quiescent until June 1940, when France fell to the German blitzkrieg and Japan took advantage of the situation by manoeuvring its way into the French colony of Indochina. Alarmed by the Japanese advance, the British War Office warned Ottawa that "Japan is very close to making war against Great Britain." Canadian authorities decided to reinforce the West Coast, though the army believed that neither "scales of attack nor availability of troops in Canada justified the posting of a large 'standing army' in a 'West Wall' type of defence at the Coast. If attacks suddenly threatened, dispositions must be planned at short notice to resist them. Enemy moves must be anticipated with a sufficient, but not excessive, margin of safety, both of time and degree." The British, though concerned about a war in southeast Asia, did not think Canada needed strong defences along the Pacific coast, suggesting that against "the opposition of the United States Navy a Japanese land thrust at Canada was 'not considered to be a possible operation of war.'"[7]

As for the Royal Canadian Air Force (RCAF), with the outbreak of war in September 1939, its Western Air Command "was the least prepared [of the three services] for the fray." It did little better in the months that followed, and by the summer of 1940, its entire aircraft strength consisted of two Stranraers, fourteen Sharks, and four Deltas, all of obsolescent design.[8] In fairness, the situation was not much better across the northern border with the United States, where Alaska also suffered from a short supply of "top-of-the-line warplanes."[9] The governments of both countries had their sights elsewhere. Moreover, as Major-General Maurice Pope, who was closely involved in Canada-US military planning in Washington, observed, the thought of the Japanese invading the home of 150 million people struck wartime policy-makers as absurd.[10]

Canada's armed services never fought Japanese forces on Canadian soil, and their one encounter with them overseas, at Hong Kong, was a catastrophe. The genesis of the decision to send two partially trained and poorly equipped battalions to Britain's Chinese colony remains somewhat murky, but it probably occurred at a July 1941 meeting between Canadian Major-General Harry Crerar and British Major-General A.E. Grasett. Travelling through Canada after a posting to Hong Kong, Grasett told his former classmate from Canada's Royal Military College that "the addition of two or more battalions" would make the garrison strong enough to withstand a long siege by the Japanese.[11] This simple military justification for extra forces was "progressively played down" in subsequent months, "while the diplomatic and political aspect [was] correspondingly emphasized," according to historian Carl Vincent. The minister of defence, J.L. Ralston, later related how he felt that "Japan was to be given a show of strength which might cause them to hesitate, and China would be reassured."[12] The British advised Canadian authorities in October 1941 that the Chinese would attack with ten divisions should Japanese forces move on Hong Kong. It was also expected that if the garrison ran into difficulties, it could be evacuated by sea, as had been done at Dunkirk, Greece, and Crete.[13]

Not unreasonably, the Canadian government concluded that the risks were manageable, especially after Crerar, the chief of the general staff, pronounced the scheme feasible (though he had not, as yet, disclosed his July conversations with Grasett). With Australian, New Zealand, and South African troops already in action in North Africa and elsewhere, it was difficult for Canada to refuse the formal British request for help, which arrived in September 1941.[14] Two regiments, the Royal Rifles of Canada and the Winnipeg Grenadiers, were duly chosen a few weeks later to cross the Pacific. They were not part of 4th or 6th Division, then forming, and already had garrison experience in Newfoundland and Jamaica, so the choice was a simple one. With a force of 1,972 all ranks, the Canadian group was to replace forces on the island proper so they could form a brigade on the mainland. Joining up with the Middlesex Regiment, the two Canadian battalions formed a brigade of their own.[15] When Japanese forces attacked in December 1941, however, the Chinese army was unable to render assistance, and the Royal Navy was too occupied on other fronts to conduct an evacuation. When what was left of the garrison surrendered on Christmas Day, the Royal Rifles of Canada and the Winnipeg Grenadiers became the only two Canadian battalions to suffer 100 percent casualties in a single Second World War battle.

Those who had survived combat continued to have death as a constant companion. Their inadequate diet, amounting to about 900 calories a day, was reduced after a failed escape attempt in August 1942. Diseases such as pellagra and beri beri took their toll. Diphtheria alone killed 50 Canadian soldiers in the fall of 1942, even though rations had been re-established at

Figure 6.1 Canadian prisoners of war after liberation, and after initial treatment for malnutrition and other medical conditions. This photo was taken in Manila, when the Canadians were on their way home. *Front row, left to right:* Grieves, Fiddler, and Duve. *Library and Archives Canada, Department of National Defence collection, PA-137745.*

Figure 6.2 The confiscation of these fishing boats from Japanese Canadians in December 1941 ended the livelihoods of about a thousand families. *Library and Archives Canada, Department of National Defence collection, PA-134074.*

normal, if meagre, levels. One group of about 500 sent to Japan in 1943 to work in shipyards fared better than most Allied prisoners of war in the Far East, suffering only a 4.5 percent fatality rate, including 11 who succumbed to pneumonia. Overall, however, of the 1,686 Canadians who surrendered in December 1941, 128 died in Hong Kong after the surrender, 4 more were executed for attempting to escape, and a further 136 lost their lives in Japan.[16]

In hindsight, it is clear that Britain and the United States, as well as the other colonial powers, seriously underestimated Japan's ability to launch a multi-fronted campaign, and Hong Kong was just one colony to fall in the offensive that swept across Malaya, the Dutch East Indies, and the Philippines. In British Columbia, the reaction to the Japanese victories was swift, as citizens throughout the province demanded increased military protection from Ottawa.[17] The RCN sprang quickly into action, although its first large operation of the Pacific war was directed not against the Imperial Japanese Navy, but against the thousand or so fishing boats owned by British Columbia residents who had been born in Japan or whose parents had come from there. It was the first step in a policy that would eventually lead to the forced removal of 22,000 Japanese Canadians from coastal areas.

The Royal Canadian Mounted Police (RCMP) found no evidence of subversive activity among Japanese Canadians, but military authorities were suspicious.[18] Though Lieutenant Commander F.R. Gow, the naval intelligence officer at Esquimalt, noted that Japanese Canadians were "for all intents and purposes, very good citizens,"[19] he also suspected some of them had undergone military training in Japan.[20] Commodore W.J.R. Beech, Commanding Officer Pacific Coast, shared these suspicions, writing that "many of the Japanese communities, if not the majority of them, are culturally, socially and ethically Japanese."[21] Therefore, immediately after the attack on Pearl Harbor, Beech decided to round up Japanese-Canadian fishing vessels even though some fishermen had already offered to place their boats in government service and Hugh Keenleyside of the Department of External Affairs had warned that such an action was ill-advised.[22] Operations to round up the fleet began on 8 December and were completed by the end of the month, though at least two high-ranking sailors, the naval officer in charge of Prince Rupert and the commanding officer of Naden barracks, complained to Beech about the unnecessary drain on their resources.[23]

The urgency with which these operations were conducted was not matched in Ottawa, where higher authority briefly considered the possibility of Japanese operations against the West Coast and then quickly discounted it. On 11 December, four days after the attack on Pearl Harbor, the chiefs of staff committee advised the minister of national defence and his cabinet colleagues "that such fears were unwarranted on military grounds and that they should ignore the inevitable demands from the public for a strengthening of the home defence forces"; in fact, the Committee pointed out, "the situation had actually improved now that the powerful resources of the US were completely involved."[24] On 18 March 1942, however, the Mackenzie King government decided to reinforce the army in Canada for political considerations of its own – keeping troops at home to defend British Columbia kept them out of harm's way overseas – and it authorised an RCAF Home War Establishment of forty-nine squadrons.[25]

The army's build-up continued until the early summer of 1943, when its strength in British Columbia peaked with an operational force of 34,000 soldiers in twenty-eight battalions. The 6th Division was responsible for the Vancouver Island area, the 8th prepared to defend northern British Columbia, while the 19th Brigade was held in reserve in and around Vernon (see Figure 6.3).[26] For the RCAF, meanwhile, the outbreak of war meant "an era of abundance and expansion such as it had never dared contemplate in its wildest dreams."[27] By early 1942, the Western Air Command had eleven squadrons on strength, so that it was better equipped than its American counterparts in the northwestern US, although it served in "an atmosphere of sustained suspense rather than direct confrontation with the foe."[28]

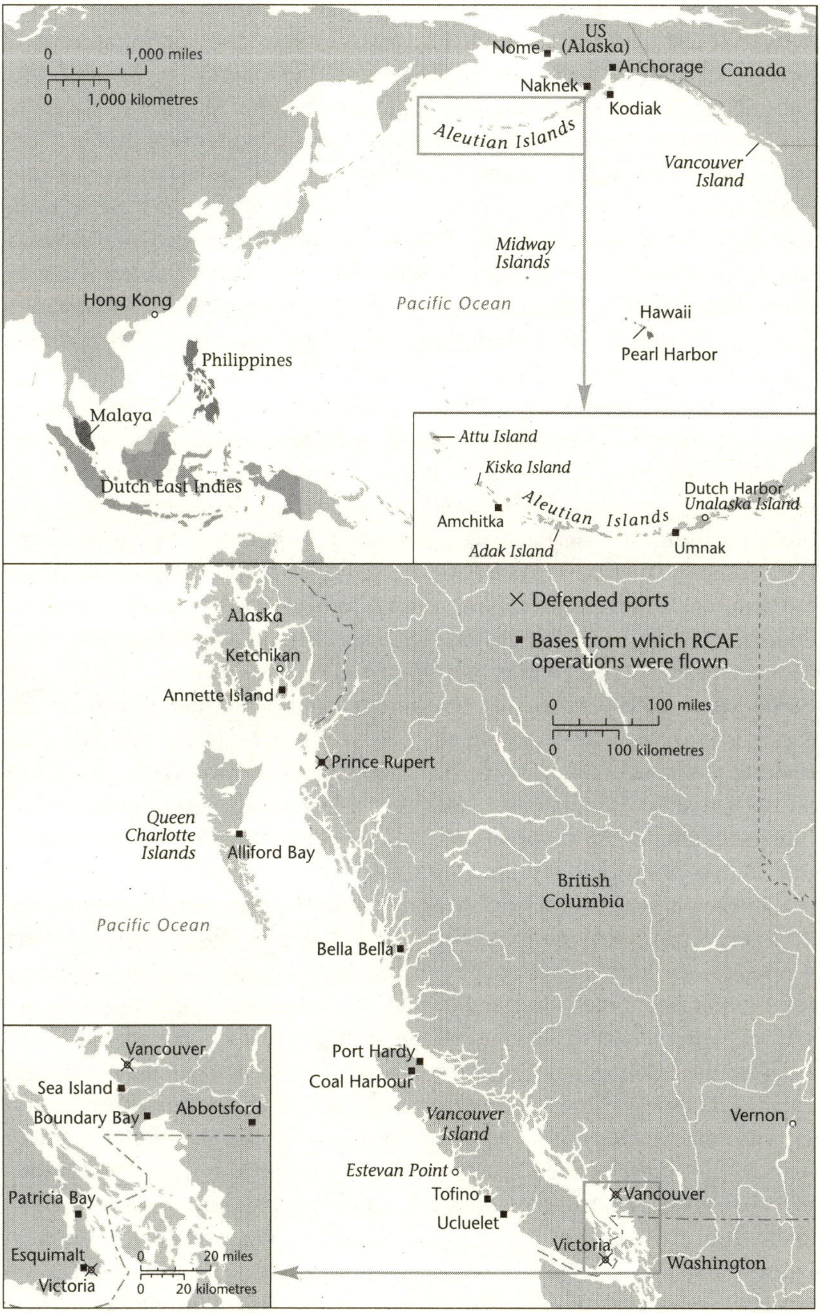

Figure 6.3 Map of North Pacific

Typical of the wartime activities of Western Air Command was an incident beginning on 8 October 1942, by which date the command had almost doubled in size to fourteen squadrons.[29] That evening, RCAF Seal Cove, opposite the Queen Charlotte Islands, reported sighting a ship "on scale of moderate cruiser" headed towards the BC coast. "Navy inform that no Canadian vessel reported there and that US forces at Ketchikan always inform movement of their vessels." A general alert was sounded and the chief of air staff himself ordered out patrols.[30] These eventually reported "negative results" – the ship was identified as the USS *Charleston* – and the alert wrapped up two days after it began. In the course of 1942, the RCAF's Western Air Command recorded over 5,600 sorties for more than 57,000 flying hours; twenty-five crashes killed forty-five airmen.[31]

Not all the RCAF's defensive operations were in the air. An Aircraft Detection Corps had been formed soon after war broke out in Europe, and by January 1941, it had established communications links with the US Warning Service.[32] One scheme involved placing watchers on the uninhabited coast of the Queen Charlotte Islands to serve as an early warning system for Prince Rupert. Teams were normally made up of a woodsman, another man "with some cooking and camping ability," and two wireless/telegraphy operators. Each unit was put ashore "with an outfit of supplies to find their own salvation in areas that provided a good view to seaward, and towards harbour entrances suitable for enemy landing operations." It was not an easy posting. One officer described an isolated tour on Hibben Island, overlooking the Inskip Channel, in the following terms: "Detachment site is located on small island, about 350 yards in length and width and 200 feet high, separated from main island by a channel which can be crossed on foot at one point at low tide and only in very calm weather. The lookout and radio cabin are on the edge of a cliff some 150 feet high ... There is little or no protection anywhere and there are no beaches. During the trip there were eight successive days when landing with any safety for man, boat or cargo was impossible." By the end of 1942, there were eight hundred observers scattered along the coast in five hundred observation posts.[33]

As for the RCN, which was also responsible for defending BC's coast and islands, its task was greatly eased by ABC-22, a Canadian-American hemispheric defence plan approved by US President Franklin D. Roosevelt on 29 August 1940 and by the Canadian cabinet on 15 October. In accordance with its provisions, the USN took care of deep water operations some distance from the coast, while the RCN focused on security closer to its own bases.[34] Operating out of Esquimalt, Vancouver, and Prince Rupert, nine vessels conducted various patrols, their numbers increasing as a few new ships, built in British Columbia, were retained on the west coast instead of being sent to the Atlantic. Only two incidents of note broke the RCN's routine patrols: the sinking of the merchant vessel *Fort Camosun* on 19 June

Figure 6.4 Estevan Point, shown here in the late 1930s, consisted of a lighthouse, fog-alarm building, and residences. It was the only community in British Columbia to be attacked by Japanese forces. *Library and Archives Canada, PA-164424.*

1942,[35] and the shelling of the Estevan lighthouse by a Japanese submarine the very same day.[36]

These two episodes confirmed the worst fears of British Columbia residents who felt that the federal government and its armed services were inclined to downplay the threat posed by Japan's forces. And there was soon more to worry them, as the Imperial Japanese Navy (IJN), seeking a decisive battle with the USN, proposed to attack Midway, an island within striking distance of Hawaii. The Imperial Japanese Army (IJA) opposed this plan and favoured a landing in the Aleutians. As control of these islands would protect the northern flank of the Midway operation and divert American troops northward, the two autonomous services soon reached an agreement. The overall plan for the operation in late May or early June 1942 was straightforward: "While a massive IJN armada would entice the USN into a murderous ambush near Midway, the Aleutian task force's goal was 'to capture or demolish points of strategical interest in the western Aleutians in order to check the enemy's air and ship manoeuvres in the area.'" Garrisons would be placed on Kiska and Attu Islands, but their occupation was expected to be temporary.[37]

By late May, American intelligence, which had cracked several Japanese military codes, was aware of the plan to attack Midway, with a diversion against Dutch Harbor in the Aleutians and the occupation of Attu and Kiska. As a result, the United States deployed its air squadrons based in Alaska further west and requested that two RCAF squadrons, one bomber and one fighter, replace them. The first Japanese strike against Dutch Harbor occurred on 2 June; 8 (RCAF) Bomber Reconnaissance Squadron arrived in Yakutat, 800 miles up the Alaska panhandle, the next day.[38] Getting it there, however, was not managed without some wrangling. The RCAF worried that the two squadrons might be little more than a sacrificial force, while the chief of the general staff, Lieutenant-General Ken Stuart, was concerned about exposing British Columbia at a time when the enemy was obviously still on the offensive. Authorities in Alaska worked the circuit in Washington, where Pentagon officials reminded Major-General Maurice Pope of the wartime agreements under which Canada and the United States promised to react jointly to threats against North America. Pope required only a few hours to convince the RCAF to move the squadrons; following the bombers, the fighters arrived on 8 June.[39]

The RCN arrived in the Aleutians later, in August 1942, with Force D, made up of five vessels. Three of them were armed merchant cruisers converted from Canadian Pacific ships, which concentrated on escorting American convoys between Kodiak Island and Dutch Harbor, a six-hundred mile journey.[40] Two RCN corvettes carried out anti-submarine patrols to the west of Dutch Harbor, helped escort a force that carried out an unopposed landing on Adak Island, and then escorted convoys of materials being used to reinforce that island. The harsh climate proved to be Force D's major challenge. The tropical Japan current clashed with the cold dry Siberian air mass over the Aleutian chain to create some of the worst weather anywhere. An ever-present dense fog blanketed the region, and Arctic storms and strong winds, known locally as "williwaws," constantly buffeted all who dared put out to sea. According to historian Brian Garfield, "it was perhaps the only place on earth where high winds and thick fog attacked simultaneously – round-the-clock Aleutian gales sometimes reached 140 miles an hour, yet most of the islands had no more than eight or ten clear days in a year. There was no calm or dry season."[41]

The Canadian deployment to the Aleutians was not large, but it was sufficient to provide the government with ammunition when the question of Canada's contribution to North American defence came to the fore. One forum for such exchanges was the Permanent Joint Board on Defence (PJBD), a binational committee created by ABC-22 to examine continental security. When, on one occasion, Jack Hickerson, the PJBD's American secretary, challenged the Canadians on their participation in the Aleutian campaign, Pope retorted "that not only were RCAF squadrons serving in Alaska but that the RCN were playing a useful part in convoying US supply ships from northwest American ports to Anchorage."[42]

Successful RCAF and RCN activities in the Pacific northwest encouraged some Canadian authorities to consider making a contribution on the ground as well. In April 1943, Major-General George Pearkes, commanding the army in British Columbia, raised the matter with Lieutenant-General John L. DeWitt, commander in Alaska, and suggested that Canada might help retake Attu and Kiska, which the Japanese had occupied in June 1942.[43] The issue soon came up for discussion in the PJBD, where Hickerson suggested that Japanese forces in the Aleutians represented a threat to the continent as a whole and that Canadian troops should be part of the formation that ejected them. He added, however, that "from his own point of view a mere token force would be adequate."[44]

Pope passed these comments to Stuart, observing that the "bread cast upon the American waters by Pearkes was returning." The chief of the general staff, who was anxious to give his troops some battle experience, favoured the idea. He also thought that a campaign against the Japanese might help the government reduce growing hostility towards its conscripted soldiers, who were only required to serve in the western hemisphere.[45] Operations in the Aleutians would give them an opportunity, whether they wanted it or not, to perform tasks more warlike than guarding bridges and canal locks.[46] At a meeting of the cabinet war committee on 27 May, Mackenzie King repeated many of these arguments, noting that recapturing the islands would raise morale, provide battle experience, demonstrate Canada's interest in the Pacific to its allies, and emphasize the partnership with the United States. He warned, however, that such a contribution would mean little credit if things went well, but a share of the blame if the operation failed. Cabinet decided that the potential benefits outweighed the risks and granted authority to proceed.[47] A brigade group would be formed, composed of those units closest to having their full war establishment strength. Using conscripts would pose no legal difficulties, as permission to use them in Alaska had been granted as early as September 1942. The 13th Brigade Group would come under the command of Lieutenant-General S.B. Buckner, Commanding General, Alaska Defence Command, and would be composed of the Canadian Fusiliers, the Winnipeg Grenadiers (reformed after their destruction at Hong Kong), the Rocky Mountain Rangers, and the Régiment de Hull.[48]

Ground operations in the Pacific northwest were not pleasant. In addition to the cold and foggy climate, the Aleutian Islands are marked by especially rugged terrain. Volcanic in origin, the islands are largely composed of stony beaches, swampy muskeg, and craggy hills and mountains with little vegetation. Later, a trench poet would write that "Maybe God was tired when he made this little isle / So he grabbed the things left over and put them in a pile / He dropped them in the ocean and paused for a spell / Then he said 'I'll call it Kiska. The earth shall have a hell.'"[49]

As the Canadians prepared to attack this inhospitable island chain in an operation called Greenlight, bringing the brigade up to strength was complicated by the fact that instructions from Ottawa excluded anyone who had less than four months of training. In addition, medical boards rejected many others as unfit.[50] Learning how to use American equipment was yet another challenge. Captain Tom Lawson of the Canadian Fusiliers later recalled how "men were issued A bags, then B bags, then sleeping bags, then battle bags, then pack bags. The A bags were to be carried in the B bags and the sleeping bags in the battle bags and both in the pack bag. This order was subsequently cancelled as no one could understand it. A new bag issue replaced them all. This was called a Rucksack and [was] designed to put a fully-trained soldier out of action after marching two miles with one on his back."[51]

Meanwhile, American forces had retaken Attu in a bitter campaign, whose lessons were quickly incorporated into the 13th Brigade's preparations for the assault on Kiska. The need for more physical hardening was especially evident, while extra training included "night manoeuvres, night shooting, indirect mortar firing, anti-tank patterns, clearing mines, evacuating casualties, combat loading of ships, unloading on beaches, preparation of meals in mobile messes and kitchens and mobile radio communications."[52] At the same time, in late July, RCAF No. 14 (Fighter) Squadron, directed its efforts at reconnoitring Japanese positions around the island's airport and harbour. Grounded by poor weather for much of the first week of August, the RCAF Kittyhawks resumed their sorties on 10 August, when they observed with some surprise that earlier signs of Japanese occupation had now disappeared.[53]

The curtain for Operation Greenlight went up on 15 August 1943. While the bulk of the Canadian force waited offshore in their transports, US forces carried out preliminary operations. To the waiting Canadians, who listened anxiously as the Americans detected and destroyed Japanese mines, the loud explosions meant only one thing: an opposed landing.[54] In fact, the Japanese had already evacuated the island, but as the Canadian Fusiliers waded ashore, neither they nor higher command was aware of that. According to Innis Hammond, "the water was calm and not particularly cold, no colder than a spring day in London, but it was a relief to get into action after the long months of training and practice. The fact that we encountered no resistance while establishing the beachhead did not surprise us because we had been told the Japanese preferred to fight from prepared defensive positions on the high ground as they had on Attu. We moved with caution to our allotted areas and immediately began to dig in and strengthen our position. Then we started to methodically explore every cave and valley. We expected underground defences because it was obvious from the damage and destruction that the Americans had dropped a lot of bombs and the garrison must have sheltered somewhere. We posted guards and changed them every hour."[55]

Unfortunately, the absence of Japanese troops did not make for a casualty-free operation; the first fatality was Lieutenant S. Vessey of the Rocky Mountain Rangers, killed by a land mine. In all, four Canadians died, with thirty other casualties. On a different note, "geographically-minded officers" quickly noticed that they were in fact in the eastern hemisphere, and were, technically, serving overseas and thus entitled to "a rebate of all income tax." National Defence Headquarters in Ottawa was skeptical, however, and insisted that since "the United States say the island is in the Western Hemisphere ... Kiska must of necessity be where its owners say it is – in the Western Hemisphere." Canadian troops continued to pay income tax as if they were on home service.[56]

The capture of the Aleutian Islands, combined with the Japanese defeat at Midway and growing Axis losses in North Africa and Sicily, eased the pressure on the Canadian government to maintain a strong and visible military presence in British Columbia. Soon after the occupation of Kiska, the chief of the general staff recommended disbanding two divisions then serving in Canada to release fourteen thousand troops for service in Europe. The 8th Infantry Division, whose main role had been to control British Columbia's 14th and 16th Brigade Groups as well as the Prince Rupert Defences, ceased to exist on 15 October 1943.[57] Similarly, although the RCAF still had thirteen squadrons deployed in ten locations in early 1944, the slow Japanese retreat back across the Pacific was quickly transforming it into "a transportation and on-the-job training organization, with only the occasional report of an enemy submarine to enliven the humdrum routine."[58]

In Ottawa, the Japanese withdrawal raised the question of Canada's role in offensive operations in the Pacific. On 6 September 1944, at a full meeting of cabinet, the chiefs of staff recommended, in writing, that Canada should be part of the final assault on Japan as a means of "avenging Hong Kong, saving face in the East and restoring Canadian military prestige." There was no disagreement on the principle, though there was much debate on the details of this policy. In particular, two cabinet ministers insisted forcefully that Canada should contribute wherever it could, while another demanded that the RCN serve with the British rather than with the Americans. The prime minister, for his part, did not want Canadian service people dying to recapture British colonies. These views noted, ministers agreed that Canadian forces would participate in the invasion of Japan and asked the chiefs of staff to draw up plans.[59]

In fact, the army had been planning for this role as early as May 1943 when the chief of the general staff initiated a series of studies on the use of Canadian troops in the Aleutians, northwest Asia, and the southwest Pacific.[60] In

July of that year, Major-General Pearkes told some of his officers that Kiska "was one of the first steps on the road to Tokyo and that Canada should be prepared to follow it up and stay with it to the end." From the fall of 1943, he later recalled, the policy was changed "from keeping the 6th and 8th Divisions keyed up as much as we could against the possibility of an attack, to one in which the 6th Division was to prepare itself for any commitment which might occur in the Pacific."[61] After Germany surrendered in May 1945, National Defence Headquarters decided to form a 6th Canadian Division organized along US Army lines. Plans were to move it to the United States beginning 20 August, but the war ended five days before that deployment began.[62] The Canadian Army Pacific Force, as it came to be known, cost some $35.5 million, even though it was never sent overseas, compared with $13.75 million for the expedition to Hong Kong and $10.75 million for the assault on Kiska. The divisions raised to defend British Columbia had cost a total of $252 million.[63]

The RCAF's experience in planning for the Pacific war was in many ways similar. In January 1944, C.G. "Chubby" Power, the minister responsible for the air force, suggested sixty or seventy squadrons could be sent to the Pacific after the war ended in Europe. The RCAF's leading officers welcomed the opportunity to press for a large and self-reliant air force that would have a major postwar role. It was far more than cabinet was willing to contribute, and in late 1944 the force was pared down to twenty-five squadrons, with thirty-three thousand men. Meanwhile, the British saw a need for construction personnel to build and maintain the airfields that Commonwealth forces would need, and asked for ten thousand such specialists from Canada. The latter might be especially important since, after US forces captured Okinawa in May 1945, Air Vice-Marshal Hugh Lloyd, who would command the Commonwealth air forces, warned that "the Americans distrust us. They think we are trying to deploy our Force on the cheap." As with the army, however, the war ended before the RCAF's precise role in the Pacific could be decided.[64]

The only Canadian fighting service to participate in the various offensives of the Pacific campaign was the RCN, in the form of a single vessel, HMCS *Uganda*. The RCN hoped that the light cruiser would be the cornerstone of a sizeable Canadian Pacific fleet, ensuring the RCN's survival into the postwar era as a balanced battle formation, complete with small aircraft carriers, cruisers, powerful fleet destroyers, and all the necessary ancillary vessels. The policy foundations for such a blue water navy had been laid down as early as 1940, when the RCN determined that it did not want to experience the low status, small budgets, and, most important, tiny fleet that had been its lot in the two decades following the First World War.[65] Unlike the Atlantic, where the RCN had served mainly in an escort role for convoys, requiring small ships many of which were versions of civilian designs, the Pacific offered the opportunity to put to sea the balanced fleet that the navy felt was most appropriate.

Commissioned on 21 October 1944, the anniversary of Lord Nelson's victory at Trafalgar, HMCS *Uganda* was armed with six-inch guns. Leaving the USN ship yards in Charleston, South Carolina, it began its voyage to the Pacific on New Year's Day 1945, arriving to join the British Pacific Fleet (BPF) in early April, a few days after US forces had begun their campaign to take Okinawa. The BPF's role was to ensure that Japanese forces did not use the Sakashima Gunto, a group of islands between Okinawa and Formosa, as a staging area. HMCS *Uganda*, more specifically, was called upon to help protect British aircraft carriers against air attack, though it also had the opportunity to bombard enemy airfields.

The enemy was not, however, the only concern of *Uganda*'s crew. Canada's wartime navy was made up entirely of volunteers (as was its air force) who could be sent to any theatre of war as determined by operational requirements. Mackenzie King, determined that he would not have yet another conscription crisis, announced on 4 April, the very day *Uganda* joined the BPF, that only volunteers would be sent to the Pacific.[66] It was not sufficient for men to have volunteered for service, however; it was also necessary for them to declare their willingness to fight against Japan and sign attestation papers to that effect. Since *Uganda* was already operating in the Pacific, the issue was tricky, to say the least. Of a complement of some 900, 605 opted not to volunteer since, as one of them, Able Seaman Andrew A. Lawson, later explained: "Why should we volunteer again. We volunteered once to get here. We were quite happy to stay here. We'll do our job that we're supposed to do and then go home ... I was one of the ones who did *not* volunteer. I was prepared to stay there, but if they were going through this nonsense of volunteering (which was all it was) I wasn't going to volunteer again."[67] Other factors affecting the men's decisions were tropical illness, the strict discipline on board a cruiser (most of the crew had previously served in corvettes, which were less formal), and the difficulty many men had volunteering for further service when others were returning to their families and to civilian jobs. With so many opting to return home, Ottawa decided that *Uganda* would make its way to Esquimalt, where it would fill out its complement with volunteers.[68]

It could not, however, leave the BPF until a replacement arrived, and so HMCS *Uganda* continued to operate as part of the fleet's anti-aircraft defence, helping to fight off a kamikaze attack on 9 May.[69] On that occasion, and in carrying out early air warning picket duty in subsequent weeks, the ship was fortunate in not being targeted by such suicide aircraft. The campaign to capture Okinawa ended on 25 May, and the BPF moved on to other operations, including a bombardment of Truk, the largest of the Japanese bases to be isolated in the US island-hopping campaign. *Uganda* left the fleet in July, intending to work up its new complement in September. Another cruiser, HMCS *Ontario*, was expected to have on board an all-volunteer crew by mid-July.[70] With other ships being allocated to the war against Japan, there was the possibility that, if the war lasted another year or two as anticipated, the RCN would have a Canadian Pacific fleet to operate alongside the BPF.

The nuclear attacks against Hiroshima and Nagasaki, and Japan's subsequent surrender on 15 August 1945, abruptly cancelled these plans. As a result, Canada's total commitment to the war in the Pacific remained relatively modest: two battalions, both destroyed, and a couple of warships, along with individuals such as radar operators who were seconded to various allies. With war in Europe a higher priority, and the need to provide formations to defend British Columbia, none of the fighting services was able to make what it considered to be an appropriate contribution to victory against Japan. The country had, in effect, three armies in the field by 1944 (one in Italy, another in northwest Europe, and a third in Canada), two air forces (one in Britain and northwest Europe, the other in Canada), and a navy escorting convoys across the Atlantic and into the Soviet Union. These extensive commitments and the government's determination to avoid the slaughter (and resulting conscription crisis) of the First World War explain why Canada's armed services never deployed large forces to the Pacific.

The war had important consequences for Canada's long-term relationship with Japan. It brought to a boil the racial tensions in Canada that had been largely contained since the riots of 1907. The wartime internment of Japanese Canadians (and their postwar deportation) created tensions and resentments that hindered close postwar relations between Ottawa and Tokyo. As Patricia Roy points out in Chapter 9 of this volume, it would take almost two decades just to begin to resolve some of these issues. Canadian POWs, who resented Tokyo's unwillingness to acknowledge their brutal treatment, nursed a parallel grievance long after the war ended and viewed with suspicion Ottawa's efforts to normalize relations.[71] More important, the war convinced Ottawa that the Pacific was an American region, and it swept away the burgeoning interest in Japan and a Pacific foreign policy that John Meehan saw developing in the 1930s. Instead, as John Price discusses in detail in the next chapter, Canada's interest in Japan narrowed sharply as the war ended and cold war with Moscow gripped Asia.

Notes

1 Cited in Galen Perras, *Stepping Stones to Nowhere: The Aleutian Islands, Alaska, and American Military Strategy, 1867-1945* (Vancouver: UBC Press, 2003), 15.

2 Ibid., 36.

3 Army Headquarters (hereafter AHQ) No. 1, "Fixed Coast Artillery Defences on the Pacific Coast," 8 May 1944, p. 1, Department of National Defence Records (hereafter DNDR), vol. 6921, Library and Archives Canada (hereafter LAC).

4 Ibid., p. 2, DNDR, vol. 6921, LAC.
5 AHQ No. 2, "The Anti-Aircraft Defences of the Pacific Coast," 22 September 1944, p. 1, DNDR, vol. 6921, LAC.
6 AHQ No. 3, "The Employment of Infantry in the Pacific Coast Defences," 1 June 1944, pp. 1-2, DNDR, vol. 6921, LAC; Pope to Ashton, 21 September 1938, C-8293, 3498-9, LAC; Memorandum from the Chief of the General Staff (hereafter CGS) to the General Staff (hereafter GS), 13 February 1939, C8293, 3498-10, LAC.
7 AHQ No. 3, pp. 5-6, DNDR, vol. 6921, LAC; Under-Secretary of State for External Affairs (hereafter USSEA) to the High Commissioner of Canada in the UK (hereafter HCCUK), 27 June 1940, C5476, 20-1-17, LAC; Secretary of State for Dominion Affairs to HCCUK, 8 July 1940, C5476, 20-1-17, LAC.
8 J.D.F. Kealy, "Coastal Command Narrative No. 1," May 1974, pp. 6 and 43, 89/97, box 2, file 2, Directorate of History and Heritage, Department of National Defence (hereafter DHH).
9 Perras, *Stepping Stones to Nowhere*, 67.
10 Maurice A. Pope, *Soldiers and Politicians: The Memoirs of Lt-Gen Maurice A. Pope* (Toronto: University of Toronto Press, 1962), 219.
11 Brereton Greenhous, *"C" Force to Hong Kong: A Canadian Catastrophe, 1941-1945* (Toronto: Dundurn Press, 1997), 15.
12 Carl Vincent, *No Reason Why: The Canadian Hong Kong Tragedy – An Examination* (Stittsville, ON: Canada's Wings, 1981), 29, 33.
13 Greenhous, *"C" Force to Hong Kong*, 17-18.
14 Canadian Military Headquarters (hereafter CMHQ) No. 163, "Canadian Participation in the Defence of Hong Kong," 14 November 1946, pp. 1-2, DNDR, vol. 6920, LAC.
15 Ibid., 3, 20; CGS to Minister of National Defence, 30 September 1941, C5477, 20-1-20, LAC.
16 Bill Rawling, *Death Their Enemy: Canadian Medical Practitioners and War* (Montreal: Athena Editions, 2001), 232-36.
17 Reginald H. Roy, *For Most Conspicuous Bravery: A Biography of Major-General George R. Pearkes* (Vancouver: UBC Press, 1977), 176.
18 For one example, see E. Vancouver Island Section to Officer Commanding (hereafter OC) E Division, 4 June 1941, Records of the Royal Canadian Mounted Police (hereafter RRCMP), vol. 3564, file C11-19-2-24, LAC.
19 Lieutenant Commander F.R. Gow to Admiral R. Nugent (Ret'd), 1938, ES-05-28, RDND, vol. 11879, LAC.
20 Naval Staff Officer, Esquimalt to Director Naval Intelligence and Plans, 9 February 1938, NSS1023-18-2, mf C5853, LAC.
21 Commanding Officer Pacific Coast (hereafter COPC) to Naval Secretary, 12 September 1941, DNDR, vol. 2769, file HQS 6615-6 v.4, LAC.
22 H. Keenleyside to Commander P.B. German, 14 August 1941, Department of External Affairs Records (hereafter DEAR), file 1698-C-40, vol. 2859; OC E Div to Commissioner, 3 December 1941, RRCMP, vol. 3564, file C11-19-2-24, LAC.
23 Naval Officer-in-Charge (hereafter NOIC) Prince Rupert to COPC, 5 January 41, DNDR, vol. 11,867, file DE10-7-1, LAC; Commanding Officer, RCN Barracks memorandum, "Strategic Employment of Ratings," 23 April 1942, DNDR, vol. 11,867, file PC014-21-17, LAC.
24 J.D.F. Kealy, "Coastal Command Narrative No. 2," July 1975, p. 1, 89/97, box 2, file 3, DHH.
25 Kealy, "Coastal Command Narrative No. 2," p. 1; Chief of Air Staff (hereafter CAS) to Minister of Air, 16 March 1942, Air 2 5260, Public Record Office (hereafter PRO).
26 AHQ No. 3, p. 24, DNDR, vol. 6921, LAC.
27 J.D.F. Kealy, "Coastal Command Narrative No. 1," p. 46, 89/97, box 2, file 2, DHH.
28 Kealy, "Coastal Command Narrative No. 2," pp. 33, 35, 37; Plant to Air Officer Commanding, 20 February 42, 181.009 (D3583), DHH.
29 Kealy, "Coastal Command Narrative No. 2," p. 57, DHH.
30 Pacific Command Victoria to Defensor Ottawa, 9 October 1942, and CAS to ACC Western Air Command (hereafter WAC) Victoria, 9 October 1942, DNDR, vol. 5215, file S19-5-4, LAC.
31 Kealy, "Coastal Command Narrative No. 2," p. 59; CAS to Minister, 9 March 1943, 181.009 (D6823), DHH.

32 Kealy, "Coastal Command Narrative No. 1," p. 45.
33 Kealy, "Coastal Command Narrative No. 2," pp. 39-40, 58; Chiefs of Staff Committee, 158th Meeting, 193.009 (D53), DHH.
34 "Operational Plan of Royal Canadian Navy to Implement Joint Canadian-United States Basic Defence Plan, 1940 (Short Title – Joint Plan 1940)," 19 December 1940, DNDR, vol. 11,764, file PC010-9-1 vol. 1, LAC.
35 Captain T.F. Eggleston, "Report on Sinking of Fort Camosun," undated, DNDR, vol. 11,845, COPC 8852-F96, LAC.
36 W.A.B Douglas, Roger Sarty, and Michael Whitby, *No Higher Purpose* (Toronto: Vanwell Publishing, 2002), 355-57.
37 Perras, *Stepping Stones to Nowhere*, 68-69.
38 Kealy, "Coastal Command Narrative No. 2," pp. 42-43, 46.
39 Perras, *Stepping Stones to Nowhere*, 73-74.
40 HMCS Prince Robert ROP, 2 September 1942, NHS NSS1926-314/3 vol. 1, DHH.
41 Brian Garfield, *The Thousand Mile War* (New York: Bantam Books, 1969), 57, 131, 141.
42 Pope, *Soldiers and Politicians*, 214.
43 Roy, *For Most Conspicuous Bravery*, 185.
44 Pope, *Soldiers and Politicians*, 214.
45 Roy, *For Most Conspicuous Bravery*, 185-86.
46 AHQ No. 6, "The Canadian Participation in the Kiska Operations," 16 October 1944, pp. 5-6, DNDR, vol. 6921; PCS 5 June 1943, Appx. 3, C5491, 20-3-12-11, LAC.
47 Minutes of the War Committee of the Cabinet, 27 May 1943, Privy Council Records (hereafter PCR), Microfilm Reel C-8475, LAC.
48 AHQ No. 6, p. 8, DNDR, vol. 6921, LAC; PCS 5 June 1943, Appx. 7, C5491, 20-3-12-11, LAC. See also C.P. Stacey, *Six Years of War* (Ottawa: Queen's Printer, 1955), 498.
49 Bill Corfield, *Silent Victory: The Canadian Fusiliers in the Japanese War* (Surrey, BC: Timberholme Books, 2003), 35, 48.
50 AHQ No. 6, p. 11, DNDR, vol. 6921, LAC; "Lessons Learned from Operations on Attu," DNDR, vol. 15,182, War Diary, Régiment de Hull, July 1943, LAC.
51 Corfield, *Silent Victory*, 41.
52 AHQ No. 6, p. 24, DNDR, vol. 6921, LAC; see also Corfield, *Silent Victory*, 40.
53 Kealy, "Coastal Command Narrative No. 2," 63.
54 AHQ No. 6, p. 32, DNDR, vol. 6921, LAC; War Diary, Winnipeg Grenadiers, 16 August 1943, DNDR, vol. 15,292, LAC.
55 Corfield, *Silent Victory*, 48.
56 AHQ No. 6, pp. 33, 49, 50-51, DNDR, vol. 6921, LAC; War Diary, 13th Canadian Infantry Brigade, 16 August 1943, Microfilm Reel (hereafter MFR) T12400, LAC; War Diary, Winnipeg Grenadiers, 22 August 1943, DNDR, vol. 15,292, LAC; War Diary, 13th Brigade, 8 September 43, MFR T12400, LAC; War Diary, 13th Brigade, September 1943, Appx. 47 and 48, MFR T12400, LAC.
57 AHQ No. 2, p. 27, DNDR, vol. 6921, LAC; Roy, *For Most Conspicuous Bravery*, 203; AHQ No. 11, p. 24, DNDR, vol. 6921, LAC; Murchie to Minister, 13 January 1944, C5471, 20-1-5, LAC.
58 J.D.F. Kealy, "Coastal Command Narrative No. 3," January 1976, 89/97, box 2, file 4, p. 24, DHH; Kealy, "Coastal Command Narrative No. 2," p. 69.
59 Norman Hillmer, "Turning towards Japan," February 1993, 94/168, 2/26, p. 16-17, DHH.
60 Perras, *Stepping Stones to Nowhere*, 192-93.
61 Roy, *For Most Conspicuous Bravery*, 196, 204.
62 AHQ No. 16, "The Canadian Army Pacific Force," 15 July 1947, p. 27, DNDR, vol. 6922, LAC; Deputy CGS (A) to CGS, 11 June 1945, C8434, 9131-6, LAC.
63 AHQ No. 16, p. 59, DNDR, vol. 6922, LAC.
64 Hillmer, "Turning towards Japan," 2, 3, 20, 35, 40.
65 "Canada's Post-War Navy," 11 November 1943, DNDR, vol. 8344, NSS 1017-10-34, LAC.
66 Canada, House of Commons, *Debates*, 4 April 1945, 435.
67 Report of Hal Lawrence's Interview with Able Seaman Andrew A. Lawson, 1987, Biog, Lawson, DHH.

68 Admiralty (hereafter ADM) to Naval Service Head Quarters (hereafter NSHQ) and Commander-in-Chief British Pacific Force, 29 May 1945, DNDR, vol. 11,732, file CS 153-15-7, LAC.

69 Mainguy to Commanding Officer (hereafter CO) 4th Cruiser Squadron, 10 May 1945, ADM 199/590, PRO.

70 Secretary of the Naval Board to CO Pacific Coast, 9 July 1945, DNDR, Acc 83-84, 167, box 4043, file 8970-CCL-31, LAC; RCN Depot to NSHQ, 7 July 1945, DNDR, vol. 11,731, file CS 153-10-1, LAC.

71 Charles G. Roland, *Long Night's Journey into Day* (Waterloo, ON: Wilfrid Laurier University Press, 2001), 327.

7

Rethinking the Occupation: E.H. Norman, Canada, and the American Empire in Asia, 1945-51

John Price

The occupation of Japan followed a devastating fifteen-year war in the Asia-Pacific region in which an estimated thirty million people died. It was a war with roots in Japan's imperial competition with Euro-American powers for control over China; it began in 1931 with Japan's annexation of Manchuria, escalated with an all-out but undeclared war on China in 1937, and exploded into a pan-Pacific conflict with Japanese attacks on Southeast Asia and Pearl Harbor in December 1941. The conflict came to a cataclysmic end in August 1945 with the atomic bombing of Hiroshima and Nagasaki by the United States and the occupation of defeated Japan by Allied forces. While Canada did not send troops to participate in the occupation, it nonetheless played an active part in Allied debates over occupation policy and the subsequent peace treaty with Japan.

No one has systematically studied Canada's role in the occupation, although several scholars have covered the subject in a cursory manner,[1] tying Canadian policy closely to the controversial career of diplomat Herbert Norman.[2] The son of Methodist missionary parents and an authority on Japanese history, Norman joined the Department of External Affairs in 1939 and became one of its foremost experts on Japan before his career was eclipsed in the late 1940s by allegations that he was a communist. In refuting these unwarranted charges, scholars have tended to downplay any differences between Norman and Canada and US policy-makers over Japan. Instead, the dominant view in the literature depicts Norman and Canada as strong supporters of the initial Allied occupation policies of democratization and demilitarization, whose influence on policy declined following the US decision in 1947 to "reverse course" and roll back earlier reforms.[3] This chapter, however, draws on recently declassified Canadian records to reassess this interpretation. It argues that Norman and Canada often challenged MacArthur and US policy during the earliest phases of the occupation and in the Far Eastern Commission, an inter-Allied body set up in 1946 to oversee policy. Canada's emerging cold war alliance with Washington, however, soon caused

Prime Minister William Lyon Mackenzie King's government, and Norman, to line up firmly behind US imperial policy in Asia. In postwar, as in prewar, Asia, Canada's attitude to Japan was largely conditioned by the interests and preoccupations of its imperially minded great power allies.

Norman and Konoe Fumimaro

During the first year of the occupation, Norman filled positions in Tokyo and Washington that brought him into close contact with US policy-makers, revealing sharp differences in Canadian and American approaches to postwar Japan. In September 1945, Norman arrived in Japan, where he was seconded to the intelligence staff of US General Douglas MacArthur, the Supreme Commander of Allied Powers (SCAP) in Japan until January 1946. After acting as Canada's delegate to the Washington-based Far Eastern Commission (FEC) in the spring, he returned to Tokyo in August 1946 as head of the Canadian mission to occupied Japan. In each of these three roles, Norman was primarily concerned with assessing responsibility for the war and revising Japan's constitution.[4]

Norman's dispute with SCAP over the fate of the former prime minister, Konoe Fumimaro, illustrates clearly the difference in view that divided Norman and MacArthur from an early date. In October 1945, both MacArthur and his political advisor, George C. Atcheson, met with Konoe and suggested that he begin to examine constitutional revision.[5] Konoe had been head of the government at the time of Japan's invasion of China in July 1937, had helped construct the national defence state, and, during his second term as prime minister, had proclaimed the Greater East Asia Co-Prosperity Sphere. Unable to resolve Japan's growing differences with the United States, Konoe resigned as prime minister in October 1941 and was not in power when Japan attacked Pearl Harbor. MacArthur and Atcheson's rapprochement with Konoe in October 1945 reflected an American tendency to perceive Japanese imperialism as a product of the military leadership, which was thought to have usurped the throne. It also reflected the US penchant to confine questions of war guilt to the Pacific phase of the war; that is, for aggression against the United States. As both a civilian and a politician who had resigned prior to Pearl Harbor, Konoe appeared to be a moderate in American eyes.

Norman's appreciation of the stages of the war and those responsible for it was radically different. He thought that the first phase of the war against China was just as important as the conflict after Pearl Harbor. He argued that responsibility for this war of colonial aggression should be assigned to Japan's oligarchy, in which he included the monarchy, the financial conglomerates (*zaibatsu*), the government bureaucracy, and the military. Although Norman used the term "military" and "military clique" as a form of shorthand, he was quite clear that civilians such as Konoe were part of this group.[6]

Figure 7.1 E.H. Norman with General Douglas MacArthur, Supreme Commander for the Allied Forces, in Japan, 1947. *Courtesy of US Army.*

It was precisely this point that he made in his 1947 review of Edwin Reischauer's book, *Japan Past and Present.*[7] In other words, civilians in positions of power had to be held accountable. Thus, MacArthur's reliance on Konoe quickly encountered objections from Norman, who began to compile a dossier on a number of key civilian figures he felt were instrumental in putting Japan on its path to imperial aggression. While some historians have argued that Norman was simply trying to divert responsibility from Emperor Hirohito, it seems clear that this was the last thing on his mind, given his analysis of the war's origins.[8]

Norman's submissions on Konoe's war guilt were crucial in forcing SCAP to distance itself from Konoe, who was subsequently listed as a suspected war criminal.[9] In their accounts of this incident, Nakano and Bowen refer to what they consider Norman's personal attacks against Konoe.[10] While this point is well taken, it should not obscure the more significant issue: Norman pursued Konoe not out of personal pique but rather from a profound difference with MacArthur over the nature of and responsibility for the war. Though Norman, like MacArthur, did not wish to put the emperor on trial, he did call for a full investigation into the imperial monarchy, a move the American blocked. Thus, from his arrival in Japan, Norman challenged the US-centred, liberal imperial view of the war.

Norman and the Far Eastern Commission

This basic difference in policy also coloured the approach to Japanese constitutional issues pursued by Norman and Canada in the FEC. Initially, the Allies were to provide advice to the United States on the occupation through a Far Eastern Advisory Council.[11] However, several allies, particularly the Soviet Union, objected to this body's limited advisory role and demanded a full commission with the power to supervise MacArthur. The resulting compromise created a commission of thirteen countries, including Canada. The United States, Soviet Union, and Great Britain could veto FEC decisions, though Washington retained the power to issue interim orders when a consensus could not be reached. While the commission would eventually prove impotent, it seemed to have some power, particularly in constitutional matters, when it was established in December 1946.

Ottawa assigned Norman as its representative on the FEC while he was still in Tokyo. Just before leaving for home, he reported back to headquarters on a meeting between MacArthur and members of the FEC, who were visiting Tokyo. During the meeting, the imperious general complained that the creation of the FEC had taken Japan's constitutional affairs from his jurisdiction, and he invited the FEC to work on the issue.[12] When his staff, however, insisted that SCAP had the power to direct constitutional reform until the FEC issued its own directives, MacArthur instructed his government section to draft a model constitution for Japan. On 4 February, General Courtney Whitney, the Section's head, informed his staff that they would effectively sit as a constitutional assembly to draft Japan's postwar constitution. This sudden reversal caught observers in Japan and abroad by surprise.

MacArthur's unexpected determination to retain control over the process may well have derived, as John Dower asserts, from his desire to protect the emperor and to re-establish the monarchy within a constitutional framework.[13] However, the new policy created havoc, both with the Matsumoto commission, established by the Japanese government to study constitutional change, and with the FEC, which was scheduled to begin deliberations in

Washington in late February. To forestall the commission, MacArthur issued guidelines in the first week of February, specifying that the emperor would remain head of state, that Japan would renounce war as a sovereign right, and that feudalism would be abolished.[14] Working non-stop, his staff drafted a complete constitution, translated it, and submitted it to the Japanese government on 13 February, with an indication that SCAP would brook no opposition on the document's key provisions.

Like other observers, Norman, who left Japan on 2 February, was astonished by this turn of events, which would preoccupy the FEC over the next few months. Though Lester Pearson, the ambassador to the United States, was the formal head of the Canadian delegation to the FEC, he relinquished much of the responsibility to Norman as his alternate. Norman sat on the FEC's constitutional and legal affairs committee, which drafted criteria for the commission to judge the proposed constitution. Unwilling to allow MacArthur to run roughshod over it, the FEC adopted a policy statement on 20 March 1946, insisting on its right to approve any constitutional proposal before it was adopted by the Japanese Diet. Moreover, the commission indicated that MacArthur's draft did not reflect its views and hoped that the Japanese would consider other suggestions. MacArthur was not impressed. He quickly telegraphed Major General Frank McCoy, the US chairman of the FEC, accusing the multilateral body of "reversing American policy." In a remarkable declaration of US imperial interests, MacArthur insisted that the FEC risked not only the occupation but the very well-being of the United States:

> What is at stake in this matter? It is not merely the unimportant question of a division of authority between various agencies but is the retention of American influence and American control which has been established in Japan by the American government in a skilful combination of checks and balances designed to preserve American interests here. There is a planned and concerted attack to break this down. It exists in the Far Eastern Commission in a most definite and decisive form under the veneer of diplomacy and comradeship therein. There is an implacable determination to break down the control of the United States which that country exercises through SCAP. I beg of you to protect in every possible way, including the veto power, the position and policy of the United States Government. Appeasements, small as they may seem, rapidly become accumulative to the point of danger. If we lose control of this sphere of influence under this policy of aggressive action, we will not only jeopardize the occupation but hazard the future safety of the United States.[15]

MacArthur's intervention put McCoy in a difficult position. In addition to working with the other countries on the FEC, the American chairman had to balance MacArthur's views with those of other US government departments, whose opinions varied widely. Indeed, John Carter Vincent, later to become a victim of McCarthyism, advised US Secretary of State George Marshall that most State Department officials believed MacArthur should "not have approved the draft constitution."[16] Through MacArthur and McCoy, however, the Pentagon remained the dominant influence on American policy, and as the constitutional drama unfolded, it became clear that it would be hard for FEC members to challenge their views.

Norman and the FEC constitutional committee were at the centre of the debate again in May, when the constitutional issue came to the fore. In a remarkable series of memoranda, Pearson outlined the dynamics shaping the debate in the commission. The first major dispute centred on the guiding principles the FEC would adopt in its deliberation on the constitution. The constitutional committee, supported by Canada but with the United States and Great Britain reserving their judgment, agreed that the Diet should be "encouraged to initiate popular and governmental discussion and study of a new Constitution." However, the Diet should not actually adopt a constitution because it had not been elected as a Constituent Assembly. Instead, the Japanese people should express their will on a new constitution through a referendum formulated either by a Constituent Assembly or a Diet specifically elected to serve as one.[17]

The committee further recommended empowering the Diet to amend the old Meiji constitution as necessary to allow time for the drafting process to unfold. This position, presented by Norman, who had often acted as its chairman as it refined its views, constituted a major challenge to MacArthur. When the US representative bluntly told the steering committee on 7 May that the recommendation was unacceptable, Pearson worried that MacArthur planned to have the current Diet discuss and adopt the draft constitution. Most members of the constitutional committee found that unacceptable, since approval by the existing Diet of a constitution largely drafted by SCAP "could hardly be 'the free expression of the will of the Japanese.'"[18] Pearson recommended that Canada support the principles embodied in the committee's recommendations, but that if no agreement was reached, the commission should advise the Diet to take no final action pending instructions from the FEC.

At a special meeting of the FEC on 13 May, Pearson reported that the United States and Great Britain opposed the recommendations on constitutional process. The Dutch representative expressed the majority sentiment best when he emphasized the FEC's responsibility to ensure that the "free will" of the Japanese people was respected, insisting that "the present Diet cannot be considered as adequate for the task."[19] Under pressure to compromise, McCoy proposed an alternative: "If the Japanese people should desire to adopt a new Constitution through media other than the present

Diet, they should not be discouraged from so doing, provided complete legal continuity is maintained from the Constitution of 1889 to the new Constitution."[20] At the request of the Indian delegate, the United States agreed to replace "not be discouraged" with the phrase "be given every opportunity." Norman asked whether a suggestion by the New Zealand delegate to include the word "encourage" could not be added. At this point, the Soviet delegate turned Norman's suggestion into a formal motion. Norman's reaction was significant. According to Pearson's account, to "avoid what obviously would have become a deadlock and to prevent any misunderstanding of our position, Mr. Norman immediately moved that in the interests of obtaining some agreement, the United States draft of paragraph 2, as amended by Sir Girja Bajpai should be adopted."[21] The Soviet delegate objected to this proposal, and the small concession that had been gained from the United States was lost. This was an important experience for Norman and Canada, as they clearly engaged in cold war politics – withdrawing their position in order to avoid its being identified with the Soviet Union.

Norman left Washington on 7 June to take up his position as head of Canada's liaison mission to occupied Japan. While delayed in Ottawa, he watched the looming confrontation in the FEC, where the debate over constitutional questions was entering its final phase. In late July, after a series of intense discussions in the Department of External Affairs, J.R. Maybee, an official in its third political division, sketched the issues for Hume Wrong, the associate under-secretary. After reviewing the commission's terms of reference and the positions adopted by the United States and the Soviet Union, Maybee concluded that "neither the United States nor the USSR appears to have a clear-cut case. While it is in our interest to maintain the authority and prestige of international bodies such as the Far Eastern Commission, it would probably not be desirable to oppose the United States in this constitutional issue since their interest in internal Japanese affairs is far greater than ours."[22] Maybee reiterated these points in a cable to Pearson on 18 July and added that the United States remained "in a position to block effective Commission action on constitutional matters."[23] Norman endorsed this view.[24]

The decision not to oppose the United States over the constitutional process, when the Canadian position was both distinct and principled, is an important example of how Canada's government was willing to sacrifice its support for the democratic process and multilateralism to the imperial view that Asia generally, and Japan specifically, were part of an American "sphere of influence." The FEC had been rendered powerless, stripped of its potential authority by the new cold war coalition lining up to support US hegemony in East Asia. Norman's role in the Konoe affair and the differences in the FEC over Japan's constitution undermine Roger Bowen's claim that "MacArthur's policies ... did not differ significantly from Canada's, and hence

Norman's in virtually every respect, at least through 1947."[25] It seems more likely that the opposite was true, and that Norman and his government initially disagreed with major elements in Washington's post-surrender policy before the two countries' policies began to converge because of Ottawa's growing deference to US control of Japan.

Reverse Course, or Rendering the Occupation Illegal?

By the late summer of 1947, a peace treaty with Japan was firmly on the international agenda. MacArthur had suggested in March that the occupation's basic objectives – demilitarization and democratization – had been achieved and that it was time for a treaty. The US State Department proposed in July that the FEC begin work on an accord, using a two-thirds majority to decide major differences. Commonwealth countries, which met in Canberra in August and September, also concluded that a peace treaty was desirable. The Canberra conference envisaged a meeting of the FEC plus Pakistan and possibly Burma; voting would be by a two-thirds majority, and the treaty should be completed by 1948.[26] But, by the end of 1948, the prospect of an agreement seemed more remote than ever.

Most historical accounts identify the major stumbling blocks to an early peace as being Soviet objections to the American proposal to use the FEC as the negotiating forum, and the two-thirds majority voting procedure. A thorough review of the documentary record, however, suggests that this interpretation is misleading. The Soviet objection to the US suggestion that the FEC draw up the treaty, and Moscow's counter-proposal that the Council of Foreign Ministers (CFM) handle it were not as far-fetched as later accounts contend. A US working group on the peace treaty had clearly envisaged the CFM as a possible venue for negotiations as recently as 1946.[27] In correspondence with the Soviet Union, the United States recognized that "the CFM was constituted on a basis which would have permitted its use for the preparation of a Treaty of Peace with Japan, provided the members of the Council subsequently agreed."[28]

The legitimacy of Soviet policy becomes even clearer when the Chinese government's position is taken into consideration. On 17 November 1947, the Chinese endorsed the US proposal that a special session of the FEC be convened on a date to be decided by the four big powers, adding that those same powers be given a veto in the deliberations. In other words, the Chinese government had come partway to meet the concerns of the Soviet Union that it retain a veto and that the big powers remain in control of the process.[29] Moscow unwisely rejected the Chinese proposal, but so too did the United States, and the Commonwealth countries of New Zealand, Australia, and Canada, which rejected the veto. In fact, the US government's July 1947 proposal was a unilateral American initiative that bypassed the precedents established both for the CFM and the FEC. What scuttled the peace treaty was not Soviet obstinacy regarding the veto, a right that the Chinese were also demanding, but rather, a remarkable shift in US foreign policy towards an imperial anti-communism that had been building throughout 1946 and 1947. While Commonwealth representatives met in Canberra, conservative forces in Washington, led by US diplomat George Kennan, were busy constructing a new strategy for President Harry Truman's administration based on an ideology of imperial anti-communism in Asia.[30]

Kennan emerged as the leading proponent of this policy in 1946. A career foreign service officer, he had been posted to Moscow from 1944 to 1946. In his "long" telegram of February 1946, he argued that the United States should quarantine the Soviet Union, spurning the policy of co-existence that had largely characterized the early postwar relationship. As part of his grand strategy, he called for the strengthening of both Germany and Japan as regional centres of capitalist development. His views attracted the attention of conservatives within Truman's administration, and when Kennan returned from Moscow, he was placed in charge of the Policy Planning Staff, a high-powered think tank within the State Department. Kennan first articulated his belief that discussions on a peace treaty should be set aside and the occupation prolonged in a memorandum to Marshall in October 1947.[31] The Policy Planning Staff study concluded that there were "great risks in an early relinquishment of Allied control over Japan. It [the United States] has no satisfactory evidence that Japanese society would be politically or economically stable if turned loose and left to its own devices at this stage. If Japan is not politically and economically stable when the peace treaty is signed, it will be difficult to prevent communist penetration."[32] Kennan cautioned that these interim views required verification through a visit to Japan. In the meantime, treaty talks should be exploratory and non-binding until he could deliver his final report. Nonetheless, the study had an immediate impact. Discussion of a peace treaty came to a standstill, and as early as January 1948, the United States told the FEC that its priority was the development of a "self-supporting economy in Japan."[33] In the spring, Kennan went to Japan to test his interim conclusions and recommended on his return that Washington "should not press for a treaty of peace at this time."[34]

The Canadian government knew that a major shift in American policy was afoot, and the stalled peace treaty discussions became the subject of close consultations among Canada, the United States, and Great Britain in the spring and summer of 1948. While visiting Japan in March 1948, Kennan had met with Norman, who warned Ottawa that the Americans wanted to delay the peace treaty and reverse occupation policy.[35] Significantly, Kennan left the meeting convinced that Canada might not welcome his proposal to continue the occupation. Consequently, he urged Marshall to allow him to take "the first opportunity to impress on the Canadians the necessity for a new approach to the questions of occupational policy in Japan and the peace treaty" and to correct the "serious divergence of view between the Canadians and ourselves."[36] US Secretary of State Marshall and his deputy, Robert Lovett, approved a proposal that Kennan visit Ottawa for discussions with Canadian officials, and endorsed a suggestion that if the opportunity arose, Kennan should share his secret strategic views with Canadian officials and cabinet ministers so that they would "feel that we were taking them into our confidence generally."[37]

Kennan travelled to Ottawa in early June, advising key officials in the Department of External Affairs that the US government now believed that a peace treaty should be delayed.[38] He brushed aside Canadian doubts, confiding that among the emerging cold war coalition partners, only Canada and Great Britain were being consulted. Echoing the unhappy FEC deliberations on the constitution, Canadian objections were overshadowed by emerging Anglo-American differences over Japan. This became clear in late July, when British Prime Minister Clement Attlee warned Prime Minister W.L. Mackenzie King that the United States appeared to "be dominated by what they believe to be the aim of the Soviet Union, viz. to obtain control of Japan as being the only Far Eastern country at present with any real industrial potential."[39] The Truman administration, Attlee continued, was determined to prolong the occupation "to retain the United States' strategic position in Japan." Although Attlee shared American suspicions of Soviet motives, he felt that the idea of fully restoring Japan's economy was open to "grave objection." He contended that the United States could ensure its position in Japan by simultaneously concluding a peace treaty and a defence pact with Japan and inviting "other friendly Powers" to accede to these agreements. Attlee explained that the "indefinite occupation by the United States without a treaty would on the contrary be difficult to defend except on grounds of pure expediency."[40]

Pearson, now undersecretary of state for External Affairs, drafted what became the basis of the Canadian position.[41] Ottawa supported the American "policy of denying Japan's industrial potential to the Soviet Union." While Pearson hoped for an early peace conference, he saw no justification for pressing the Americans if they did not think it "wise" at this time.[42]

Secure in the knowledge that the Canadian and British governments would not dissent, Kennan and the State Department extended the occupation of Japan and delayed the peace treaty. As Kennan recounted in his memoirs, in "the refusal of the Russians and Chinese to go along [with the treaty], we had been luckier than we deserved."[43] In retrospect, Kennan's remarks reflect the fact that the debates within the FEC provided a useful screen behind which the Truman administration was able to undercut the peace treaty process for its own purposes. Acquiescence through consultation meant that the Canadian government played the role of an enabler and was confirmation that Canada would support Washington as it pursued an emerging cold war agenda in which Japan was to act as an economic bulwark against communism. But what of values or international law? If, as all parties to the occupation seemed to agree, "the freely expressed will of the Japanese people" had completed the process of "democratization and demilitarization" and chosen "a peacefully inclined and responsible government,"[44] the Potsdam Declaration made it incumbent on them to sign a peace treaty and withdraw their forces. That was also expressed in the US "Initial Post-Surrender Policy for Japan."[45] In other words, the people of Japan could have regained their sovereignty in 1948, but the cold war meant that the occupation dragged on for another four years. In abetting this imperial agenda, Ottawa helped undermine both international norms and democratic values.

Canada and the San Francisco Peace Treaty

With the exception of Okubo's compendium in Japanese of the complete works of Norman, a common problem in the study of Herbert Norman, in both English and Japanese language sources, is that his work during the early 1950s is treated as a hiatus in his career.[46] To the extent that it is discussed at all, it is portrayed as a period of victimization, when Norman was recalled from Japan in October 1950 because of charges of disloyalty raised in the US Senate, after which he suffered interrogation and rehabilitation, only to fall suspect once again. However, as the primary documentation becomes increasingly available, it is possible to reconstruct a fuller view of Norman and his role in shaping Canadian occupation policy in the years immediately before the conclusion of a peace treaty at San Francisco in the fall of 1951.[47] Here again, Canadian policy towards postwar Japan conforms to an increasingly familiar pattern: persistent doubts about the wisdom of US behaviour in Japan are eventually subordinated to the overarching demands of its cold war alliance with the United States.

The prospect of peace talks emerged in 1949, when the US government raised the matter, but progress was slow since the US military demanded continued unfettered access to bases in Japan, a demand that the State Department opposed as incompatible with a peace agreement.[48] Commonwealth foreign ministers, who discussed the question at the Colombo Conference in January 1950, also felt that the time had come for a treaty and recommended that negotiations begin as soon as possible.[49] The outbreak of the Korean War in June 1950 made Washington's need to tie Japan closely to the West more urgent. In April 1950, Truman appointed John Foster Dulles, a Republican lawyer aligned with US conservatives, as a consultant to resolve internal differences over the future US military posture in Japan and to secure Republican support for the outcome.

Dulles moved quickly, and by October, preliminary elements of a draft treaty were circulating. Despite the constant spectre of incrimination and possible discharge, Norman persevered in preparing the Canadian position regarding the peace treaty, a job he was well qualified to take on. Prior to the treaty discussions in Canberra in 1947, Norman wrote a large number of memoranda detailing options for it and led much of the discussion for the Canadian delegation.[50] Pearson appointed Norman head of the American and Far East Division in December 1950, and he took up his duties after receiving a top security clearance in January 1951. In March, the US government submitted a draft peace treaty to Canada. From this point on, Norman was the main coordinator of Canadian policy on peace with Japan.

In Norman's division, which discussed the American draft in early April, there was a broad consensus that it "foreshadowed a very generous peace settlement for Japan."[51] Canadian officials feared that this would make it difficult to offer Germany lesser terms and endorsed Norman's demand for a war guilt clause, since its absence might promote cynicism among some countries, who would look askance at the lengths the United States was willing to go to "gain the cooperation of an ex-enemy." The department worried too that Communist China and the Soviet Union would use its omission in their anti-Western propaganda and that the absence of limitations on Japanese rearmament might set a precedent for Germany.[52]

Regarding territorial issues, the department recommended that the treaty force Japan to renounce its claims to its former colonial territories without specifying to whom they were ceded. This was especially crucial in the case of Formosa (Taiwan), which was claimed by both Communist China and the breakaway Republic of China. The department accepted provisions giving US control of Okinawa. Other provisions that attracted Canadian attention included a clause extending most-favoured nation (MFN) treatment to Japan, subject to reservations to restrict low-cost imports, as well as clauses on shipping and civil aviation. The department proposed incorporating a draft human rights clause and recommended including a clause to regulate the North Pacific fisheries.

While the American and Far Eastern division solicited the opinions of other government departments, Norman travelled to Washington where he held talks with John Allison, Dulles's main assistant in preparing the peace treaty. He quickly learned how little give there was in the US position. Allison saw no link between the Japanese and German treaties because Japan was an isolated island whereas Germany was occupied by several powers, including the nearby Soviet Union. He rejected a war guilt clause outright, and argued that limitations on rearmament would be accomplished through the US-Japan security treaty that Washington planned to sign simultaneously with the peace treaty. Allison did not disagree with Norman's observation that it would be "undesirable" to use the treaty to tie Japan to the Nationalist Chinese government of Taiwan. Nevertheless, he indicated that the United States hoped to have the Nationalist government sign the treaty. Norman concluded by suggesting that Japan be required to carry out key occupation reforms and by noting two particular Canadian concerns: a fisheries convention and Japan's gold assets held in neutral countries as part of any reparations package. Allison made no promises.[53]

The rigid American posture was also apparent in the State Department's discussions with other countries regarding the draft treaty. After an exchange of views between British and American officials, Norman told Arnold Heeney, the under-secretary of state for External Affairs, that the British seemed prepared to concede on most points except economic ones, while the United States refused to budge on any item that might make the treaty seem "restrictive or ungenerous." The Americans were carrying this to "ludicrous" extremes, even opposing publication of a map with Japan's new territorial limits, lest it have "an undesirable psychological effect upon the Japanese."[54] The division head told Heeney that he believed that the Canadian government should not hesitate to put forward its views on such matters as war guilt, in deference to US sensitivities.

In late April, the Department of External Affairs asked Canada's ambassador to the United States, Hume Wrong, to seek an official State Department clarification on the four issues "of central importance" – the precedents established by the peace treaty for Germany, the question of Chinese representation at the signing ceremony, the disposition of former Japanese territories, and the security aspects of the treaty. On these issues, the memorandum reiterated the concerns raised by Norman regarding Germany; called for China's seat at the peace conference to remain empty, with the possibility of Chinese accession later; requested Japan's renunciation of all former colonial possessions, but without assigning them to any specific country; and asked how a supplementary security agreement might limit Japanese rearmament.[55]

The US responded in early May. Its position had not changed substantially since Norman's interview with Allison. Dulles told Wrong bluntly that Washington saw no link between the Japanese and German peace treaties, took note of the suggestion for later Chinese accession, as well as the idea that Sakhalin and the Kuriles be simply renounced, and that this not be contingent on the Soviet Union signing the treaty. He also reassured the Canadian representative that a US-Japan military agreement would make it clear that Japan would not be allowed to possess armaments that "could be an offensive threat."[56]

Dulles's clarifications had little impact on the final Canadian response to the US draft treaty.[57] On 18 May, Norman sent a copy of the Canadian government's formal reply to the Canadian embassy in Washington and made sure that Dulles received a copy personally before he left for London for talks with the British. Of particular concern to Canadian authorities was the fisheries issue, and the fisheries minister, R.W. Mayhew, met with Dulles in late May to overcome American opposition to a fisheries convention as part of the treaty. Eventually, the two men agreed on a compromise whereby the Japanese government agreed that no fishing would take place in north Pacific waters until further trilateral discussions had taken place.[58]

Ottawa continued to hope that Allied consultations with the United States might prompt Washington to amend the most worrying features of its treaty. In June, Norman headed to London to consult with his British counterparts, as they too sought changes from Dulles. On 14 June, American and British negotiators reached agreement on the main issue dividing them, the representation of China. London abandoned its demand for Communist Chinese participation at the peace conference in exchange for a US commitment not to press the claims of the nationalist Republic of China government on Formosa.[59] The compromise was not especially reassuring and drew the attention of Chester Ronning, who had returned to Ottawa from his post as chargé d'affaires in Nanjing, in the spring of 1951.

The veteran China-hand was skeptical of British hopes that Japan would be subsequently free to work out arrangements with both Nationalist and Communist governments. The US, he argued, would pressure Tokyo to recognize the Nationalists, and Beijing would refuse to deal with a government that sought relations with both the mainland and Formosa.[60] In Ronning's view, the United States was getting what it wanted "with little compromise involved." Moreover, he warned, a treaty that did not include the Soviet Union and Communist China could not "provide for stable relations in the area" and would make it more difficult to settle the Korean War. The deputy under-secretary, Escott Reid, took these points up with Pearson, who agreed in late June that Wrong might raise them informally with the State Department.[61] Wrong dutifully met Dean Rusk, the assistant secretary of state for far eastern affairs, who dismissed Canadian concerns, noting that Great Britain did not share Ottawa's worries.[62]

Despite Rusk's claims, Canadian doubts did not go away. Indeed, they became more serious. On 27 July, the Department of External Affairs informed cabinet that it had "doubts about the timing of the treaty" because of the difficulties it might create for a settlement in Korea.[63] Another factor also gave the department pause; Asian states did not agree on the treaty. Burma was refusing to sign it, the Philippines were unhappy about limitations on reparations, while India, Pakistan, and Indonesia seemed prepared to sign. Despite the drawbacks, the department recommended that Canada sign the accord because it was "part of the United States' arrangements for the defence of the Pacific, and the responsibility for appearing to threaten those arrangements by refusing to sign would be very grave."[64]

The department continued to monitor international reaction to the draft treaty during early August. The views of the Asian states were now clearer, Heeney informed Pearson, and India had decided that it would not sign a treaty "which would in effect make Japan a United States bastion against

China."[65] The under-secretary assured the minister that Wrong had informed the US administration of his concerns about the timing of the treaty and his doubts about the security clauses. These, Heeney reiterated, were not "legally necessary and are the ones to which China and the USSR could not reasonably be expected to agree."[66] He added that there was mounting opposition to the treaty from other countries, including the Netherlands. More important, he told Pearson of legal division's view that the "renunciation by Japan of her rights and titles in Formosa, the Pescadores, Sakhalin and

Figure 7.2 Secretary of State for External Affairs Lester B. Pearson signing the Japanese Peace Treaty, September 1951. *Acme News Pictures, Library and Archives Canada, C-20131.*

the Kuriles provides China and the U.S.S.R. respectively with legal title to the territories."[67] Given the treaty's evident shortcomings and lukewarm international support, Heeney thought that any Canadian statement in favour of it should be moderate. Indeed, the under-secretary asked Pearson whether the department should "support India's stand in respect to the security clauses or whether we should leave it to the Indian government to argue this point alone with the United States government."[68]

Pearson's reply is not recorded, nor does it appear that he shared the concerns raised in Heeney's memorandum with his cabinet colleagues, who approved the treaty on 22 August. Indeed, at the San Francisco Conference to finalize the treaty, Pearson made it abundantly clear where his sympathies lay. Disregarding Heeney's cautious recommendation that Canada give only moderate support to the treaty, the minister vigorously defended it. He praised MacArthur and Dulles for their work and directly challenged India's hesitations. His support for the US government was undiluted: "It [the treaty] reflects also the wisdom and basic democracy of the United States government and people in refusing to embark on the imperialistic course of making Japan a mere appendage to the United States; or more subtly perhaps, of attempting to refashion Japan in the image of America."[69] That Communist China was not at the conference, he suggested, was its own fault because it had committed its forces to aggression in Korea. "The Peiping government must realize that it cannot shoot its way into the United Nations," he stated, echoing the very words of the US State Department.[70]

Conclusion

The evidence presented in this chapter challenges the conventional view that Canadian and American views of the early stages of the occupation were similar. While Ottawa and Washington generally agreed on the post-surrender objectives of democratization and demilitarization, they differed profoundly in the application of those policies. That Norman and MacArthur, and the two countries they represented, disagreed is clear in both the Konoe affair and the FEC confrontation over Japan's postwar constitution. Norman's critical perspective and his knowledge of Japanese history led him to adopt views that were largely antithetical to those of the paternalistic MacArthur.

This chapter also suggests some broader reflections about the place of Japan in Canada's postwar foreign policy. Ottawa's decision in the FEC to abandon its principled position regarding Japan's constitutional process in the face of US objections was one in which democracy and multilateralism were sacrificed in order to keep peace with US policy. East Asia was, in the opinion of Pearson and External Affairs, part of the "American sphere of influence." A similar dynamic governed Canada's approach to the long-delayed peace treaty and Kennan's "reverse course." The abandonment of

Canadian positions in deference to US cold war preoccupations underlines how much Canada's postwar approach to Japan was played out against the country's basic continentalist – rather than internationalist – orientation.[71] At least in the immediate postwar period, an independent Canada-Japan relationship was subordinated to the larger cold war concerns of Canada's imperial ally, the United States.

Notes

The author gratefully acknowledges the financial assistance for research related to this paper from the University of Victoria and the Social Sciences and Humanities Research Council.

1 See Arthur Menzies, "Canadian Views of United States Policy toward Japan, 1945-1952," in *War and Diplomacy across the Pacific, 1919-1952*, ed. A. Hamish Ion and Barry Hunt (Waterloo, ON: Wilfrid Laurier University Press, 1988), 155-72; Klaus H. Pringsheim, *Neighbours across the Pacific* (Westport, CT: Greenwood Press, 1983), ch. 3; John W. Holmes, "Canada's Postwar Policies towards Japan" (paper presented at the International University Symposium on Japan and Postwar Diplomacy in the Asia-Pacific Region, International House of Japan, 18-19 March 1983); Michael G. Fry, "Canada and the Occupation of Japan: The MacArthur-Norman Years," in *The Occupation of Japan: The International Context*, ed. Thomas Burkman (Norfolk, VA: The MacArthur Foundation, 1984), 130-59; Roger Bowen, *Innocence Is Not Enough: The Life and Death of Herbert Norman* (Vancouver: Douglas and McIntyre, 1986), ch. 4 and 5.

2 Accounts of Norman's life in English include Roger Bowen, ed., *E.H. Norman: His Life and Scholarship* (Toronto: University of Toronto Press, 1984); and Bowen's biography, *Innocence Is Not Enough*; John Hilliker, "'Sleeping with an Elephant': Canada, the United States and Herbert Norman" (paper presented at the 1998 Annual Meeting of the American Political Science Association, Boston); Peyton Lyon, "The Loyalties of E. Herbert Norman" (report for External Affairs and International Trade, 18 March 1990); Charles Taylor, *Six Journeys: A Canadian Pattern* (Toronto: Anansi Press, 1977); James Barros, *No Sense of Evil: Espionage, The Case of Herbert Norman* (Toronto: Deneau, 1986); and a short pamphlet, Greg Donaghy, ed., *Herbert Norman: A Documentary Perspective* (Ottawa: Department of Foreign Affairs, 1999). In Japanese, see Nakano Toshiko, *H. Nōman – aru demokuratto no tadotta unmei* [H. Norman: The Fate that Befell a Democrat] (Tokyo: Riburopōto, 1990); Kudō Miyoko, *Higeki no gaikōkan: habato nōman no shōgai* [Tragedy's Diplomat: The Life of Herbert Norman] (Tokyo: Iwanami shoten, 1991).

3 See Bowen in response to Michael Fry's paper, "Canada and the Occupation of Japan," in Burkman, *The Occupation of Japan*, 156.

4 The re-creation of events relating to the constitutional work in Japan is based on Robert E. Ward, "Presurrender Planning: Treatment of the Emperor and Constitutional Changes"; Theodore H. McNelly, "'Induced Revolution': The Policy and Process of Constitutional Reform in Occupied Japan"; and Tanaka Hideo, "The Conflict between Two Legal Traditions in Making the Constitution of Japan," all in *Democratizing Japan: The Allied Occupation*, ed. Robert E. Ward and Sakamoto Yoshikazu (Honolulu: University of Hawaii Press, 1987), 1-41, 76-106, and 107-32 respectively; John Dower, *Embracing Defeat: Japan in the Wake of World War II* (New York: WW Norton/New Press, 1999); Kyoko Inoue, *MacArthur's Japanese Constitution* (Chicago: University of Chicago Press, 1991). In Japanese, Kudō Yoroshi, *Ruporutaajyu Nihonkoku Kempō* [Reporting on the Japanese Constitution] (Tokyo: Asahi Shimbun, 1997); Satō Tatsuo, *Nihonkoku kempō seiritsu-shi* [History of the Establishment of Japan's Constitution], 2 vols. (Tokyo: Yūhikaku, 1962, 1964). This part of the chapter also draws on my article, "E.H. Norman, Canada and Japan's Postwar Constitution," *Pacific Affairs* 74, 3 (2001): 383-405.

5 Bowen, McNelly, Tanaka, and Nakano all refer to Norman's role.

6 Norman's distinct emphasis on this was pointed out as early as 1974 by Dower in his edited work, *Origins of the Modern Japanese State: Selected Writings of E.H. Norman* (New York: Pantheon, 1974), 26-27.
7 The oligarchy consisted of representatives of the "armed services, business, bureaucracy, and court"; in Herbert Norman, "Review of Edwin O. Reischauer, *Japan Past and Present,*" *Pacific Affairs* 20, 3 (1947): 359.
8 Norman, "Memorandum for the Officer in Charge," 8 November 1945, contained in Ōkubo Genji ed., *Historical and Political Writings [MSS] by Herbert Norman* (Tokyo: N.p., 1978), Special Collections, Main Library, University of British Columbia.
9 See Dale Hellegers, "The Konoe Affair," in *Legal Reform in Japan,* ed. L.H. Redford (Norfolk, VA: MacArthur Memorial,1979), 173-74; and *Kudō, Ruporutaajyu Nihonkoku Kempō,* 174-76.
10 See Bowen, *Innocence Is Not Enough,* 123; Nakano, *H. Nōman-aru demokuratto no tadotta unmei,* 116.
11 See Michael Schaller, *The American Occupation of Japan* (New York: Oxford University Press, 1985), 57-61.
12 Norman, "General MacArthur's Remarks to the Far Eastern Advisory Council," 29 January 1946, as cited in Katō Shūichi and Nakano Toshiko, *Nihon Senryoku no kiroku (1946-48)* [E.H. Norman Reports from Occupied Japan, 1946-48] (Tokyo: Jinbun Shoin, 1997), 16. That the staff had stopped work on the constitution is confirmed by Tanaka, "The Conflict between Two Legal Traditions," 108.
13 See Dower, *Embracing Defeat,* 362-64. This view had been articulated by the Japan crowd in the State Department, including former ambassador to Japan, Joseph C. Grew. For details on pre-surrender planning, see Ward, "Presurrender Planning."
14 "Three basic points stated by Supreme Commander to be 'musts' in Constitutional Revision," SCAP files of Commander Alfred R. Hussey, Document No. 5, National Diet Library, Tokyo, Japan.
15 MacArthur's full message is contained in Max W. Bishop of the Office of the Political Adviser in Japan to the Secretary of State, 15 April 1946, reprinted in Department of State, *Foreign Relations of the United States, 1946* (hereafter *FRUS*), vol. 8: *The Far East* (Washington: US Government Printing Office, 1972), 204-5.
16 Memorandum by the Director of the Office of Far Eastern Affairs (Vincent) to the Secretary of State, 19 April 1946, reprinted in *FRUS, 1946,* 8:211.
17 FEC, Steering Committee -012/4, as contained in Canadian Ambassador to the US to Secretary of State for External Affairs (hereafter SSEA), 8 May 1946, Department of External Affairs Records (hereafter DEAR), vol. 2654, file 4606-40, Library and Archives of Canada (hereafter LAC).
18 Canadian Ambassador to US to SSEA, 8 May 1946, DEAR, vol. 3649, file 4606-A-40, LAC.
19 Canadian Ambassador to US to SSEA, 14 May 1946, DEAR, vol. 3649, file 4606-A-40, LAC.
20 Ibid.
21 Ibid.
22 Positions of people are based on John Hilliker and Donald Barry, *Canada's Department of External Affairs,* vol. 2: *Coming of Age, 1946-1968* (Montreal and Kingston: McGill-Queen's University Press, 1995).
23 J.R. Maybee, First Secretary, Political 3 Division, to the Canadian Ambassador in the US, telegram EX-1790, 18 July 1946, DEAR, vol. 3649, file 4606-A-40, LAC.
24 Norman to Collins, telegram EX-1784, 18 July 1946, DEAR, vol. 3649, file 4606-A-40, LAC.
25 Bowen, *Innocence Is Not Enough,* 130-31.
26 Defence Minister Brooke Claxton's report on the conference is contained in Brooke Claxton Papers, vol. 99, Canberra Conference file, LAC. Extracts are reprinted in Norman Hillmer and Donald Page, eds., *Documents on Canadian External Relations* (hereafter *DCER*), vol. 13: *1947* (Ottawa: Minister of Supply and Services, 1993), 227-34. Norman's submission, included in the preparatory materials provided to Claxton and the delegation, are contained in Canberra Conference Book 2, Claxton Papers, vol. 99, LAC.
27 Working Group on Japan Treaty, Notes on Meeting, reprinted in *FRUS, 1946,* 8:349.

28 United States Aide-Memoire to the Soviet Government of 12 August 1947, reprinted in Robin Kay, ed., *Documents on New Zealand External Relations* (hereafter *DNZER*), vol. 3: *The ANZUS Pact and the Treaty of Peace with Japan* (Wellington, New Zealand: Historical Branch, Department of Internal Affairs, 1985), 206.
29 Chinese Embassy, London to United Kingdom Government, contained in Secretary of State for Commonwealth Relations to the Minister of External Affairs, 19 November 1947, reprinted in Kay, *DNZER*, 3:219.
30 For details, see Schaller, *The American Occupation of Japan*, 98-106; and Howard B. Schonberger, *Aftermath of War: Americans and the Remaking of Japan, 1945-1952* (Kent: Kent State University Press, 1989), 178-80.
31 Memorandum by the Director of the Policy Planning Staff (Kennan), 14 October 1947, and Annex, reprinted in Department of State, *FRUS, 1948*, vol. 4: *Eastern Europe and the Soviet Union* (Washington: US Government Printing Office, 1975), 536-43.
32 Ibid., 537.
33 Statement to Be Made to Far Eastern Commission by United States Member and Transmitted to SCAP for Information and Released for Publication, reprinted in *FRUS, 1948*, 4:654.
34 Report by the Director of the Policy Planning Staff (Kennan), 25 March 1948, reprinted in *FRUS, 1948*, 4:691-96.
35 Cited in Bowen, *Innocence Is Not Enough*, 153.
36 U.S. National Archives, Occupation of Japan, Part 2: US and Allied Policy, 1945-1952, 3-H-21.
37 Ibid., 1.
38 The record of the discussions with Kennan are contained in Arthur Menzies, United States Policy for Japan, 3 June 1948, DEAR, vol. 4730, file 50061-40, LAC.
39 Personal Message for Mr. Mackenzie King from Mr. Attlee, 21 July 1948, DEAR, vol. 4730, file 50061-40, LAC.
40 Ibid.
41 Pearson wrote Canada's high commissioner to the United Kingdom, Norman Robertson, on 4 August explaining that Mackenzie King was preoccupied with the Liberal convention (at which he would retire) but that Robertson might share with British authorities the content of the draft reply. He also told Robertson that they had shared their views with Kennan and that the matter was basically closed. Pearson to Robertson, telegram 1245, 4 August 1948, DEAR, vol. 4730, file 50061-40.
42 Personal Message for Mr. Attlee from Mr. Mackenzie King, 23 July 1948, DEAR, vol. 4730, file 50061-40, LAC.
43 George F. Kennan, *Memoirs, 1925-1950* (Boston: Little, Brown, 1967), 376.
44 "Potsdam Declaration," as reproduced in Supreme Commander for the Allied Powers, *Appendices: Political Reorientation of Japan, September 1945 to September 1948* (Washington: US Government Printing Office, 1948), 413.
45 In the ultimate objectives of the occupation, U.S. policy stated that "(d) The Japanese people shall be afforded opportunity to develop for themselves an economy which will permit the peacetime requirements of the population to be met," in "United States Initial Post-Surrender Policy for Japan," in *Supreme Commander for the Allied Powers, Appendices*, 423.
46 Herbert Norman, *Hâbâto Nōman zenshū* [Complete Works of Herbert Norman], trans. and ed. Ōkubo Genji (Tokyo: Iwanami, 1997-98).
47 As the Historical Section of the Department of Foreign Affairs continues its efforts to produce the invaluable resource, *Documents on Canada's External Relations*, an increasing number of files are being released for scrutiny. On the peace treaty, see especially Greg Donaghy, ed., *Documents on Canadian External Relations,* vol. 17: *1951* (Ottawa: Canada Communication Group, 1996).
48 For background on the peace treaty, see John Price, "A Just Peace? The 1951 San Francisco Peace Treaty in Historical Perspective," published by the Japan Policy Research Institute (Working Paper No. 78, June 2001), or a longer version, "Cold War Relic: The 1951 San Francisco Peace Treaty and the Politics of Memory," *Asian Perspective* 25, 3 (2001): 31-60.
49 Pearson's remarks on the peace treaty during the Colombo conference are reprinted in Kay, *DNZER*, 3:305-7. Pearson's report is reprinted in Greg Donaghy, ed., *DCER*, vol. 16: *1950* (Ottawa: Canada Communication Group, 1995), 1,196.

50 Kay, *DNZER*, 3:156.
51 Memorandum Regarding the Japanese Peace Treaty, 10 April 1951, DEAR, vol. 4615, file 50051-40, LAC.
52 Ibid.
53 Ibid, 2. "Japanese Peace Treaty: Memorandum of Conversation on April 12 between Dr. E.H. Norman and Mr. John M. Allison," 14 April 1951, NAC, RG 25, vol. 4615, file 50051-40, pt. 11, p. 1-5.
54 Norman, Memorandum for the Under-Secretary of State for External Affairs (hereafter USSEA), 28 April 1951, DEAR, vol. 4615, file 50051-40, LAC.
55 SSEA to Canadian Ambassador in the US, telegram EX-941, 30 April 1951, reprinted in Donaghy, ed., DCER, vol. 17: *1951* (Ottawa: Canada Communication Group, 1996), 1802-4.
56 Canadian Ambassador in the US to SSEA, telegram WA-1936, 8 May 1951, reprinted in Donaghy, *DCER*, 17:1805.
57 Memorandum on the Japanese Peace Treaty, 9 May 1951, DEAR, vol. 4615, file 50051-40, LAC. I do not summarize this document because of space limitations, although it is of interest because of the divergent views expressed by the various parties.
58 SSEA to the Canadian Ambassador in the US, telegram EX-1144, 25 May 1951, reprinted in Donaghy, *DCER*, 17:1816-22.
59 High Commissioner for Canada in the UK (hereafter HCCUK) to SSEA, 14 June 1951, DEAR, vol. 4615, file 50051-40, LAC.
60 Chester Ronning, Memorandum for the Minister, 14 June 1951, DEAR, vol. 4615, file 50051-40, LAC.
61 SSEA to Ambassador in the US, telegram EX-1408, 11 July 1951, reprinted in Donaghy, *DCER*, 17:1823.
62 Ambassador in the US to SSEA, telegram WA-2830, 13 July 1951, reprinted in Donaghy, *DCER*, 17:1825.
63 Memorandum from SSEA to Cabinet, 27 July 1951, reprinted in Donaghy, *DCER*, 17:1826.
64 Ibid., 1826.
65 Memorandum from USSEA to SSEA, 8 August, 1951, reprinted in Donaghy, *DCER*, 17:1829.
66 Ibid., 1830.
67 Ibid.
68 Memorandum from SSEA to Cabinet, 21 August 1951, reprinted in Donaghy, DCER, 17:1833.
69 Pearson's speech is reprinted in US Department of State, *Conference for the Conclusion and Signature of the Treaty of Peace with Japan: Record of Proceedings* (Washington: Department of State, 1951), 215-19.
70 Ibid., 218.
71 I explored this theme recently in my article "The 'Cat's Paw': Canada and the United Nations Temporary Commission on Korea," *Canadian Historical Review* 85, 2 (June 2004): 297-324.

8
Two Other Solitudes: Encounters between Japanese Canadians and French Canadians, 1900-50

Greg Robinson

> Les Canadiens à qui on demande en quoi leur pays se distingue des États-Unis devraient répondre en français.
>
> (When Canadians are asked what is the difference between their country and the United States, they should answer in French.)
>
> – Attributed to Lester B. Pearson

Japanese immigrants and their descendants contributed in important ways to the development of Canada during the early twentieth century. The presence of Japanese Canadians and their struggle for equality had a significant impact on Canadian social relations. In turn, the hostility and discriminatory treatment accorded them, climaxing in their wartime confinement by the federal government, shaped the course of diplomatic relations between Canada and Japan. Although Japanese Canadians, like members of other minority groups, tended to interact primarily with the dominant English Canadian community, French Canadians played an influential role in their experience in the country. French-Canadian political leaders in Ottawa worked with the Japanese government to determine the conditions under which Japanese immigrants came to Canada, in the process helping to inaugurate an independent Canadian foreign policy, and supported their mass "repatriation" immediately after the Second World War. Conversely, French Canadians in Quebec offered homeless Japanese Canadians a wartime refuge and a particular welcome.

The history of the French Canadian–Japanese Canadian encounter begins with the wave of Japanese immigration to Canada at the end of the nineteenth century. The vast majority of these Japanese immigrants settled in British Columbia, where they became active in agriculture, lumbering, and the fishing industry. By 1907, there were some 10,000 Japanese immigrants in Canada. As David Sulz shows in Chapter 3 of this volume, Japanese immigration proved a contentious issue in British Columbia, where local whites, anxious over labour competition and inflamed by racial bias, protested the Japanese presence. Beginning in 1897, British Columbia's legislature passed a series of laws to restrict Japanese immigration. The federal government disallowed these laws in order not to disturb British imperial foreign policy towards its Japanese ally. Emotions in British Columbia peaked on 7 September 1907, when a mass demonstration called by the Asiatic Exclusion League in Vancouver erupted into a race riot. White thugs attacked the city's Chinese and Japanese neighbourhoods, damaging property and looting shops.[1]

During these years, many French Canadians expressed a general ambivalence or hostility towards immigration to Canada. Immigration to Quebec, where most French Canadians lived, had been minimal from 1867 to 1896, but it expanded dramatically in the years afterwards.[2] Between 1901 and 1915, 292,296 immigrants took up residence in Quebec. The Catholic Church, which dominated French-Canadian intellectual life, so stressed the importance of immutable racial and/or religious identities in opposing entry by Italians, Jews, and other groups that one scholar claimed that the Church regarded immigration as "a horrid experience which caused individuals to lose their ties and sense of attachment to family and community values."[3] In addition, many educated French Canadians, influenced by prevailing social Darwinist ideas, viewed immigrants from outside Western Europe as inferior and even dangerous on racial grounds. A cartoon from the journal *Le Canard,* dating from 1900, for example, presented the new immigrants, whether Asian, Jewish, or Eastern European, in stereotyped fashion to emphasize their undesirability (see Figure 8.1). French-Canadian liberals, who had supported Confederation as a means of striking a balance of power between English and French, opposed immigration by members of other nationalities as a destabilizing force.[4]

At the same time, the mass of French Canadians concentrated in Quebec remained largely distant from and indifferent to the specific question of Japanese immigration. Commentary in the French-language press on Japanese immigrants was scanty and neutral.[5] In early 1907, *La Presse* expressed opposition to anti-Japanese legislation, not on racist grounds but because it hindered development: "If British Columbia wishes to keep its anti-Japanese laws, so be it, but our country, being young, must follow the example of the United States, and as far as the development of our railroads is concerned, the policy of the Canadian people should be: whether you are black, yellow, red or white, come work!"[6]

Despite the general indifference, French-Canadian politicians, notably Prime Minister Wilfrid Laurier, occupied a central role in the exclusion of Japanese immigrants. Scholars of Canada's anti-Asian movements, notably Peter Ward and Patricia Roy, have described Laurier as generally respectful towards Japan, whose political and military progress he admired. As he wrote

L'IMMIGRATION

SIFTON: Voici un joli lot d'immigrants que j'ai eu pour presque rien. MLLE CANADA: Mon Dieu! Combien va-t-il m'en coûter pour les renvoyer?

Figure 8.1 "L'Immigration," *Le Canard,* August 1900. Clifford Sifton, the federal minister in charge of immigration, actively promoted immigration from central and eastern Europe, much to the consternation of some French Canadians. Sifton is saying, "Here's a nice lot of immigrants I got for almost nothing." Miss Canada replies, "My God! How much will it cost to send them back?"

privately, the "Japanese has adopted European civilization, has shown that he can whip European soldiers, has a navy equal man for man to the best afloat, and will not submit to be kicked and treated with contempt, as his brother from China still meekly submits to."[7] Fearing to confront Japanese power, and hindered by imperial ties, Laurier refused to be drawn into the movement for exclusion.

After the 1907 Vancouver riot, the Laurier government was forced to act. As a conciliatory gesture towards Japan, the prime minister sent the deputy minister of labour, and future prime minister, William Lyon Mackenzie King, to Vancouver as head of a commission to examine claims for damages caused by the riot. Meanwhile, Laurier sought some means of limiting Japanese immigration that would placate British Columbian restrictionists without alienating Japan, disturbing the Anglo-Japanese naval alliance, or violating the Anglo-Japanese Treaty of Commerce, to which Canada was a signatory.[8] Laurier's trusted lieutenant, Labour Minister Rodolphe Lemieux, volunteered to visit Tokyo and negotiate with the Japanese government an informal

Figure 8.2 Rodolphe Lemieux, Laurier's lieutenant who negotiated the Gentleman's Agreement. *Library and Archives Canada, Topley studio fonds, PA-027994.*

understanding to limit immigration visas, on the model of the "Gentlemen's Agreement" that Japanese leaders were in the process of concluding with US President Theodore Roosevelt.[9] In addition to his closeness to Laurier, Lemieux was selected for this mission, the first independent démarche of Canadian diplomacy, because of his fluency in French, then the international language of diplomacy.[10]

Lemieux arrived in Tokyo in December 1907. Although his hosts refused any explicit undertaking that would signify Japanese inferiority, Japan valued the preservation of friendly foreign and trade relations more than immigration rights. As a result, Lemieux succeeded in obtaining from First Minister Count Hayashi a private promise that Japan would henceforth permit only four hundred Japanese each year to enter Canada.[11] On his return in January 1908, Lemieux reported to Parliament on his mission and hailed Japan's willingness to cooperate in limiting immigration. In a long passage discussing the history of the "Japanese problem," he made it clear that unrestricted Japanese immigration posed a menace to the western "Anglo-Saxon" civilization in which he included French Canadians such as himself:

> In an Anglo-Saxon country like ours, where democratic institutions prevail, the introduction in large numbers of foreign races unfamiliar with our principles of self-government can only be considered dangerous. These orientals belong to a civilization formed over the centuries in ways radically and totally different from ours. It is thus clear that British Columbians must oppose this vast foreign colony – exclusive, inscrutable, unassimilable, retaining their particular customs and characteristics.[12]

Laurier backed his minister with a two-hour speech of his own. While he expressed great regard towards the Japanese government and its constructive attitude, Laurier saw no contradiction between esteem for Japan and advocacy of international friendship, on the one hand, and a hostile and exclusionary policy on the domestic side. He made the case for a restrictive immigration policy in apocalyptic and racially charged terms: "In all the nations where they have met, the white and mongol races have demonstrated their antagonism. The population of British Columbia is small, and it is understandable that they fear if the wave of Asian immigration is not contained, power will soon pass from one race to another."[13] The Gentlemen's Agreement was approved by a large majority in Parliament, and swiftly became a cornerstone of Canadian-Japanese relations. It remained in force (with amendments in the mid-1920s that reduced the annual number of visas issued from 400 to 150) until the Second World War.

Following the outbreak of the crisis in British Columbia, French-Canadian newspapers shifted rapidly from neutrality towards an anti-immigrant line. The September 1907 issue of the satirical humour magazine *Le Canard* depicted Japanese immigrants in dehumanized terms as a swarm of insects, although it also satirized the exaggerated nature of British Columbian xenophobi (see Figure 8.3). *La Presse,* which had blamed the Vancouver riot on the provocations of "unassimilable" Asians, devoted generous coverage to Lemieux's visit to Tokyo.[14] The week of his return, it reported indignantly

NOTRE IMMIGRATION!
CB: Wilfrid, protège-moi contre ces maudites bêtes!

Figure 8.3 "Notre Immigration," *Le Canard,* September 1907. Like *La Presse, Le Canard* had some sympathy for British Columbia's desire to keep out the Japanese as British Columbia asked Laurier to protect it from the "accursed beasts."

that "a horde" of "oriental demons" had attacked three firemen in Victoria.[15] Following Lemieux's report and the announcement of the Gentleman's Agreement, *La Presse,* which referred to both Laurier's and Lemieux's speeches as "magisterial exposés" of the Asian problem, expressed outspoken support for Japanese exclusion. *Le prix courant* and *Le moniteur de commerce,* which spoke for the francophone business community, were even more extreme. According to historian Fernande Roy, in the months after the Vancouver riot and Lemieux's visit to Japan, they published "several hate-filled articles demanding that the government halt entirely all immigration by Blacks, Asians and Jews."[16]

As anti-Japanese agitation in British Columbia subsided following the Gentlemen's Agreement and a consequent sharp reduction in Japanese immigration, so too did attention to Japanese Canadians among French Canadians. So far, I have found only a handful of references to Japanese Canadians in works by French Canadians in Quebec over the following decades. For example, Emile Miller's 1912 textbook, *Terres et peuples du Canada,* spoke of British Columbia's "8000 proud and combative Japanese" as part of an "invasion jaune" (yellow invasion) that threatened the future of the country.[17] Louis Marie Le Jeune's 1931 *Dictionnaire général* described Japanese immigrants as the least desirable element among Asians, incontestably talented but inassimilable and resentful of their inferior status.[18]

During these years, a tiny community of ethnic Japanese settled in Montreal.[19] Shaw T. Nishimura settled in Montreal in 1900 as a representative of the Japan Central Tea Association,[20] the Yokohama silk company sent agents, and a Japanese consulate opened downtown in 1902 before moving to Ottawa shortly afterwards. Joseph Ogawa, a Japanese circus strongman who came to Canada in 1882, married Nellie Rowlands, an Irish immigrant woman in Montreal, while her sister married a McGill student, Yasuhara H. Kato. Saburo Yamamoto, a cook, arrived in 1905 with his wife Catherine. A trio of cousins, Shinsaburo Koga, Tomitaro Yamashita, and Manzo Yoshida, settled in the city around 1911.[21] The Hayakawa family settled in Montreal in the 1920s; S.I. Hayakawa, future linguist, college president, and United States Senator, received his MA from McGill University in 1928. In 1937, S. Hayakawa, Secretary of the Canada Nippon League of Montreal, sent a letter to the *Ottawa Citizen* opposing a boycott of Japanese goods following the Japanese invasion of China.[22] Naomi Yamamoto, a young Nisei (the first generation of Japanese born in Canada), contributed chronicles from Montreal for the Los Angeles newspaper *Rafu Shimpo* in 1939-40.

The Japanese attack on Pearl Harbor in December 1941, and the outbreak of war between Canada and Japan unleashed a new wave of anti-Japanese hysteria in British Columbia against the local ethnic Japanese population. White farmers, merchants, and political leaders, seizing the opportunity to rid themselves of their long-despised ethnic Japanese competitors, accused the Japanese Canadians of being spies and saboteurs for Tokyo and called for drastic action to protect the West Coast. In response to the political pressure, on 24 February 1942, the government issued order-in-council P.C. 1486, which authorized the minister of justice to require "any or all persons regardless of their citizenship" to leave the "protected area," a 100-mile zone inland from the Pacific Coast. The next day, Prime Minister Mackenzie King announced that all people of Japanese ancestry would be excluded from the "protected area." The order led to the expulsion from their homes of 22,000 Canadian Japanese, of whom 61 percent were Nisei; 70 percent of the Canadian-born were under twenty-one years of age. Families were separated as able-bodied men were sent to work in road labour camps, while women and children were transported to what were euphemistically known as the interior housing centres, mainly in largely abandoned mining towns. To keep their families together, some Japanese Canadians accepted employment on the sugar beet farms of Alberta and Manitoba. In order to discourage them from returning to the West Coast, the government confiscated their land and possessions. In addition, a federal official, the Custodian of Enemy Alien Property, sold off their property for a fraction of its value.[23]

In 1945, a new order-in-council presented Japanese Canadians with a stark choice: agree to resettle permanently east of British Columbia, or sign up for "voluntary repatriation" to Japan. Most Japanese Canadians moved east of the Rockies, and new communities grew up in and around cities such as Toronto, Montreal, and Winnipeg. In the first years after the war, the Canadian government, hoping to appease racist public opinion in British Columbia, maintained its restrictions on Japanese Canadians, although there was clearly no longer any conceivable military danger. Under the direction of the minister of justice, Louis St. Laurent, in December 1945 the government issued an order-in-council to deport the 10,000 Japanese Canadians who had "agreed" to "voluntary" repatriation. By this time, however, the war had ended, and there was increasing criticism of the injustice of the government's actions. Progressive and religious groups joined Japanese Canadians to form the Co-operative Committee on Japanese Canadians, which organized legal challenges to the involuntary deportation of Japanese Canadians. Although the Supreme Court of Canada (and subsequently the British Privy Council) upheld the constitutionality of mass deportations in 1946, the government ultimately abandoned that policy in the face of public opposition. The nation's West Coast was finally reopened to Japanese Canadians on 1 April 1949.[24]

In the days following Pearl Harbor, the anti-Japanese hysteria on the West Coast found little echo in Quebec, where both the war and the government's conscription law remained unpopular. (Montreal's mayor Camillien Houde, imprisoned for counselling resistance to conscription, became a martyr to many French Canadians.) At first, the French-Canadian press even rang a supportive note. *La Patrie* reported that none of the seventeen people in Montreal's tiny Japanese colony, most of whom were outspokenly pro-British, had been arrested for disloyal activity.[25] One resident, H.S. Kobayashi, the article noted, was a Canadian First World War veteran.[26] Ten days later, all Canadian residents of Japanese ancestry were ordered to register with the federal government. A correspondent for *La Presse* referred to those concerned as the "Japanese whose loyalty to Canada is undoubted, except in a few isolated cases."[27] As the movement for mass expulsion of Japanese Canadians grew, the prevailing tone among Quebec newspapers remained one of indifference. Newspaper coverage of the government's policy was scanty and consisted in large part of wire service dispatches or verbatim reports of government statements. Interestingly, French-Canadian newspapers devoted much greater attention to the contemporaneous anti-Japanese movement in California and to the removal of Japanese Americans than to events in British Columbia.

This said, those French-language press reports that did appear revealed strong anti-Japanese hostility and editorial support for official policy, and editors showed few signs of sympathy for Japanese Canadians. On 25 February, even before the government announced its policy of evacuation of all ethnic Japanese from the West Coast, *La Patrie* devoted prominent space to a speech by Ian Mackenzie, a Liberal member of Parliament from British Columbia and the chief instigator of evacuation within the cabinet. Mackenzie bluntly declared that Japanese Canadians would be entirely removed from the West Coast. "First we will remove the men. Later we will take care of their families."[28] Shortly afterwards, *La Patrie* ran a headline referring to the Japanese Canadians in British Columbia as "the Yellow Peril."[29] The monthly nationalist magazine *L'Action Nationale* deplored what it referred to as a government plan to send more soldiers overseas and to relieve the consequent farm labour shortage by bringing over Japanese Canadians, whom the magazine referred to as "a swarm of spies, or, in any case, unassimilable people who have up until now been the despair of our compatriots in British Columbia."[30] Similarly, in March 1942, *Montréal-Matin* printed on its editorial page an article by H.H. Stevens, a former minister of trade and commerce in R.B. Bennett's Conservative government. As a member of Parliament from British Columbia from 1911 to 1940, Stevens had often campaigned against Asian immigration and was the author of a notorious anti-Asian pamphlet, "The Oriental Problem." Stevens repeated all the familiar canards about Japanese spies and saboteurs and insisted that Japanese Canadians had already formed military units for mobilization in support of a potential Japanese invasion.[31] The newspaper's editors agreed with Stevens on the necessity of removing all Japanese Canadians to the interior, where they could be "under control and observation." The editorial stated that "the Question of military defence must be discussed by experts but that of the presence of Japanese in strategic areas does not require any military knowledge."[32]

The dispersion of Japanese Canadians from the Canadian Pacific Coast marked a turning point in the encounter between Japanese Canadians and French Canadians. Beginning in 1942, Japanese Canadians, predominantly Nisei, began to leave the West Coast or the camps and move East.[33] The *New Canadian*, the organ of the Japanese Canadian Citizens League, published repeated accounts by its editor, Tom Shoyama, extolling Montreal as an ethnically diverse city free of discrimination, where Japanese Canadians could easily find jobs. As a result, Montreal's Japanese population jumped from 25 in January 1942 to 334 by the end of 1943.[34] The trickle became a torrent following the government's 1945 order requiring ethnic Japanese in Canada to "repatriate" to Japan or relocate outside British Columbia, as the majority accepted resettlement in the East. The largest fraction of migrants, most of whom were young, unmarried Nisei, settled in agricultural southern Ontario or near Toronto (whose Board of Control refused to allow Japanese Canadians to reside within city limits until 1946). However, approximately one-tenth of the migrants resettled in Montreal, despite the vocal opposition of Premier Maurice Duplessis, the right-wing French-Canadian nationalist who had returned to power shortly before. In the end, the newcomers to Quebec settled almost exclusively in the Montreal area,[35] whose Japanese population reached 1,247 by the end of 1946 and over 1,300 in 1949, making it the largest Japanese community in the francophone world.[36]

The full story of Japanese-Canadian settlement and adaptation in Montreal is beyond the scope of this chapter, but a few general statements can be made. Many of the newcomers discovered that public opinion was less negative against them than in British Columbia, and some were able to find professional work in areas such as nursing, teaching in the public schools, and accounting. Koryo Shimotakahara even set up a popular ladies' fashion store on rue St. Catherine.[37] Nevertheless, Japanese Canadians in Montreal encountered significant racial prejudice, especially in housing and employment. Many Nisei, irrespective of their qualifications, were forced to take menial labour jobs, particularly in domestic service, where 74 out of a total of 240 employed Nisei were working at the end of 1943.[38] Another significant fraction of Nisei found work in the garment factories of Montreal's Jewish community.[39]

The Nisei formed a number of community institutions for mutual support and sociability. In 1944, a group of Nisei Christians led by Taira Yasunaka formed a Friendship Club, and a group of young workers and university students formed a Nisei Fellowship Club in 1946. With the aid of a United Church minister, the Rev. Kosaburo Shimizu, the two clubs united to create the Montreal Japanese United Church in 1946-47.[40] Shortly afterward, the Montreal Buddhist Church was founded, although Duplessis refused to grant it official recognition as a religious institution.[41] In May 1946, Japanese Canadians in Montreal launched a monthly community newsletter, *The Montreal Bulletin*.[42]

The migration to Quebec brought French Canadians and Japanese Canadians into large-scale association for the first time. Many of the migrants settled in the historically French neighbourhoods of Villeray and St. Michel, and the Nisei interacted daily with French Canadians on the streets, in school, and in the workplace. Perhaps not surprisingly, there was a measure of confusion and wariness among the locals at their first contact with the newcomers. As one Nisei later described, he was a figure of curiosity at his new job: "The French Canadians with whom I worked asked me if I was Chinese; I told them no. Then they asked where I came from; I told them British Columbia ... Then I told them what had happened during the war. They could not believe it. They simply could not understand it."[43] Still, many Nisei made friends with their French neighbours and co-workers, and there were a number of marriages between members of the two groups during the postwar years. One Nisei later explained that he felt a warmer welcome from the French group. "I was impressed by the French Canadians. They are interested to know you; they are simple, ordinary people ... with a rather friendly curiosity ... The English ... not every one of them is bad. But as a group ... you have to be on your guard."[44]

One striking contemporary description of the relations between Japanese Canadians and French Canadians in Montreal comes from the memoir of an unnamed Nisei who relocated to Montreal in October 1942.[45] Unable to find a job due to employment discrimination, the narrator was befriended by a French-Canadian restaurant manager, who hired him as a dishwasher. Soon after, a Nisei friend explained that, even if French Canadians speak English, Japanese Canadians' assimilation and job prospects would be eased if they learned French:

> The French, whether they are of the higher or lower station in society, are a proud people. Just as you or I appreciate anyone knowing something of the culture and language of Nippon, the French learn to appreciate those who take an interest in their heritage. If one knows their language, they feel some vague sense of security that their heritage is held in respect. In turn, they feel that you respect them as individuals and as a people.
>
> Quebec, they consider as their own, which is, I think, a true way of looking at it; a country within a country. You do not try to ignore this fact by not attempting to learn the new language.
>
> Sure, it's hard and perhaps a little discouraging at first, but once you're determined, you'll find that it's a beautiful language which you'll ... want to show off.[46]

The narrator duly proceeded to study French, and in the process gained many French-Canadian friends.[47]

Meanwhile, leaders within both the city's English and French communities were divided over the issue of how to deal with the Japanese-Canadian "problem." The city's politically dominant English community initially reacted to the newcomers with some hostility. In October 1944, McGill College, which was notorious for its longstanding discriminatory policies against Jews and other ethnic minorities, became the first Canadian university officially to close its doors to Japanese-Canadian students.[48] The English-language newspaper, the *Montreal Star,* editorialized in May 1944 about the need to "clear out lock stock and barrel" and deport the entire Japanese-Canadian population.[49] However, liberals and religious groups supported the rights of Canadian citizens. Canon P.S.C. Powles, a former missionary in Japan, organized the Montreal Committee on Japanese Canadians to help the newcomers resettle and find jobs and housing. McGill sociology professor Forrest La Violette (an American of French-Canadian ancestry) denounced anti-Nisei racism and warned that discrimination at home would hinder Canada's postwar international role.[50] McGill's Students Society sponsored a mass meeting protesting the university's exclusion policy, and the university Senate voted to lift the exclusion in the autumn of 1945.[51] The United Church organized aid to the migrants, and Sir George Williams University accepted a number of Nisei students.

The French community reaction was rather different. From the beginning, a number of French-Canadian organizations, especially Catholic groups, organized to support the Japanese Canadians. In 1945, Mother Saint-Pierre and the Soeurs du Christ-Roi, who had served as missionaries in Japan, opened a hostel for young Nisei women. In 1944, Archbishop Joseph Charbonneau of Montreal formally approved a plan to aid Japanese Canadians in Montreal.[52] Later, when Father Jean-Claude Labreque returned to Montreal from a mission to Japan in 1950, he devoted himself primarily to assisting Japanese Canadians. The Université de Montreal accepted Nisei students.[53] However, the institutional response of French Canadians was overwhelmingly one of indifference, and even Duplessis's hostility did not translate into restrictive legislation.

The issue of deportation, however, gained widespread attention within the French community, dividing it sharply. As in the era of Wilfrid Laurier, French-Canadian officials led anti-Japanese forces within the federal government. In Mackenzie King's cabinet, St. Laurent, dubbed "the King of Quebec," campaigned hard for the deportation of as many Japanese Canadians as possible following the war. When liberal groups challenged St. Laurent's orders-in-council, Maitre Aimé Geoffrion was assigned to defend the government's position on mass deportation before the Supreme Court. The court ruled in the government's favour in February 1946, but split over the issue of whether women and children could be involuntarily deported. Among the minority who supported the extreme position were the court's two French-Canadian judges, Chief Justice Thibaudeau Rinfret and Associate (later chief) Justice Robert Taschereau, who ruled that the orders-in-council gave the government authority to strip any Canadian citizens of Japanese ancestry of their citizenship and to deport whom it chose. During the months that followed, as public opinion turned against discrimination, and the government hesitated to enforce its orders, St. Laurent continued to push for mass deportation. At a cabinet meeting on 22 January 1947, he called for the renewal of orders-in-council restricting people of Japanese ancestry, insisting that they would be "troublesome" if they were not deported, and warning that their continued presence would lead to pressure "to have the Japanese in Canada given the same rights as the white population."[54]

In contrast, French Canadians outside government circles lined up to support the citizenship rights of the Nisei. The French section of the Canadian Welfare Council unanimously adopted a resolution asking the prime minister to grant full rights to Canadian citizens.[55] In 1947, Benoît Michaud, a French-Canadian Liberal member of Parliament from Restigouche-Madawaska, New Brunswick, spoke out in the House of Commons against the extension of the War Measures Act, stating that as "a member of a minority race in Canada, I must oppose such legislation."[56] The nationalist Saint Jean-Baptiste society joined the YMCA and the Canadian Jewish Congress in sponsoring the Montreal Committee on Canadian Citizenship/Le Comité pour la défense de la citoyenneté canadienne to support the rights of Japanese Canadians. A group of progressive French-Canadian civil libertarians and political activists connected with the Co-operative Commonwealth Federation, including Thérèse Casgrain, Jacques Perrault, and Roger Ouimet, joined its executive committee.[57] The committee, which denounced the deportation policy as "dangerous and attacking the fundamental rights of minorities," mobilized to awaken public opinion and to raise funds in order to appeal the Supreme Court ruling to the Privy Council.[58] As Casgrain explained in her memoirs:

> An event that profoundly moved me during this period was the treatment, ignoble and unjust in my opinion, of a group of our citizens ... Seeing the difficulties in which these unhappy people [Japanese Canadians] were caught, in 1943 a group of Canadians, of whom most were from the CCF, decided to come to their assistance. In several Canadian cities, such as Toronto, Montreal, Vancouver and Ottawa, groups formed for this purpose. Thus I had the chance to work with Frank Scott, Paul Baby, Roger Ouimet and professor Forrest La Violette in a group formed in Montreal. In 1945, at the war's end, the Canadian government hoped to send the citizens born in Japan back to their native country. A long legal battle ensued and our committees across the nation fought against this deportation, which would be even more tragic as it would separate families.[59]

Quebec newspapers also expressed support, albeit indirectly, for Japanese Canadians. *La Patrie* ran a photo of a Japanese Canadian reading a book on citizenship and explained that any "deportation" of such people would be expulsion, as they were born in Canada and would be strangers in Japan.[60] *Montréal-Matin* ran a story on a Japanese Canadian serving with Allied intelligence in Asia, G. Suzuki, which featured the headline "Long Live Democracy."[61]

In the end, the federal government, despite its victory in the courts, was forced to abandon its plan for mass "repatriation" of Japanese Canadians. The publicity efforts of the Co-operative Committee on Japanese Canadians aroused sufficient opposition to the plan among voters and newspaper editors that King was unwilling to risk political capital to put it into effect. The level of anti-Japanese sentiment in British Columbia soon eased, thereby removing the primary prop for the expulsion policy. Also, as Patricia Roy notes elsewhere in this volume, Canada's leaders feared that permanent exclusion of Japanese Canadians would harm Canada's international image and help turn Japan towards Moscow. Ultimately, the government announced on 24 January 1947 that mass deportation was "no longer necessary" and that only those who expressed a desire to return to Japan would be sent away from Canada. Although the government continued its exclusion policy and travel restrictions, the West Coast was finally reopened to Japanese on 1 April 1949.

As first Toronto, and later the Pacific coast, were reopened to Japanese Canadians, over one-third of those who had initially resettled in Montreal left the city in what they called the "second evacuation." Quebec's society remained unfamiliar to them, and their lack of French fluency limited their employment and business prospects.[62] Nevertheless, the majority preferred to stay in their adopted city, where they had put down roots and started families and careers. Many Nisei considered Montreal a far less hostile environment than their previous homes, and they were able to become absorbed into the wider society.[63] In the following decades, the Montreal community was reinforced by new arrivals, and by 1971 it numbered 1,670 people.[64] The community boasted a few well-known figures during these years, including anthropologist Toshio Yatsushiro, actor Robert Ito, jazz trombonist Jiro "Butch" Watanabe, and Ikebana specialist Seisho Kuwabara (who was awarded the Order of Canada in 1978), as well as francophone Japanese immigrants such as novelist Aki Shimazaki and painter Miyuki Tanobe. Much later, in 2004, Kent Nagano, an American of Japanese ancestry, would occupy a prominent position in city life as conductor of the Orchestre Symphonique de Montréal.

In sum, French Canadians and Japanese Canadians reacted to each other in a variety of ways during the first half of the twentieth century. Both groups defined themselves primarily in relation to the dominant anglophone community, and their interactions were mediated through their respective postures towards its principal locus of power, the federal government. French Canadians who associated themselves with the federal government tended to be indifferent, or even actively hostile, to the rights of the Japanese immigrants and their descendants. This is exemplified by the case of the French-Canadian ministers and judges in Ottawa who fought for exclusion of Japanese immigrants at the turn of the century or who supported mass postwar deportation of Japanese Canadians. In taking nationwide responsibilities and working with Canadians from other provinces, they may have absorbed widespread anti-Japanese-Canadian sentiment. Or perhaps, like the French of a bygone era, who were said to be "more royalist than the King," they sought to establish themselves as "more federalist than the English," and championed racist policies in order to distance themselves from more marginal minorities. Yet, French Canadians outside official circles, such as Thérèse Casgrain, offered Japanese Canadians their sympathy and support.

Throughout these decades, the average French Canadian in Quebec remained neither friendly nor malevolent in his attitude towards Japan. That neutrality extended as well to Japanese Canadians. Knowing little of the "Japanese question" in British Columbia or of their wartime confinement, the Québécois were at first bewildered by the new Japanese migrants – sometimes wary, sometimes curious, often indifferent – but almost never hostile. Their tolerant attitude was not necessarily the result of a cosmopolitan outlook – they simply had more important things to worry about. Perhaps their very indifference represents an example of what American political scientists and statesman Daniel Patrick Moynihan, in another context, later called "benign neglect." In the first postwar years, Japanese Canadians were generally happy to be thus left alone, and many of them showed their gratitude by remaining in Montreal and building their lives there, long after the Canadian Pacific Coast reopened to them.

Notes

1 Ken Adachi, *The Enemy That Never Was: A History of the Japanese Canadians* (Toronto: McLelland and Stewart, 1976), 41-46; W. Peter Ward, *White Canada Forever: Popular Attitudes and Public Policy toward Orientals in British Columbia* (Montreal and Kingston: McGill-Queen's University Press, 1978). See also Chapters 3 and 4 in this book.

2 Norman McDonald, *Canada, Immigration and Colonization, 1841-1903* (Aberdeen: Aberdeen University Press, 1966), 187; Paul-André Linteau, René Durocher, and Jean-Claude Robert, *Histoire du Québec Contemporain*, vol. 1: *De la Conféderation à la crise 1867-1929* (Montreal: Boréal Express, 1979), 46, 176.

3 Denise Helly, *Les Chinois à Montréal, 1877-1951* (Montreal: éditions de l'IQRC, 1979), 179.

4 Fernande Roy, *Progrès, harmonie, liberté: Le liberalisme des milieux d'affaires francophones à Montréal au tournant du siècle* (Montreal: Boréal, 1988), 238 *passim*.

5 I do not focus in this chapter on the French-language press in Manitoba; however, it seems also to have been virtually silent on the question of Japanese immigration before 1907 and generally hostile to the Japanese presence thereafter.

6 "Un véritable péril national," *La Presse* (Montreal), 16 January 1907, 16, "que la législation provinciale de la Colombie Britannique contre les japonais reste en force, soit ... Notre pays, étant jeune, doit suivre l'exemple des États-Unis, et en autant que le développement de nos voies ferrées est concerné, la politique du peuple canadien doit être: que vous soyez noirs, jaunes, rouges ou blancs, venez travailler!"

7 Ward, *White Canada Forever*; Laurier quoted in Patricia E. Roy, *A White Man's Province: British Columbia Politicians and Chinese and Japanese Immigrants, 1858-1914* (Vancouver: UBC Press, 1989), 189.

8 Roy, *A White Man's Province*, 197.

9 *La Presse* (Montreal), 29 January 1908, 13.

10 René Castonguay, *Rodolphe Lemieux et le Parti Liberal 1866-1937: le chevalier du roi* (Sainte-Foy: Presses de l'Université Laval, 2000).

11 Adachi, *The Enemy That Never Was,* 81.

12 *La Presse,* 29 January 1908. "Dans un pays anglo-saxon comme le nôtre, où les institutions démocratiques prévalent, l'introduction en grand nombre de races étrangères, non familières avec nos principes de self-government ne pouvait être vu sans danger ... Ces orientaux appartiennent à une civilisation formée par les siècles, sur mode radicalement et totalement différent du nôtre. Il est donc établi que les Colombiens s'opposent à cette vaste colonie étrangère – exclusive, inscrutable, non-assimilable, peu exigeante, conservant intacts leurs coutumes particulières et caractéristiques ... ne pouvant ni désirant s'amalgamer."

13 Ibid. "Dans tout les pays où elles sont rencontrées, les races blanches et mongole ont fait preuve d'antagonisme ... la population de la Colombie Britannique est petite et l'on craint, cela se comprend, que si le courant d'immigration asiatique n'était pas endigué, le pouvoir passerait bientôt d'un race à l'autre."

14 *La Presse,* 12 September 1907.

15 *La Presse,* 2 January 1908.

16 Fernande Roy, *Progrès, harmonie, liberté,* 238.

17 Emile Miller, *Terre et peuples du Canada* (Montreal: Beauchemin, 1912), 142.

18 "Japonais" in Louis Marie Le Jeune, *Dictionnaire général de biographie, histoire, littérature, agriculture, commerce, industrie et des arts, science, moeurs, coutumes, institutions politiques et religieuses du Canada.* vol. 1 (Ottawa: University of Ottawa Press, 1931), 335.

19 Interestingly, the first recorded protest against nativism by a Japanese North American – K.T. Takahashi's 1897 pamphlet, "The Anti-Japanese Petition: Appeal in Protest against a Threatened Persecution" – was published in Montreal by the Montreal Gazette Press, but Takahashi appears to have been a Vancouverite.

20 "Prominent Americans Interested in Japan and Prominent Japanese in America," supplement to *Japan and America,* January 1903, 85.

21 Ibid.; Toyo Takata, *Nikkei Legacy: The Story of Japanese Canadians from Settlement to Today* (Toronto: NC Press, 1983), 108.

22 Arthur Lower, *Canada and the Far East: 1940* (Westport, CT: Greenwood Press, 1973), first published 1940 by International Secretariat, Institute of Pacific Relations, New York. While the French-language press ran a number of articles on the Sino-Japanese conflict in 1937-38 and the boycott movement, they tended to oppose the embargo on exports to Japan, and did not speak about Japanese Canadians. Ibid., 40. I am indebted to Serge Granger for calling my attention to this information.

23 See, for example, Adachi, *The Enemy That Never Was,* 199-306; Ann Gomer Sunahara, *The Politics of Racism: The Uprooting of Japanese Canadians during World War II* (Toronto: Lorimer, 1981).

24 Stephanie D. Bangarth, "Politics of Rights: Canadian and American Advocacy Groups and North America's Citizens of Japanese Ancestry, 1942-1949" (PhD diss., University of Waterloo, 2003) and *Voices Raised in Protest: Defending North American Citizens of Japanese Ancestry, 1942-49* (Vancouver: UBC Press, 2007). See also Patricia E. Roy, "Lessons in Citizenship, 1945-1949: The Delayed Return of the Japanese to Canada's Pacific Coast," *Pacific Northwest Historical Quarterly* 93 (Spring 2002): 69-80, and *The Triumph of Citizenship: The Japanese and Chinese in Canada, 1941-1967* (Vancouver: UBC Press, 2007).

25 *La Patrie,* 10 December 1941, 6.

26 A Montreal Nisei, Private David Tsubota, son of James Jitsuei Tsubota, another Canadian World War One veteran, joined the Black Watch of Canada before the start of the war. Tsubota took part in the disastrous raid on Dieppe, where he was taken prisoner, and he remained in a German prisoner of war camp until his liberation by the allies in 1945. See Roy Ito, *We Went to War: The Story of Japanese Canadians Who Served during the First and Second World Wars* (Stittsville, ON: Canada's Wings, 1984).

27 "Les Japonais, dont la loyauté au Canada n'est pas mise en doute, sauf dans les cas isolés ..." *La Presse,* 16 December 1941.

28 "Nous déplaçons les homes les premiers. Plus tard, nous nous occuperons des familles." "L'Évacuation des Japonais," *La Patrie,* 25 February 1942, 20.

29 "Le Péril jaune," *La Patrie,* 16 March 1942, 21.

30 "Une idée saugrenue," *L'Action Nationale,* February-March 1942, 105: "une nuée d'espions ou, en tout cas, des gens inassimilables et qui ont fait jusque içi le désespoir de nos compatriotes en Colombie."
31 H.H. Stevens, "Le problème japonais en Colombie-Britannique," *Montréal-Matin,* 3 March 1944.
32 "L'article de M. Stevens," *Montréal-Matin,* 3 March 1942, 4: 1-2. "La question de la défense militaire doit être discutée par des experts mais celle de la présence des japonais a des endroits stratégiques ne nécessite aucune connaissance militaire."
33 As with newspapers, I have not considered the interactions between Japanese Canadian migrants and French Canadians in Western Canada (such as the experience of Roy and Arthur Miki in the francophone community of Saint-Agathe in Manitoba), because there were few such interactions and there is little documentation of them.
34 Canada, Department of Labour, *The Re-establishment of Japanese in Canada 1944-1946* (Ottawa: King's Printer, 1947).
35 Late in 1946, an additional three hundred Japanese Canadians were briefly resettled in a hostel in Farnham, Quebec, after which they passed though Montreal.
36 *Vancouver Sun,* 17 March 1945, cited in Forrest La Violette, *The Canadian Japanese and World War II* (Toronto: University of Toronto Press, 1948), 239; Montreal Japanese Canadian survey, 1953, cited in Keiko Minai, "The Japanese in Montreal: Socio-economic Integration and Ethnic Identification of an Immigrant Group" (MA thesis, McGill University, 1977), 9.
37 Toyo Takata, *Nikkei Legacy,* 56. For the story of the Issei physician Kozo Shimotakahara's studies in Montreal, see also Gordon G. Nakayama, *Issei: Stories of Japanese Canadian Pioneers* (Toronto: Gordon Nakayama, 1983), 55-69.
38 See Masako Iino, "From B.C. to Montreal – the Resettlement of Japanese Canadians in the East," *Journal of American and Canadian Studies* 8 (Autumn 1991): 60-61.
39 Japanese Canadian History and Archives Committee, Ganbari: *Reclaiming Our Home/Ganbari: Un chez-soi retrouvé* (Montreal: Montreal Japanese Canadian History Committee, 1998), 9.
40 Roland M. Kawano, ed., *A History of the Japanese Congregations in the United Church of Canada* (Scarborough, ON: The Japanese Canadian Christian Churches Historical Project, 1998) 98-102; Isobel McFadden, *Kosaburo Shimizu: The Man Who Knew the Difference* (Toronto: United Church of Canada Board of Information, 1965).
41 Terry Watada, *Bukkyo Tozen: A History of Jodo Shinshu Buddhism in Canada, 1905-1995* (Toronto: Toronto Buddhist Church, 1995), 245-54. Buddhism remained unrecognized as an official religion in Quebec into the mid-1990s, with the result, among other things, that Buddhist clergy could not perform marriages.
42 For the Montreal Bulletin and its community influence, see Kuniko Kondo, "Les Canadiens d'origine japonaise à Montréal: Leur processus d'intégration dans la vie canadienne" (MA thesis, Université de Montréal, 2000), 121-26 *passim.*
43 "Repartir à zero: L'expérience des Canadiens d'origine japonaise à Montréal, 1942-1952," *Tribune Juive* 5, 1 (1987): 15-16.
44 Ibid., 16.
45 "From B.C. to Quebec – One of the First Nisei to Settle in French Canada, as told to Howard Ikebuchi," contest entry, National JCCA's Japanese Canadian History Contest, 1958, Memoirs and History Contest, Japanese Canadian Citizens Association Papers, Library and Archives Canada (hereafter LAC).
46 Ibid., 11
47 Ibid., 12
48 La Violette, *The Canadian Japanese and World War II,* 183.
49 Ibid., 307.
50 "Canada's Jap Problem Cited," *Montreal Star,* 13 February 1945; "Jap Problem Here Outlined at Club," *Montreal Gazette,* 13 February 1945. Three years later, La Violette published *The Canadian Japanese and World War II,* the first book to examine the wartime experience of the Nisei.
51 "Stand on Japs 'Neutral'," *Montreal Gazette,* 16 November 1944; "Senate Will Study Japanese Problem," *Montreal Star,* 6 November 1944.

52 Translation, Letter, Joseph Charbonneau to Louis St. Laurent, 27 May 1944, Ministry of Labour, RG 27, vol. 169, LAC. The plan was evidently submitted by one Rev. Father Gagnon.
53 Japanese Canadian History and Archives Committee, *Ganbari: Reclaiming Our Home/Ganbari: Un chez-soi retrouvé,* 10, 12.
54 Cited in W.L. Mackenzie King Diary, 22 January 1947, 3, King Diary, King Papers, LAC.
55 *La Patrie,* 10 December 1945, 10.
56 "Order in Council to Continue," *Nisei Affairs,* April 1947, 5.
57 Patricia Roy, J.L. Granatstein, Masako Iino, and Hiroko Takamura, *Mutual Hostages: Canadians and Japanese during the Second World War* (Toronto: University of Toronto Press, 1990), 178; Ross Lambertson, *Repression and Resistance: Canadian Human Rights Activists, 1930-1960* (Toronto: University of Toronto Press, 2005), 133.
58 *Montreal Gazette,* 28 February 1946.
59 Thérèse F. Casgrain, *Une femme chez les hommes* (Montreal: Éditions du Jour, 1971), 154-56.
60 "Que veut dire déportation?" *La Patrie,* 22 January 1946, 25.
61 "Vive la démocratie!" *Montréal-Matin,* 16 February 1946, 9:1. In a somewhat more neutral vein, *La Patrie* responded by publishing in its 26 March 1946 issue a photo of George Tamaki, a Japanese Canadian appointed as a legal counsel in Saskatchewan by the Co-operative Commonwealth Federation, a social democratic party.
62 Takata, *Nisei Legacy,* 168.
63 Iino, "From B.C. to Montreal," 53 *passim.*
64 Census of Canada, cited in Adachi, *The Enemy That Never Was,* 413. The total ethnic Japanese population of the province of Quebec was 1,745.

9
Reopening the Door: Japanese Remigration and Immigration, 1945-68

Patricia E. Roy

> The rusty hinges of Canada's immigration door for Japanese is once again slowly opening, however limited. This, however, is not reason to get carried away with joy, as one need only look back at the historical pattern of Canada's immigration – the opening and slamming shut of its doors have been the cause of untold grief to countless Japanese Canadians for half a century.
>
> Takaichi Umeziki, *The New Canadian,* 3 March 1965

Takaichi Umeziki, the editor of *The New Canadian,* the Japanese-Canadian newspaper, was justifiably less than enthusiastic about the 1965 white paper on immigration that promised to remove racial considerations from Canada's immigration policy. Through the Gentlemen's Agreement of 1907 and its revisions, Canada had reduced Japanese immigration to a trickle for most of the twentieth century.[1] Despite a postwar policy of encouraging as many immigrants as could "advantageously be absorbed in our national economy," Prime Minister William Lyon Mackenzie King in 1947 had warned that "large-scale immigration from the Orient would change the fundamental composition of the Canadian population" and might cause social and economic problems and "serious difficulties" in international relations.[2] Thus, Canada extended its wartime ban on immigration from Japan into the postwar era.[3] Ottawa also made it extremely difficult for Japanese strandees (individuals born or resident in Canada who were caught by the war in Japan) and repatriates (individuals who returned to Japan during or after the war) to return home to Canada. This was true even of those Japanese with an irrefutable claim to Canadian residency or citizenship. For over two decades, the Japanese Canadian Citizens Association (JCCA) lobbied for the relaxation and elimination of the discriminatory treatment that effectively made them "second class citizens." While the JCCA played a major role in reuniting strandees and repatriates with their families, Japan's re-emergence as a major economic and political power, and changed attitudes to race relations in Canada largely explain the end of racial restrictions as they applied to the Japanese.

In the spring of 1945, the King government had tried to resolve the "Japanese problem" in British Columbia by requiring all Japanese in Canada to move east of the Rockies or agree to "voluntary repatriation" to Japan after the war.[4] With the peace, King softened his policy ever so slightly.[5] In introducing measures to exclude postwar immigration from Japan, he suggested that a future Parliament could reopen the door. The prime minister feared that permanent exclusion might embarrass Canada at the new United Nations (UN) and encourage Japan to support the Soviet Union and its communist allies in the cold war confrontation with Canada and the Western democracies. For the time being, however, he was far more concerned with popular sentiment in British Columbia.[6] Though fading, hostility towards Japanese immigration was still evident there. Even as late as 1949, for instance, a report that 3,200 strandees and repatriates wanted to return led the Vancouver *Sun* to assert that Canada need not admit these "most loyal Japanese in the world."[7] The report prompted the Departments of Immigration and External Affairs to reassure Howard Green, the Progressive Conservative member of Parliament for Vancouver South and a strident opponent of Asian immigration, that only "certain former residents" were re-admissible and that their number was "very small."[8]

Indeed, some officials and cabinet ministers would have been happier to halt Japanese immigration altogether. In particular, as Chapter 8 on French Canada also notes, Justice Minister Louis St. Laurent favoured deporting all Japanese who had agreed to repatriation, lest a demand for equal civil rights by an increased Japanese-Canadian population cause problems at the UN.[9] But this would not be easy to do. Under the Canadian Citizenship Act of 1947, repatriates born in Canada and naturalized Canadians who had not acquired another nationality or lost their Canadian residency had a right to return to Canada. And denying that right would require legislation "of a rather unsavoury type."[10] Nevertheless, the Department of External Affairs effectively excluded them from Canada by refusing assistance with travel funds or exit documents. On instructions from cabinet, the Foreign Ministry directed Canadian representatives in Tokyo to issue passports only to those repatriates with an exit permit and passage.[11] Raising passage money was difficult.[12] As late as 1956, Harold Hirose, president of the Manitoba JCCA, reminded National JCCA members that there were "still Canadian Japanese – born and brought up in Canada – who are stranded in Japan and cannot return."[13]

The lot of Japanese Canadians in postwar Japan was not a happy one. Not only did they suffer general privations, but many Nisei (first-generation Canadian-born Japanese) repatriates had limited Japanese language skills.

Wartime repatriates faced special hardships. One complained that "the Occupation Forces regard us as Japanese while the Japanese themselves, because we were born abroad, regard us as being non-Japanese, and then are unable to see why we can not give them soap, cigarettes, and clothing." Not surprisingly, there was some resentment directed towards the repatriates, who were sometimes seen as fair-weather friends. A Canadian journalist reported in 1950, for example, that Japanese nationals sometimes argued that Nisei who came to Japan in "palmy" pre-war days should stay to help rebuild "a better Japan."[14]

The JCCA shared the suspicion that some of those Japanese Canadians who had spent years in Japan might be "uncomfortable in Canada" and then, feeling "frustrated and left out," long for a "Japan where they might have suffered privation but not from lack of companionship."[15] The JCCA, however, set aside these doubts, and exploiting the provisions of the new Citizenship Act, began to press the government in 1947 to admit the 1,692 strandees who wished to rejoin their families.[16] The first strandee, Tsuru Fujiwara, a Japanese national who had obtained Canadian residency before a pre-war visit to Japan, returned to Canada in April 1948. Muriel Kitagawa, the real-life daughter of the absent mother in Joy Kogawa's novel, *Obasan*, spent two years wrestling with red tape to get her mother home, writing almost weekly letters to Ottawa, the American proconsul in Japan, General Douglas MacArthur, and the Canadian mission in Tokyo.[17] Such efforts, however, were often futile, and the strandees trickled home very slowly. By October 1949, fewer than 150 had returned to Canada.[18]

The exact number of strandees was unclear, reinforcing the government's reluctance to act too quickly. In 1947, Herbert Norman, Canada's representative in Tokyo, estimated that 5,000 to 6,000 Canadian-born Japanese resided in Japan, of whom 2,606 were postwar repatriates.[19] In 1952, the JCCA estimated a maximum of about 1,500 relatives and close friends;[20] the Department of External Affairs believed that fewer than 3,000 could return and that they would scatter across the country to settle near relatives. The Department of Immigration, however, calculated that 10,000 to 12,000 were admissible as Canadian-born or near relatives of Canadians, and that those without kin would congregate in British Columbia.[21]

The Japanese immigration problem was made worse by the narrow criteria set out in the 1930 order-in-council 2115 that governed Asian immigration. These regulations prohibited the immigration of persons of the "Asiatic race" apart from the spouse and unmarried children under the age of eighteen of a Canadian citizen legally resident in Canada and capable of caring for them.[22] The JCCA, however, had files on many other relatives of strandees and repatriates with valid claims to Canadian citizenship. They included children born to Japanese Canadians during visits to Japan before the war, adopted children, and the spouses of Canadian citizens. There were also cases of elderly parents (including a veteran of the Canadian Expeditionary Force from the First World War), who had lost Canadian residency but whose children resided in Canada, and Canadian women, who lost their citizenship by marrying Japanese nationals. One woman, a 1946 "repatriate," was born in Japan and married a Nisei in Canada, with whom she had three Canadian-born children. Canada would readmit her husband and children but decreed that as a naturalized Canadian she had lost her citizenship with "repatriation."[23] At the end of 1948, the JCCA had over sixty cases of individuals with some claim to Canadian status. It secured admission for seven, including a Nisei who was briefly forced to serve in the Japanese armed forces, two Nisei who were repatriated with their parents during the war, and four Issei, who were postwar repatriates.[24]

As long as Asians could not sponsor the entry of close relatives other than spouses and children, *The New Canadian* declared in January 1951, they did not have "the full status of citizenship equal in respects to other Canadians." It argued that immigration laws that caused "undue hardship" were "contrary" to the UN Declaration of Human Rights, which described the family as "the natural and fundamental group unit of society ... entitled to protection by society and the State." Invoking the deepening cold war, *The New Canadian* warned that such discrimination played "directly into the hands of those who are attempting to wean Asia from the side of the free world."[25] In a public brief for the immigration minister, Walter Harris, the JCCA cited cases of individuals who could not be reunited with their families and asked for equal treatment for Japanese Canadians in respect to the immigration of relatives.[26] The plea received some sympathy. The Toronto *Globe and Mail,* for instance, noting that such discrimination contradicted the spirit of the pending peace treaty with Japan, argued, "we cannot offer freedom to a Japanese in his own country without recognizing his freedom in ours."[27]

Ratification of the Japanese peace treaty in April 1952 did not change the situation, though it meant that the Japanese were no longer regarded as enemy aliens. Old Japanophobes expressed themselves forcefully during the Parliamentary debate on the treaty. Liberal Senator Tom Reid from New Westminster averred that it could mean the return of three thousand Japanese, all of whom would settle in British Columbia.[28] In the House of Commons, Green revived pre-war panic as he gloomily argued that with ratification, the JCCA would seek "to bring about substantial immigration of Japanese." Strandees and repatriates, he claimed, would want their families too, "and the first thing we know there may be several thousand." Secretary of State for External Affairs Lester B. Pearson quickly reassured him that the government had no desire "to make it any easier in the future for them [Japanese] to get here than it has been in the past – and it has not been very easy in the past."[29]

The New Canadian complained that the peace treaty offered "relative freedom" to the people of Japan but did "not recognize this freedom to live in Canada."[30] Columnist Toyo Takata described the continued inability of Japanese Canadians to bring family members to Canada as "the final obstacle to our full and unqualified recognition as bona fide Canadian citizens."[31] As a result, the JCCA expended much of its efforts in the early 1950s on family reunification. On behalf of individual families "living in forced separation," it lobbied ministers of immigration, presented briefs to parliamentary committees, and secured the support of CCF Members of Parliament such as M.J. Coldwell and Angus MacInnis.[32] It advised members to get letters of sympathy and support from Canadian friends or employers if they wanted to bring relatives into the country.[33] A file of supportive letters did not guarantee admission, but it sometimes helped. After submitting a petition from the local Liberal Association, for instance, Teiji Kobayashi of Kamloops was able to bring his Japan-born daughter to Canada in 1956.[34] By using such tactics, the JCCA gradually secured an increase in the number of Japanese immigrants to Canada; in 1954 there were ninety-one.[35]

Limited success with individual cases did not remove the discriminatory ban on Asian and Japanese immigration. Though Harris, the immigration minister, promised the JCCA a new immigration policy following ratification of the peace treaty, nothing was immediately forthcoming.[36] The wait was long because the government simply could not devise a policy that would eliminate "the appearance of discrimination against all Asians while at the same time maintaining the exclusion of Asians, or providing for only a very small inflow of Asian immigrants."[37] With the resumption of normal diplomatic and trade relations after 1952, however, the government came under increasing pressure to relax its policy. Of immediate concern was the expectation that in discussing a treaty of trade and commerce, Japan might suggest reviving the Gentlemen's Agreement.[38] The Immigration Department thought a new agreement would show that Canada was not discriminating against Japan and would regulate the immigration flow but noted it would give preference to a former enemy over other Asians who remained subject to P.C. 2115.[39] The prime minister's office took a hard line and recommended keeping Japan under the general Asiatic ban as long as possible because of "very strong objection to any Japanese immigrant whatever for some time."[40]

Canadian officials knew that Japan regarded Canada's discriminatory regulations as "an important prestige problem." Ottawa's first postwar ambassador in Tokyo, Robert Mayhew, who had been chosen for the post partly for his knowledge of British Columbia, reported being frequently asked: "What is Canada's immigration policy?" It was a good question, but Ottawa had only evasive answers. The Department of External Affairs, for instance, advised Mayhew to keep the flow and volume of admissible immigrants at a reasonable level and to avoid "any sudden large movement which might be opposed in certain parts of Canada."[41] When Prime Minister Louis St. Laurent visited Japan shortly after, he evaded a journalist's question about Canada's restrictive immigration policies by referring to Canada's housing shortage![42] Similarly, when C.D. Howe, the powerful minister of trade and commerce, visited Japan in 1956, Canadian diplomats reminded him not "to give any encouragement to the press in Japan to foresee increased immigration to Canada from Japan."[43]

The JCCA was quick to exploit the added leverage that Japan enjoyed after the ratification of the peace treaty. Despite regarding itself as an organization of Canadian citizens, "mainly concerned with those problems which affect Japanese Canadian families,"[44] its astute executive contacted the Japanese ambassador in Ottawa for help.[45] And indeed, Japanese diplomats informally inquired about immigration policy, specifically asking about the apparent special treatment for Chinese fiancées and the discrepancy between the annual admission of two to three thousand Chinese and only twenty to thirty Japanese. Worried lest the Japanese embassy become the champion of Japanese Canadians, Jules Léger, the under-secretary of state for External Affairs, urged the Immigration Department in March 1957 to allow Japanese Canadians to bring over their fiancées without a formal *démarche* from Japan.[46]

About the same time, the JCCA and the Toronto-based Chinese Canadian Association (CCA) tried to increase their impact on the government's attitude by making a joint presentation to J.W. Pickersgill, then minister of citizenship and immigration. They had reason to believe he might be sympathetic. In his 1954 Christmas message in *The New Canadian,* Pickersgill had asserted that "Canadians of Japanese origin belong to our wider Canadian family."[47] Moreover, he had persuaded a reluctant cabinet to open the door to some elderly parents of Canadian Japanese who had lost their Canadian status by accepting repatriation.[48] In their 1957 brief, the CCA and JCCA told the influential minister and St. Laurent confidante that so few Asians could enter that the policy was eliminating "Canadian citizens of Asian background from the population of Canada."[49] They sought the removal of race-based restrictions to put "Canadian citizens of Asian ancestry on an 'equal plane'" with other Canadians in sponsoring various categories of relatives as immigrants.[50] In its own brief, the JCCA expressed satisfaction with two hundred cases of reunification that gave many families "the peace of mind and happiness which are the fundamental rights of all citizens." Then, after reminding Pickersgill that Japan was now a UN member, the JCCA asked that "the stigma of the war ... be cast off" and that Asian Canadians be put on the same basis as other Canadians in respect to sponsoring relatives as immigrants. It had applications for eighty prospective immigrants including nephews, nieces, mothers, brothers, sons, daughters, and fathers. The sons were all over twenty-one, as were the brothers and sisters.[51]

Pickersgill seemed sympathetic. He agreed to admit the fiancées of both Canadian citizens and landed immigrants of two years standing and to lower the minimum age for elderly parents. However, he promised only to consider the more far-reaching changes suggested by the JCCA.[52] As *The New Canadian* had earlier observed, Pickersgill thought that "non-English speaking Europeans can contribute more to Canadian progress than non-English speaking Japanese. It's not advantageous for politicians to admit so, but this very misconception (which we can only see as prejudice) is basic for Canada's virtual ban on Japanese immigration."[53] This was not an inaccurate characterization, and in private, Pickersgill told colleagues that he was "rather afraid of the public reaction to Japanese immigration, especially of domestics."[54] Mackenzie King's policy directive of 1947, to increase the population "without altering the fundamental character of the people as a whole," the minister wrote to one petitioner, remained valid.[55]

But Pickersgill was soon gone, swept away in the federal election of June 1957 by the Progressive Conservatives under John Diefenbaker, who had a reputation as a strong advocate of human rights. While the 1958 federal election delayed their campaign, the JCCA solicited support from Canadian religious and labour groups. Once the election confirmed the Progressive Conservatives in office, the JCCA quickly pressed the new minority government to remove "such inequalities still written into the Immigration Act ... [that were] inconsistent with the rights of Canadian citizens" and the UN Declaration of Human Rights.[56] The CCA and JCCA, in what appears to have been their last formal joint effort, sent copies of their brief to Ellen Fairclough, the new minister of citizenship and immigration, the press gallery, and members of Parliament. A sympathetic Progressive Conservative member, John Drysdale from Burnaby-Richmond, described for Parliament the problems faced by "repatriates" who wished to return to Canada,, and Japanese Canadians who wanted to have parents who were not yet senior citizens join them.[57] That a Conservative MP from coastal British Columbia would champion the Japanese was telling evidence of changed attitudes. So too was the presence of another British Columbia Conservative MP, Douglas Jung from Vancouver Centre, a Chinese Canadian, in the joint JCCA-CCA delegation that met Fairclough in June 1958. The delegates stressed that they were only "asking for equal rights and privileges as Canadians."[58] Fairclough merely said the cabinet would soon consider revising immigration policy. True to her word, that fall she told cabinet in a discussion of Chinese and Japanese immigration that it would be easier to deal with immigrants from Japan "because Japanese customs were more like those of western nations and security screening was possible in Japan." The cabinet, however, deferred its decision.[59]

Meanwhile, the JCCA concentrated on family reunification and blamed the "stigma of race and colour" for their second-class status in bringing their relatives to Canada. Reporting that only 928 Japanese had landed in Canada between 1946 and 1958 and that most were "strandees," the JCCA emphasized there would be no large-scale immigration to "change the fundamental composition of the Canadian population."[60] The widely distributed brief yielded an interview on the CBC-TV national news for Edward Ide of the JCCA, but most MPs who responded were non-committal, as was Fairclough who only repeated her willingness to consider individual cases.[61]

Japan's embassy also approached the new government to seek changes in Canadian immigration law. It explained that it was not seeking to solve a population problem but, as a matter of principle, was concerned about discrimination against its nationals. Though it denied having anything to do with the recent JCCA brief, its *aide-mémoire* specifically mentioned relatives of Japanese Canadians and long delays in granting visas to businessmen. In a subsequent discussion, a counsellor at the Japanese embassy "insisted" on comparing the numbers of Chinese and Japanese admitted to Canada and argued that the differences suggested "discrimination against the Japanese."[62] Nothing arose directly from these talks. Japan did not abandon the cause but carefully avoided becoming involved in Canadian domestic issues. This was especially evident during the visit to Ottawa of Prime Minister Nobusuke Kishi and Foreign Minister Aiichiro in 1960. *The New Canadian* urged the two Japanese politicians to discuss Canada's "restrictive immigration policy" that hindered family reunification and limited "some groups solely for reasons of race or color." The paper admitted that opening Canada's "doors completely to Japanese immigrants" might be unwise, but proposed a small annual quota.[63] Ambassador Toru Hagiwara agreed that a quota or a kind of gentlemen's agreement might be the answer, but said that Canadian citizens must press Ottawa for it.[64]

Prime Minister Kishi was more concerned about the difficulty that Japanese firms planning to expand into Canada had in securing the entry of a small number of managers and technical personnel to run their affairs.[65] The Department of Immigration was sympathetic but insisted on dealing with admissions on a case-by-case basis, admitting such personnel and their families on annual non-immigrant visas. These could be extended, but there was no guarantee of renewal.[66] For the Japanese firm that proposed to build farm pumps in Saskatchewan, such visas did not provide adequate security. Because the Department of External Affairs was anxious to develop Canada's relations with the rising Asian political and economic powerhouse, it urged its minister, Howard Green, to seek cabinet's support for liberalized measures to provide for the admission of Japanese businessmen, but the Japanophobic minister declined since "it would restrict the Government's freedom of action."[67]

The Immigration Department also continued to reject suggestions for a revived gentlemen's agreement or quota, lest Japan or other countries demand a review of immigration policy relating to their nationals.[68] Ambassador W.F. Bull, who succeeded Mayhew in 1957, and the Department of External Affairs, however, believed that admitting technicians and supervisors would "do much to assuage Japanese sensitivities" and resentment of the discriminatory policy that admitted limited numbers of other Asians but only close relatives of Japanese Canadians.[69] This made sense to Diefenbaker, and soon after the new Japanese prime minister, Hayato Ikeda, visited Ottawa in 1960, Ottawa agreed to make satisfactory arrangements.[70] Thus, when Diefenbaker visited Tokyo in October 1961, he announced that Canada would consider applications for the permanent admission of up to 150 key personnel and their dependents from Japanese businesses wishing to locate operations in Canada. The Japanese Foreign Office was pleased, and the Japanese press carried extensive reports of the announcement.[71]

In Canada, where popular opinion was beginning to outpace government policy, there was a sense that this was not sufficient. The *Toronto Star* called the new policy "grudging concessions," an "insult to Japan," and "national self-interest carried to the point of lofty arrogance," since it was made only to draw investment and to sell Canadian products.[72] Others argued that because of trade considerations, Canada should admit more Japanese. Now a member of the official opposition, Pickersgill even suggested that reviving the gentlemen's agreement to permit limited Japanese immigration might benefit trade.[73] In British Columbia, the *Grand Forks Gazette* urged the minister of citizenship and immigration to "open the door at least an inch or two further to allow for a reasonable amount of Japanese immigration."[74] British Columbia's minister of mines, Kenneth Kiernan, reported that the people he met in Japan while on a trade mission in 1961 could not "understand our no-Japanese policy." He too recommended accepting a small annual quota of immigrants to relieve discrimination and assist trade. In reporting this, J.K. Nesbitt, a Vancouver *Sun* columnist, observed that on his own visit to Japan, he "was ashamed because we close our doors, slam-bang in Japanese faces." He also advocated some kind of token immigration program.[75] Other Canadians, ranging from an officer of the Canadian Federation of Business and Professional Women to United Church congregations, endorsed increased Japanese immigration to Canada.[76]

In response to evidence of this shift in public opinion, the Immigration Department was rethinking its policies. George Davidson, the deputy minister, gave several speeches in the spring of 1961 warning Canadians that the international situation might force them "to change their own attitude towards immigrants, get rid of 'seeds of smugness,'" and admit newcomers including those from Asia, Africa, and the West Indies as "equals on social and political levels."[77] By January 1962, the government had a new policy.

Fairclough announced that "any suitably qualified person, from any part of the world, can be considered for immigration to Canada entirely on his own merit, without regard to his race, colour, national origin or the country from which he comes." Immigrants would be selected on the basis of their skills. This, she added, would particularly benefit Asians, Africans, and people from the Middle East and Central and Latin America.[78] At the last minute, however, the Immigration Department added a clause to the regulations apparently designed to prevent an influx of non-European relatives.[79] The new regulations still prevented Asians and most Africans from sponsoring other than certain very close relatives, and *The New Canadian* accurately dismissed claims that the new regulations would wipe out discrimination saying that they were "amusing" and "to be taken with not much more than a grain of salt."[80] A Toronto *Globe and Mail* correspondent reported that people in Japan greeted Canada's new policy "with something less than wild enthusiasm."[81] The JCCA offered to assist new immigrants in settlement and preparation for citizenship but insisted that the new policy, which favoured technicians, was still discriminatory.[82] Indeed, George Imai, president of the Toronto JCCA, denounced the policy as "a kind of falsified Gentlemen's Agreement to display to the rest of the world that Canada has no discriminatory laws."[83]

Lester B. Pearson's Liberal government, which was elected in April 1963, further eased immigration restrictions by admitting personnel of Japanese-owned enterprises as immigrants without numerical restrictions and shortening the waiting period for repatriates who had lost Canadian citizenship.[84] René Tremblay, the minister responsible, did not expect large-scale immigration but told Japan's foreign minister that Canada hoped for "a growing movement" of "qualified professional and technical workers and their families."[85] The Japanese press took note, but the embassy in Tokyo received only a few enquiries about emigration.[86] Tremblay believed this was because the Japanese preferred to emigrate in groups rather than as individuals, whereas Canada's immigration system was based on individuals and their families.[87] Despite its own labour shortages, Japan was interested in sending to Canada knowledgeable technicians who were "eager to become good Canadian citizens" and would give "Canadians a good opinion of the Japanese people."[88] Canada sent considerable information about occupations in Canada to Japan's Emigration Bureau, which gave some publicity to the available opportunities. The subsequent increase in the number of immigration inquiries at the Tokyo embassy prompted the Department of Immigration to suggest attaching an official to the embassy "to screen and counsel applicants."[89]

Cabinet was already considering the matter. When Pearson asked about concern in British Columbia, Tremblay assured him that Ron Basford, chair of the BC Liberal caucus, had advised that posting an immigration officer in

Tokyo would be well received in the province.[90] A few weeks later, J.R. Nicholson, the member of Parliament for Vancouver Centre, became minister of citizenship and immigration and instructed his officials to arrange for the appointment. Still, the government took few chances. Thus, in public, Nicholson only said that discussions had been held with Japan, while quietly sending Vitus Meilus of the Department of Citizenship and Immigration to act as immigration attaché at the embassy.[91]

Canadian efforts to open the immigration door were well-received in Japan. In the first half of 1965, the embassy received over three thousand inquiries from prospective immigrants compared to thirty to fifty the previous year.[92] In response to the overwhelming demand, it opened an immigration office in Tokyo in September 1966. Despite being located on the Ginza, it gained the reputation of being "one of Canada's most low-keyed immigration promotions anywhere." Japan supported its establishment but did not let it advertise. Some Japanese citizens visited the office, but language problems discouraged skilled trade and technical personnel from leaving, and the Canada-Japan Trade Council reported that such professionals would only come for attractive job offers, since most "are enjoying employment in prestige posts."[93]

More significant than the opening of the new immigration office was the announcement in Tokyo on 20 September 1966, by Nicholson's successor, Jean Marchand, that he would soon release a white paper on immigration policy.[94] That white paper was not the result of specific concern with Japanese immigration but followed a lengthy review of immigration policy that had focused on "Canada's economic needs in terms of manpower" and "the need to overcome discrimination in sponsorship privileges as between different groups of Canadian citizens."[95] While the review was under way, the department became the Department of Manpower and Immigration, a not inappropriate change given the white paper's concern with reconciling the shortage of skilled labour in Canada and the difficulties of the unskilled in finding work.[96] In announcing the white paper, Marchand frankly admitted that a "white Canada" policy had existed but denied it was ever law and promised no racial or religious discrimination in law or regulation in the future. Dealing specifically with the Japanese, he said Canada wanted skilled immigrants, would offer them the same assisted passages as it gave to Europeans, and would let immigrants sponsor relatives who might not be otherwise qualified.[97]

Press comment in British Columbia was limited but favourable. In a thoughtful analysis, the Vancouver *Sun* admitted that a generation earlier, Marchand's going to Tokyo "to beat the drum for increasing numbers of Japanese immigrants," would have been "unthinkable," and two generations earlier might have caused riots in Vancouver. The *Sun* explained that Canadians had "grown up," had become internationally minded, and had

"Give Me Your Skilled, Your Rich, Your Coddled Few . . ."

Figure 9.1 "Give Me Your Skilled," *Montreal Star*, 17 October 1966. Using an ironical image of the Statue of Liberty, cartoonist Ed McNally illustrated how the White Paper still limited immigration. *Permission by Copyright Board of Canada.*

developed strong ties in trade and finance with Japan. Moreover, the Japanese immigrants would be skilled workers.[98] That sharp contrast to what the *Sun* had argued two decades earlier was strong evidence of how opinion in British Columbia had changed. Similarly, no British Columbia newspaper gave much prominence to a Canadian Press story quoting Ralph Loffmark, the provincial minister of trade and commerce, as saying the new policy would mean a "flood" of Japanese.[99] *The New Canadian*, then published in Toronto, however, asserted that Loffmark's remarks had "the undertones of a Neo-Yellow-Peril campaign redolent of the early 1900s."[100] When the JCCA protested, Loffmark easily assuaged them by producing the original *Victoria Daily Colonist* report quoting him as having said that the "social differences" between the Japanese and other British Columbians were "minimal," that the Japanese would assimilate well, and that he looked forward to successful joint business ventures with Japan.[101]

Shortly after returning to Ottawa, Marchand released the white paper that promised to "create uniformity of standards for admission for all countries" and let citizens sponsor, "on a universal basis, a broader range of relatives than at present."[102] Amendments to the regulations retained the sponsorship system but without geographic or racial restrictions and introduced the "points system" by which most potential immigrants were rated on a score sheet that gave them specific marks in such categories as education, occupational skills and employability, age, knowledge of English and/or French, and an immigration officer's assessment of their personal qualities. The white paper, of course, dealt with immigration from all parts of the world. As for potential Japanese immigrants, Marchand denied that trade influenced his plans to abolish discrimination and to give the Japanese the same access to assisted passages as European immigrants.[103] It is difficult to believe that trade and diplomatic considerations did not affect policy, but widespread concern in Canada about human rights may also have been a factor. Although the St. Laurent government had only reluctantly subscribed to the UN Universal Declaration of Human Rights, many Canadians, not just the JCCA, were inspired by references to international human rights to seek better ways to safeguard the freedoms and liberties of Canadians.[104]

What can be concluded from this survey of Canada's Japanese immigration policies in the two decades after the Second World War? First, Ottawa remembered British Columbians' antipathy to the Japanese long after most of the province's citizens, except for such staunch Japanophobes as Howard Green, had abandoned their prejudices.[105] Second, despite turnover in the Department of Citizenship and Immigration, both in the bureaucratic and ministerial ranks, officials saw themselves as doorkeepers and were cautious in relaxing regulations.[106] Yet, the persistent campaign of Japanese Canadians for equality in treatment in immigration eventually paid off. Because of discriminatory franchise laws before the war, they had had limited experience in Canadian electoral politics, but they learned quickly, using those skills to generate widespread political support for their quest for full equality with other Canadian citizens. Yet, their quest might not have succeeded were it not for other factors. Generally, respect for human rights had superseded racial discrimination in Canada by the late 1950s. In addition, Japan had re-emerged as an economically powerful nation. Not only was it determined to establish the equality of its people, but Canadians recognized that any of its citizens who wished to come to Canada could be "advantageously absorbed" without changing the "fundamental composition" of its population or causing social and economic problems. Thus, Canada could reopen its doors to immigrants from Japan.

Notes

1 See my *A White Man's Province: British Columbia Politicians and Chinese and Japanese Immigration, 1858-1914* (Vancouver: UBC Press, 1989), 209-13 and *passim*; and *The Oriental Question: Consolidating a White Man's Province, 1914-41* (Vancouver: UBC Press, 2003), 82-85 and *passim*.

2 Conscious of objections to discrimination, Mackenzie King noted that his government was repealing the exclusionary Chinese Immigration Act to let Chinese who were Canadian citizens have their wives and unmarried children under the age of 18 join them.
3 Canada, House of Commons, *Debates* (hereafter HCD), 1 May 1947, 2644-46.
4 Of the approximately 24,000 Japanese in Canada, 10,813 either signed for repatriation themselves or were the children of signers. After the war, many tried to revoke their applications. Under pressure from churches and civil libertarians, the government cancelled the repatriation program early in 1947. By then 3,964 Japanese Canadians, of whom 51 percent were Canadian born, had been repatriated to Japan. See Canada, Department of Labour, *Report on the Re-Establishment of Japanese in Canada, 1944-46* (Ottawa: Department of Labour, 1947).
5 These policies are discussed at length in most histories dealing with the Japanese in Canada during the Second World War. One source is Patricia E. Roy, J.L. Granatstein, Masako Iino, and Hiroko Takamura, *Mutual Hostages: Canadians and Japanese during the Second World War* (Toronto: University of Toronto Press, 1990), 139-91.
6 Some officials shared this opinion. See Gordon Robertson to Mackenzie King, 23 April 1947, Library and Archives Canada (hereafter LAC), W.L.M. King Papers, #390360-2.
7 *Sun* (Vancouver), 1 March 1949.
8 Memorandum, Japanese Immigration, 1 March 1949, Department of Immigration Records (hereafter DImm), vol. 87, file 9309/19, LAC; Escott Reid, Memorandum for the Minister, 2 March 1949, Department of External Affairs Records (hereafter DEAR), vol. 3977, file 9890-40, LAC; HCD, 3 March 1949, 1086.
9 W.L.M. King, Diary, 22 January 1947 and 1 May 1947. From 1936 to 1949, Immigration was a branch of the Department of Mines and Resources. It was the Department of Citizenship and Immigration from 1949 to 1966. In 1966, the Department of Manpower and Immigration was created. For convenience, it will be referred to as the Department of Immigration.
10 *Victoria Daily Times,* 2 May 1947; *Prince Rupert Daily News,* 5 May 1947; R.G. Robertson to A.D.P. Heeney, 6 December 1946, LAC, Department of Labour (hereafter DLab), vol. 639. The six-year rule could be extended if passage was unavailable, as happened during the war.
11 H.H. Wrong to Director of Immigration, 15 August 1946, DEAR, vol. 3766; Cabinet Conclusions, 10 October 1947, LAC, Privy Council Records (hereafter PCR), MfT2365.
12 The fact that the government financially aided European refugees but not the Nisei galled *The New Canadian. The New Canadian,* 1 June 1949, 27 July 1949, 1 October 1949, and 25 August 1950.
13 *The New Canadian,* 11 January 1956.
14 Fumiko Tabata to George Tanaka, 8 September 1948, LAC, Japanese Canadian Citizens Association Records (hereafter JCCA), MFC12827; Bill Herbert in Vancouver *Sun,* 15 December 1950.
15 *The New Canadian,* 27 July 1949. Hugh Keenleyside, the deputy minister responsible for immigration, agreed that they had been "imbued with the Japanese educational background." See Report to Provincial JCCA Chapters, 5 July 1948, JCCA, MfC12827.
16 *The New Canadian,* 17 July 1947; Tanaka to Deputy Minister of Mines and Resources, 8 December 1947, JCCA, MfC12827; *The New Canadian,* 26 May 1948.
17 *The New Canadian,* 12 May 1948.
18 A handful came later as contract farm workers; others returned with Japanese-born wives and children by joining the Canadian Forces fighting in Korea. See Tanaka to Canadian Liaison Mission, Tokyo, 25 February 1950, JCCA, MfC12827; Vernon Chapter, JCCA, Resolution of March 1952, copy in JCCA, MfC12826; *The New Canadian,* 21, 25, and 29 August 1951, and 28 November 1951; Tanaka to Ted Aoki, 14 March 1952, JCCA, MfC12821.
19 Memo to Cabinet Committee on Japanese Problems, c. April 1947, PCR, vol. 84, file J-25-1.
20 Tanaka to Walter Harris, 23 June 1952, JCCA, MfC12825.
21 C.S. Gadd to McCardle, 23 April 1952, DEAR, vol. 128. Immigration did not believe that "voluntary repatriates" who lost their citizenship should be allowed to return.
22 The age limit was later raised to twenty-one.

23 Tanaka, "Why We Must Help Excluded Strandees in Japan," *Ontario Bulletin*, September 1949. Although the Canadian government referred to these people as repatriates, some of them had been born in Canada and had not previously been to Japan.
24 National JCCA Committee on Future Projects, meeting, 9 January 1949, JCCA, vol. 2, file 27.
25 *The New Canadian,* 21 February and 14 March 1951.
26 Tanaka to Minister of Citizenship and Immigration, 27 June 1951, JCCA, MfC12826.
27 *Globe and Mail* (Toronto), 10 September 1951, quoted in *The New Canadian,* 12 September 1951.
28 Canada, Senate, *Debates*, 2 April 1952, 146-47.
29 HCD, 16 June 1951, 3300-1.
30 *The New Canadian,* 5 December 1951.
31 *The New Canadian,* 8 March 1952.
32 *The New Canadian,* 7 April 1954. The executive contemplated a campaign to get a mass of letters from Caucasian Canadians to Members of Parliament supporting reunification of Japanese families. Tanaka to Aoki, 3 February 1952, JCCA, Mf12821.
33 *The New Canadian,* 2 February 1952. A fisherman born in Steveston visited Japan and married a Japanese woman. He applied to bring her to Canada but the war intervened. As soon as he was permitted to go back to fishing, he returned to Steveston. Despite favourable letters from three Caucasians, the managers of the cannery, the Royal Bank in Steveston, and a building contractor, the Immigration Department ruled that his wife was a Japanese citizen and therefore non-admissible, but their son born in 1941 and a second born after a visit in 1950 were. The correspondence is in JCCA, MfC12827. Illustrating the individual variations on policy, in an earlier case, the Immigration Department admitted a Japan-born woman who had married a Canadian before 1947. *The New Canadian,* 22 September 1951.
34 *The New Canadian,* 1 December 1956.
35 HCD, 24 March 1955, 2331.
36 *The New Canadian,* 9 January 1952.
37 Heeney to Harris, 29 December 1950, PCR, vol. 166, f. I-50-3.
38 E.H. Norman to Consular Division, 5 May 1952, and IGETP Meeting, Minutes, 12 May 1952, DEAR, vol. 2838.
39 Department of Citizenship and Immigration, Memo, 17 November 1952, LAC, Department of Citizenship and Immigration Records (hereafter DCIR), vol. 128. The full document is reprinted in Greg Donaghy, ed., *Documents on Canadian External Relations* (hereafter *DCER*), vol. 20: *1954* (Ottawa: Canada Communication Group, 1997), 1841-51. In bringing the matter of Japanese immigration to the cabinet in January 1954, the minister of immigration drew on this memorandum (Cabinet Conclusions, 14 January 1954, PCR, vol. 2654). On 5 March 1954, the secretary of state for external affairs (hereafter SSEA) sent a message to the Canadian Ambassador in Tokyo that also drew heavily on it. See DEAR, vol. 3977.
40 R.G. Robertson to J.W. Pickersgill, 8 August 1952, PCR, vol. 237, file T-50-4-J.
41 Mayhew to Under Secretary of State for External Affairs (hereafter USSEA), 7 January 1954, DEAR, vol. 6153; SSEA to Canadian Ambassador, Tokyo, 5 March 1954, DEAR, vol. 3977; Department of Citizenship and Immigration, Memorandum, 8 March 1954, in Donaghy, *DCER*, 20:1852. A decade later, the Immigration Department admitted that the potential return of three thousand Japanese-Canadians and their approximately seven thousand dependants was the "primary reason" for its refusal to establish an immigration quota for Japan; in fact, there had been no significant movement to Canada of such people. (Memo prepared by the Immigration Branch, June 1964, with C.M. Isbister to Minister, 5 June 1964, LAC, L.B. Pearson Papers (hereafter LBPP), vol. 207, file 572).
42 He also repeated that the several thousand Canadian citizens in Japan could return to Canada once transportation was arranged. See Press Conference of Louis St. Laurent in Tokyo, 11 March 1954, DEAR, vol. 6653.
43 Report on Japanese Immigration prepared for Mr. Howe's visit, 8 October 1956, DEAR, vol. 3977. With its overpopulation problem, Japan was promoting emigration. The chief inspector of its overseas offices visited Toronto in 1955 but does not appear to have contacted the Department of Immigration. *The New Canadian*, 28 September 1955.

44 Tanaka to M. Takada, 10 January 1953, JCCA, MfC12831.
45 JCCA, Executive Committee Meeting, 6 November 1955, JCCA, MfC12819.
46 Leger to Fortier, 4 March 1957, DCIR, vol. 128. The embassy denied having anything to do with JCCA petitions. It said, "the legal ties of the Japanese Canadians with Japan are completely broken" in an informal complaint about long delays in approving the entry of Japanese nationals, including relatives of Japanese Canadians and Japanese businessmen. Japanese Embassy, Aide Memoire, July 1958, DCIR, vol. 128.
47 *The New Canadian,* 22 December 1954.
48 Minister of Citizenship and Immigration to Cabinet, 18 April 1955, reprinted in Greg Donaghy, ed., *DCER,* vol. 21: *1955,* 1634-35; Department of External Affairs, Memorandum, 6 May 1955, DEAR, vol. 3977; Cabinet Conclusions, 20 April 1955, PCR, vol. 2657. External Affairs considered them "harmless" individuals who would not permanently increase Canada's Japanese population, and whose admission would avoid criticism from Japan where children were expected to care for their aged parents. See Jules Leger to L.B. Pearson, 22 November 1955, in Donaghy, *DCER,* 21:1636-37; Laval Fortier to Pickersgill, 11 November 1955, Pickersgill Papers, vol. 45, file I-2-437; Pickersgill to Deputy Minister, 26 November 1955, J.W. Pickersgill Papers (hereafter JWP), vol. 45, file I-2-437.
49 Chinese Canadian Association and Japanese Canadian Citizens Association to Pickersgill, 9 March 1957, JCCA, MfC12826; also in LAC, JWP, vol. 45.
50 Stan Hiraki and Ruth Lor to Pickersgill, 9 March 1957, JWP, vol. 45.
51 JCCA to Minister of Citizenship and Immigration, 9 March 1957, in JWP, vol. 45, and JCCA, MfC12826.
52 Pickersgill to Hiraki and Pickersgill to Lor, 12 March 1957, JWP, vol. 45.
53 *The New Canadian,* 1 December 1956.
54 Pickersgill to Perry S. Bower, 22 July 1955, JWP, vol. 45. The Department of Citizenship and Immigration, however, agreed with a proposal from the Japanese Embassy that it send a handful of young Japanese men to learn Canadian agricultural techniques by working on Canadian farms for seven months, provided the program was not "identified as an 'immigration movement.'" The program operated over several years, but no more than five or six students came each year. They were placed mainly in Ontario. See correspondence in DImm, vol. 914.
55 Pickersgill to Rev. E.E. Long, 4 May 1957, JWP, vol. 79.
56 JCCA, Executive Meeting, 19 February 1958, JCCA, MfC12819.
57 HCD, 21 May 1958, 328-29. Shortly before the 1957 election, E. Davie Fulton, MP (Progressive Conservative, Kamloops), offered to help a Japanese Canadian constituent who wanted permission to allow his sons to remain in Canada. See Fulton to C. Nakamura, 29 March 1957, LAC, E.D. Fulton Papers, vol. 12.
58 CCA and JCCA to Minister, June 1958, copy in LAC, H.W. Herridge Papers, vol. 40; Report of Delegation, 20 June 1958, JCCA, MfC12826.
59 Privy Council Office, Cabinet Conclusions, 24 October 1958, PCR, vol. 1899.
60 National Report to the Sixth National JCCA Conference, Toronto, 1-3 September 1961, JCCA, Mf C12829; National JCCA to Ellen Fairclough, 19 July 1960, John Diefenbaker Papers, #102886, LAC. Copies are also in the papers of H.W. Herridge, L.B. Pearson, and the JCCA.
61 *The New Canadian,* 23 July and 31 August 1960, and 11 February 1961.
62 Japanese Embassy, Aide Memoire, July 1958, with USSEA to Deputy Minister, Citizenship and Immigration, 18 July 1958; Deputy Minister of Citizenship and Immigration to Director, 1 October 1958; and Aide Memoire from Japanese Embassy, 8 October 1959, all in DCIR, vol. 128. The Embassy was also concerned about the need for medical examinations of such non-immigrants as businessmen and long delays in granting them visas.
63 *The New Canadian,* 16 January 1960.
64 Toru Hagiwara to *The New Canadian,* 6 February 1960, in DImm, vol. 871, file 557-3-478; *The New Canadian,* 6 February 1960, and 9 and 19 August 1961. However, in anticipation of a meeting with Fairclough and her deputy, Hagiwara asked the JCCA for a report on immigration cases. See JCCA executive meeting, 25 January 1961, JCCA records, MfC12819.

65 HCD, 25 January 1960, 258. In December 1948, the Immigration Branch requested cabinet approval to admit Japanese businessmen who were engaged in international trade, had sufficient funds, and were approved by the Canadian Liaison Mission. Memorandum to Cabinet, 30 December 1948, PCR, vol. 83.
66 W.R. Baskerville to Undersecretary of State for External Affairs, 10 March 1960, DEAR, vol. 5081.
67 Director of Immigration to Deputy Minister, 21 March 1961, DCIR, vol. 128.
68 W.E. Collins, Memo for file, 23 June 1960, and "Visit to Ottawa of Japanese Foreign Minister, Zentaro Kosaka, 14-16 September 1960," DEAR, vol. 5081.
69 J.M. Teakles to Consular Division, 5 May 1961, and Teakles to Far East Division, 8 May 1961, DEAR, vol. 5081.
70 H.M. Jones to Minister of Immigration, 21 June 1963, DImm, file 557-8-578.
71 Zentaro Kosaka to W.F. Bull, 1 November 1961, and Tokyo to SSEA, 27 December 1961, DEAR, vol. 5082, file 4606-C-21-1-40.
72 *Toronto Star,* 30 October 1961.
73 HCD, 10 February 1961, 1946.
74 *Grand Forks Gazette,* 11 August 1960, quoted in *The New Canadian,* 20 August 1960.
75 *Sun* (Vancouver), 24 and 29 June 1961.
76 *The New Canadian,* 10 June 1959, and 9 March and 3 September 1960.
77 *The New Canadian,* 29 March and 31 May 1961.
78 HCD, 18 January 1962, 10.
79 See Freda Hawkins, *Canada and Immigration: Public Policy and Public Concern* (Montreal and Kingston: McGill-Queen's University Press, 1972), 131.
80 *The New Canadian,* 27 January 1962.
81 *Globe and Mail,* 29 March 1962.
82 JCCA, Executive Meetings, 24 September 1963, 28 April and 20 May 1965, JCCA, MfC12919.
83 *The New Canadian,* 4 September 1963.
84 Operations Memorandum to All Immigration Officers, 12 December 1963, DImm, vol. 871, file 557-3-578; National JCCA, Meeting, 15 April 1964, JCCA, MfC12819.
85 *The New Canadian,* 8 April 1964; Memo prepared by Immigration Branch with C.M. Isbister to Minister, 5 June 1964, LBPP, vol. 207, file 572; HCD, 14 August 1964, 6823.
86 Tokyo to Ottawa, 8 May 1964, DEAR, vol. 10192. Some skilled Japanese did come. The first, arriving in July 1962, was an architect who had won a competition sponsored by the Canadian Embassy in Japan. Over the next few years, a trickle of professionals including a nurse, a skilled builder, a draftsman, a printer, and a potter from Brazil arrived. The fact that *The New Canadian* reported individual arrivals underscores how few came. *The New Canadian,* 18 July 1962.
87 HCD, 14 August 1964, 6823.
88 *The New Canadian,* 27 May 1964; Tremblay to Pearson, 26 January 1965, LBPP, vol. 207, file 572. In 1967, the Japan Emigration Service opened an orientation program for emigrants to Canada with a twenty-five-day familiarization course, which focused on English language instruction. *The New Canadian,* 27 May 1967.
89 H.F. Clark to Embassy, 2 December 1964, DEAR, vol. 10192.
90 C.N. Isbister to Tremblay, 4 November 1964, DCIR, vol. 128.
91 J.R. Nicholson to Pearson, 22 February 1965, LBPP, vol. 207, file 572; HCD, 22 February 1965, 11564.
92 Tokyo to SSEA, 29 July 1965; DEAR, vol. 10192; *The Financial Post,* 14 August 1965.
93 For example, *Victoria Daily Times,* 21 September 1966.
94 The colour referred to the cover of the document, not to its contents.
95 Cabinet Conclusions, 5 March 1964, PCR, vol. 6264, LAC.
96 A succinct but critical summary of the white paper may be found in Hawkins, *Canada and Immigration,* 159ff.
97 *Victoria Daily Times,* 20 September 1966. The *Times* gave the announcement a front page headline, but the Vancouver *Sun* and the *Victoria Daily Colonist* both gave shorter versions of the same Canadian Press stories and put them on inside pages. The Vancouver *Province*

report, from AP-Reuters, was practically identical in content and appeared on page 1 under the heading "Ottawa to Overhaul Immigration" (21 September 1966).

98 *Victoria Daily Times,* 21 September 1966.

99 *Victoria Daily Times,* 23 September 1966; *Sun* (Vancouver), 23 September 1966. Neither paper gave the report much prominence: the *Victoria Daily Times* had it on page 8; the *Sun*, page 64!

100 *The New Canadian,* 28 September 1966.

101 *Victoria Daily Colonist,* 22 September 1966; Meeting, 16 November 1966, JCCA, MfC12819.

102 HCD, 8 July 1966, 7377.

103 *Province* (Vancouver), 1 October 1966.

104 Christopher MacLennan, *Toward the Charter: Canadians and the Demand for a National Bill of Rights, 1929-1960* (Montreal and Kingston: McGill-Queen's University Press, 2003), 60.

105 In 1941, 95.4 percent of the Japanese in Canada resided in BC; in 1951, 33 percent; in 1961, 35.7 percent; and in 1971, 36.4 percent. Calculated from Ken Adachi, *The Enemy That Never Was* (Toronto: McClelland and Stewart, 1976), 423.

106 Hawkins, *Canada and Immigration,* 141, 377.

10
Under the Radar: Japanese Investment in Canada since 1945

Carin Holroyd

The re-establishment of commercial relations between the former combatants of the Second World War and the rapid re-emergence of Japan as an economic power in the postwar period stand as one of the most remarkable developments of the twentieth century. Ostracized for its aggressive behaviour before the war and badly damaged by years of bombing and war-induced hardships, Japan seemed destined to be relegated to the economic margins after 1945. Even as the Allied powers, especially the United States, assisted Japan with its phoenix-like emergence from the rubble of the war, future trade and investment relations with Canada were in doubt. Initial prospects were unpromising, as a series of economic and social crises in Japan limited business ties until the mid-1950s. Yet, by the early 1960s, Japan was again a significant international economic influence and by the early 1970s had established itself as Canada's second-largest trading partner and as a major investor in Canadian natural resources. Japan's commercial interest in Canada expanded during the boom of the 1990s, and remained strong even after the "bubble economy" burst.

Though Japanese businesses returned to Canada quickly and decisively in the postwar period, they provoked surprisingly little awareness and even less understanding among Canadian businesses and governments, which maintained the studied lack of interest that has long characterized Canada's relationships with its international economic partners other than Great Britain and the United States. Canadians did not react as much as Americans to the influx of Japanese investment and consumer goods; in fact, they showed little interest or concern in the growing presence of Japanese firms in their economy.[1] Today, as Canada and Japan reconsider their trade and investment ties, it is useful to reflect on the postwar era, when Japan emerged to become Canada's third most important source of foreign direct investment (FDI). After outlining the evolution and scope of Japanese investment in Canada, this paper evaluates this investment in light of the broader patterns of Japan's economic expansion and Canada's postwar economic development strategies.

Japanese Investment in Canada, 1945-90

As a country with few natural resources and few friends in postwar Asia, Japan had little choice but to look overseas to guarantee itself the supplies of raw materials – copper, iron, lead, zinc, and potash – it needed to fuel its industrial revitalization. Japan's approach to Canada was distinct and low profile: Japanese trading companies began by lending money to local companies for the development of mines and other resource industries in Canada and were repaid from profits. Over the course of the 1960s, Japanese interest in the Canadian market expanded, and Japanese companies began making equity investments, usually 50.1 percent, in a series of ventures. The trading companies later sought to have the loans repaid with stock in Canadian corporations before choosing to enter into joint ventures with Canadian companies.[2] The focus in the 1970s was on joint ventures, often arranged by trading companies like Mitsui, Mitsubishi, and Marubeni, which rarely took a controlling interest in the new projects. In 1974, Japan's consul general explained that "the Japanese Government prefers that its investors form joint ventures involving local labor, materials and sites in the country in which the investments are being made."[3] Japanese companies, at least where Canada was concerned, followed this pattern closely.

It is difficult to gauge the full extent of Japanese direct investment in Canadian resources in the 1960s because close to half of it came in the form of loans, including corporate bonds and debentures, and many loan repayments were subsequently converted to equity in joint ventures.[4] In addition, much of the loan capital did not come directly from Japan, but was raised by Japanese commercial banks with offices in Canada or New York. Japanese companies deliberately kept their investment understated since Canadians, concerned about high-profile American investment, worried that Canada was being sold out to foreign interests. Guaranteed purchase agreements and loans seemed, on the surface, less obtrusive and worrisome than American takeovers. Few Canadians recognized the growing Japanese presence in their country, partly because Japanese firms put comparatively small amounts of money into a large number of firms, thereby distributing both the commercial and public relations exposure.[5] While this arrangement gave the Japanese control of the enterprise, with Japanese featuring prominently on its board of directors, a Canadian was almost always installed as the president and public face of the venture. In fact, between 1961 and 1967, the only known case of a Japanese serving as president of a joint venture was at Canadian Motor Industries (CMI) in Nova Scotia, which was about 60 percent controlled by Japanese investors.[6]

Throughout the 1960s, as Japan's remarkable economic expansion took hold, investor interest focused on raw materials, especially in minerals in British Columbia. The first significant postwar example was Sumitomo Metal Mining Company's investment in Bethlehem Copper Corporation (BCC) in 1961. Initially, Sumitomo advanced Bethlehem $5 million, before the loan was liquidated in 1963.[7] Sumitomo received about one-third of BCC shares and appointed three of its nine board members. Sumitomo also enjoyed the exclusive right to purchase, at market prices, all the copper that Bethlehem produced until 1971.[8] Granisle Mining Company, which opened in 1966, borrowed money from Sumitomo and Mitsubishi and their subsidiaries in return for an option to purchase stock and a ten–year contract for exclusive purchase of the minerals produced.[9] Similarly, Mitsubishi Metal Mining formed a joint venture (Minoca Mines) with Noranda Mines to develop a copper mine on northern Vancouver Island, while Sumitomo Metal financially supported New Imperial Mines copper development in the Yukon.[10]

Reporting on mounting Japanese investment in 1968, newspaper stories typically gushed with enthusiasm for the "magic" that was putting new excitement into an industry for which fresh money is increasingly hard to find. A veteran mining developer commented that several recent developments in British Columbia and the Yukon made "them the hottest mineral area in Canada, that never would have got off the ground unless Japanese money appeared on the scene – either to finance development directly, or to set up outside financing by okaying long-term contracts."[11] Indeed, this Japanese involvement was integral to the development of the industry in British Columbia. Of the fifteen copper mines opened there from the early 1960s to the mid-1970s, only one did not have some form of Japanese participation through a loan, an equity position, a long-term purchase agreement, or simply as customers. In 1967, for instance, shipments to Japan represented 25 percent of the total value of British Columbia's mineral production.

Japanese firms helped launch a number of new mines through long-term purchase agreements. Falconbridge Nickel Mines attributed the opening of the Westfrob Mines in the Queen Charlotte Islands to a ten-year contract with Mitsubishi International for iron and copper concentrates. In the 1970s, Japanese firms held long-term contracts with Cowichan Copper, Craigmont Mines, Texada Mines, Brynor Mines, and Coast Copper, among others. Similarly, the Northeast Coal project in British Columbia in the 1980s was developed almost entirely because Japanese steel producers, who wanted a guaranteed supply of coal, were willing to sign a multi-year purchase agreement. That persuaded the federal and provincial governments to construct the necessary $2.1 billion infrastructure, which included new rail lines, a deep water terminal, and the town site of Tumbler Ridge. The viability of

Figure 10.1 The Bullmoose Mine. *Courtesy of Teck Cominco.*

the Quintette and Bullmoose mines depended on the fifteen-year supply contract and on continuing price stability for the coal delivered.

By the time the mine opened, the price of coal had fallen, sparking a major dispute over the product's appropriate price. Critics argued that the Japanese steel industry had deliberately encouraged excess capacity by offering long-term supply contracts at premium prices to mines around the world and then, after the market was flooded, attempting to renegotiate price and tonnage. The Japanese responded that they had no idea that steel production would not reach the anticipated levels and would therefore require less coal nor that world coal prices would decline markedly. Given the situation, they saw no reason to pay prices dramatically above the world level.[12] Three major mines – Quintette and Bullmoose at Tumbler Ridge, and Gregg River, a $200 million, open pit coal mine located 40 kilometres southwest of Hinton, Alberta – opened in 1983 but closed in 2000 and 2003.[13] (The Tumbler Ridge region has reopened recently, ironically, to meet the surging demand in China for raw materials.)[14]

In the mid-1960s, Japanese interests in Canada broadened to include pulp and paper, and a small amount of secondary manufacturing for the Canadian market. Although the geographic focus on Japanese companies shifted eastward, with important investments in Alberta and Saskatchewan, and even minor forays into the Atlantic provinces, half of Japanese investment in Canada remained in British Columbia.[15] Commentators in the 1970s claimed that investment might have been considerably higher except for fears of nationalization and government interference in resource development by the left-wing New Democratic Party, which governed the province from 1972 to 1975.[16]

Forestry, a vital economic sector in Canada, has a long history of Japanese involvement. The first recorded shipment of Canadian lumber to Japan was in 1886, and early in the twentieth century, Japanese trading companies actively sought to buy Canadian forest products.[17] These sales revived after 1945 and by the 1960s, forest products were Canada's leading export to Japan. Wood and articles of wood remain Canada's largest export to Japan by a substantial amount; wood pulp usually ranks as the third most important export by value, with paper in tenth place. Investment in timber peaked early in the 1970s, although there was a resurgence of investment in pulp and paper between 1987 and 1994. It remains significant today. The Daishowa Paper Manufacturing Company began purchasing wood chips and shipping them to Japan for processing in the mid-1960s. In December 1969, it set up Cariboo Pulp and Paper Company, a 50-50 joint venture with Weldwood of Canada to build a pulp mill in Quesnel, BC. Other ventures in British Columbia included Finlay Forest Products (a joint venture with Sumitomo and Jujo Paper Manufacturing), the QC Timber pulp mill, and the Quesnel River Pulp Company, which Daishowa, in conjunction with West Fraser Mills, established in 1981. Honshu Paper, Mitsubishi Corporation, and the Ontario Municipal Employees Retirement Board owned Crestbrook Forest Industries, which operated three sawmills and a softwood pulp mill in southeastern British Columbia.[18]

Manufacturing investments also grew in the 1970s. Sony, Matsushita, and other producers of consumer goods opened Canadian distribution plants. Some Japanese companies shipped in components to be reassembled in Canada, capitalizing on Canadian tariffs and other domestic production regulations. Other significant investments included Toyobo and Marubeni's purchase of Bruck Mills in Quebec and Japanese investments in, or establishment of, such firms as YKK Zipper in Quebec, Cirtex Knitting in New Brunswick, the Prince Hotel in Toronto, and Trans Pacific Tours, a joint venture between Canadian Pacific Airlines and C Itoh.[19] Japanese companies also participated in crude oil exploration and development in Alberta, whaling operations off the coast of Newfoundland, and establishing a barbed wire factory in Saskatchewan.[20]

Investments and purchase agreements in a number of other sectors have made Japanese involvement in Canada, particularly British Columbia, much deeper and more influential than most observers realize. A look at British

Columbia's north coast fishery reveals that Japan has been either the primary or sole market for a substantial proportion of the catch including sockeye salmon (90 percent), coho salmon (50 percent), geoduck clams (100 percent), sea cucumber (100 percent), sea urchins (100 percent), herring roe on kelp (100 percent), and black cod (100 percent). Japanese companies have been important for Canada's aluminum industry too. As recently as the mid-1990s, almost 60 percent of the production of the Aluminum Company of Canada's Kitimat smelter went to Japan.[21]

Japan's investment presence in Canada developed steadily through the 1980s, but its commercial interest rarely registered on the Canadian consciousness. Even in those areas that attracted the greatest amount of investment – northern British Columbia being perhaps the best example – interest in the scale of Japanese involvement was never high. Japan had nonetheless become Canada's third-largest investor, behind the United States and Great Britain. Following the Plaza Accord (which restructured currency rates and sparked Japan's "bubble economy"), and the conclusion of the Canada-US Free Trade Agreement (CUFTA) and the North American Free Trade Agreement (NAFTA), Japanese investment in Canada increased dramatically, though the impressive investment gains remained small in comparison to Japanese investment in the United States. As Table 10.1 illustrates, Japanese investment in Canada increased almost eightfold from $605 million in 1980 to $5,222 million in 1990.[22]

The lion's share of this new investment was concentrated in British Columbia and Ontario, followed by Quebec, at a significant distance, and

Table 10.1

Japanese direct investment in Canada, 1920-2004

Year	Japanese investment (stock, Cdn$ million)
1960	0
1965	10
1970	103
1975	257
1980	605
1985	2,250
1990	5,222
1995	6,987
2000	8,041
2004	10,583

Sources: Statistics Canada, *Canada's International Investment Position: Historical Statistics 1926 to 1996*, Catalogue 67-202; Statistics Canada, *Canada's International Investment Position: Historical Statistics 2001*, Catalogue 67-202 (1990-1998); Statistics Canada, *Canada's International Investment Position: Historical Statistics 2004, First Quarter Report*, Catalogue 67-202 (1999-2003).

Alberta. Japanese investors during the 1980s moved into a broader range of investments, including automotive assembly and automotive parts manufacturing, newsprint, and services such as hotels, banking, and construction. Honda established a manufacturing presence in Canada in 1986, followed by Toyota two years later, and CAMI Automotive (a Suzuki-General Motors joint venture) in 1989. By 1993, the three plants, all located in southern Ontario, were responsible for over 15 percent of total Canadian motor vehicle production. Over time, the three plants expanded significantly and, along with the auto parts manufacturers that service them, became a substantial economic force in Ontario.[23] Diversity in investment was also evident between 1986 and 1990 as Japanese investors purchased at least fifteen hotels and resorts, particularly in Vancouver and Whistler, BC, in Banff, Alberta, and in Niagara Falls, Ontario – all areas that appealed to Japanese tourists.

Investment in natural resources, however, continued to represent a major share of the Japanese portfolio in Canada. As late as 1989, pulp and paper and mining still constituted about 40 percent of total accumulated investment, with key sectors attracting considerable attention in certain time periods: wood and paper from 1988-94, chemicals from 1990-95, minerals and metals in 1990. Japanese service companies, mainly trading firms and banks, followed the investment dollars, setting up branches in Canada to support the export and import sectors. As David Edgington, a Canadian geographer specializing in the study of Japanese business activity, points out, in 1986, Canadian subsidiaries of Japanese banks handled close to 90 percent of Japanese financial activity in Canada. At roughly the same time, a growing number of Japanese companies came to Canada to take advantage of lower labour costs and to overcome protectionist sentiment, which was rising in the face of Japan's massive trade surplus. Production in Canada, particularly after NAFTA, allowed access to the US market without the tensions and hostile reaction that production in the United States routinely brought.[24] Table 10.2 offers a summary of Japanese investment by sector through the 1970s and 1980s. The focus on wood, mining, and oil and gas is evident, as is the dramatic jump in manufacturing and financial investment at the end of the 1980s.

Japan's growing presence in the Canadian economy attracted little public notice and very little of the nervousness evident in the United States, where popular fear of Japanese economic domination propelled Michael Crichton's 1992 novel, *Rising Sun,* to the ranks of the bestsellers. In sharp contrast, as studies of Japanese investment in northern British Columbia and northern Alberta reveal, Canadians were largely oblivious to the extent of Japanese engagement with the regional and national economy and indifferent to the rapid growth of Japanese activity in key economic sectors.[25] There was little regional awareness of the scale of Japanese investment and no campaigns to limit Japanese involvement in the Canadian economy.

Table 10.2

Japanese direct investment in Canada by industry, 1960-89 (Cdn$ million)

Year	Wood and paper products	Other manufacturing	Oil and gas	Mining	Merchandising	Finance	Other
1965					1	8	1
1970	55	3	5	26	11	3	
1975	83	23	3	75	54	7	12
1980	99	59	49	68	257	27	45
1985	51	147	477	238	709	268	33
1989	1,174	662	84	309	853	836	187

Source: Statistics Canada, *Canada's International Investment Position: Historical Statistics 1926 to 1992*, Catalogue 67-202.

Japanese Investment in Canada after 1990

While Japanese investors had largely operated below the radar in the 1970s and 1980s, the climate in Canada for Japanese investment had changed significantly by the 1990s. Tokyo's soaring economy, mounting media and business interest in Japanese business practices, and widespread approval of Japan's commitment to high quality production meant that Canadian politicians trumpeted new Japanese investments as a sign that Canada was "open for business," and they offered handsome inducements to Japanese firms. The new approach was not Japan-specific, but in an era of growing openness of markets and greater enthusiasm for international investment, deep-pocketed Japanese firms seemed particularly attractive.

What is particularly interesting in the 1990s is that, unlike the United States where expanding Japanese involvement sparked a xenophobic reaction in some quarters, the Canadian response remained muted. In 1990, Daishowa purchased High Level Forest Products in northern Alberta and opened a $580 million pulp mill near Peace River, Alberta, that was then the largest pulp mill in the world (there is now a larger mill in Indonesia). The company signed a renewable twenty-year forestry management agreement to harvest an area of more than 24,000 square kilometres, and the province spent $65 million on road and rail access, including a new bridge, to be used only by the mill.[26] Alberta-Pacific (a joint venture of three primarily Japanese-owned entities, with Mitsubishi Corporation as the dominant interest) built a second pulp mill between Athabasca and Lac La Biche. Alberta-Pacific had the forestry management rights to a 61,000 square kilometre area in northeast Alberta and received $275 million in subordinated debentures from the Alberta government, which also invested about $75 million in infrastructure costs.[27] In total, these two Japanese multinationals obtained the management rights to approximately 8 percent of Alberta. Yet, there were few protests; in fact, most Canadians remained blissfully unaware of the concessions used to lure the Japanese investors. Incredibly, these inducements may not have been necessary, since the investors wanted access to the timber.

During the 1990s, Japanese companies moved into value-added industries. From 1990 to 1997, for instance, Mitsubishi Canada and Chugoku Pearl and Company operated the world's largest chopstick manufacturing operation in Fort Nelson, BC. Mitsui Homes established a prefabricated homes manufacturing plant in Langley, BC. The major investments, however, were in Ontario, where the Toyota, Honda, and CAMI automotive plants continued to expand.[28] By 2004, the three ventures represented a combined investment of $6.13 billion, employed 10,400 people, and produced over 670,000 cars annually. Supporting these three companies were thirty-six Japanese manufacturers of automotive parts and related materials, and nine machine tool operations, employing approximately 14,000 people. The Japan Automobile Manufacturers Association estimated that when head offices and vehicle dealerships are included, Japanese automotive companies employed 56,000 people in Canada in 2003.[29]

Japan was, as of 2003, the third largest investor in Canada.[30] Save for a few areas – southern Ontario in particular – there is little awareness of the variety and complexity of Japanese investment. While investments by Americans and even smaller investors like the People's Republic of China, have generated considerable public comment, the reaction to Japanese investment since the Second World War has been surprisingly limited. Japan re-entered Canada cautiously, structuring its investments in creative ways that minimized public awareness of, and reaction to, its presence in the country. Canadians became accustomed to Japanese capital flowing into the country but have rarely viewed it as an intrusion or imposition.

Pattern and Meaning in Japanese Investment in Canada

Although Japan's postwar investment in Canada was substantial and had a marked impact on Canadian economic development, Canada's share of overall Japanese FDI has always been small, particularly when compared with that of countries such as Australia, Singapore, Great Britain, and the Netherlands. From 1951 to 1970, the Canadian share of total FDI was nearly 6 percent of all Japanese investment. By the 1980s, this had dropped to under 3 percent in most years. In fact, as Table 10.3 demonstrates, from 1951 to 2001 cumulatively, Canada only received 1.7 percent of total Japanese FDI.[31] And at the end of the twentieth century, Canada was only the fifteenth largest destination for Japanese foreign investment.

There are crucial aspects of its investment situation that Canada cannot address: its relatively small population, investor preference for accessing

Table 10.3

Japanese foreign direct investment, 1951-2001

Country	% share	Value (US$ million)
United States	38.6	310,515
United Kingdom	11.1	89,430
Netherlands	5.6	45,091
Australia	4.0	32,244
Indonesia	3.3	26,373
China	2.7	21,949
Singapore	2.1	16,626
Thailand	2.0	15,677
Brazil	1.7	13,929
Canada	1.7	13,790

Source: Japan External Trade Organization, *Nippon 2003 Business Facts and Figures* (Tokyo: JETRO, 2003), 42.

the Canadian market from an American base, and the inability of the small Japanese-Canadian community to provide a conduit to the Japanese market comparable to that supplied to the People's Republic of China by Hong Kong and Chinese émigrés. Canadian political and industrial factors have also hindered Japanese investment. Federal-provincial jurisdictional conflicts worried Japanese investors. Indeed, by the early 1960s, provincial politicians and business leaders blamed federal tariff barriers for interfering with British Columbia-Japan trade.[32] Japanese investors were also concerned with Canada's unsettled labour climate from the 1960s to the 1990s, especially its generally low levels of industrial productivity. Investors were uncertain too about dealing with the federal government's Foreign Investment Review Agency (FIRA), which reviewed FDI for its benefits to Canada from 1975 until 1988, when Conservative Prime Minister Brian Mulroney abolished it, famously declaring that "Canada was open for business."

More important, Japanese investment was shaped by a lack of interest in Canada, concerns about Canadian taxation policy, the limited Canadian interest in Japan's culture, language, and business environment. And, until the 1960s, as Patricia Roy points out in Chapter 9, Japanese managers and technicians confronted bureaucratic hurdles in seeking to gain long-term admission to Canada. It was also hampered by the failure of Canadian business to recruit investors in Japan, and the comparative attractiveness of other markets, especially Australia, the United States, Korea, and China, which provided opportunities in high-growth industries. Most Japanese investment in Canada has been the result of Japanese, not Canadian, initiative.

One of the most striking aspects of Japanese investment overseas is how quickly and quietly most of it took place. At the end of the Second World War, Canadians were unsympathetic towards their recent enemy and were not eager to re-establish the relationship or take constructive steps towards rebuilding their limited pre-war economic links. However, despite these limitations, and with very little active cultivation by Canada, Japan emerged as Canada's second-largest trading partner by 1973 and became a significant source of investment capital and market demand, which permitted the development of a variety of resource projects in Canada. Its corporations also stimulated considerable manufacturing activity in Canada. While a number of the Japanese investments might have been controversial, the low-profile approach of the investors meant that few Canadians were aware of Japan's involvement in mineral exploration or understood the size and extent of the forestry management rights held by Japanese companies in northern Alberta.

The history of Canada's postwar investment relationship with Japan offers some insight into Canada's status as a target for international investment. The pattern of investment that Japan pursued during the 1960s and 1970s laid the crucial groundwork for the current relationship. During those decades, Canada made raw materials easily available at relatively low costs, and Japan capitalized on this. For a time, this was mutually advantageous, bringing cash into Canada, producing thousands of jobs, and creating entire communities. This pattern, however, reinforced Canada's dependence on the resource trade, a reality that became only too obvious when the sector experienced a prolonged downturn in the 1990s.

As Japan shifted from a heavy-industry intensive economy to a more sophisticated and diversified economy, Canada received a disproportionately smaller percentage of Japanese overseas investment. Unlike Australia, which embraced Asia in the 1970s, Canada has been reluctant to conceptualize itself as a nation with compelling interests in the Pacific. It remained instead a country with overwhelming North American connections. As a result, it proved very passive in its approach to Japanese investment; but when Japanese companies approached Canada, governments often took aggressive steps to attract investment that would likely have come without incentives of the magnitude offered. In a number of these cases, Japanese companies, following a model widely adopted by international companies, played provinces, cities, or regions against each other, inducing them to outbid each other in order to attract investment into their region.[33]

There are costs associated with the patterns evident in Canada's investment relations with Japan. The continued reliance on natural resources and primary processing stands out as a legacy of the country's history of resource dependency. The lack of responsiveness to changes in the world's second-largest economy clearly reflected systemic challenges within the Canadian system, as did the general lack of concern about the nature and extent of foreign investment in key commercial sectors. Perhaps, however, the greatest lesson rests in the realization of what Canada has lost by not cultivating the Japanese market more assiduously. Consider one simple comparison. If, over the 1951-2001 period, Canada had attracted the same amount of Japanese investment as Australia (not an unrealistic expectation), it would have received US$20 billion in additional investment, plus all of the accompanying benefits of construction, employment, and taxes.

It is no surprise that Canadians are preoccupied with the opportunities and threats posed by the American market. It is the most powerful nation in the world, and Canadian prosperity rests substantially on the continued development of opportunities there. Opportunity can become dependence, however, and an overwhelming reliance on American trade has tended to limit Canada's interest in non-North American markets. As Greg Donaghy documents in the next chapter, Prime Minister Trudeau's concern about Canada's growing integration with the United States economy resulted in the creation of the "third option," a specific attempt to cultivate trade and investment relations with Europe and Japan as a means of offsetting American control. The Trudeau government soon found that Canadian businesses did not share its enthusiasm for shifting attention towards Japan, and efforts to build stronger economic ties fell far short. Trudeau, himself, soon lost interest as the growing threat of Quebec separatism drew his attention away from international economic relations.

This is not to say, of course, that Canada has been indifferent to foreign investment and trade. The country's "open for business" attitude has meant that expressions of interest from foreign investors have been welcomed, even if they were not actively or aggressively solicited. In this situation, and Japan is perhaps the best example of this process (with Chinese business possibly set to reproduce the pattern), foreign investors have been able to set the agenda and determine the trajectory and pace of investment-driven growth. Canada's general passivity has meant that, despite rapid growth after 1945 and an increasingly comprehensive reach through its economy, there is still surprisingly little understanding of the shape, nature, and extent of Japanese investment in Canada. The pattern of flying below the radar, established after the Second World War to facilitate overseas investment in a climate of considerable suspicion, served Japan well; it is much less clear that this Japanese investment model has benefited Canada to the same extent.

Notes

1 The issue of Japanese investment in Canada has attracted surprisingly little attention, particularly compared to the scholarship and journalism devoted to this topic in the United States. Certainly, there is no Canadian version of Michael Crichton's *Rising Sun*, which fed on fears of Japanese domination of the American economy. (The appearance of books such as *China Inc.: How the Rise of the Next Superpower Challenges America and the World*, by Ted Fishman, suggests that the paranoia about Japan in the 1980s and 1990s has a new focus.) There have, nonetheless, been some useful studies of Japanese investment in Canada, including Frank Langdon, *The Politics of Canadian-Japanese Economic Relations 1952-1983* (Vancouver: UBC Press, 1983); Carin Holroyd and Ken Coates, *Pacific Partners: The Japanese Presence in Canadian Business, Culture and Society* (Toronto: James Lorimer and Company, 1996); David Edgington, "Japanese Direct Investment in Canada: Patterns and Prospects" in *The North Pacific Triangle: The United States, Japan and Canada at Century's End*, ed. Michael Fry et al. (Toronto: University of Toronto Press, 1998); Stephanie LeBlond, "Trends in Japanese Foreign Direct Investment to the Year 2000," Canadian Embassy Japan, 1994, unpublished internal document; Klaus Pringsheim, *Neighbors across the Pacific: The Development of Economic and Political Relations between Canada and Japan* (Westport, CN: Greenwood Press, 1983); David Edgington, *Japanese Direct Investment in Canada: Recent Trends and Prospects* (Vancouver: UBC Department of Geography, 1992); Masanao Nakamura and Ilan Vertinsky, *Japanese Economic Policies and Growth: Implications for Businesses in Canada and North America* (Edmonton: University of Alberta Press, 1994); R. Stern, *Trade and Investment Relations among the United States, Canada and Japan* (Chicago: University of Chicago Press, 1989); Carin Holroyd, *Government, Trade and Laissez-Faire Capitalism: Canada, Australia and New Zealand's Relations with Japan* (Montreal and Kingston: McGill-Queen's University Press, 2002); Carin Holroyd, "Japan and Northern British Columbia," *Proceedings of JSAC 1994: The Global Role of Modern Japan*, Japan Studies Association of Canada annual conference, 1994 (Edmonton: Japan Studies Association, 1994).

2 "Japan Buys a Share of Canada's Economy," *Globe and Mail*, 1 February 1967, B-5; "Bethlehem Copper" *Globe and Mail*, 28 June 1961, 19.

3 Robert Turner, "Japanese Prefer Joint Ventures in B.C.," *Globe and Mail,* 15 February 1974.
4 Dennis Stephens, "Ottawa Likes the Money to Promote Growth, but Restrictions Pinch," *Globe and Mail,* 1 February 1967, B4.
5 "Japan Buys a Share of Canada's Economy," *Globe and Mail,* 1 February 1967, B-5.
6 Ibid., "CMI Control Transferred to Three Japanese Firms," *Globe and Mail,* 5 July 1966, B-2.
7 "Mining Firm Gets Backing from Japanese," *Globe and Mail,* 5 February 1964, B-4.
8 "Japan Buys a Share of Canada's Economy," *Globe and Mail,* 1 February 1967, B-5.
9 "Japanese Firms' Loan Aids Granisle Copper," *Globe and Mail,* 29 September 1964, B-14.
10 "Japan Buys a Share of Canada's Economy," *Globe and Mail,* 1 February 1967, B-5.
11 Ken Smith, "Japanese Investment in Canada Expected to Soar," *Globe and Mail,* 16 January 1968, B-14.
12 Holroyd and Coates, *Pacific Partners,* 120-22.
13 Ibid.
14 Teck Cominco Web site, "About Us, History," http://www.teckcominco.com/Generic.aspx?PAGE=About+Us+Pages%2fHistory&portalName=tc, accessed 14 August 2007.
15 "Japan Buys a Share of Canada's Economy," *Globe and Mail,* 1 February 1967, B-5.
16 "Japanese Investment in B.C. Slows Down," *Globe and Mail,* 14 February 1974, B-1.
17 Holroyd and Coates, *Pacific Partners,* 106.
18 Ibid., 140-41. Crestbrook is no longer operating.
19 "Japanese Penetration Greatest in B.C. Pulp Mills," *Globe and Mail,* 14 February 1974, B-9; "Loans Favoured over Equities in Mining," *Globe and Mail,* 14 February 1973, B-9; "Cirtex Knitting," *Globe and Mail,* 14 June 1974, B-12.
20 "Japan Buys a Share of Canada's Economy," *Globe and Mail,* 1 February 1967, B-5.
21 Holroyd and Coates, *Pacific Partners,* 122-24.
22 Statistics Canada, *Canada's International Investment Position: Historical Statistics 1926 to 1996,* Catalogue 67-202.
23 Holroyd and Coates, *Pacific Partners,* 144.
24 Ibid., 133-35.
25 Carin Holroyd, "Japan's Economic Impact on Northern British Columbia," *Northern Review* 15/16 (Winter 1995/Summer 1996), 113-38; Larry Pratt and Ian Urquhart, *The Last Great Forest: Japanese Multinationals and Alberta's Northern Forests* (Edmonton: NeWest, 1994).
26 Pratt and Urquhart, *The Last Great Forest,* 86.
27 Ibid., 151.
28 JAMA Canada, *JAMA Canada 2004 Annual Review,* http://www.jama.ca.
29 Ibid.
30 Statistics Canada, CANSIM Table 376-0051.
31 Japan External Trade Organization [JETRO], *Nippon 2003 Business Facts and Figures* (Tokyo: JETRO, 2003), 42. The matter of Canada's comparative performance is discussed in "The Cost of Falling Behind: Canada's Economic Relationship with Japan," *Canada-Asia Commentary* 38 (February 2005), 11.
32 "The Provinces Trade with Japan," *Globe and Mail,* 27 May 1966, B-1.
33 "Ottawa Likes the Money to Promote Growth, but Restrictions Pinch," *Globe and Mail,* 1 February 1967, B-4.

11
"Smiling Diplomacy" Redux: Trudeau's Engagement with Japan, 1968-76

Greg Donaghy

Securing Quebec's place within Confederation was Pierre Trudeau's primary motivation for entering Parliament and seeking the leadership of the Liberal Party (and the prime ministership) in 1968. Despite his domestic preoccupations, the new prime minister, who had participated actively as a cabinet minister in the previous government's foreign policy discussions, had firm ideas on the need to recast Canada's place in the world. Convinced that Canada lavished too much attention on the United States and Western Europe, Trudeau wanted a foreign policy that extended the country's reach beyond the North Atlantic. "Because of past preoccupations with Atlantic and European affairs," he told Canadians during his first election campaign in the spring of 1968, "we have tended to overlook the reality that Canada is a Pacific country too."[1]

But except for the recognition of Communist China in October 1970, Trudeau was slow to show any substantial interest in the Pacific region. Relations with Japan continued to proceed smoothly and undisturbed, much as they had since the early 1950s. Widely regarded in Ottawa as tightly bound within Washington's political and diplomatic embrace, postwar Japan seemed to have little to offer Canada. When diplomats and politicians from the two countries met, as they sometimes did following the creation of a joint ministerial committee in 1961, they congratulated each other on their good relations and engaged in what Derek Burney called "smiling diplomacy."[2] The limited substance at the core of the relationship was defined almost exclusively by trade. From the mid-1950s, Japan's expanding postwar industrial economy provided an inexhaustible market for Canadian raw materials and foodstuffs. Though Ottawa routinely pressed Tokyo to liberalize its domestic market and import more processed and manufactured Canadian goods, the huge trade surpluses enjoyed by Canada provided a soothing balm for this perennial complaint.

Trudeau's first visit as prime minister to Japan, in response to an invitation to attend Expo 70 at Osaka, did little to change this stagnant but

Figure 11.1 Prime Minister Pierre Trudeau greets a Japanese monk during his visit to Osaka in 1970. *Courtesy of Sun-Media Corp.*

comfortable state of affairs. At the prime minister's end, where the visit was handled by his executive assistant, Gordon Gibson, it was decided early on that the trip would be designed to obtain the "maximum possible domestic impact," with a mix of activities chosen to enhance the prime minister's "image" in Canada.[3] Trudeau's substantive agenda was therefore left largely in the hands of T.M. Burns, the general director of the office of area relations in the Department of Industry, Trade, and Commerce (ITC), who trotted out the usual list of trade desiderata. That surprised the Japanese, who had hoped that the two prime ministers would simply exchange generalities.[4] However, neither Trudeau nor the Japanese prime minister, Eisaku Sato, needed much briefing on bilateral issues, for they spent most of their short meeting politely debating Canada's plans to recognize the People's Republic of China.[5]

Nevertheless, Japan was beginning to attract some limited attention in the Department of External Affairs. In March 1971, spurred on by the growing volume of trade between Canada and Japan, which was poised to become Canada's second most important export market, and the "staggering" number of official contacts across an array of new issue areas, senior officials asked an interdepartmental committee to review relations with Japan in order to develop a coordinated approach to Tokyo.[6] The exercise had barely started when a series of US measures introduced to strengthen the American dollar in August 1971 – the first of US President Richard Nixon's "shokku" – sparked a period of global economic uncertainty and sidelined the study.

The US action had more important consequences for Canada's relations with Japan. The measures resulted in a thorough review of Canada-US economic relations in Ottawa and a decision to reduce Canada's overdependence on the nearby American market with a policy of trade diversification. The "third option," as the strategy was usually called, targeted Europe and Japan as obvious counterweights to the United States.[7] In Tokyo, a second American shock – Kissinger's surprise visit to China – produced a similar review of relations with Washington and a decision to diversify Japan's economic and political relations.

What this meant for Canada was not immediately clear, though the initial signs seemed promising. The Canada-Japan ministerial meeting in September 1971, recalled Arthur Andrew, director-general of the Bureau of Asia-Pacific Affairs, "was unprecedented in its candour."[8] His recollection assumed even greater significance when placed against the growing number of Japanese feelers on trade, economic and scientific cooperation, and political consultation. Tokyo's apparent interest in "deepening" its relations with Canada was confirmed in early January 1973, when Japan's foreign minister, Masoyoshi Ohira, told Ross Campbell, Canada's ambassador to Tokyo, that he hoped that bilateral relations could be "broadened beyond trade and economic spheres to political and cultural matters."[9] Ottawa took the hint, and by the spring, External Affairs was laying the groundwork for a sustained, interdepartmental review of Canada-Japan relations.[10]

Despite the interest of Mitchell Sharp, the secretary of state for External Affairs, progress on this study was slow. Even after departments clarified what Sharp wanted to achieve with a questionnaire that he distributed in May, several ministries, including the Departments of Finance and ITC, refused to let officials in External Affairs handle any parts of the survey touching on matters within their jurisdiction.[11] By December, the study was so bogged down in interdepartmental squabbling that the responsible foreign service officer gave up, insisting that she no longer had time to wrestle replies from recalcitrant departments.[12]

The deadlock continued into the New Year before it was suddenly broken in February 1974 by Ivan Head, the prime minister's foreign policy advisor. To divert attention from the government's failure to conclude a trade agreement with Europe as part of its diversification strategy, Head wanted to include a reference to plans to seek a trade agreement with Japan in the forthcoming throne speech. The reaction in the Pearson Building, the new headquarters of the Department of External Affairs, was skeptical. Stephen Heeney, who took over the Japan desk in the fall of 1973, doubted that

Japan was as open to a Canadian *démarche* as it had once seemed, and observed that "there are grounds for thinking they accord a lower priority [to Canada] than would presumably be warranted in a period of energy crisis."[13] Peter Lee, the economic counsellor at the mission in Tokyo, echoed this analysis and warned Head that without strong interdepartmental agreement, any initiative might be misunderstood by the Japanese and prove counterproductive.[14]

Head dropped his plans to feature Japan in the throne speech, but remained determined, as he put it, "to move into high gear with the Japanese."[15] The need for speed reflected both the government's domestic worries as well as Head's concern that Nixon might launch his own Japan initiative, overshadowing Canadian efforts. In Head's view, the government should begin by determining – "more or less instantly" – how it wanted to shape its relations with Japan, identifying goals and dangers. For this purpose, Head proposed to send a kind of "matrix" or open-ended questionnaire to departments, giving them only three weeks to outline how they could contribute to a closer relationship with Japan. The Department of External Affairs would collate the replies, but Head would analyze them to identify precise aims and areas on which the government should focus. These would be given to the Japanese in April in preparation for a detailed discussion at the Canada-Japan ministerial committee slated for May in Tokyo.[16]

Work had hardly begun on the matrix when Campbell called Head with a scheme of his own. The ambassador argued that Canada would not attract the attention of senior Japanese policy-makers unless the prime minister himself intervened, and he urged Head to visit Tokyo.[17] Head was intrigued, but Heeney rightly worried that "moving too fast on our side could put us in the position of petitioners," and that the visit might simply irritate Japanese ministers, who would resent being bypassed.[18] Head was undeterred, and after consulting Campbell, went to Tokyo in early April for meetings with both Foreign Minister Ohira and Prime Minister Kakuei Tanaka.

Armed with a letter from Trudeau that outlined potential areas of co-operation, the prime minister's emissary began by explaining the rationale behind Ottawa's search for a more diversified foreign policy and how that gave rise to an interest in a "deep and broad relationship with Japan." Canada had a real political and economic interest in maintaining Japan's strength as a trade partner and an important source of international stability. Noting that the recent oil crisis had exposed Japan's vulnerability in foodstuffs, raw materials, and energy, Head indicated that Canada "wished to use the assets which we had – space, air, land, water, skilled labour force, etc – to reduce Japan's vulnerability while deepening our bilateral relationship." In exchange for these valuable and scarce resources, Canada sought Japan's help in its efforts to increase manufactured exports, to develop domestic industries, and to reduce regional disparities. With a little imagination, Head insisted, it should be possible to find mutually beneficial ways to meet these objectives, a search he hoped would begin in earnest at the next joint ministerial meeting.[19]

Understandably, the Japanese interpreted Head's remarks as the opening salvo in yet another "hard sell" campaign to introduce Canadian manufactured goods into Japan. Indeed, after almost a day and a half of talks, Head and Campbell realized that their "message was not really getting through," largely because they could not provide concrete proposals for bilateral co-operation.[20] At the political level, however, the results were more encouraging. Tanaka had responded to news of Head's impending visit by inviting Trudeau to meet with him in Paris after the funeral of French President Georges Pompidou. Meanwhile, in Tokyo, the Japanese prime minister impressed Head as a "politically sensitive individual [who] has understood the true thrust of Canadian policy."[21]

This was confirmed for Trudeau during his meeting with Tanaka in Paris. The Japanese politician listened to the Canadian's pitch and endorsed it fully. Tanaka's remarks "underlined the similarity between the basic aspirations and foreign policies of the two countries" and demonstrated that he understood Canada's need "for more processing of its exports."[22] This, the two leaders agreed, was the basis for expanding and strengthening bilateral relations. Head shared this view, and on his return from Tokyo, urged Trudeau forward. Discounting the skepticism he encountered among Japanese officials, he insisted that "Japan's needs are so great that the opportunity exists for Canada to derive much of the benefit of our 'third option' from this one country without suffering any of the disadvantages that have accrued in the Canada-US relationship." For good measure, Head included a short primer on responsible government: "Canadian officials will plead for more time. They are not ready to advise on policy. There are too many unknowns. To all of this you will be able to reply that a game plan has now been designed by Ministers. The goals have been chosen by Ministers. The limits within which activity can proceed are for Canada to set down. It is for the government, in short, to devise the preferred strategy, and it is for officials to advise the government of the applicable constraints."[23]

Encouraged by the Prime Minister's Office (PMO), officials from the five departments most closely involved – External Affairs, ITC, Finance, Agriculture, and Energy, Mines, and Resources (EMR) – soon worked up a detailed program for the May ministerial meeting. They recommended replacing the 1954 Canada-Japan trade agreement with a "general agreement on trade, commerce, and economic relations" that would serve as a framework for closer bilateral relations. The new treaty would provide for the exchange of Most Favoured Nation (MFN) treatment on tariffs and shipping, and include an arbitration mechanism for settling trade disputes. It would also create a consultative body to consider matters arising from the treaty and to discuss such recurring subjects as Japan's need for security of supply and Canada's desire for assured markets.[24] Officials also suggested that ministers explore the idea of a broad cultural agreement, covering academic exchanges and the arts.[25]

Although the ministerial meeting was cancelled when Trudeau's minority government fell in early May, a team of officials from Ottawa, led by Campbell, presented the Canadian program in Tokyo. The Japanese listened, but were unimpressed. They questioned the value of amending the 1954 trade agreement unless it was broadened to protect capital transactions, foreign investment, and labour mobility, provisions incompatible with the Trudeau government's economic nationalism. Moreover, they wondered about the impact of a revised agreement on Japan's growing stake in Western Canada's natural resources, since they were a provincial responsibility. The Japanese admitted that perhaps more could be done on the cultural side, but for their own parliamentary reasons, they were reluctant to consider a formal cultural agreement.[26]

This sobering encounter left officials feeling "fairly pessimistic."[27] Campbell, who had shared Head's initial, naive expectations for speedy progress with the resource-deficient Japanese, was forced to revise his own views quite drastically. In part, he concluded, Japanese hesitations resulted from a natural desire to see what changes might be brought about by the federal election. More important, he suggested that Japan's view of its place in the world was profoundly at odds with the perspective in Ottawa. Tokyo's hard line, Campbell wrote Head, "reflects a Japanese judgement that they have the money and a choice of sources of supply throughout the world that puts them in a position of not needing to make any concessions to Canada to overcome their own vulnerabilities. In the short run they might be right, but in the longer run are almost certainly wrong. To me it seems they will have to go the longer run and suffer the pinch ... before they will be ready to talk turkey."[28]

Campbell's grim assessment was confirmed as preparations got under way during the spring and summer for Tanaka's visit to Ottawa in September 1974. Japanese negotiators, who reasonably insisted that any new agreement must meet their outstanding needs too, firmly rebuffed the ambassador's repeated efforts to engage Tokyo in detailed discussions on the revised trade treaty. Poor tactics, especially the haste with which Ottawa wanted to act, further weakened the Canadian position. This urgency, complained the embassy in Tokyo, "will no doubt make the Japanese feel they are in a better position to demand stronger language on points of interest to them."[29]

Progress on other, less important elements of the visit was slightly more promising. Japan agreed in principle to seek a broad cultural treaty, but declined to start negotiations until directed to do so by Tanaka and Trudeau. Tokyo was prepared to extend its existing program for funding Japanese studies in Europe and the United States to Canada with a grant of a million dollars over five years. A few weeks later, the Canadians learned that the money came with a catch: given Japan's severe foreign exchange difficulties, Tanaka insisted on a matching grant for the promotion of Canadian Studies in Japan, and East Asian studies in Canada. As this was the only concrete accomplishment likely to result from Tanaka's visit, Ottawa could hardly turn it down without signalling an end to its Japan initiative. Cabinet provided the funds.[30]

Nevertheless, Head remained optimistic. With the Japanese premier facing charges of corruption, he argued that Tanaka's "own political vulnerability may make him highly susceptible to our suggestions." Moreover, Head was convinced that Trudeau could persuade Tanaka that "Canada possesses assets needed by Japan, and *not available from any other country* (i.e., that Canada is qualitatively distinct from Brazil or Indonesia or Australia. We are unique.) In short, that we are necessary to Japan's continued prosperity and viability."[31]

The Department of External Affairs was much more restrained. An examination of the entire Japan initiative, which was quietly slipped into the prime minister's briefing notes, revealed obstacle after obstacle. It began bluntly: "Established Canadian trade patterns, the early stage of many of our own domestic economic policies and the general absence of a dirigiste approach to commercial relations in Canada will likely preclude an immediate significant increase in the rate at which we find a new 'opening to Japan.'"[32] The department insisted that Japan paid very little attention to Canada, which it regarded "primarily as an American sphere of influence and resource hinterland." This conclusion had recently been confirmed in spades when Tanaka insisted on including a side trip to Washington as part of his Ottawa visit.[33] Most important, as Campbell's discussions in the spring and summer demonstrated, Japan simply did not need Canada. "They are working to play a world role," the briefing note observed, "and although there is room in their scheme for countries like Canada, we must acknowledge that Canada is going to be a much lower priority than it might have been in Japan's days of economic weakness." While Tanaka's visit hinted at a "glimmering of high-level" interest among some Japanese in deepening their relationship with Canada, engaging Tokyo was clearly going to be a difficult and lengthy exercise.

Tanaka's visit to Ottawa did little to dispel this gloomy prediction. Nor did it resolve the differences in perspective that divided politicians from their officials on both sides of the Pacific. Trudeau apparently got on well with the Japanese prime minister, whom Head described as "a dynamic little man ... a political scrapper of some skill and force."[34] Observers reported that the visiting premier "showed imagination and a readiness to achieve future harmony in our expanding relationship" during his talks with Trudeau.

Figure 11.2 Prime Ministers Pierre Trudeau and Kakuei Tanaka during the latter's visit to Ottawa in September 1974. This visit signalled the start of a renewed effort to "deepen and broaden" relations. *Courtesy of Department of Foreign Affairs and International Trade.*

The high-level talks, which seemed to herald closer relations, were "constructive and a success."[35] Beyond the pomp and ceremony, however, the gulf dividing the two nations remained. In a meeting with their Canadian counterparts, the senior officials accompanying Tanaka were much more skeptical. These talks "achieved little," a view indiscreet Japanese officials spread widely in Tokyo and Ottawa.

For Campbell, the ambiguous results of the Tanaka visit called for a redoubling of the Canadian effort, which paled in comparison with the time and energy being poured into the search for a renewed link with Europe. "I was particularly struck," the ambassador noted in late November, "by the contrast between, on the one hand, the apparent warmth, if not zeal, with which we offered to cooperate with France in a variety of areas ... and on the other hand, the indifference we have shown to repeated Japanese expressions of interest in the same area ... We have in fact allowed a specific Japanese offer of financial and technical cooperation in the tar sands development to go unanswered while soliciting such bilateral cooperation from the French."[36]

Heeney, however, was less certain how to proceed, since Tokyo had effectively rejected Canada's initial offering of a revised trade agreement. He turned to the Interdepartmental Committee on Commercial Policy (ICCP) for help. The brainchild of Michel Dupuy, an assistant under-secretary with heavy responsibilities for international economic policy, the ICCP had been set up in 1972 to coordinate Canadian trade policy, despite some unhappy grumbling from ITC about External Affairs "taking over other people's work."[37] Under Dupuy, the committee had proven "indispensable" in exerting the department's influence over commercial policy. Worried that the ICCP had come to focus too much on Europe, Dupuy welcomed suggestions that it broaden its focus to include Japan.[38]

The ICCP met in early January 1975 and promptly asked a working group headed by Gerry Shannon, director of the Commercial Policy Division, to propose ideas for the next step. Shannon's draft report to the ICCP, which reflected the list of obstacles prepared at the time of Tanaka's visit, painted a bleak picture of the prospects for progress. Shannon was especially uncertain how to handle negotiations over the revisions to the 1954 trade agreement. Simply put, he wrote, "the problems are all on our side; in all except a few very circumscribed areas, we are demandeurs."[39] The situation was made worse by the lack of guidance the department received from the new secretary of state for External Affairs, Allan MacEachen. A cautious politician, with a tendency to absent himself from files in which the prime minister was interested, MacEachen left his officials unsure of how far they could challenge established policies and other departments in their search for new ideas.[40]

ITC did not share Shannon's diffidence. It was confident that Canada had the necessary leverage to bring Japan to the table on its terms and insisted that "in the context of Japanese concerns over security of supply and investment, [the] advantage is inherent in Canada's relatively stable economic environment, its creditable supply performance, and its larger resource base and already substantial resource exports to Japan." The economic department argued that the government should ignore the revised trade agreement and press the Japanese to begin a joint examination of specific sectors of the industrial economy in search of practical areas for cooperation.[41]

Shannon and his colleagues worried that the ITC proposal did not specifically identify what sectors Canada would pursue and what precisely this approach would mean for industrial cooperation with Japan. They also suspected that ITC was simply advancing another campaign to promote Canadian exports to Japan, or as Dupuy put it, "to put old problems into new wrapping."[42] Nonetheless, the sectorial plan seemed to represent a step forward. It at least had the virtue of avoiding an intractable confrontation

Figure 11.3 Duncan Macpherson's image captures the ambiguities and difficulties involved in wooing Japan, which remained more interested in relations with Washington. *Toronto Star*, 24 September 1974. Copyright Duncan Macpherson. *Reprinted with permission by Torstar Syndication Services.*

with Tokyo over which general principles to include in a revised trade agreement. In late March, the ICCP agreed that ITC's sectorial plan should be presented to the Japanese at the ministerial meeting in June.[43]

Even though a parliamentary crisis meant that Foreign Minister Kiichi Miyazawa appeared only momentarily, and that most of his colleagues missed the second day of meetings, the June encounter in Tokyo exceeded Ottawa's expectations. The Canadian delegation, led by MacEachen, surprised its Asian hosts by its extensive knowledge of Korean affairs and persuaded Tokyo to co-sponsor a UN resolution on South Korea. Ottawa believed that the Korean discussion and talks on Canada's recent decision to upgrade its safeguards on nuclear exports gave a "significant impetus to the process of political consultation."[44] Better yet, Japanese ministers agreed to proceed with a joint examination of the two economies with a view to identifying industrial sectors where there might be a basis for bilateral cooperation. A delighted

Campbell called the breakthrough "a minor miracle."[45] Dupuy too was pleased, but more restrained. After all, Miyazawa accepted the Canadian proposals by observing wryly that "there may be something in it and we have nothing to lose."[46]

Trudeau, however, was less impressed with the mission's results, and he told colleagues that he hoped "strong political will could be imparted to the follow-up."[47] He was soon disappointed. The Bureau of Asia-Pacific Affairs tried to convince colleagues to increase their contacts with Japanese diplomats to encourage "the habit of consultation" but were rebuffed. Rejecting this plea, Yvon Beaulne, director-general of Africa and the Middle East Bureau complained that "Japanese diplomats are reputed to be incorrigible gossipers and quite unable to keep any confidential information to themselves."[48]

On the economic front as well, progress was difficult. A meeting of Canadian and Japanese officials in November 1975 to start the joint examination yielded little. In a report to the provinces, MacEachen claimed to be "encouraged," citing Tokyo's agreement to send three mixed industry/government teams to explore opportunities in Canada's oil sands, uranium mines, and coal pits. But there was bad news too. Japanese officials remained much more interested in Canadian primary resources and repeatedly reverted to urging Canadian manufacturers to work harder to access Japan's markets. Still more disturbing, Tokyo indicated that its long-term investment program would focus less on Canada and more on the undeveloped third world, where there were greater resources and cheaper labour.[49]

This was not the kind of report the prime minister wanted to hear. When MacEachen recommended a visit to Japan during the coming year, an unenthusiastic Trudeau replied that he would go only if the Japanese understood how unhappy he was with the state of relations and the visit "mark[ed] a substantial degree of progress."[50] The prime minister's letter, with its casual dismissal of the efforts of the previous year, irked the Department of External Affairs.[51] It was disconcerting moreover to see that Trudeau's expectations remained so stubbornly high, prompting MacEachen to warn the prime minister against expecting a speedy breakthrough in 1976. The effort to mesh Canadian domestic economic objectives with Japanese needs and desires, he noted, had barely begun and was made daily more difficult by the deteriorating international economic situation.[52]

But Trudeau's letter also provided External Affairs with the means to overcome the objections of those departments, particularly ITC and EMR, whose lack of enthusiasm threatened to halt planning for the prime minister's visit. Officials in the Bureau of Asian and Pacific Affairs were happy enough with plans for the visit's political and cultural elements but fretted about the absence of a significant economic dimension. Largely responsible for the success or failure of the prime minister's trip, they justifiably resented the continued failure of the major economic departments to identify sectors for cooperation. Thus, they proposed their own economic objectives. There were two. First, they thought Trudeau's visit might be used to achieve a "symbolic" breakthrough in the manufacturing sector by concluding a cooperative arrangement in a field where Canadian products were particularly competitive. Specifically, they hoped Japan might be interested in either de Havilland's short take-off and landing (STOL) aircraft or in Atomic Energy of Canada Limited's popular CANDU nuclear reactor.[53]

Second, External Affairs suggested that Ottawa seek an economic cooperation agreement similar to the one just signed with Europe. This would "serve as an umbrella for mutual efforts to develop economic cooperation projects" and commit both governments to facilitating joint economic projects. Moreover, the agreement would provide a way for the federal government "to insert itself in the management of our economic relationship with Japan," possibly giving Ottawa some leverage to intervene in Tokyo's close relationship with resource-producing provinces in Western Canada. MacEachen concurred, and after some prodding, so too did the economic ministers, who agreed that securing a Japanese market for CANDU and signing a bilateral economic cooperation agreement should form the centrepiece of the prime minister's visit to Tokyo.[54] In late May, the prime minister finally pronounced himself pleased with MacEachen's efforts.[55]

Because there was insufficient time to secure a firm indication of Japanese interest in either the CANDU reactor or the STOL project before Trudeau's visit, final preparations focused on negotiating an agreement for economic cooperation. Canadian representatives found the going tough from the start, a reflection of the simple fact that, as the Japanese ambassador to Ottawa later put it, "Japan was not the demandeur." Divisions among the Canadian negotiators complicated their work. The embassy in Tokyo, where Bruce Rankin had replaced Campbell in early 1976, was not keen on the cooperation agreement, which it thought downplayed bilateral political relations. It favoured a broad and general communiqué, an idea it shared with Japan's foreign ministry. Thus, when Peter Towe, who took over the file from Dupuy in the spring of 1976, raised the agreement with his Japanese counterpart, he was surprised to discover that Japan was thinking in terms of the kind of communiqué favoured by Rankin. After firmly underlining the discrepancy in the Canadian position, Bunroku Yoshino, Japan's deputy minister of foreign affairs, agreed that something "general in nature and involving no substantive obligations" might be concluded in time for Trudeau's visit.[56]

An inoffensive and non-binding draft of the proposed "Economic Cooperation Framework Agreement" was quickly prepared in Ottawa and handed to Japanese negotiators, who indicated in an early meeting with embassy staff that Japan was ready to sign the agreement since it was "harmless." That being so, the Japanese team continued, Tokyo would prefer that it not be called an "agreement," a term which implied new rights and obligations.[57] As this change would make the accord less significant than the agreement signed with Europe, Ottawa rejected the Japanese position and instructed Rankin to appeal to the foreign minister. When Miyazawa proved no less determined that the title be altered, Towe invited Yoshino to Ottawa to resolve the impasse.[58] Yoshino too was tough and unyielding, and he forced Towe to retreat. As Tokyo wished, the bilateral arrangement would be called a "Framework for Economic Cooperation."[59]

Tokyo's steadfast refusal to accept Canada's terminology was discouraging. Louis Rogers, director-general of the Asia-Pacific Bureau, concluded after the Yoshino visit that Trudeau's trip "hardly seemed worthwhile."[60] There were other disturbing developments in Tokyo, where the Japanese prime minister, Takeo Miki, was in deep political trouble. Worried that Canadians might wonder why their prime minister could only get in to see Japanese premiers who were on the verge of being deposed, Rogers suggested postponing the trip.[61] Trudeau agreed, but rather than take the initiative, he left the final decision to Miki, who urged the Canadian to come and promised to "do his best to make the visit a most productive one."[62]

Miki did, and by the time Trudeau was done, the two men could point to a small but impressive pile of accomplishments: a cultural agreement initialled, the Canadian Studies program in Japan inaugurated with a book presentation, and the Framework for Economic Co-operation signed. During the visit, Trudeau enjoyed two lengthy meetings with the Japanese prime minister and similar sessions with four senior Japanese ministers. The talks were "frank and thorough," and ranged across the multilateral and the bilateral spectrum, with the two prime ministers demonstrating an encouraging "symmetry in perceptions" on the need to further strengthen the relationship. Ambassador Rankin described Miki's opening remarks as "the most understanding and comprehensive canvas of the bilateral relationship ever heard from a Japanese prime minister."[63] Rogers and Derek Burney, the tough-minded realist in charge of the Pacific Division, even mustered up sufficient enthusiasm to observe that after "two years of effort on the broadening and deepening exercise, we do so seem to have produced an echo."[64]

Trudeau's framework, however, provided only a context for closer economic cooperation and depended on the private sector in both countries to make it work. And on both sides of the Pacific, it was impossible to motivate the business community. Japan's cultural and linguistic barriers intimidated many Canadian firms, who preferred to do business with their more familiar neighbours to the south. Even de Havilland, to the astonishment

Table 11.1

Direction of Canadian trade in goods, 1972-84 (Cdn$ millions)

Year	US	UK	Japan	Other EEC	ROW	Total
Exports						
1972	13,973	1,385	965	1,178	2,649	20,151
1974	21,399	1,129	2,231	2,175	4,708	32,442
1976	25,901	1,898	2,399	2,712	5,565	38,475
1978	37,175	2,007	3,062	2,912	7,686	52,842
1980	48,174	3,245	4,374	6,338	14,028	76,159
1982	58,074	2,695	4,788	4,777	14,226	84,560
1984	85,026	2,493	5,971	4,510	14,219	112,219
Imports						
1972	12,878	949	1,071	1,215	2,556	18,669
1974	21,387	1,126	1,430	1,920	5,859	31,722
1976	25,801	1,150	1,524	1,991	7,028	37,494
1978	35,246	1,600	2,268	3,036	7,787	49,937
1980	48,614	1,974	2,796	3,574	12,316	69,274
1982	47,072	1,939	3,552	3,752	10,424	66,739
1984	65,890	2,293	5,476	5,843	11,991	91,493

Note: ROW denotes Rest of World.
Sources: Figures for 1972-78 are from Statistics Canada, *Canada Year Book, 1980-81* (Ottawa: Minister of Supply and Services, 1981), 733; those for 1980 are from Statistics Canada, *Canada Year Book, 1985* (Ottawa: Minister of Supply and Services, 1985), 691; and those for 1982-84 are from *Canada Year Book, 1988* (Ottawa: Minister of Supply and Services, 1987), 21-28.

of officials in External Affairs, reportedly told its majority shareholder – the federal government – that it was uninterested in the Japanese market. Although Japan took in just over 9 percent of Canada's exports in 1980, by the time Trudeau left office in 1984, its share of Canadian goods had shrunk to 6.7 percent, almost exactly where it had been in 1972. Similarly, imports from Japan remained relatively static as a percentage of overall imports (see Table 11.1).

Just as important, Trudeau's Japan initiative faltered as the prime minister turned away from foreign policy in the mid-1970s to deal with the separatist threat in Quebec. Without the continued application of the high level of political pressure that made the initiative possible in the first place, the sustained follow-through required at the official level was not forthcoming. In its stead, during the second half of the Trudeau mandate, Canada-Japan relations were marked by a sense of drift, a return to the "smiling diplomacy" of the 1960s, but a diplomacy increasingly interrupted by crises over uranium, fisheries, and cars.

Notes

The views in this article are the author's alone and do not represent the official position of the Government of Canada or of Foreign Affairs and International Trade Canada.

1 Pierre Trudeau, "Canada and the World," 29 May 1968, Canada, Department of External Affairs, Statements and Speeches, No. 68/17.

2 Cited in Klaus Pringsheim, *Neighbours across the Pacific: Canadian-Japanese Relations, 1870-1982* (Oakville, ON: Mosaic Press, 1983), 167.

3 Gordon Gibson, Executive Assistant to the Prime Minister to Allan McGill, Senior Assistant to the Secretary of State for External Affairs (hereafter SSEA), 17 December 1969, and Richard Gorham, Department of External Affairs Press Office, to Ivan Head, 16 March 1970, Department of External Affairs Records (hereafter DEAR), vol. 9244, file 20-Cda-9-Trudeau-Pac, Library and Archives of Canada (hereafter LAC).

4 Burns to Ralph Collins, Assistant Under-Secretary of State for External Affairs (hereafter AUSSEA), 27 January 1970, and Tokyo to Ottawa, telegram 543, 4 May 1970, DEAR, vol. 9244, file 20-Cda-9-Trudeau-Pac, LAC.

5 Tokyo to Ottawa, telegram 578, 8 May 1970, DEAR, vol. 8755, file 20-1-2-JPN, LAC.

6 John Harrington, Director of Pacific Division, to A.E. Ritchie, Under-Secretary of State for External Affairs (hereafter USSEA), 26 July 1971, DEAR, vol. 8755, file 20-1-2-JPN, LAC. New issue areas included technological and scientific cooperation, shipping, fisheries, the law of the sea, and the environment.

7 J.L. Granatstein and Robert Bothwell, *Pirouette: Pierre Trudeau and Canadian Foreign Policy* (Toronto: University of Toronto Press, 1990), 60-68.

8 Arthur Andrew, Director-General of Asia-Pacific Affairs, to Ritchie, 14 April 1972, DEAR, vol. 8755, file 20-1-2-JPN, LAC.

9 Tokyo to Ottawa, telegram 69, 11 January 1973, DEAR, vol. 8755, file 20-1-2-JPN, LAC.

10 Thomas Wainman-Wood, Director of Pacific Division, to Geoffrey Pearson, Director of the Policy Analysis Group, 26 January 1973, and following correspondence on file DEAR, vol. 8755, file 20-1-2-JPN, LAC.

11 Andrew to Departments, 16 July 1973; Andrew to Departments, 8 August 1973; and Ian Ferguson, Pacific Division, to Wainman-Wood, 31 August 1973, DEAR, vol. 8755, file 20-1-2-JPN, LAC.

12 Dorothy Armstrong, Pacific Division, to Pearson, 11 December 1973, DEAR, vol. 8755, file 20-1-2-JPN, LAC.

13 Stephen Heeney, Deputy Director of Pacific Division, to Andrew, AUSSEA, 21 January 1974, DEAR, vol. 8755, file 20-1-2-JPN, LAC.

14 Peter Lee, Economic Counsellor in Tokyo, Memorandum on the Throne Speech, 19 February 1974, DEAR, vol. 8755, file 20-1-2-JPN, LAC.

15 Heeney to file (via Pam McDougall, Director-General of the Bureau of Economic and Scientific Affairs), 25 February 1974, DEAR, vol. 8755, file 20-1-2-JPN, LAC.

16 Ritchie to Mitchell Sharp, Secretary of State for External Affairs (hereafter SSEA), 1 March 1974, and Head to O.G. Stoner, Deputy Minister of Transport, 1 March 1974, DEAR, vol. 8755, file 20-1-1-JPN, LAC.

17 Ivan Head and Pierre Trudeau, *The Canadian Way: Shaping Canada's Foreign Policy, 1968-1984* (Toronto: McClelland and Stewart, 1995), 276.

18 Heeney to Ritchie, 11 March 1974, DEAR, vol. 8755, file 20-1-2-JPN, LAC.

19 Ottawa to Tokyo, telegram GPO-312, 1 April 1974, Tokyo to Ottawa, telegram 899, 5 April 1974, and Tokyo to Paris, telegram 909, 5 April 1974, DEAR, vol. 8755, file 20-2-1-JPN, LAC.

20 Tokyo to Paris, telegram 909, 5 April 1974, DEAR, vol. 8755, file 20-2-1-JPN, LAC.

21 Ottawa to Tokyo, telegram GPO-312, 1 April 1974, DEAR, vol. 8755, file 20-1-2-JPN, LAC.

22 Paris to Ottawa, telegram 1286, 8 April 1974, DEAR, vol. 9239, file 20-JPN-9-Tanaka, LAC.

23 Head, Memorandum for the Prime Minister, 10 April 1974, DEAR, vol. 8755, file 20-1-2-JPN, LAC.

24 Ritchie to Sharp, 30 April 1974, and attached Memorandum to Cabinet, 22 April 1974, and Ottawa to Tokyo, telegram GPO-430, 3 May 1974, DEAR, vol. 8819, file 20-1-2-JPN-1, LAC.

25 Ibid.

26 Tokyo to Ottawa, telegram 1484, 15 May 1974, DEAR, vol. 8819, file 20-1-2-JPN-1, LAC.
27 Ross Campbell, Ambassador in Tokyo, to Andrew, 23 May 1974, DEAR, vol. 8819, file 20-1-2-JPN-1, LAC.
28 Campbell to Head, 23 May 1974, DEAR, vol. 8819, file 20-1-2-JPN-1, LAC.
29 Tokyo to Ottawa, telegram 2387, 14 August 1974. See also Ottawa to Tokyo, telegram ECL-1321, 18 June 1974, and Tokyo to Ottawa, telegram 2409, 15 August 1974, DEAR, vol. 15675, file 37-3-1-JPN, LAC.
30 Ritchie to Sharp, 10 September 1974, and attached Memorandum to the Cabinet, 11 September 1974, DEAR, vol. 13178, file 56-23-JPN-3, LAC.
31 Head, Memorandum for the Prime Minister, 13 September 1974, DEAR, vol. 9239, file 20-JPN-9-Tanaka, LAC. Emphasis in original.
32 "Canada/Japan Relations: A Context for the Tanaka Visit," 23-26 September 1974, DEAR, vol. 9239, file 20-JPN-9-Tanaka, LAC.
33 Sharp, Memorandum for the Prime Minister, 12 July 1974, DEAR, vol. 9239, file 20-JPN-9-Tanaka, LAC.
34 Head, Memorandum for the Prime Minister, 13 September 1974, DEAR, vol. 9239, file 20-JPN-9-Tanaka, LAC. See also Head and Trudeau, *The Canadian Way*, 277.
35 Campbell to Louis Rogers, Director-General of Asia-Pacific Affairs, 23 January 1975, DEAR, vol. 8819, file 20-1-2-JPN-1, LAC.
36 Tokyo to Ottawa, telegram 3268, 6 November 1974, DEAR, vol. 8756, file 20-1-2-JPN, LAC.
37 Lee to Michel Dupuy, AUSSEA, 8 March 1972, DEAR, vol. 13840, file 37-1-1-ICCP, LAC.
38 On the ICCP's success, see E.P. Black, Director-General of Europe, to McDougall, 13 May 1974. On the addition of Japan to its agenda, see Gerry Shannon, Director of Commercial Policy Division, to Dupuy, 13 January 1975, DEAR, vol. 13840, file 37-1-1-ICCP, LAC.
39 Shannon, "External Draft Report to the ICCP, 12 February 1975," DEAR, vol. 13840, file 37-1-1-ICCP, LAC.
40 Heeney to H.B. Robinson, USSEA (via McDougall and Andrew), 4 February 1975, Andrew, Memorandum for the Minister, 14 February 1975, and Heeney to the office of the USSEA, 25 March 1975, DEAR, vol. 8756, file 20-1-2-JPN, LAC.
41 Maldwyn Thomas to Shannon, 27 February 1975, and the attached "Canada/Japan Economic Cooperation," 26 February 1975, DEAR, vol. 13840, file 37-1-1-ICCP, LAC.
42 Heeney, Memorandum for file, 22 May 1975, and Robinson to A.J. MacEachen, SSEA, 29 May 1975, DEAR, vol. 8819, file 20-1-2-JPN-1, LAC.
43 Heeney to file, 24 March 1975, DEAR, vol. 8756, file 20-1-2-JPN, LAC.
44 Dupuy, "Canada/Japan Ministerial Committee Meeting," 23-24 June 1975, DEAR, vol. 8819, file 20-1-2-JPN-1, LAC.
45 Tokyo to Ottawa, telegram 2157, 4 June 1975, DEAR, vol. 8819, file 20-1-2-JPN-1, LAC.
46 Dupuy, "Canada/Japan," DEAR, vol. 8819, file 20-1-2-JPN-1, LAC.
47 James Midwinter to Robinson, 23 June 1975, DEAR, vol. 8819, file 20-1-2-JPN-1, LAC.
48 USSEA to All Canadian Missions, Letter GPO-(M)-596, 5 September 1975, Rogers to Directors-General, 10 September 1975, and Yvon Beaulne to Rogers, 16 September 1975, DEAR, vol. 8756, file 20-1-2-JPN, LAC.
49 MacEachen to Provincial Premiers, 14 January 1976, DEAR, vol. 13840, file 37-1-1-ICCP, LAC.
50 MacEachen, Memorandum for the Prime Minister, 13 November 1975, and Trudeau to MacEachen, 19 December 1975, DEAR, vol. 9242, file 20-Cda-9-Trudeau-Japan, LAC.
51 Tokyo to Ottawa, telegram 137, 13 January 1976, DEAR, vol. 9242, file 20-Cda-9-Trudeau-Japan, LAC.
52 MacEachen to Trudeau, 9 January 1976, DEAR, vol. 9242, file 20-Cda-9-Trudeau-Japan, LAC.
53 Robinson to MacEachen, 31 March 1976, DEAR, vol. 9242. file 20-Cda-9-Trudeau-Japan, LAC.
54 MacEachen to Donald Jamieson, 6 April 1976 (with similar letters to Gillespie and Donald Macdonald), MacEachen, Note for Mr. Jamieson, 14 April 1976, and replies, DEAR, vol. 9242, file 20-Cda-9-Trudeau-Japan, LAC.

55 Trudeau to MacEachen, 25 June 1976, DEAR, vol. 9242. file 20-Cda-9-Trudeau-Japan, LAC.
56 Peter Towe, "Memorandum for GPO," 30 June 1976, DEAR, vol. 9242, file 20-Cda-9-Trudeau-Japan, LAC.
57 Tokyo to Ottawa, telegram 428, 22 July 1976, DEAR, vol. 9242, file 20-Cda-9-Trudeau-Japan, LAC.
58 Tokyo to Ottawa, telegram 531, 28 July 1976, DEAR, vol. 9242, file 20-Cda-9-Trudeau-Japan, LAC.
59 USSEA to the Canadian Embassy in Tokyo, Numbered Letter GPO-880, 30 September 1976, and enclosed Record of Conversation, DEAR, vol. 14072, file 35-1-1, LAC.
60 D.H. Burney, Director of Pacific Division, Memorandum for file, 9 November 1976, DEAR, vol. 9242, 20-Cda-9-Trudeau-Japan, LAC.
61 MacEachen, Memorandum for the Prime Minister, 13 September 1976, DEAR, vol. 9242, file 20-Cda-9-Trudeau-Japan, LAC.
62 Ottawa to Tokyo, telegram GPO-900, 27 September 1976, and Ottawa to Tokyo, telegram GPO-908, 28 September 1976, DEAR, vol. 9242, file 20-Cda-9-Trudeau-Japan, LAC.
63 Tokyo to Ottawa, telegram PMDEL 007, 24 October 1976, DEAR, vol. 9242, file 20-Cda-9-Trudeau-Japan, LAC.
64 Summary Report of the Prime Minister's Visit to Japan, 28 October 1976, DEAR, vol. 9242, file 20-Cda-9-Trudeau-Japan, LAC.

12
North Pacific Neighbours in a New World: Canada-Japan Relations, 1984-2006

John Kirton

Canadian policy towards Japan under the leadership of Prime Ministers Brian Mulroney and Jean Chrétien has inspired much the same scholarly debate that unfolded over previous periods in the Canada-Japan relationship and in Canadian foreign policy as a whole.[1] Has Canada's involvement with and influence over Japan been declining, holding steady, or ascending? Have Canada's own interests and values, those of the multilateral order, or those of a predominant United States driven Canada's approach?

The first school, the declinists, asserts that Canada, as a fading power in the world, had limited involvement in and influence over a Japan that still deferred to its dominant US ally in its own dangerous region and around the world.[2] Canada's longstanding limits were reinforced from 1984 to 1993 by the continuing cold war and great power rivalries in Asia among Japan, China, Russia, and India. During the Chrétien decade, Canada's relations with Japan were similarly constrained by the crash of Japan's bubble economy, China's soaring economic strength, and Canada's preoccupation with its new free trade partners, the United States and Mexico.[3] Further fuelling Canada's decline in Japan were the US's cold war victory and economic resurgence under President Bill Clinton, Canada's preoccupation with its national unity crisis and fiscal deficits, and the fascination of Chrétien's Liberal Party with a booming China as Canada's key Asia-Pacific partner. As a result, even as the twenty-first century began, Canada was very slow to mount the major foreign policy overhaul required to deal with Japan, which, by some economic indicators, ranks as the world's number two power and is certainly a regional leader.[4]

A second school, featuring liberal internationalist continuity, sees Canada's relations with Japan primarily through the prism of multilateral institutions and norms. It focuses on the emergence of Japan as the second largest financial contributor to the United Nations, a growing partner of Canada in peacekeeping and official development assistance (ODA), and a soulmate in promoting diplomatic solutions to global security concerns.[5] Beneath this broad multilateral level, however, lies unfulfilled a more direct potential partnership between Canada and Japan, who share similar worldviews and basic broad values, but seldom cooperate to give them international life.[6] Even in the face of Japan's economic, political, and social reforms in the 1990s, these analysts argue, Canada's response was too slow and small.[7]

A third school highlights Canada's growing partnership with Japan in an emerging North Pacific triangle, where the American, Japanese, and Canadian poles and bilateral relationships increasingly move towards having more equal weight. In its mainstream variant, this school sees a reviving Japan becoming a twenty-first century partner for Canada. From this perspective, Japan's portfolio and direct investments in Canada are likely to reach new highs, accompanied by a significant advance in economic, political, and security ties between the two countries. Thus, as one scholar cautions, "even though it has become fashionable to write Japan off as a fading power, Canadian business leaders and policy-makers would be ill advised to follow suit."[8] Policy-makers responsible for managing the bilateral relationship share this view of a rapidly increasing partnership in the past and potential for the future, even if it is still largely invisible to those outside.[9]

In its most ambitious expression, this third school suggests that the Canada-Japan side of the triangle was beginning to move beyond a normal state-to-state relationship towards the sort of close, broad, multilayered, and significant relationships Canada and the United States and the United States and Japan have long had. It argues that this relationship is acquiring the same intimacy and intensity that has long prevailed between Canada and the United States and is broadening from economics to peace and security issues, and extending to joint leadership in the global order. This Canada-Japan partnership in the Mulroney and Chrétien years and beyond was driven by the growing vulnerability of the once dominant US to energy, financial, and terrorist threats in an era of intensifying globalization, and by the relatively lower vulnerability that both Canada and Japan enjoyed.[10]

This chapter follows the third school as it explains how stronger and wider bilateral relations came from the revival of trade, investment, and technological cooperation, as demonstrated by Chrétien's choice of Japan as the first non-developing country to receive a visit from his high-profile Team Canada trade mission. Canada's burgeoning investment in a more open Japan and the mutual interest in freer trade arrangements also encouraged closer relations. On the politico-military front, the Canada-Japan partnership, taking place largely within both the plurilateral (limited membership) framework and the wider multilateral framework, expanded into peacekeeping, arms control, human security, regional security, postwar reconstruction, and fighting together as military allies in the war against terrorism. Initiatives and successes in global leadership came as the two worked together to combat financial crises, strengthen global environmental protection, combat terrorism and weapons proliferation, and bring the democratic revolution to the former Soviet Union, the Balkans, Asia, Africa, and the Middle East.

Several systemic forces propelled this enriched, extended global partnership after 9/11. The first was Japan's growing need for support from partners like Canada because of its continuing cold war with communist China and North Korea, as well as its great power rivalries with China, Russia, and India. The second was the personal friendships their respective leaders developed during summit diplomacy, especially within the Asia Pacific Economic Co-operation (APEC) forum, the Association of South East Asian Nations (ASEAN), the G7 (or, after Russia joined in 1997, the G8), and the Group of Twenty (G20). Cooperation arose here on the shared priorities of environmental protection, human security, conflict prevention, counterterrorism, and financial stability. The third force was the emergence in both Canada and Japan of leaders who recognized the need to promote the "soft power" values they shared, as the United States under Republican President George W. Bush adopted a foreign policy marked by a more unilateral approach focused on national security.[11]

To explore this post-1984 trend towards global partnership between Canada and Japan, this chapter first examines the overall political importance each country has accorded the other in its national and foreign policy priorities, both in high-level declarations and in the material distribution of resources that often reveal what a country's real priorities are. Second, it explores the economic dimension of the relationship, especially bilateral trade, investment, and technology ties. Third, it considers the broader security and more intense domestic policy relationship, as well as the two countries' shared leadership in global governance through the United Nations (UN), G7/8, and APEC. And fourth, it assesses the relative strength of the systemic, state, and societal level forces that have thrust the two countries towards closer partnership on a global scale. The chapter concludes by suggesting that these systemic drivers continue to strengthen this global partnership.

The Strengthening Priority Partnership

From 1984 to 2004, in setting their national and foreign policy priorities, neither Canada nor Japan identified the other as a leading concern on a narrow bilateral plane. However, as each moved beyond bilateralism to exercise a stronger, more expansive global voice, each discovered that the other was of growing importance to its national objectives and the improved world order it sought to build. Yet, Canada rarely devoted to Japan alone the attention Japan deserved on the basis of her strength. Nevertheless, Canadian policy increasingly emphasized the plurilateral institutions, such as the G7/8 and APEC, and the values, such as conflict prevention and human security, that she shared with Japan.

While Japan had been a temporary target of economic opportunity for Prime Minister Pierre Trudeau in the 1970s, it had not been a priority in its own right under Mulroney. Under Chrétien, who focused on the G7/8, Japan disappeared as a bilateral partner but became relevant as a full-strength, permanent plurilateral partner on the global issues that Canadians cared most about. From 1984 to 2004, as measured by mentions in Speeches from the Throne, Japan stood as Canada's primary Asian partner, with references to it outranking those to China by a margin of seven to two.[12]

During the Mulroney years, Canada's formal foreign policy statements gave Japan an increasing, ever more global place as an important priority. While the Mulroney government's initial set of objectives in 1985 focused on Canada's relationship with the United States, its December 1986 white paper signalled a broader international vision. Once the Canada-US Free Trade Agreement (CUFTA) was safely secured, the Mulroney government embarked on a "going global" thrust that put Japan in the first rank of its foreign policy priorities.[13]

Chrétien's first formal foreign policy statement of 7 February 1995 went even further, placing Asia-Pacific at the centre of Canadian foreign policy for the first time.[14] In the opening text, he underlined Asia's growing significance to Canada: "Canada's geographic location gives it an important advantage as new poles of political and economic power emerge in the Pacific and Latin America." He affirmed that "Canada's cultural heritage gives it privileged access to the homelands of Canadians drawn from every part of the world who make up its multicultural personality" – this implicitly acknowledged that Canadians of Chinese origin had become the third-largest component of Canada's multicultural society and perpetuated the traditional tilt of Liberal governments towards China. However, Japan was brought back to the centre of Canadian policy when Chrétien stated, "Canada can further its global interests better than any other country through its active membership in key international groupings, for example, hosting the G7 Summit this year and the APEC Summit in 1997." While China joined both Canada and Japan in APEC, it was not a member of the democratic G7.

Under Mulroney, Japan assumed a prominent place in the distribution of Canada's diplomatic posts and personnel abroad.[15] In 1989, the fourth largest number of Canadian foreign officers serving abroad (after the US, the UN, and Great Britain) was in Japan. In 2003, Canada had twice as many diplomats in China as in Japan.[16]

Institution building between Canada and Japan showed a similar strengthening and broadening partnership. The effort to create bilateral institutions began in 1961 with the creation of the Canada-Japan Ministerial Committee, and continued in 1970s, when the annual Canada-Japan Consultations on United Nations Questions and a bilateral Joint Economic Committee were set up. This pace accelerated sharply under Mulroney, who created three new bodies covering the full array of policy fields: the 1990 Canada-Japan Business Committee; the strategic 1991 Japan-Canada Forum 2000; and the action-oriented 1991 Committee to Follow-Up the Recommendations of the Forum. Moreover, from 1980 to 1988, while the United States maintained its wide historic lead with 121 new bilateral treaties with Canada, Japan with nine stood almost equal to Germany, Canada's foremost European partner, which had ten. Creating and using bilateral institutions and agreements quickly became routine behaviour for Ottawa and Tokyo. These spread down into the bureaucracy and across issue areas to embrace defence and security, social policy, the natural environment, space, and cultural concerns. By 2006, there were "over 40 governmental and non-governmental consultative schemes between Japan and Canada."[17]

It was, however, at the summit level, in a plurilateral framework, where the new Canada-Japan relationship was really forged.[18] From 1984 to 1990, the Canadian and Japanese prime ministers met on nineteen occasions, with seventeen of these meetings taking place within the context of the G7 summits. Moreover, eleven were linked to meetings with the United States, showing the importance of the North Pacific triangle's primary pole. The G7 was thus emerging as the great Canada-Japan connector, although the heavy influence of the United States remained.

Between 1984 and 1993, Mulroney visited his Japanese counterpart on eleven occasions, with the majority of these visits coming during his second mandate from 1989 to 1993. The powerful pull of the G7 gave Japan almost one-third of the summit diplomacy attention that Canada devoted to the United States.[19] Because APEC leaders began meeting annually in 1993 – and the Canadian and Japanese leaders, unlike their American counterpart, always attended – Canada's summit level diplomacy with Japan intensified. Indeed, Japan ranked fourth in the world as a destination for visits by the prime minister. This is even more striking when it is realized that, during his first term, Chrétien made almost two-thirds the number of visits to Japan as he did to the United States. During his second term (1997-2001), Chrétien made eleven visits to Japan — almost as many as he made to the United States (14) or to the United Kingdom (12). The strong equalizing effects of the plurilateral summit-level institutional forums of the G7/8 and APEC overwhelmed the counter-pull of the Eurocentric North Atlantic Treaty Organization (NATO), the Organization for Security and Co-operation in Europe (OSCE), and the Liberal Progressive Leaders' Conferences (from which Japan, with its succession of conservative governments, was excluded).

The Economic Relationship

If Canada and Japan were pulled together as global partners from the top through the plurilateral forums of the G7/8 and APEC, they were also building their partnership from the bottom up in the economic fields of trade, foreign direct investment (FDI), and technology cooperation. This process unfolded despite a variety of pressures exerted in the opposite direction in Japan, Canada, and the United States. Following its collapse in 1992, the Japanese economy continued to struggle, hindered by restrictions on trade and investment and an aging population. Burdened by debt and deficits, and hard hit by the fall in commodity exports that accompanied the 1997-99 global financial crisis, the Canadian economy was also sluggish. These two dampening effects were further magnified by the counter-pull of the economically surging United States, which was more tightly connected to Canada than ever before in an integrated North American trade and investment bloc.[20]

Nonetheless, Canadian exports to Japan steadily climbed from 1991 to peak in 1995, before declining in value in 1998 (see Table 12.1), as the Asian financial crisis, Japanese stagnation, and plunging Canadian commodity prices exerted their toll. Even so, the decline proved temporary, and by mid-1999, growth had returned. In May of that year alone, Canadian exports to Japan leapt by 9.3 percent.[21]

Canadian imports from Japan initially experienced a similar cadence, rising in 1991, briefly dipping in 1996, and cresting in 1998. As a result, Canada's trade deficit with Japan peaked at Cdn$3.3 billion in 1992 and moved into a surplus position in 1996, before posting a record deficit of Cdn$5.4 billion in 1998. While this development troubled analysts with a mercantilist mentality, it demonstrated that Canada, as a good G7/8 major power partner, was playing its role as a spender of last resort for crisis-afflicted Japan, which was driven by a declining yen and domestic recession to find markets abroad for an export-led recovery.

There were other signs of resilience amid the shocks of the 1990s. In many sectors, it was simply the value, not the volume, of trade that declined. For

Table 12.1

Canada's exports and imports with Japan, 1990-98 (Cdn$ million)

Year	Exports	Imports
1991	7.2	10.3
1995	12.1	12.1
1998	8.6	14

instance, there was rapid growth in high technology sectors such as telephony, telecommunications, and agrifood. Throughout that difficult decade, Canada maintained its position as the eleventh most important source of imports for Japan. More important, as the financial crisis receded, there was a significant policy-driven strengthening of bilateral trade relations. In the vital automotive industry, Canada eliminated tariffs on parts imported from overseas by Japanese assemblers in Canada. Following a ruling by the World Trade Organization (WTO) in response to a complaint by Japan and the European Union against the Canada-US Autopact, Canada reduced its 6.1 percent tariff on imports of assembled automobiles, effectively generating closer trade ties with Japan.[22]

The prime ministerial "Team Canada" trade mission to Japan in September 1999 was of particular value in a country where direct exposure is useful for understanding the different business systems and forging the personal contacts required for long-term relationships.[23] As this was the first Team Canada mission to a developed country, it dealt with far more than trade promotion and provided a boost for a broad range of economic and political activities. The willingness of leading Canadian premiers and senior representatives of 260 firms to accompany Chrétien to Japan underscored the importance that influential Canadians attached to Japan and endowed the relationship with an entrenched political foundation. A "Think Canada" mission in 2001 centred on each country's major research universities and generated many multilateral and bilateral follow-ons that further broadened and deepened the bonds. Since its start in 1987, Japan's JET (Japan Exchange and Teaching) Programme has welcomed over 13,500 young Canadians, whose continuing links with Japan gave the bilateral relations a broad personal basis. At the post-secondary level, the 181 exchange agreements between 94 Japanese and 41 Canadian universities reinforced the close connections among people and future elites.[24]

During the first few years of the twenty-first century, Japan remained Canada's second-largest market, absorbing 2.1 percent of Canada's global exports, increasingly in such high valued-added sectors as aircraft, software, telecommunications, as well as resource and environmental products and services. However, in 2001, Canadian exports to Japan decreased by 0.5 percent to Cdn$8.2 billion, and Canada's imports from Japan in 2002 grew 5.3 percent to Cdn$15.2 billion. Behind these trends lay relatively slow growth and demand in Japan, relatively good growth and demand in Canada, and the attraction of the vibrant American and Chinese economies that saw, for example, China surpassing Japan by 2003 to become Canada's number two source for imports and thus trade overall.[25] Serious regulatory barriers and systems, especially those relating to natural resources, food, and agricultural products also inhibited trade. The discovery of mad cow disease in both Japan and Canada, for example, quickly led to market closures that were relaxed very slowly.[26]

In contrast, a more revitalized relationship arose in the field of foreign direct investment (FDI).[27] Investments encountered fewer impediments than trade from embedded multilateral or regional regimes. The World Trade Organization's failure to take up investment issues left the plurilateral codes of the Organization for Economic Co-operation and Development (OECD) as the predominant forum for Canadian-Japanese investment cooperation, notwithstanding the OECD's failure to conclude the Multilateral Agreement on Investment (MAI). From 1993 to 1998, the stock of Japanese FDI in Canada increased 29 percent, from Cdn$6.2 billion to Cdn$8.1 billion. This made Japan the fourth-largest source of FDI in Canada (after the United States, Great Britain, and the Netherlands), though Canada attracted only 1.5 percent of Japanese FDI. More than half of the total Japanese investment was driven by major new investments totalling almost Cdn$5.1 billion by Toyota and Honda in the automotive industry, which remained at the core of the Canadian manufacturing economy.[28]

Canadian FDI in the relatively closed Japanese economy was more volatile. From its peak of Cdn$3.4 billion in 1994, it plummeted to Cdn$2.6 billion in 1996, rebounding to Cdn$3.1 billion by 1998. The following year, it jumped sharply, fed by Manulife Financial's decision to invest almost one billion dollars in a new joint venture with Daihyaku Mutual Life Insurance. As this was only the second investment by a foreign firm in the Japanese insurance market, it pointed to a future in which a Japan far more open to FDI would attract Canadian investment in a broadening range of sectors, and in those high value-added service sectors where Canada had particular global strengths.[29]

Technological and scientific exchanges also fuelled an intensifying bilateral economic relationship. This was particularly evident in the business alliances made by smaller Canadian companies in such core sectors as automotive products, with large "flagship" corporations in both the United States and Japan.[30] They did so within an overall business network that enhanced the autonomy of the Canadian firms and enabled them to flourish in a number of global markets. In other sectors, such as aerospace, defence, or health products, where American national security restrictions and federal regulations made Canada-US partnerships problematic, firms from Japan served as attractive flagships. Mirroring changes in the automotive industry, regional and global rationalization in marketing and distribution, supply, and research and development brought Canadian, Japanese, and US firms into the common embrace of a single business network.

In the realm of government-to-government science, cooperation increased in several sectors, including environmental protection, where Canada and

Japan focused on developing sustainable cities and managing Pacific Ocean fisheries. They also worked actively with the United States and other G8 partners on the International Space Station.

Paradoxically, the Japanese had a favourable if fuzzy concept of Canada as a nice country renowned for peacekeeping, a pristine natural environment, and abundant raw materials, but not as a pioneer in those areas that were expected to dominate the twenty-first century economy.[31] This "Anne of Green Gables" vision had obvious advantages in promoting Japanese tourism and Canadian exports in the agrifood sector, but it hurt when it came to selling Canadian culture and technology or cooperation in those fields. The Japanese generally perceived Canada as a weak cultural power (with few artistic exports beyond Céline Dion, Cirque de Soleil, and jazz musicians Oscar Peterson and Diana Krall) and were almost wholly unaware of Canada's technological prowess. It is noteworthy that the Japanese assigned the highest priority to culture when determining the importance of other countries.

The Security and Functional Relationship

During the Mulroney and Chrétien years, Canada-Japan cooperation embraced many new issues, especially in the peace and security field. Traditionally, cooperation on these issues had been confined to UN-based efforts at arms control and development assistance.[32] Under Chrétien, the two countries started to flesh out emerging concepts of "soft power" and found themselves working together on peacekeeping missions in the Middle East and the Balkans. They also worked together on a shared domestic and social policy agenda, as Ottawa's emphasis on promoting culture and values coincided with Japanese efforts to construct a "caring world." The partnership thus acquired a more comprehensive, full-strength, and multilayered character.

Canada and Japan have progressed from being Second World War enemies to being fellow UN peacekeepers, to their current twenty-first century status as de facto military allies waging war on terrorism in the Indian Ocean. This progression began with peacekeeping within the safe institutional setting of the multilateral UN, with Japan serving alongside Canada as a ceasefire observer in Cambodia in 1992-93. It continued when Japan joined Canada in 1994 as a peacekeeper on the distant and dangerous Golan Heights, overseeing the precarious peace between Israel and Syria. This, Japan's only peacekeeping involvement for many years, saved Canada badly needed defence dollars and liberated Canadian troops for other, more combat-oriented assignments. It further signalled that Japan was a permanent and global, rather than merely Asian, partner in the provision of this international public good. Significantly, by the spring of 1999, Canada was participating in peacekeeping training sessions with Japan and other members of the ASEAN Regional Forum (ARF).

This process of coming together to foster security in regions experiencing deadly conflict encouraged more bilateral military consultations.[33] Despite the absence of a formal bilateral security treaty, under Chrétien, senior military officers began to meet annually in the Canada-Japan Military Staff Study. High-level visits between the defence ministries became more frequent. Canada's naval officials, for example, visited Japan every two years and participated in goodwill visits with their Japanese counterparts. Formal navy-to-navy talks began in Ottawa in September 2003. Only funding restrictions in Canada's Department of National Defence prevented more intensive exchanges.

The process of coming to stand shoulder-to-shoulder in actual combat theatres progressed rapidly after the 1999 war over Kosovo and the subsequent reconstruction effort in the Balkans. The Japanese had tended to see Kosovo – in remote Europe – in human security terms, and had strong reservations about the military interventionist approach taken by Canada and the United States, as NATO members. However, Japan did not publicly criticize its North American allies and eventually became a vocal critic of Serbian dictator Slobodan Milosevic's aggressive behaviour. Moreover, Tokyo joined the Western coalition in contributing to the reconstruction effort. Japan discussed with Canada the prospects for joint activity in relief and development, citing their shared experience in Bosnia on de-mining as a precedent.

Japan and Canada largely reversed roles later in Asia, during the conflict over the independence of East Timor. While other regional powers shared the lead, Canada's military contributed logistics to help secure a region of immediate interest to Japan. This regional division of labour gave way to more global forms of cooperation with the terrorist attacks on North America on 11 September 2001. The ensuing war in Afghanistan brought Canada and Japan together as actual allies in combat. Their two navies served together in the Indian Ocean, and in April 2003, they signed a new agreement under which Japanese Maritime Self-Defence Forces refuelled Canadian warships operating there.[34]

In the American-led coalition invasion of Iraq in 2003, neither country supplied ground troops during the initial phase of the conflict, though Japan later sent its Self-Defence Forces to Iraq for a humanitarian mission aimed at postwar reconstruction. Canada declined to send troops to Iraq, but left its military officers on exchange assignments with American and British forces in place during the invasion, contributed Cdn$300 million in relief aid, and trained Iraqi security forces in Jordan. Both countries, however, cooperated in the G8 in 2003 and 2004 to bring the Iraqi mission under UN and Iraqi control, and to promote the effective democratization of the broader Middle East and North Africa under US and G8 leadership.[35]

During the Chrétien years, Ottawa and Tokyo also became major partners in arms control and disarmament. Their willingness to pioneer and accept the ban on anti-personnel land mines, generated through the Ottawa Process, showed that both were willing to work outside a UN process that, however venerable, seemed likely to fail. Moreover, unlike the United States, Tokyo and Ottawa were willing to accept the convention despite the defensible argument that anti-personnel land mines might still prove useful on the Korean Peninsula, where Canadian forces had fought from 1951 to 1953 and from which Japan still faced an immediate security threat from a nuclear-arming North Korea. Both Japan and Canada provided Cdn$100 million for the de-mining effort and worked together in de-mining operations along the Peru-Ecuador border.

Canadian-Japanese comprehensive security cooperation started with political-military discussions that resulted in an action plan made public in 1999. This document moved cooperation from peacekeeping through post-conflict peace building to human security and conflict prevention. Consistent with Canada's approach, a bilateral dialogue was initiated in 1998 in Vancouver with a series of symposia, involving government departments and non-governmental organizations (NGOs).[36] Another symposium, aimed at identifying possibilities for cooperation, took place in Tokyo in September 1999, as part of the broader program of activities that accompanied Chrétien's Team Canada visit.

Subsequently, the two countries began to work together on civil and political peace support, focused on Japan's involvement in East Timor. This eventually expanded into a full-blown interest in human security, with explorations of the content and compatibility of their respective approaches to the subject. They shared a substantive set of core beliefs but also had distinctive and different emphases. Canada's well-defined concept, developed through the Eurocentric Lysøen Group, focused on stopping the trade in small arms and ending the use of child soldiers. Japan's more recent notion contained an economic dimension that emphasized poverty eradication, human dignity, and social issues such as drugs and child labour. Nonetheless, the Japanese became active on small arms, hosted a conference on child soldiers, and eventually sought membership in the Lysøen Group, which was at the heart of the international human security network.

At the start of the twenty-first century, Canada and Japan also launched a series of bilateral initiatives in several other areas that were more domestically intrusive and that had long been left to the plurilateral forums of the traditionally Eurocentric OECD. The most important field was the environment, on which annual consultations and ministerial visits took place. In another major area, health care and demographic policy, there was substantial interest in comparing experiences, conducting research, and identifying best practices. In cultural policy, the two countries examined the possibility of joining together to develop products for a global audience. The Canada-Japan relationship thus started to move towards becoming the full-powered, comprehensive, multilayered, deeply domestically penetrating partnership that the Canada-US relationship had long been.[37]

Leadership in Global Governance

The broadening partnership between Ottawa and Tokyo was most evident in the realm of global governance, where the two Pacific nations came together to lead in an expanding array of subjects and forums. In the 1990s, when they realized that the UN was unlikely to function as its founders had intended, both Canada and Japan began to look beyond the world organization to build new, very different mechanisms for global governance, particularly the G7/8 and such new international financial institutions as the Financial Stability Forum and the G20. On the national security front, where the bilateral US-Japan security treaty of 1951 had once defined the security regime in the Pacific, Canada and Japan increasingly developed a close regional connection through APEC and the ARF.

At the core of the shared Canadian-Japanese vision for promoting human security stood the G7/8, which had come to serve as one of the international community's central mechanisms for responding to major economic and security challenges. Japan stood out as the only G7/8 member from Asia and the only one to consistently host successful summits. In 1986, when Japan hosted the annual G7 summit, Canada was able – due to American support – to create the G7 finance ministers group with Canada as a full member. In 1993, when Japan again hosted, Canadian Prime Minister Kim Campbell used the summit to help conclude the overdue Uruguay Round of multilateral trade negotiations. In 2000, during the G8 Summit at Okinawa, with Russia present, Ottawa worked closely with Tokyo to advance measures to prevent conflict, to protect cultural diversity, to bridge the North-South digital divide, to promote development in Africa, and to encourage growth in renewable energy.

Canadian hosting saw a similar coming together in expansive ways. When Mulroney hosted the Toronto G7 meeting in 1998, Japan adjusted its policies to support the Canada-US Free Trade Agreement, even though its own Miyazawa Initiative on Middle Income Debt made little progress. At Halifax in 1995, Canada and Japan again teamed up to press successfully for progress on sustainable development. At Kananaskis, Alberta, in 2002, the first G8 Summit after the terrorist attacks of 11 September 2001, the two countries and their G8 colleagues launched their historic G8 Africa Action Plan for the democratic development of Africa; the Global Partnership against Weapons and Materials of Mass Destruction, designed to help partially disarm a still dangerous Russia; and a plan to bring Russia fully into the G8 summit club. Despite its ongoing territorial dispute with Russia over the latter's occupation of the Kurile Islands, Japan joined Canada, the United States, and their G8 partners in making a financial contribution to the Global Partnership's work.

Similarly, during the global financial crisis of 1997-99, Canada and Japan worked together closely and effectively through the G7/8 and the International Monetary Fund (IMF) to provide leadership in crisis response and system reconstruction, particularly when the United States was unable to do so.[38] In the initial phases of the crisis, in September 1997, the United States and Canada united to defeat a Japanese proposal for an Asian fund to assist beleaguered Thailand. As the crisis spread in the autumn, however, the United States joined Japan in providing money for a second line of defence for Indonesia. Subsequently, both the United States and Canada (and the rest of the G7) joined Japan to extend help to South Korea in December, and later Canada (but not the United States) helped rescue Thailand in April 1998. Japan was similarly supportive as the crisis spread beyond Asia to Europe and South America. Specifically, Tokyo contributed through the General Arrangements to Borrow, the New Arrangements to Borrow, and the IMF when the crisis spread to Russia in the summer and to Brazil in the autumn of 1998.

In the effort to construct a stronger international financial system at the Birmingham G8 Summit in May 1998, Canada and the United States together told Japan bluntly to clean up its bad bank loans. Again, as the crisis proceeded, Canada and Japan identified a number of common interests that Washington subsequently accepted, most notably the need to relax the neoliberal "Washington Consensus" that guided IMF adjustment programs, allowing much greater social spending and fiscal stimulus in the recovery packages for Indonesia and other hard-pressed Asian countries.

A similar pattern of Canadian-Japanese cooperation was evident on the G8's security agenda after the human security breakthrough over Kosovo. At the meeting of the G8 foreign ministers in June 1999 in Cologne, when Canadian Foreign Minister Lloyd Axworthy introduced a draft text announcing a new program for conflict prevention, his Japanese colleague, Masahiko Komura, was his most vigorous supporter. Although the United States was reluctant to include Axworthy's text in the communiqué, combined Canadian-Japanese pressure forced Washington to compromise. Conflict prevention later became a major theme for Japan as host of the next G8 Summit.[39]

On the key issue of climate change, the G7/8 has also been a productive forum for taking Canadian-Japanese global cooperation to a new level. Since signing the Kyoto Protocol in 1997, Ottawa and Tokyo have worked to find a way to bring the regime to life through a formula that both the enthusiastic Europeans and reluctant Americans could accept. At the 2001 Genoa Summit, soon after the newly elected American president, George W. Bush, rejected the Kyoto accord, Canada and Japan joined with Russia to agree that they would all ratify the protocol, thereby giving it the minimum support necessary to bring it into force as a global regime. Canada, Japan, and Russia agreed to ratify the protocol to give the minimum support necessary. Unlike the land-mines convention, where Canada and Japan had a sympathetic ally in the American president, Bill Clinton, and the support of coalitions of senators and NGOs, on Kyoto, Canada and Japan exercised global leadership on a protocol that the US Senate had voted against by a margin of 97 to 0. To do so, Japan had to overcome its longstanding suspicions about Russia. At the Genoa G8 Summit, over Kyoto, a new North Pacific Triangle for effective global leadership came to life.[40]

Nevertheless, this pattern of fluid trilateral leadership is also evident in the growing number of new plurilateral forums in which Japan and Canada ranked among the most powerful members, along with the United States. Ottawa and Tokyo supported Clinton's initiative at the Vancouver APEC Summit in November 1997 to create a G22 in order to bring major emerging economies into the process of creating a stronger, more meaningful international financial system. From this emerged the G20 finance ministers' forum, which has held effective ministerial meetings annually since 1999. Canada and Japan are also leading members of the Financial Stability Forum, created in the spring of 1999 by the G7 to implement, *inter alia*, Canadian plans for strengthening the professional supervision of national banking and financial systems.

Intensifying trilateral cooperation was also clearly evident during the 1990s within APEC. Though Japan succeeded in destroying the Early Voluntary Sectoral Liberalization trade program that Canada and the United States had led, Ottawa and Tokyo cooperated to good effect on problems such as the Food, Energy, Environment, Economic Development, and Population (FEEEP) program. Japan participated, with Canada in the professional lead, in the ARF session on peacekeeping training. In 2000, at the APEC leaders' meeting, the two united to support the effective military intervention that brought independence to East Timor. In 2004, the ASEAN connection was strengthened too, as the Asian organization contemplated a free trade agreement with Japan and sought advice from Canada, which had experience with CUFTA and NAFTA.

Causes of the Canada-Japan Global Partnership

Several systemic forces in a rapidly changing world drove the emergence of a more intense, broader, global Canadian-Japanese partnership between 1984 and 2004. These forces were more important than the state-level shift within Canada from a Progressive Conservative government, which has historically favoured Japan, to a Liberal government, with its traditional tilt towards China, or the limited societal connections and pressures for cooperation between Canadians and Japanese.

A first systemic force was the new vulnerability caused by the sequence of shocks associated with the proliferating process of globalization. While Canada and Japan were relatively invulnerable to these blows, proving resilient and capable of quickly adapting, the United States was comparatively vulnerable. In the economic field, for instance, the Mexican peso crisis in 1994 and the global financial crisis of 1998 threatened the United States, but left both Canada and Japan largely untouched at home.[41] The Asian crisis, especially, encouraged Japan to look beyond the United States for new principal power partners, such as Canada, who could help rescue Thailand and the other stricken countries of Asia while reconstructing an international financial system to withstand the threats of the twenty-first century. These two crises, along with the rapid economic rise of neighbouring China, also helped policy-makers in Tokyo recognize that Japan needed a more open and deregulated economy, which would embrace FDI in many major sectors, including the financial service and insurance field, and would encourage bilateral free trade.

In the security sphere, the terrorist attacks by Al-Qaeda on the United States in 1993 and 2001 demonstrated the new physical vulnerability of the US homeland. For Japan, the defining moment was the 1995 sarin gas attacks on the Tokyo subway, which led to the creation of the G7's ministerial forum for counterterrorism at Ottawa within a year. Canada, where no one has died from terrorist attacks since 1970, stood as a secure partner for a terrorist-sensitive Japan. At the same time, the death in June 1985 of Japanese baggage handlers at Narita Airport from a bomb planted in a plane that originated in Vancouver, tragically demonstrated that Canada and Japan were together involved in the war against transnational terrorism.

Those changes in vulnerability were reinforced by changes in capability, especially with the equalization of power once again among the three Pacific nations, in a world where power more broadly was again starting to diffuse. The 11 September 2001 terrorist attacks on the United States, compounded by the crash of the dot.com stock market the year before, and the subsequent decline in the American dollar, strengthened Canada and Japan relative to the United States and the G7 as a whole.

The second systemic force was the continuing cold war and great power rivalries in Japan's dangerous Asia-Pacific region. In the face of rising regional dangers, Canada stood as a militarily forceful, rather than fading, power, of ever greater value to a Japan shaken by crises over the Taiwan Straits in 1996 and the launch by North Korea of a missile over Japan in 1998.

The third systemic force was the growth of consequential plurilateral institutions in which Canada and Japan stood alongside the United States as ranking members, with positions in the inner leadership. The G7/8 system, long the pioneer in this regard, was strengthened by its central role in the war over Kosovo and its response to the global financial crisis. That crisis bred new international groupings, notably the Financial Stability Forum and G20.[42] The events of 11 September 2001 and the war on terror added several other plurilateral security cooperation ventures, with the G8 and APEC as the generative forums. These include the Proliferation Security Initiative (PSI), the Container Security Initiatives, and the Safe and Facilitated International Travel Initiative (SAFTI) concluded at the G8 Sea Island Summit in June 2004.[43] The development of APEC and the ARF, and new processes such as the human security network, reinforced the trend.

The fourth systemic factor was the growing compatibility between Canada and Japan as states emphasizing human security and soft power, compared with the United States under George W. Bush, which was moving into more unilateral expressions of hard, military power to maximize its national security. To be sure, the new institutional forums of the G7/8 and APEC helped governments in Canada, Japan, and the United States recognize and emphasize their shared democratic values amidst the economic and political shocks produced by a globalizing world, especially since 9/11 had an intensifying effect on those shocks. These democratic networks helped leaders identify such common social problems as health care or aging populations and find better ways to address them. An early sign of this cooperation in addressing issues once at the heart of domestic policy is the leadership role exhibited by the United States and Japan since 1994, with Canada's full support, in the G7's new forum for labour ministers.[44]

Nonetheless, the replacement in January 2001 of Democratic President Bill Clinton, with his foreign policy of engagement, by President George W. Bush, with his more unilateral and militarily intrusive approach, increasingly moved the United States out of the old North Pacific triangle. Its departure brought Canada and Japan closer together, in order to promote multilateral regimes without and against America. They did so not only for conflict prevention, socially secure financial liberalization, land-mines control, and financial support for Thailand as before, but more broadly for climate change, arms control, and the International Criminal Court (ICC). Most important, they worked closely to bring Bush's spring 2003 invasion of Iraq under a UN umbrella. While not as strong and direct as the August 1971 economic restrictions that directly assaulted Canadian and Japanese trade interests, this new burst of American unilateralism similarly brought Canada and Japan together. It led the senior members of the Chrétien government to favour a strategy of inculcating, as an interest rather than an instrument, a culture of multilateralism that would encourage the United

States to respect multilateralism in general, as Canada, along with Japan and others, built respect for the rule of law in the WTO, the ICC, and elsewhere.[45]

At the state level, political leadership beyond the socializing effect of plurilateral summitry played only a small part in transforming relations between Ottawa and Tokyo during the final decades of the twentieth century. Indeed, the Canada-Japanese partnership continued to intensify under Chrétien, whose Liberal Party had traditionally favoured non-democratic and anti-American China rather than democratic and pro-American Japan as its primary major power partner in the Asia-Pacific region. By the end of the 1990s, pressure for closer bilateral relations came from Japanese Prime Minister Keizo Obuchi. As foreign minister, Obuchi had developed a personal relationship with Lloyd Axworthy, which helped prompt Obuchi to overrule the Japanese foreign policy bureaucracy and support Canada's human security agenda. In the case of land mines, Obuchi himself decided to support the Canadian initiative, over the opposition of a foreign ministry that was impressed with the heavy pressure exerted by the United States.[46]

Chrétien, like Trudeau before him, focused first on China rather than Japan, and on trade rather than human rights, in his approach to Asia. Nonetheless, through the G8 and APEC, Chrétien became intimately acquainted with Japanese leaders and their preoccupations. In cabinet, Finance Minister Paul Martin emerged as an energetic advocate of APEC and Asia. Chrétien's first trade minister, Roy MacLaren, began his tenure by declaring Asia to be his top priority, leading a trade mission to Japan (as well as to China and South Korea) in March 1994 and making overtures for bilateral free trade arrangements with Japan and other APEC members.

Additional evidence that the growing Canada-Japan relationship was driven primarily by a rational summit-driven state response to systemic pressures comes from the still fragile, if growing, connections between Canadians and Japanese. Within Parliament, the emergence of the separatist, Quebec-based Bloc Québécois after 1993 kept the Chrétien government's attention firmly focused on the separatist threat in Quebec. Canada's business community, labour movement, and NGOs tended to look south to the United States or east to their well-developed, linguistically familiar European confrères. Similarly, despite a growing flow of tourists and students between Canada and Japan, supported by private sector and government exchange programs, there was no large-scale permanent migration between the two countries. Nor did the mass media provide an impulse towards closer relations. According to a survey of Canada's major daily newspapers for nine months during the period from 1982 and 1990, only 5 percent of all international news dealt with the Asia-Pacific region. Television coverage was also thin and stereotypical, and no Canadian news organization had a resident correspondent in Japan. Coverage of this bilateral relationship fell from 3 percent in 1982 to 2 percent in 1992, and Japan's ranking slipped from fifth to seventh.[47] In view of this slender and skewed media portrait, it is all the more remarkable that the Canadian public strongly recognized Japan's growing importance. In both 1993 and 1996, Canadians ranked APEC's major members as the countries in the world on which Canada should place a priority. In February 1996, Canadians chose as priority countries the United States first (94 percent) and Japan second (56 percent). In November 1996, 77 percent of Canadians agreed Canada should be part of a Pacific Rim alliance to promote trade, and 63 percent agreed that Canada should enter into a free trade agreement with its members. This rational Canadian public support sustained the summit-socialized prime ministers from both major parties in their steady strengthening of Canada's global partnership with Japan.[48]

Epilogue: The Progress of Partnership in the Martin and Harper Years

Because the partnership between Canada and Japan has been driven primarily by systemic rather than state or societal forces within Canada, it has continued to expand even when Canadian prime ministers and parties in power changed. It thus flourished with little disruption during the minority governments of Liberal Prime Minister Paul Martin, who took office in December 2003, and Conservative Prime Minister Stephen Harper, elected on 6 February 2006.

In January 2005, the distribution of Foreign Affairs employees at Canada's embassies abroad saw Japan stand second with thirty-two, behind the United States with fifty-two, and ahead of France with thirty, Britain with twenty-eight, and China with twenty-seven.[49]

Despite the constraints of a minority government, Martin, in January 2005, took a summit tour of Asia focusing on Japan and its two other rising powers, China and India. He had already met Japan's Prime Minister Koizumi at the June 2004 G8 summit in Sea Island, Georgia, and at the November 2004 APEC leaders meeting in Chile. They met again at the July 2005 G8 summit in Gleneagles, Scotland, and at the November 2005 APEC leaders' meeting in South Korea. Showing again how such plurilateral summitry provides an opportunity for a strengthening bilateral relationship, while he was prime minister, Martin met Koizumi abroad on six occasions, including a separate meeting at the Gleneagles G8.

In the sphere of policy, Martin moved into serious discussions of bilateral free trade deals with Japan and South Korea. Driven by an outpouring of concern from the Canadian public, in response to the deadly tsunami that struck Indonesia, Thailand, and Sri Lanka on 26 December 2004, Martin joined with Japan and the United States to place Canada in the front ranks of countries providing assistance. In earth remote sensing, where Canada and Japan had world-leading systems, the G8's 2004 Sea Island Summit endorsed efforts to develop a Global Earth Observation System of Systems (GEOSS) to address the looming challenge of climate change. In 2005, Canada secured the lead in APEC to strengthen human security against the deadly avian flu then attacking Asia, in recognition of Canada's experience in combating the SARS assault on Canada and Japan in the spring of 2003.

At the UN's World Summit in September 2005, Martin also secured support from Japan for his cherished and successful effort to have the UN adopt the revolutionary principle of the international Responsibility to Protect (R2P) endangered citizens when their own governments cannot or will not. But he did not reciprocate by supporting Japan's failed bid for a permanent seat on the United Nations Security Council. Nor did Japan provide the vital support needed to bring to life Martin's preferred institutional addition to global governance – a summit of the twenty or so leaders of the world's systemically significant countries (L2O) based on the membership of the G20.

Conservative Prime Minister Stephen Harper has also intensified Canada's partnership with Japan in several ways.[50] He promised to seek free trade agreements with Japan and India as a key plank in his electoral platform.

Figure 12.1 Prime Ministers Junichiro Koizumi and Stephen Harper after their Ottawa meeting in June 2006. Koizumi was one of Harper's first international contacts. *Courtesy Prime Minister's Office.*

He promised and subsequently produced the Pacific Gateway initiative, so that Canada could better take advantage of the booming markets across the Pacific. He signalled his openness to joining the Asia Pacific Partnership for Clean Development and Climate as part of Canada's effort to engage the US in effective climate change control.

On 27-28 June 2006, four months after he assumed office, Harper welcomed, as his fourth foreign visitor to Canada, Japanese Prime Minister Junichiro Koizumi. During the visit, which covered an extensive agenda, Harper agreed to reconsider Canada's current opposition to Japan's quest for a permanent seat on the Security Council, a position he had inherited from the Liberal governments of Martin and Chrétien. Koizumi arrived two months after Harper had first met with US President Bush in Cancun, Mexico, making these two members of the North Pacific triangle early partners of a new, internationally inexperienced Canadian prime minister. By the autumn, following Harper's visit to APEC and his bilateral meeting there with Japan's new Prime Minister Shinzo Abe, Japan stood as the country whose leader Harper had met most often, tied for first along with the United States and Mexico, with four meetings each. Bilateral solidarity and global partnership were what the twenty-first century Canada-Japan relationship had become.[51]

Notes

I am grateful to Laura Sunderland for her research assistance.

1 John Kirton, *Canadian Foreign Policy in a Changing World* (Toronto: Thomson-Nelson, 2006); Duane Bratt and Christopher Kukucha, eds., *Readings in Canadian Foreign Policy: Classic Debates and New Ideas* (Toronto: Oxford University Press, 2007); Kim Richard Nossal, *The Politics of Canadian Foreign Policy* (Scarborough: Prentice Hall, 1997), 52-66; and Andrew Cooper, *Canadian Foreign Policy: Old Habits and New Directions* (Scarborough: Prentice Hall, 1997), 6-21. For overviews of the field of Canadian foreign policy in political science, see Michael Hawes, *Principal Power, Middle Power, or Satellite?* (Toronto: York Research Programme in Strategic Studies, 1984); Maureen Appel Molot, "Where Do We, Should We, or Can We Sit? A Review of Canadian Foreign Policy Literature," *International Journal of Canadian Studies* 1-2 (Spring-Fall 1990): 77-96; Denis Stairs, "Will and Circumstance and the Postwar Study of Canadian Foreign Policy," *International Journal* 50 (Winter 1994-95): 9-39; and Daizo Sakurada, "The Contending Approaches to Canadian Foreign Policy and Canada-U.S. Relations: A Reinterpretation of Literature," *Proceedings of the Sixth Tsukuba Annual Seminar on Canadian Studies* (University of Tsukuba, 18-19 November 1994, Tokyo).

2 Norman Hillmer and Maureen Appel Molot, eds., *Canada among Nations 2002: A Fading Power* (Toronto: Oxford University Press, 2002). Journalist John Hay noted in 1997 that since Chrétien took power in 1993, "Canada's relations with Asia and the Pacific Rim have commanded more attention from the Canadian public and policymakers than at any time in our history," but concluded "Canada is a small country by Asia-Pacific standards, with limited power to act on its own or influence others." John Hay, "Asia-Pacific: Questions and Choices," *Canadian Foreign Policy* 5 (Fall 1997): 105, 112.

3 Carin Holroyd, "The Costs of Falling Behind: Canada's Economic Relationship with Japan," *Canada Asia Commentary* 38 (February 2005), 1–11; Anna Turinov and Yuen Pau Woo, "Canada-Japan Relations at 75: New Reasons to Revive an Old Relationship," *Canada Asia Commentary* 37 (October 2004): 1–8.

4 Yuen Pau Woo, "The Re-emergence of the Re-emergence of Asia," *International Journal* 58 (Autumn 2003): 615-36. The relative capability of the world's leading powers is assessed by multiplying their GDP in their national currency each year by the exchange rate of that national currency against the US dollar that year, to reflect both the overall productive performance of a country (available to be devoted to any purpose it chooses) and what the value of that production is worth in the estimate of everyone in the world who can trade in that currency (which many more can do in an increasingly globalized world). For calculations of the relative capability of Canada, Japan, and the US based on this formula, see John Kirton, "Explaining G8 Effectiveness," in *The G8's Role in the New Millennium,* ed. Michael Hodges, John Kirton, and Joseph Daniels (Aldershot: Ashgate, 1999), 58-59.

5 John Kirton and Mitsuru Kurosawa, *The Triangle of Pacific States: Contemporary United States, Canada, Japan Relations* (Tokyo: Sairyusha Press, 1995).

6 Julian Dierkes and Yves Tiberghien, "Shall We Dance?" *Globe and Mail,* 18 January 2005, A19; Charles McMillan, *Approaching the Millennium: Canada and Japan in the New Era* (Ottawa: Canada Japan Trade Council, 1999).

7 Woo, "The Re-emergence of the Re-emergence of Asia;" Yves Tiberghien, *Japan is Changing! Significant Reforms and Debates in Post-1996 Japan: Implications for Canada,* Canada in Asia Series on the Foreign Policy Dialogue (Vancouver: Asia Pacific Foundation of Canada, 2003).

8 Woo, "The Re-emergence of the Re-emergence of Asia," 622. As early as 1986, one longtime scholarly specialist argued that "the Pacific has become a region of priority for both Canada and the United States." H. Edward English, "Canada and the United States Look West: Pacific Policy Networks," in *Canada among Nations 1986: Talking Trade,* ed. Brian Tomlin and Maureen Appel Molot (Toronto: James Lorimer, 1987), 169.

9 A Japanese scholar has said that "a movement is already underway" towards a new vision, and that "although Japan-Canada cooperation on peace and security has been developed significantly, it is not yet well known by ordinary Japanese and Canadian people." Masaya Fujiwara, "Future of Japan-Canada Relations from the Perspective of the Government of Japan" (paper presented to a conference of the Japanese Studies Association of Canada, Victoria, British Columbia, 16 October 2004). A similar argument dominates Canada-Japan Forum 2006, *Report of the Canada-Japan Forum 2003-2006,* June 2006. Somewhat earlier, Raymond Chan, Canada's secretary of state for Asia-Pacific, had argued "Canada moved to strengthen its ties with Asia Pacific in the early 1970's. This was prompted mainly by ... the recognition of the emerging power of Japan's economy. The acceleration of Asian economic growth in the 1980s and its projection on to the world stage through shifting exchange rates and financial flows have further highlighted Asia's importance to Canadian and global prosperity ... As we approach what many are calling the 'Pacific Century,' strengthening Canada's relationships with Asian economies becomes crucial to our economic security." The Honourable Raymond Chan, "Canada and Asia Pacific," in *Canada among Nations 1997: Asia Pacific Face-Off,* ed. Fen Osler Hampson, Maureen Appel Molot, and Martin Rudner (Ottawa: Carleton University Press, 1977), 106. In 1999, a Canadian official added: "Asia is probably more important than ever for Canada. All the 'big picture' foreign policy priorities of the government are engaged in the region ... Japan ... still has immense reserves of capital and a per capita gross domestic product about twice the size of Canada's." Daryl Copeland, "After the Storm: Asia Pacific Prospects and Canadian Foreign Policy," *International Journal* 54 (Autumn 1999): 685-86.

10 See, for example, Michael Fry, John Kirton, and Mitsuru Kurosawa, eds., *The North Pacific Triangle: The United States, Japan and Canada at Century's End* (Toronto: University of Toronto Press, 1998); John Kirton, "The Emerging Pacific Partnership: Japan, Canada and the United States at the G7 Summit," in Fry, Kirton and Kurosawa, *The North Pacific Triangle,* 292-313; Kirton and Kurosawa, *The Triangle of Pacific States.* For more on vulnerability, please see John Kirton, *Canadian Foreign Policy in a Changing World* (Toronto: Thomson Nelson, 2007).

11 As Masaya Fujiwara puts it, "as allies of the United States, both countries share an interest in ensuring that the United States commits itself to multilateral dialogue in economic and

security fields." Masaya Fujiwara, "Future of Japan-Canada Relations from the Perspective of the Government of Japan" (paper presented to the Japanese Studies Association of Canada, Victoria, BC, 16 October 2004).

12 Parliament of Canada, "Speeches from the Throne and Motions for Address in Reply," http://www2.parl.gc.ca/Parlinfo/compilations/parliament/ThroneSpeech.aspx? accessed August 2007.

13 "Prime Minister Announces 'Going Global' Trade Development Strategy," Prime Minister's Office Press Release, 15 October 1989.

14 Department of Foreign Affairs and International Trade (Canada) (1995), "Canada in the World: Canadian Foreign Policy Review," www.dfait-maeci.gc.ca/foreign_policy/cnd-world/menu-en.asp, accessed October 2004.

15 This number three spot would appear to be the rational place for a country that was, a decade and a half later, ranked third in economic weight in the world in terms of purchasing power parity. See Woo, "The Re-emergence of the Re-emergence of Asia," 620. Relevant in expanding Canada's diplomatic representation and reach was the opening of the new Canadian embassy. See Raymond Moriyama, "The New Canadian Embassy in Tokyo: Ambassador Extraordinary," in *Canada among Nations 1992-93: A New World Order?* ed., Fen Osler Hampson and Christopher Maule (Ottawa: Carleton University Press, 1992), 29-45; Brian Job and Frank Langdon, "Canada and the Pacific," in *Canada among Nations 1993-94: Global Jeopardy*, ed. Fen Osler Hampson and Christopher Maule (Ottawa: Carleton University Press, 1993), 278-79.

16 See also Roy Rempel, *Dreamland: How Canada's Pretend Foreign Policy Has Undermined Sovereignty* (Kingston: Breakout Educational Network, 2006), 153.

17 Canada-Japan Forum 2006, *Report of the Canada-Japan Forum 2003-2006*, 1.

18 While space precludes a detailed, idiographic discussion of the context, content, and significance of each summit encounter, the broad pattern suffices to identify priorities. Here summit diplomacy is especially revealing as it requires zero-sum allocations of a fixed resource – the leaders' time – and allows for learning and decisions among the most powerful actors in the formal and often effective hierarchy in the nation state. The patterns of summit diplomacy also set precedents, expectations, and foundations for what will come in future years. In Japanese, see Daizo Sakurada, *Canadian-American Summit Diplomacy, 1948-2005* (Tokyo: Akashi Shoten, 2006).

19 See Kirton, *Canadian Foreign Policy in a Changing World*, Appendix 11, "Summit Visits, 1948-2006," updates available at http://www.kirton.nelson.com/student/appendix_updates.html.

20 For background on the Japanese economy in the 1990s, see Koji Watanabe, "Japan's Summit Contributions and Economic Challenges," in *The G8's Role in the New Millennium*, 95-105; and Richard Wright, "Japan's Post-Bubble Economic Changes: Implications for the United States and Canada," in Fry, Kirton, and Kurosawa, *The North Pacific Triangle*, 106-39.

21 These figures come from Statistics Canada data. There is a considerable discrepancy between Canadian and Japanese figures on bilateral trade, with Japanese figures widely acknowledged as being more reliable. Canadian figures, however, provide an accurate overview of the trends over time.

22 On the WTO action, see Dimitry Anastakis, "Requiem for a Trade Agreement: The Auto Pact at the WTO, 1999-2000," *Canadian Business Law Journal* 34 (February 2001): 313-35.

23 The importance of cultural awareness is examined in Rosalie Tung, "Business Negotiations: Comparing the U.S.-Japan and Canada-Japan Experiences," in Fry, Kirton, and Kurosawa, *The North Pacific Triangle*, 140-64.

24 Canada-Japan Forum 2006, *Report of the Canada-Japan Forum 2003-2006*, 11. For a history of the JET Programme, see http://www.jetprogramme.org/e/introduction/history.html. Figures obtained by email in February 2007 from Hiromi Iwamoto, JET Programme Coordinator, Embassy of Japan.

25 Rempel, *Dreamland*, 153.

26 Paul Martin and Junichiro Koizumi, "Joint Declaration by Canada and Japan" (19 January 2005), http://www.pco-bcp.gc.ca/default.asp?Language=E&Page=archivemartin&Sub=newscommuniques&Doc=news_release_20050119_395_e.htm, accessed August 2007.

27 David Edgington, "Japanese Direct Investment in Canada: Patterns and Prospects," in Fry, Kirton, and Kurosawa, *The North Pacific Triangle*. A similar dynamic arose in portfolio investment. See Woo, "The Re-emergence of the Re-emergence of Asia," 622.
28 Andrew Delios and Prescott Ensign, "Japanese Investment in Canada," *Ivey Business Journal* 64, 2 (1999): 41-45; and Keith Head and John Ries, "Rivalry for Japanese Investment in North America," in *The Asia Pacific Region in the Global Economy: A Canadian Perspective*, ed. Richard Harris (Calgary: University of Calgary Press, 1996).
29 Diane Francis, "Go East, Young Man, Go East: Japan's Door to Our Exports Is Open; We Just Have to Walk In," *Financial Post*, 18 May 1999, C03.
30 James Tiessen and Bill Merrilees, *Canadian Small and Medium-Sized Enterprises in Japan* (Ottawa: Canada-Japan Trade Council, 1999).
31 "The Canadian Image in Japan," *Canada-Japan Trade Council* (May-June 1999): 1-5.
32 For an introduction to Japan's peacekeeping activities, see Mitsuru Kurosawa, "Japanese and Canadian Peacekeeping Participation: The American Dimension," in Fry, Kirton, and Kurosawa, *The North Pacific Triangle*, 196-208.
33 Frank Langdon, "Co-operative Security in the North Pacific," in Fry, Kirton, and Kurosawa, *The North Pacific Triangle*, 167-84; and David Welch, "The Future of the U.S.-Japan Security Relationship," in Fry, Kirton, and Kurosawa, *The North Pacific Triangle*, 185-95.
34 Foreign Affairs and International Trade, Canada, "Asia Pacific: Defence Relationship," geo.international.gc.ca/asia/main/japan/peace_security_defence-en.asp.
35 The most systematic comparative analysis of Canadian and Japanese behaviour in the 2003 Iraq War concludes that Canada followed a middle-power approach and Japan a small-power approach. See Daizo Sakurada, "Kurechienseiken no taiogaiko [Diplomatic Response by the Chrétien Regime], in Daizo Sakurada and Go Ito, eds., *Hikakugaikoseisaku: Irakusense eno taiogaiko* [Comparative Foreign Policy: The Iraq War and Seven Powers] (Tokyo: Akashi Shoten, 2004), 261-94; and Daizo Sakurada and Go Ito, "Ketsuron [Conclusion], in Sakurada and Ito, *Hikakugaikoseisaku*, 295-318 (both in Japanese). On this extra-regional foreign policy issue involving America's use of force, neither Canada nor Japan had emerged as principal powers equal to the US. However, each was able, in varying degrees, to maintain a similarly divergent position, which put them in a relatively more powerful position when America's defeat in the war became clear in the Harper years.
36 In welcoming participants to Vancouver, then Canadian Foreign Minister Lloyd Axworthy called on participants to "maintain the momentum by these important initial commitments," referring to cooperative work on the Golan, naval visits, peace-building consultations, and disarmament. For more information, see the 1998 *Canada-Japan Symposium on Bilateral Peace and Security Cooperation* (Vancouver, UBC, 1998), geo.international.gc.ca/asia/main/japan/symposium-en.aspm, accessed in August 2007.
37 See, for example, Foreign Affairs and International Trade, Canada, "Asia Pacific: Canada and Japan, A Global Partnership for the 21st Century," 17 September 1999, http://geo.international.gc.ca/asia/main/japan/pmcomuniquefinal-en.asp.
38 Saori Katada, "Japan's Approach to Shaping a New International Financial Architecture," in *New Directions in Global Economic Governance: Managing Globalisation in the Twenty-First Century*, ed. John Kirton and George von Furstenberg (Aldershot: Ashgate, 2001), 113-26. John Kirton, "Canada's Leadership Role in International Negotiations: The G7, IMF and the Global Financial Crisis of 1997-99," http://www.g8.utoronto.ca/scholar/kirton199901.
39 John Kirton and Radoslava Stefanova, eds., *The G8, the United Nations, and Conflict Prevention* (Aldershot: Ashgate, 2004).
40 John Kirton and Virginia Maclaren, "Forging the Trade-Environment-Social Cohesion Link: Global Challenges, North American Experiences," in *Linking Trade, Environment and Social Cohesion*, ed. John Kirton and Virginia MacLaren (Aldershot: Ashgate, 2002).
41 While Canada and Japan were sensitive to the effects of the regional Mexican and Asian crises respectively, they were less vulnerable than they had been to the great American-initiated Nixon shock of 15 August 1971, a manifestation of the old state-to-state vulnerability that had been directly and consciously targeted at them. On the latter, see Daizo Sakurada, *A Study of Canadian Foreign Policy Perspectives: The Trudeau Era* (Tokyo: Sairyusha, 1999) (in Japanese).

42 John Kirton, "Canada and the Global Financial Crisis of 1997-98: G7 and APEC Diplomacy" (paper prepared for a conference at National Chengchi University, Taipei, Taiwan, 18 December 1998).
43 Martin and Koizumi, "Joint Declaration by Canada and Japan."
44 The G7 labour ministers met for the first time in 1994, hosted by the United States but while Italy held the G7 presidency. In 1996, at the second labour ministerial (under France's G7 presidency), the Japanese government offered to host a meeting of experts to focus on youth employment, the aging workforce, and lifelong learning; see "Conclusions of the Chair" (G7 Jobs Ministerial Conference, Lille, France, 1-2 April 1996), http://www.g8.utoronto.ca/employment/labour1996.htm. The following year, Japan hosted the Kobe Jobs Conference during the US's year as chair of the G7/8; see "Chair's Conclusions" (Kobe Jobs Conference, Kobe, Japan, 28-29 November 1997), http://www.g8.utoronto.ca/employment/labour1997.html.
45 Senior Canadian official, interview by the author, 25 November 2002.
46 Lloyd Axworthy, *Navigating a New World: Canada's Global Future* (Toronto: Random House, 2003), 143.
47 B.E. Burton, et al., "The Press and Canadian Foreign Policy: A Re-examination Ten Years On," *Canadian Foreign Policy* 3 (Fall 1995): 63.
48 Goldfarb Consultants, February 1993 and February 1996.
49 Rempel, *Dreamland*, 85.
50 John Kirton, "Harper's 'Made in Canada' Global Leadership," in *Canada among Nations 2006: Minorities and Priorities*, ed. Andrew Cooper and Dane Rowlands (Montreal and Kingston: McGill-Queen's University Press, 2006), 34-57.
51 Japanese and Canadian officials, interviews with the author, Tokyo, December 2006.

13
Canadian Chanceries in Tokyo

Marie-Josée Therrien

The evolving nature of Canada's relationship with Japan since 1929 is amply reflected in the architecture of the two stylistically very different diplomatic enclaves that Ottawa constructed in Tokyo during the last century. In the early 1930s, the first plenipotentiary minister, Sir Herbert Marler, in an unprecedented manner, assumed complete responsibility for financing and supervising the construction of the first diplomatic outpost ever built by Canada. Largely ignorant of Japan and its architectural practices, Marler erected a series of buildings inspired by a Eurocentric and postcolonial worldview. The handful of Asian architectural features belatedly integrated into his design simply underlined the gulf that divided the two Pacific countries.

Sixty years later, during the final stage of Canada's diplomatic architectural odyssey in Japan, the two countries had become much more open to each other and were ready to work in close collaboration to deliver a spectacular building, reflecting their growing cultural integration. Though incorporating elements of both cultures in the hybrid chancery of the 1980s clearly reflected the broad pressures of postwar globalization, there were also specific Canadian-Japanese factors at play, creating networks of cultural contact across the Pacific. As Masako Iino points out in the final chapter of this volume, Japan embraced the hip and modern Canada that was highlighted during Prime Minister Pierre Trudeau's 1970 visit to the Osaka world fair. Soon after, the Japanese consulate in Toronto began supplying reference materials and Japanese films to libraries across the country, an exercise in public diplomacy that would culminate in the establishment of the Japan Foundation in 1990. Canadians, too, embraced cultural diplomacy in the 1970s, anxious to assert their distinctiveness in the face of a homogenizing America. As part of the larger diplomatic initiative to strengthen relations with Japan that Greg Donaghy explores in Chapter 11, Trudeau's government promoted a program of academic exchanges with Japan in 1974. Indeed, cultural diplomacy seemed so useful a diplomatic tool that Ottawa decided in 1975 to build its major chanceries as cultural centres that would include library, auditorium, and exhibition space.[1] This policy meshed well with Ottawa's efforts to engage Japan during the 1980s, a strategy that called for a "deepening of cultural relations, involving personal contacts, academic relations, the creative and performing arts and sport."[2] This heightened cultural sensitivity clearly informed plans for the new embassy. The final result fell short of the mark for, while different in form, the modern embassy shared and was profoundly shaped by a preoccupation that had often influenced Canadian-Japanese relations: Canada's interest in attracting its share of Japanese wealth through closer trade and political relations.

Marler's initial intention for the Canadian legation in Tokyo was expressed in a proposal he submitted to Prime Minister William Lyon Mackenzie King in February 1929, only a month after his nomination. It makes clear that although Marler was a knowledgeable and experienced businessman, his understanding of Japanese culture was limited to the accounts he had read or heard from the very few Canadian experts or British officials who briefed him on the subject after his appointment.[3] As historian John Meehan persuasively argues, myths of untold Asian riches and colourful descriptions of the splendour of the Sunrise Empire, an emerging Pacific power that had recently become a member of "the imperialist club," shaped an extremely positive image of the country for Marler.[4] Typical of many Canadian businessmen, he considered Japan to be the most Westernized of the Asian countries, perhaps even ready to embrace liberalism and North America's emerging consumer culture. The new legation, Marler insisted, would be designed to help Canadians tap into Japan's potential as an economic partner.

Marler's approach to building the new legation was also conditioned by a strong pragmatic streak. After inquiring about housing conditions in Tokyo, a city that was still recovering from the earthquake of 1923, he concluded that there were no buildings suitable for a Canadian mission. That assessment was confirmed by the legation's first secretary, Hugh Keenleyside, who, in June 1929, described Tokyo's urban conditions as grim: "I fancy that many of us come here impressed with the idea of Japan as a progressive modern community. And so, in many respects it is. But in others its medievalism is impregnable. In comparison with other oriental cities I presume that Tokyo is very advanced, but in comparison with Montreal (for example), nine-tenths of it comprise a huge and filthy slum."[5]

Marler took it upon himself to produce a very detailed proposal complete with renderings for the legation (see Figure 13.1). He commissioned the Montreal architect Kenneth Rea, with whom he had previously worked on two of his own residences. Marler's Quebec roots profoundly influenced his expectations for the new legation. His status as a second generation member of an Anglo-Quebec family of notaries and his marriage to the grand-niece of Sir Hugh Allan, a well-connected financier and industrialist, contributed to his rise through Montreal's affluent anglophone society. The Marlers

Figure 13.1 K.G. Rea's rendering of the official residence, Tokyo, 1929. *Library and Archives Canada, Department of External Affairs Records, RG 25, Volume 2611, p. 37.*

Figure 13.2 Marler's home in Senneville, Quebec, as renovated by K.G. Rea in the early 1920s. *Photo by Marie-Josée Therrien.*

seemed to have been tireless hosts, if one judges by their country houses in Drummondville and Senneville, as well as their property on Redpath Crescent in Montreal's wealthy Golden Square Mile. Perhaps not surprisingly, Marler's initial renderings for the legation show an idealized version of a gentleman's country house similar to his own residence in Senneville on the West Island (see Figure 13.2). Both buildings present the same external attributes: an emphasis on the façade, with a monumental columned porch crowned by a pediment, symmetrically placed windows, and a pitched roof ornamented with the projecting brackets of a modillioned cornice.

The floor plans of the residential section of the proposed legation and the finished official residence share characteristics with Marler's other Quebec houses and reflect a spatial organization typical of Montreal's elite mansions. They are divided according to Western notions of space distribution with closed rooms and fixed walls. The two houses show a tripartite organization with large rooms for social gatherings, a cluster of private rooms for the owners, and a segregated area for the live-in servants. As in a typical English house of the affluent, staircases were arranged to limit contact between servants and owners.

For Marler, an inveterate anglophile in the matter of taste, this Georgian style reflected his strong attachment to the British Empire. Since the legation was to be built in a country populated by what some regarded as the "British of Asia,"[6] he judged this style as the most appropriate. Especially concerned with the symbolic impact of the building, Marler wanted to build a "proper and dignified accommodation" that would have "an effect on the Ministers of other countries ... and particularly on the minds of the people of Japan to whom he is accredited from a great Dominion."[7] Outlining his intentions to the prime minister, Marler, speaking in the third person, reveals a missionary-like temperament as he recalls how Reverend James Robertson, the Superintendent of the Missions of the Presbyterian Church in the North West Territories

> advised the people to build churches because he wanted to see a building as evidence of the ability and permanence of his people and that a building stood as visible evidence of such ability and permanence. This saying put in the language of the Minister commends itself as an apposite saying with respect to the position of Canada in Japan in the eyes of the rest of the world and the people of the Dominion in particular. The Minister is of the firm opinion that the people of Canada expect to have their legation as a source of pride.[8]

This comparison with missionary churches in the remote Canadian territories suggests that Marler envisioned the legation as a transplanted microcosm of a familiar social order to a country that he could not yet visualize, relying on a constructed image of the "wild west" to which the missionaries had brought "civilization."[9] Though Marler, unlike the Canadian Protestant and Roman Catholic missionaries who formed the main Canadian presence in Japan, had no intention of converting the Japanese to Christianity, he perceived his role to be part of the much broader effort to exhibit the benefits of Western civilization to the people of Japan. For the liberal and secular Marler, the religious comparison also gave moral weight to his more mercantile interests. The embassy was to be the "visible frontage"[10] of a nation in the making, eager to demonstrate its wealth, stability, and newly acquired autonomy.

Though Marler understood the sophistication of the society he was about to encounter, there is no doubt that he considered Japan a "strange country with people completely different from our own."[11] Even as he celebrated Japan's potential to become one of Canada's largest trading partners, Marler's view of Japanese society was tainted by suspicions based on racial and social prejudices. He drew a clear distinction, for instance, in his early proposal about the place of Japanese and Canadians in the legation's premises. While he planned to house Canadian domestics in the residence, he anticipated that the quarters for "Oriental" servants would be outside the legation. While it was acceptable to trade with the Japanese, Marler was not yet ready to share his private environment with them on a daily basis.

Marler's plans for the diplomatic enclave also suggest that he was not especially concerned with the legation's need to accommodate Canadian immigration services. In his preparatory documents, Marler completely ignores immigration. Though one might argue that the small annual quota of 150 Japanese applicants did not justify a separate office, the tight control of Japanese immigration was one reason that Mackenzie King established the mission.

The canny prime minister wanted to appease unhappy Japanese authorities who resented Canadian efforts to exclude immigrants by signalling his willingness to help deal with Japan's overpopulation problem. Unlike Canadian missions in Europe, this legation was not concerned with encouraging immigration, and the lack of attention paid to it underscores Marler's different set of priorities. Eventually, his omission was corrected and an examination room for prospective immigrants was placed in the chancery.

If Marler initially neglected the legation's immigration functions, he never lost sight of its commercial and diplomatic purposes. The question of comfort, for family, guests, or servants, was of paramount importance in shaping his early views of the legation. He insisted that all residents must feel at home since they were to live in a "strange land and among strange people." Providing proper accommodation for his staff implied that their lives in Japan would be made as pleasant as possible so that they could be more efficient. Marler insisted on a prestigious and wealthy looking building because he was truly convinced that a proper setting would invite business through "social intercourse and friendly conversations."[12]

Marler learned a little more about Japan in the summer of 1929 when he mingled with the Canadian expatriates who were returning to Tokyo with him onboard the *Empress of France*. During the elaborate official welcoming ceremony that greeted him, Marler discovered reassuring elements of similarity between the British and Japanese empires, with their shared passion for imperial trappings and etiquette. Marler attached great importance to the matter of royal or aristocratic lineage. The gold-braided diplomatic uniform that he so obviously loved to wear illustrates his profound sympathy for imperial protocol.

Japanese imperial history seems to have equally fascinated him. In a document accompanying the planning of the enclave, Marler explained in minute detail the rich and lively story of the Tokyo property that he purchased for the new legation. Once part of the vast domain of a local *daimyo*, the Lord of Akasaka, the storied property was seen as a symbolic link between the Japanese and British empires.[13] Avoiding any direct allusion to the shrewd transaction he had made in purchasing this centrally located property so cheaply, Marler claimed that the Viscount Tadatoshi Aoyama, the thirteenth daimyo of his line, had simply transferred his property to the British Crown for the use of Canada. This version contrasts with the rumour current in Tokyo that the property might have been haunted and "was suitable only for foreign occupation."[14] While this rumour is now considered amusing, and even worth a reference in the promotional material issued on the opening of the new chancery in 1989, Marler ignored it. Instead, he seized the opportunity to emphasize the highly symbolic value of a site with an impressive ancestral pedigree that had been passed on to Canada and which, incidentally, was located close to one of the imperial parks.

The design for the legation was in line with the Georgian aesthetic, a style which enjoyed some popularity in Tokyo and was probably much appreciated by the local elite.[15] For the Canadian diplomat, it could not better express his sense of decorum. However, his design sense was certainly challenged by Antonin Raymond, the architect he commissioned to design the compound. Raymond, who had been in Tokyo since 1919, when he went to work with Frank Lloyd Wright on the Imperial Hotel, had opened his own architectural practice in the early 1920s. Over the next decade, he became expert on Tokyo's soil and seismic conditions, and fond of the Japanese architectural tradition, a perspective he brought to bear as he worked on the new legation. Associated with the construction of the Russian, French, and American embassies, he was closely integrated into the local diplomatic circuit by the time the Marlers arrived, and he was ideally suited to build Canada's enclave. Even so, Marler, who "watched every nail that went into the residence," did not always welcome Raymond's suggestions, and both men had bitter memories of their working relationship.[16] Marler later complained that he was not entirely satisfied with Raymond's design and even listed Rea, who never set foot in Tokyo, as one of the building's architects in a transparent effort to diminish Raymond's contribution.[17] For his part, Raymond was reluctant to claim the buildings as his own and did not include a picture of the embassy in his memoirs, where he acknowledged only his role as an assistant.[18]

The three-acre property allowed Raymond to distribute the functions of the enclave into more than the one building that Marler had initially envisioned. The chancery, the legation's offices, and the official residences became two separate buildings. The Canadian servants lived in their designated area in the official residence. The enclave also included quarters for the Japanese domestics and a playground for their children. Marler, who was always concerned with the efficiency of the diplomatic household, justified the inclusion of a Japanese playground by observing that the "Japanese are devoted to their children and to give them some place in which to play will be a very great boon and induce better service."[19] The minister insisted, however, that they be screened from the main residence and its grounds by high planting.[20]

The novice diplomat made other compromises with his Asian environment. During his stay in Tokyo, he developed a keen interest in the Japanese art of landscaping, and the legation's gardens reflected a fusion of styles (see Figure 13.3). He was also prepared to include a Japanese quarter within the limits of the diplomatic enclave in accordance with local practice. He drew the line, however, at having the new building's floor plan blessed according to Shinto rituals. According to Shinto tradition, if one built a new house without the permission of the spirits, they would become angry and destroy the building. To guarantee the dweller's fortune and good health, priests usually inspected site and floor plans prior to construction. Raymond had learned to collaborate with these religious experts, who also gave advice about the orientation of certain rooms in a house. Initially, Marler staunchly opposed the practice as an unacceptable superstition. As the legation approached its opening, his views shifted, much to the disapproval of Keenleyside:

> This morning the Canadian Legation in Tokyo was officially cleansed and blessed by Shinto priests! Done secretly (even I was not informed) and with only the Minister and his private secretary in attendance, the performance is to be kept from ears of the Canadian people. The reason, of course, is the number of deaths and illnesses that have occurred since the Legation was taken over. From now on there will be no more ill-luck: all devils have been exorcised! The servants – and I rather think the Minister himself – will feel easier.[21]

Figure 13.3 A view of the gardens of the official residence, circa 1933. *Library and Archives of Canada, PA-120405.*

Marler, who was seriously ill during the final stages of the legation's construction, left no explanation for his actions.[22] Nonetheless, it is not unreasonable to suppose that his decision to allow the Shinto blessing was largely motivated by a pragmatic desire to calm the fears of his increasingly nervous Japanese employees.

The new Canadian legation, which finally opened in November 1933, was, as Marler had anticipated, a "splendid advertisement [for Canada] throughout the Orient."[23] He told Conservative Prime Minister R.B. Bennett, elected in 1930, that the enclave was designed for entertainment on a grand scale, but with a sharp focus on trade and commerce. "What pleases the prospective business client," he wrote, "is to be shown attention and no better attention can be shown him than a walk around a beautiful garden."[24] This "proper and dignified house"[25] also pleased Mackenzie King, who, at the time of its opening, was leader of the official opposition. Receiving a full account of the new legation from Prince Iyemasa Tokugawa, the first Japanese minister to Ottawa, Mackenzie King wrote Marler to thank him for so "firmly and splendidly" establishing the foundations for Canadian diplomatic relations in Asia.[26] Marler's new mission reflected in stone the ambiguous duality of the policies towards Japan. While embracing Japanese traders and businessmen in its public reception rooms and flowing gardens, officials in the chancery excluded potential Japanese immigrants from a staunchly white Canada.

Although bilateral relations developed slowly but steadily after the end of the Second World War, they assumed much more importance in the 1970s as postwar political and economic priorities shifted in response to changes in the international economy. As part of Prime Minister Pierre Trudeau's "third option" policy of diversifying Canada's foreign relations, Ottawa persuaded Tokyo in 1974 to embark on a program to intensify economic, political, and cultural ties between the two countries. During the same period, partly to counter Quebec's claim to represent French Canada on the international stage, the Trudeau government demonstrated a strong interest in cultural diplomacy and the projection abroad of Canada's distinct multicultural personality. As a result, new embassies were increasingly designed to meet not only the country's traditional political and economic needs but also its cultural objectives. Embassies would house art galleries, theatres, and libraries.

These considerations figured in early discussions about a new Canadian embassy in Japan. While Marler's original residence, which had escaped wartime damage and was one of postwar Tokyo's most distinctive buildings, retained its representational functions, the embassy offices, expanded in the 1950s, were badly outmoded. Moreover, with the growth in bilateral relations, Canadian staff were housed in offices scattered across the Japanese capital. Consequently, in 1977, the Vancouver firm McCarter & Nairne prepared a virtually complete set of drawings for a new embassy, ready for tendering.[27] The model showed a vast and unimaginative "L-shaped" three-storey office building, spread over the original and adjacent plots. Canada's mounting deficit forced Ottawa to abandon the project.[28]

Finding the money to build a new embassy, while retaining Marler's residence and high-profile site, both identified with Canada's presence in Japan, proved difficult and delayed planning until the early 1980s. As Tokyo real estate values exploded, Japanese investors devised an innovative solution. In response to a request from the Department of External Affairs for proposals, Mitsubishi Trust and Bank Company and the Shimizu Construction Company formed a consortium that offered to finance the construction of a new embassy and staff apartments provided that the site included extra commercial space that they could lease until they recouped their investment.[29] Although Canadian diplomats initially worried that the arrangement might violate an international convention that forbids countries from profiting from diplomatic properties, it eventually accepted the offer.[30]

Shimizu Construction commissioned the Canadian architect Lloyd Sankey, who was about to complete Canada's new diplomatic compound in Riyadh,

Saudi Arabia, to sketch a design for the new project. The Department of External Affairs, however, was unimpressed with Sankey's proposal, which placed too much emphasis on meeting the consortium's business plan and fulfilling the embassy's daily operational needs. Worried that the building's aesthetic did not project a forceful image of Canada, the department asked Shimizu to redraft its proposal. The Japanese company refused, but promised "to strengthen [the] design element of their project team by engaging Raymond Moriyama."[31]

Moriyama, a Canadian architect of Japanese descent, who, along with his family, had been removed from the British Columbia coast during the Second World War, had established a strong reputation in Canadian architectural circles for his sensitive modernism. Trained at the universities of Toronto and McGill in the 1950s, he had completed at the time such award-winning buildings as the Japanese Canadian Cultural Centre in Don Mills (1963), the Ontario Science Centre (1969), and the Metropolitan Toronto Reference Library (1977). Fascinated by Japanese culture, Moriyama was an ideal candidate to design a building to represent how the two societies had come to understand each other better over the previous six decades.[32]

Moriyama's chancery was the last major embassy built by Canada in the twentieth century. By then, the Department of External Affairs was quite experienced in the construction of diplomatic facilities, with a division devoted exclusively to designing, constructing, and managing its extensive real estate holdings abroad. Since the Second World War, the department had developed a set of building standards that took into consideration the evolution of diplomatic life and postwar architectural practices. Among the most important criteria stipulated in the department's generic project brief were that new diplomatic buildings should reflect the architecture of the host country and respect local practices. Significantly, this time, Canadian and Japanese authorities agreed without hesitation to start their collaboration with a Shinto blessing of the site. Indeed, Shinto rituals marked the completion of every phase of the project's progress.

Unlike Marler, Moriyama conceived a chancery inspired by both contemporary and traditional architecture. The overall shape of the building echoes the seventeenth-century Himeji Castle, erected in the Hyogo prefecture during the Momoyama period. The castle presents a stone fortification upon which is perched a more delicate wooden construction covered with plaster. In Moriyama's design, the embassy's sturdy base, with its massive corner pillars, corresponds to the stone work of the castle. The design also makes a reference to the surface treatment of the imperial palace, across the park. The triangular incline of the immense roof – reminiscent of the wooden structure of the Himeji castle – is a result of the "Law of the Sun," a municipal regulation that prohibits the construction of a building that casts a shadow onto neighbouring property. Inside, the concave ceiling of the theatre located in the first and second basements, evokes the Japanese Noh theatre. At a more abstract level, Moriyama claims to have been inspired by the simplicity of Ikebana, the Japanese art of flower arrangement. Finally, the architect constructed a dual garden on the perimeter of the fourth floor, the official entrance of the chancery. One garden represents the Canadian landscape from the Maritimes to the Rockies, while the other is a Zen garden with boulders and sand. Two reflective pools symbolize the Atlantic and Pacific oceans. This second pool, located between the Zen garden and the emblematic mountains of Canada's West Coast, represents the major geographic feature linking the two countries.

At one level, the chancery, considered by many to be one of the most outstanding examples of Canadian diplomatic architecture, emphasizes how much progress the two countries have made towards mutual understanding. Marler's hesitant suspicions have been replaced by genuine cultural sympathy. However, the building's design suggests that the primary objective of the Canadian presence in Tokyo remained unchanged: to facilitate commerce and trade. The financing agreement itself, between private Japanese commercial investors and the Department of External Affairs, provides a strong indication of the direction in which external affairs wished to guide the bilateral relationship. Moreover, in the design phase, the department agreed to sacrifice some of its space, especially the areas slated for cultural services, in order to meet the real estate requirements of its local Japanese partners.

Thus, in contrast to Canada's other recently constructed embassies in Washington and Mexico City, which offer direct access to their public areas on the ground floor, the Tokyo embassy relegated its cultural space to the basement, setting aside the first three floors for leasing. The main door on the busy Aoyamadori Street is designed for this commercial section. Diplomatic or political dignitaries, who would normally arrive by car, enter through the back entrance of the building.[33] But once on the fourth floor, visitors are to be impressed just as they would have been with Marler's gardens and reception rooms, perhaps even more as the terrace opens to spectacular surroundings (see Figure 13.4). Here, visitors can mingle and hold the friendly conversations that Marler saw as the essential basis for developing closer and more profitable relations.

Canada's two diplomatic premises in Tokyo, despite their very different styles, were both designed to encourage and nurture commercial exchange. This aspect was central to Marler's conception of the legation's architecture creating a luxurious setting, in which the minister could impress his guests and persuade them of Canada's value as an economic partner. The new chancery offers a similar environment with the addition of facilities to host

Figure 13.4 Moriyama's rooftop gardens echo Marler's earlier landscaping efforts. *Department of Foreign Affairs and International Trade.*

cultural events. Moriyama planned its remarkable bold geometric forms and intimate garden to appeal to the "gaze of the Japanese eye."[34] Not unlike Marler, Moriyama envisioned a spectacular setting that would show Japan "that we Canadians are open and accessible, that we are ready to reach out to another culture, that we are willing to bow, shake hands, and make a deal."[35]

Notes

1 See M.J. Therrien, *Au-delà des frontières, L'architecture des ambassade canadiennes, 1930-2005* (Quebec: Les Presses de l'Université Laval, 2005), ch. 3.

2 John T. Saywell, "Continuity, Discontinuity, and Asymmetry in Canada-Japan Relations," in John Schultz and Kimitada Miwa, eds., *Canada and Japan in the Twentieth Century* (Toronto: Oxford University Press, 1991), 198.

3 Herbert Marler, "The Canadian Legation in Japan: Recommendations Submitted to the Secretary of State for External Affairs (hereafter SSEA), February 1929, Department of External Affairs Records (hereafter DEAR), vol. 2611, Library and Archives of Canada (hereafter LAC).

4 John D. Meehan, *The Dominion and the Rising Sun: Canada Encounters Japan, 1929-41* (Vancouver: UBC Press, 2004), 2.

5 Hugh Keenleyside to Marler, 10 June 1929, cited in Meehan, *The Dominion and the Rising Sun,* 20.

6 Meehan, *The Dominion and the Rising Sun,* 3.

7 Marler, "The Canadian Legation in Japan [1929]," 33.
8 Ibid.
9 J.L.J. Comaroff, *Of Revelation and Revolution: The Dialectic of Modernity on a South African Frontier* (Chicago: University of Chicago Press, 1997), 2:293.
10 Ibid.
11 Marler, "The Canadian Legation in Japan [1929]," 7.
12 Ibid., 33-34.
13 Herbert Marler, "The Canadian Legation at Tokyo," [1933], R.B. Bennett Papers, Microfilm Reel M892, LAC.
14 Eber H. Rice, "Sir Herbert Marler and the Canadian Legation in Tokyo," in Schultz and Miwa, *Canada and Japan,* 82. In a footnote about this widespread rumour, Rice adds that "Mrs Marler subsequently suggested the most plausible explanation for the advantageous purchase – at least when judged from the standpoint of contemporary business customs in Japan. 'We really got it', she wrote to the former Prime Minister King, 'because we play golf with Viscount Aoyama.'"
15 Antonin Raymond, *Antonin Raymond: An Autobiography* (Rutland, VT: Charles E. Tuttle Publishing, 1973), 29.
16 Hugh Keenleyside, *Hammer the Golden Day: The Memoirs of Hugh L. Keenleyside* (Toronto: McClelland and Stewart, 1981), 292.
17 Marler to Bennett, 3 March 1933, Bennett Papers, Microfilm Reel M891, LAC. The full excerpt reads: "I deal with the chancellery. In that respect I have been delayed owing to the fact that I could not satisfy myself with the floor plans. These I drew out personally time and again before reaching a satisfactory conclusion."
18 Raymond, *Antonin Raymond,* 123.
19 Marler, "The Canadian Legation at Tokyo [1933], 166271.
20 Ibid.
21 Keenleyside, *Hammer the Golden Day,* 436.
22 Marler was so sick that he did not attend the opening of the buildings.
23 Marler, "The Canadian Legation in Japan [1929]," 34.
24 Marler, "The Canadian Legation at Tokyo [1933]," 166271.
25 Marler, "The Canadian Legation in Japan [1929]," 33.
26 Mackenzie King to Marler, 27 December 1933, W.L. MacKenzie King Papers, J8, vol. 26, LAC.
27 "Evaluation Report Embassy Redevelopment Project," 26 January 1978, Foreign Affairs Canada (hereafter FAC), file 11-9-Tokyo-C, Foreign Affairs Canada Archives (hereafter FACA).
28 Memorandum to Alan Gotlieb, Under-Secretary of State for External Affairs, 15 December 1978, FAC file 11-9-Tokyo-C, FACA.
29 J.H. Taylor, "A New Base for Promoting Canada's Interest in Japan," in David Reece, ed., *Special Trust and Confidence: Envoy Essays in Canadian Diplomacy* (Ottawa: Carleton University Press, 1996), 259-60.
30 The Vienna convention prevents countries from making money from diplomatic properties.
31 Shimizu Construction to Christina Perk, Department of External Affairs Architect, 9 December 1985, FAC file 11-9-Tokyo-C, FACA.
32 For Moriyama's account of the planning of the chancery, see his "The New Canadian Embassy in Tokyo: Ambassador Extraordinary," in *Canada among Nations: 1992-93, A New World Order?* ed. Fen Hampson and Christopher Maule (Ottawa: Carleton University Press, 1992), 29-45.
33 Since 11 September 2001, this discreet entrance at the back is definitely more secure than a front entrance.
34 Moriyama, "The New Canadian Embassy in Tokyo," 30.
35 Ibid., 34.

14

Projecting Canada in Japan: Reflections on the Japanese Association for Canadian Studies, 1979-2004

Masako Iino

In the years after 1945, Canada played an important role in helping to smooth Japan's re-entry into the community of nations and, eventually, the United Nations. For much of the postwar period, however, the Japanese people and their government were so preoccupied with the United States that they paid little attention to Canada. Despite the long-standing presence of Canadian Protestant and Roman Catholic missionaries, as explained in this volume in Chapters 1 and 2, or the existence of handsome Canadian embassies in Tokyo as described in Chapter 13, few residents of Japan had actually met a Canadian. Fewer still knew very much about Canada. Indeed, for many years, some Japanese even thought of Canada as part of the United States. Mio, a village in Wakayama prefecture in the western part of Japan, a major source of immigrants to Canada at the turn of the twentieth century, for instance, was popularly known as "America Village."[1] In the mid-1970s, buoyed by a growing nationalism at home, the Canadian government launched a sustained program of cultural diplomacy to reinforce Canadian claims to a distinct place in the world. One result of this initiative, which took advantage of a growing interest in Canada among a handful of Japanese scholars, was the creation of the Japanese Association for Canadian Studies (JACS).

As trade relations between Canada and Japan improved in the mid-1950s, the interest of Japanese scholars in Canada also grew, reinforced by the publication of a handful of books and essays on Canada. One of the first examples was the essay, "Land of Canada and Friends of America" (1954), by Kotaro Tanaka, the Chief Justice of the Supreme Court of Japan. Its description of Canada's political system and constitution gave Japanese readers a general picture of Canada. Ryozo Azuma's widely read text, *A Country Called Canada* (1955), an overview of Canadian geography, history, society, and relations with Japan, remained popular for nearly two decades. An edited volume, *The Study of Canada* (1963), produced by the Research Institute for World Economic Affairs, dealt objectively and comprehensively with the Canadian economy and its relations with Britain and the United States.

This interest continued to develop in the 1960s, as the new concept of the Pacific Rim gave the two countries a geographical link, one reinforced by the steady stream of Japanese tourists who headed to Canada, attracted by Expo '67, the world fair marking Canada's centennial. At the same time, the work of several Canadian scholars, including a history of anarchism by George Woodcock, literary criticism by Northrop Frye, and studies of Japanese history by the scholar-diplomat, E.H. Norman, were translated into Japanese. Though little of this material dealt directly with Canada, it contributed to the mounting interest in Canada and introduced Japanese to Canadians other than Anne of Green Gables, who, though important in drawing Japanese tourists to Prince Edward Island, was a fictional character! Ironically, if one book can be given credit for arousing the interest of Japanese scholars in Canada, it was the translation of *Revolution and Anti-Revolution* (1972) by the American sociologist, Seymour Martin Lipset, which alerted students of the United States in Japan to the possibility of comparative studies.[2]

Though Canadian Studies in Japan remained in an embryonic stage, it soon took a significant step forward. As Greg Donaghy reminds us in Chapter 11, the election of the charismatic Pierre Trudeau, who was determined to pursue a more diversified foreign policy, encouraged Canadian and Japanese policy-makers to think of new ways to promote closer relations between the two countries. As a result, in September 1974, Trudeau and Japanese Prime Minister Kakuei Tanaka issued a joint statement in Ottawa, committing their governments to contribute one million dollars for the promotion of Japanese studies in Canada and Canadian studies in Japan. This cultural agreement paved the way for Canada's foreign ministry to fund Canadian Studies courses at a small number of universities in Japan and to provide money for the translation of books on Canada. It also established a number of scholarships and research grants for Japanese students, and a program that enabled Japanese universities to invite Canadian scholars to offer courses on Canada.

These developments were watched carefully in Canada, where Trent University president Tom Symons was undertaking a major examination of Canadian Studies. Though primarily concerned with Canadian Studies in Canada, the Report of the Commission on Canadian Studies (commonly known as "The Symons Report") also encouraged the government to promote the study of Canada abroad. It noted "with pleasure" the Trudeau-Tanaka initiative and urged Ottawa to provide an annual grant to the Canadian Centre at Sophia University and to find more ways of fostering "a greater interest in and knowledge of Canada at other appropriate universities in Japan."[3]

In explaining the emergence of Canada's interest in promoting Canadian studies abroad, Ramsay Cook, a mentor for many Japanese scholars in the field of Canadian Studies, highlighted three general issues that worried Canadian cultural analysts and policy-makers in the 1970s. In his keynote address to the JACS Annual Conference in 1997, "Canadian Studies in a Multicultural, Postnationalist World," Professor Cook described the promoters of Canadian Studies as "those people who might loosely be characterized as Canadian nationalists," who had a fear that "the great achievements of Canada's first century, unless effectively reinforced, were in danger of withering away under ... the expanding influence of the United States whose economic potential and cultural aggressiveness threatened to 'Americanize' Canada." In Cook's view, two other factors lay behind Ottawa's early support for Canadian studies. First, there was a growing determination to counter "the growth of a new, Quebec-focused, francophone nationalism" with a federal vision of a united Canada. Second, Ottawa welcomed "cultural diplomacy" as an important instrument to help offset Canada's declining stature on the world stage, which was increasingly populated by the rising powers of Asia and Africa, as well as an integrated Europe. It was hoped that encouraging knowledge of Canada through cultural and academic exchanges would help Canada maintain a distinct international presence, promote global understanding, and enhance Canadian trade prospects.[4]

Two events in 1977 suggested that Ottawa's investment in cultural diplomacy in Japan was paying off. That year, the monthly magazine of the Japanese Institute of International Affairs published five articles about Canada. More significantly, a nucleus of eighteen scholars and researchers individually engaged in Canadian studies formed a study group called the Japan Canadian Studies Society in 1977 and held their first annual conference at International House in Tokyo in December of that year.[5] A year later, the name was changed to the Japanese Association for Canadian Studies (JACS).

Acknowledging this nascent interest in Canadian Studies, the Canadian government subsidized the translation into Japanese of three Canadian textbooks and distributed them to Japanese academic institutions and scholars.[6] As Yoshida Kensei, a former official at the Canadian embassy and now a professor at Obirin University, noted, these texts "became essential reading" for those who were interested in learning about Canada "and in many respects, provided the cornerstone for the development of Canadian studies in Japan."[7] Subsequently, several other texts and works of general interest relating to Canada were translated into Japanese, including, for example, the memoirs of Hugh Keenleyside, several studies by John T. Saywell, and collections of essays by Pierre Trudeau and Ramsay Cook. Several of the translators, particularly Nobuya Bamba and Yuko Ohara, had an important role in founding JACS.

Thus, the establishment of JACS was part of a broader Canadian national project, and it also had significant meaning for those in Japan who were interested in learning about Canada. It united more than one hundred scholars, researchers, and students who had been studying particular aspects of Canada in isolation or in small groups throughout Japan. The birth of JACS provided them with a central organization and allowed many researchers who had considered Canada only as a marginal extension of their primary specialties to see and deal with Canada as a major and distinct theme of their research. Proudly, they came to call themselves "Canadianists." With a current membership of close to four hundred, JACS holds an annual conference and a number of regional study seminars. Besides producing its *Annual Review of Canadian Studies*, the association has published several books on Canada, including *Documentary Canada*, a collection of important historical documents. In 2004, JACS celebrated its twenty-fifth anniversary along with the seventy-fifth anniversary of the establishment of diplomatic relations between Canada and Japan.

The evolution of JACS over the past twenty-five years reveals the maturation of Canadian studies in Japan. As mentioned already, with the exception of a few pioneering works, Canadian studies in Japan started with a series of books translated from English or, in a few cases, French, into Japanese. Works of translation still abound and have played an important role in introducing Canada to general Japanese audiences. Beginning in the 1990s, however, a great change in the field of Canadian Studies has been observed in Japan as the number of original books and papers about Canada by Japanese scholars and researchers has grown. These publications deal with subjects as varied as history, federalism, multiculturalism, labour law, local government, literature, diplomacy and defence, trade, economics, education, and culture. In addition, collaborative research between Canadian and Japanese scholars has increased. Noteworthy results have been published, both in Japan and in Canada, particularly in the fields of Canadian politics, Canada-Japan relations, and Japanese Canadians.[8] The variety of such work is well illustrated by the papers published in the *JACS Annual Reviews*. The 2003 issue, for example, included papers on topics as varied as Stephen Leacock, Chinese and Punjabi speakers in Vancouver, and second-language education in Canada.[9] While the number of these studies has increased, some commentators have criticized their usefulness and have suggested that few of them generate much interest beyond a small circle of experts. Others claim that, with the exception of those dealing with Canada-Japan relations and Japanese Canadians, these works are not sufficiently academically sophisticated to be published in Canada. Nonetheless, these changes should be considered encouraging signs of the maturing of Canadian Studies in Japan. At the same time, Japanese Canadianists believe that their works represent a unique addition to Canadian Studies as a whole.

A second notable change can be seen in the make-up of Japanese Canadianists themselves. Unlike the older generation of scholars who came into the field through other programmes, notably American Studies or an interest in comparative studies, a younger generation, with support from the Canadian government, has studied in Canadian universities in such fields as political science, economics, history, and sociology. Members of this younger generation are quite active in JACS and promote Canadian Studies at their home universities. JACS is now in its second generation, or even its third.

Of course, the older Japanese Association for American Studies remains much larger, with approximately thirteen hundred members, and more universities offer more courses in American than in Canadian Studies. Nevertheless, JACS members are rightfully proud of the remarkably rapid growth of Canadian Studies. The number of universities and colleges offering courses on Canada has increased from five in the 1970s to almost fifty in 2003, mainly due to the Canadian government's funding efforts and the missionary activities of JACS members. The number of Canada-related courses, programs, and lecture series at universities and colleges is now seventy, with an estimated enrolment of almost six thousand students. Several local governments and community organizations have also invited JACS members to offer popular education seminars and lecture series on Canada. Indeed, the variety and depth of the accomplishments of JACS members is so highly regarded in the academic circle in Japan that the Japanese government, which has paid much more attention to American studies, finally took notice. In 1996, in response to JACS pressure, Tokyo unveiled a new grant program to enable several Japanese Canadianists to spend three months each year researching in Canada, and an equal number of Canadian Japanologists to spend time in Japan. JACS has been responsible for selecting the Japanese recipients of this grant every year.

While Canadian Studies was developed in Canada in response to the anxieties arising from a fear of Americanization, Canadian Studies programmes in Japan have paradoxically tended to model themselves on their American predecessors. However, this too has begun to change, as the paths of the two study programs have diverged. During the late 1980s and the post-cold war era, when there was conspicuous friction between Washington and Tokyo, some Japanese scholars of American Studies felt that their field should focus more on providing scholars and the public with a broad view of American society in an effort to halt the deterioration of relations between the two countries. Although they realized that their influence would remain rather limited, they sought to restrain the Japanese media's "sensationalistic tendency and to present sober views of American affairs and U.S.-Japanese relations."[10]

In contrast, Japanese Canadianists have been increasingly drawn to the study of multiculturalism, which has been for several years a popular theme at various conferences in Japan, including at least one JACS conference. Many Japanese scholars have been interested in learning about it from a variety of perspectives: as a policy in the field of law or ethnic relations, and in the disciplines of history and sociology. To many Canadianists, the greatest difference between Canada and Japan lies in their ethnic structures. They had already observed that ethnic structure, of course, showed the greatest difference between the United States and Japan. The Japanese people are not entirely mono-ethnic, and there is a sizable population of non-Japanese permanent residents in Japan. It is undeniable, however, that Japan has a much more homogeneous population than the United States or Canada and that Japanese democracy and social tranquility depend largely on this high degree of homogeneity.

Japanese Americanists had been interested in American society with its multiracial, multi-ethnic, and multicultural population and were anxious to learn how the United States dealt with this population in a liberal democracy. Subsequently, these scholars discovered Canada and its unique and intriguing "multiculturalism" policy. At the time, Japan had started to receive a large number of immigrants from South America and southeast Asia and was engaged in a heated discussion on immigration policy, and on whether the door should be open or closed. The Japanese people have much to learn from the experiences of the people of Canada. Thus, a comparison of Canadian and American multiculturalism policies drew the interest of Japanese Canadianists. The views of Japanese Canadianists, of course, can also be a unique addition to Canadian Studies as a whole.

Now, as "globalization" replaces "multiculturalism" as a keyword in twenty-first century Canadian Studies, Japanese Canadianists can have an important role in bringing a comparative perspective to Canadian Studies. The popular recent themes at JACS conferences have been security matters, health care systems, and international contributions such as peacekeeping operations and non-governmental organizations.

Where should JACS head next? When I was president of JACS (1996-2000), I made it clear that JACS must let the outside world know about the research and studies being carried out in the field of Canadian Studies in Japan. The period for simply learning from Canadian scholars was long past, and it was now time to share. In other words, I tried to convince JACS members that we should share with Canadianists in other nations what we have been doing in Japan. It would raise the level of our scholarship, as we would learn not only from Canadian scholars in Canada but from Canadianists in other countries. At the same time, we would contribute to Canadian Studies in Canada and elsewhere by offering our unique vision of the Canadian experience, past and present. Recently, JACS has begun to move in this direction.

Let me conclude by citing three recent accomplishments that collectively aim to bring JACS more into the Canadian Studies mainstream. First, like many academic organizations, JACS is trying to encourage broader linkages by developing its web page (http://www.jacs.jp) in three languages: Japanese, English, and French. Second, the association is working to overcome the relative isolation imposed by the Japanese language, and has encouraged its members to publish more in English (or, to a lesser extent, in French), a step possible due to the increased number of Canadianists who have been educated in Canada. Third, JACS has been working to incorporate itself more closely in the international network of Canadian Studies associations. In 1998, JACS organized, with the support of the Canadian government, the Asia-Pacific Conference on Canadian Studies in Tokyo, bringing to Japan leading Canadianists from Asia, Australia, and New Zealand, as well as from Canada and the United States. Its great success led to subsequent conferences in Australia and Korea and has sparked hopes that this dialogue in the international Canadian Studies community will continue and expand, benefiting all Canadianists, wherever they are. Although I am fully aware of the limit of area studies, I also believe strongly that area studies can contribute a great deal to international relations.

Notes

1 Patricia Roy, Jack Granatstein, Masako Iino, and Hiroko Takamura, *Mutual Hostages: Canadians and Japanese during the Second World War* (Toronto: University of Toronto Press, 1990), 5.

2 This paragraph and the previous one draw on Yoshida Kensei, "Canadian Studies in Japan," in *Canada and Japan in the Twentieth Century*, ed. John Schultz and Kimitada Miwa (Toronto: Oxford University Press, 1991), 213-23, which provides many other examples.

3 T.H.B. Symons, *To Know Ourselves: The Report of the Commission on Canadian Studies* (Ottawa: Association of Universities and Colleges of Canada, 1975), 2:55.

4 The speech was published as Ramsay Cook, "Canadian Studies in a Multicultural, Postnationalist World," Japanese Association for Canadian Studies, *Annual Review of Canadian Studies*, 18 (1998): 49-62.

5 A chronological history of JACS can be found at its website: http://www.jacs.jp/English/index.html.

6 These books were Kenneth McNaught, *The Pelican History of Canada* (London: Allan Lane, 1976); Ian M. Drummond, *The Canadian Economy: Structure and Development* (Georgetown, ON: Irwin-Dorsey, 1972); and John Saywell and J. Ricker, *How Are We Governed?* (Toronto: Clarke Irwin, 1961).

7 Kensei, "Canadian Studies in Japan," 214.

8 One recent example is Mitsuru Kurosawa and John Kirton, eds., *The Triangle of Pacific States: Contemporary United States, Canada, Japan Relations* (Tokyo: Sairyusha, 1995).

9 The tables of contents for the *Annual Reviews* since 1979 are listed on the JACS website, http://www.jacs.jp/English/index.html.

10 Tadashi Aruga, "Japanese Scholarship and the Meaning of American History," *Journal of American History* 79 (September 1992): 511.

Conclusion

Patricia E. Roy and Greg Donaghy

Canada's relations with Japan in the twentieth century were ambiguous and often contradictory. Nevertheless, as the essays collected in this volume demonstrate, Japan has long been an important point of contact between Canadians and their world. Though progress was rarely steady, over the past century, Canada has slowly entered into a more multifaceted relationship with Japan, but one that is still complex, uncertain, and incompletely understood. Perhaps, as Prime Minister Stephen Harper suggested during the visit in June 2006 of his Japanese counterpart, Junichiro Koizumi, because recent relations have been "relatively irritant free," the two countries "haven't tended the relationship as closely as we should."[1]

Contradictions in the Canada-Japan relationship have a long history. Canada's relations with Japan in the late nineteenth and early twentieth centuries were surprisingly vibrant and warm, despite the racism that generally characterized attitudes towards the Japanese. As the opening chapters of this collection emphasize, the early relationship was largely rooted in Canada's membership in the British Empire. Canadians welcomed the emergence of modern Japan and were enthusiastic in finding their country allied with Tokyo under the Anglo-Japanese Treaty of 1902. Trade followed the empire and the "all-red" route to Asia, fuelled by visions of unparalleled riches. "Take it for granted," Lord Grey, the governor-general, crowed in 1908, "we are on the eve of a growing demand for flour and wheat which will grow to enormous dimensions at first from Japan, and later on from the great continent of which Japan is only the porch."[2]

Canadian Protestant and Catholic missionaries also flocked to Japan. Chapters by Hamish Ion and Richard Leclerc remind us that despite their linguistic and theological differences, the two groups had remarkably similar goals and not very dissimilar methods. Canadian missionaries established a beachhead in Japan with their educational and social work, but they won few followers. Though they enjoyed a prominent voice in national discussions on how Canada should deal with Japan, their efforts did little to defuse the hostility that many Canadians long felt towards Japanese immigrants.

Her other imperial partner – the United States – played an important role, too, in influencing Canada's early encounters with Japan. Much British Columbia rhetoric against Japanese immigration was borrowed from California, while the Gentlemen's Agreement that regulated it after 1907 was based on an American model. Immigration and its restrictions created an enduring source of bilateral resentment. Fear of Tokyo's intentions in the Pacific compounded these sentiments. Though Canadians depended on Japan to patrol its western shores during the First World War, by the 1920s, some viewed the island chain with suspicion and fretted about being trapped in an imperial rivalry between Washington and Tokyo.

During the interwar period, relations with Japan remained uncertain and were marked by contradictory urges towards cooperation and conflict. While the Orient's legendary wealth continued to beckon, prompting the government to open a diplomatic mission in Tokyo in 1929, Ottawa's antipathy to Japanese immigration cast a shadow over bilateral relations. Even greater dangers lurked in the Pacific. Japan's seizure of Manchuria in 1931 and its assault on China in 1937 sparked a divisive debate among Canadians over their ties to Tokyo and how to handle Japanese aggression. Anglo-American differences over the Japanese threat in the Pacific troubled Ottawa as well, and underlined the dangers of great power rivalry for a small country like Canada.

Mounting concern with the American strategic stake in Asia largely shaped Canada's wartime and postwar attitude towards Japan and persuaded a generation of policy-makers that Canada had no independent interest in relations with Tokyo. During the Pacific War, from 1941 to 1945, Ottawa emphasized home defence. In doing so, it responded to domestic demands for protection, retained control of its coastal defences, and gave priority to the much larger Canadian effort in Europe. The war destroyed the process of discovering Japan that had engaged missionaries, traders, and diplomats in the interwar decades. Worse, the removal of Japanese Canadians from the West Coast and the harsh treatment of Canadian POWs in Japanese camps reinforced the long tradition of animosity that had always been a brake on bilateral relations. Any prospect that Canada might re-engage Japan quickly receded during Allied negotiations over occupation policy. Washington's determination to dictate the peace in Japan for cold war reasons warned off Canadian diplomats, who directed their efforts elsewhere.

Even so, over the next two decades, elements of the Canada-Japan relationship slowly evolved in response to outside forces. The defeat of Nazi Germany and the ideological nature of the cold war gave renewed impetus to human rights, encouraging Ottawa to dismantle its restrictive immigration policies. The Japanese, too, showed a new interest in Canada as their booming postwar economy drove them overseas in search of markets and plentiful sources of raw materials. And in both countries, technological change and the wealth that accompanied postwar economic expansion encouraged trans-Pacific travel and personal contact.

Prime Minister Pierre Trudeau sensed the change and responded with a search for deeper and broader relations with Tokyo. Building on manifestations of mutual interest was not and has not been easy or straightforward. Despite the efforts at cross-cultural understanding explored by Masako Iino and Marie-Josée Therrien, popular prejudices remain complicating factors in the relationship. Though the Canadian embassy in Tokyo echoes Japanese design values, Therrien insists that older, more dangerous influences linger nearby. This historical inheritance, though clearly no longer as strong as it once was, still matters, giving rise to sharp disagreement about the intensity of the contemporary relationship.

Carin Holroyd's position is clear: the seductive presence of the United States, an economic and cultural superpower on Canada's doorstep, continues to constrain relations with Japan, often pulling Canadians south rather than west. In contrast, John Kirton insists that the American influence is increasingly offset by larger international forces, which have slowly brought Canada and Japan closer together since 1945. Despite differences in subject and emphasis, this theme finds an echo in most of the volume's chapters dealing with the postwar period. Kirton perhaps overstates his case, exaggerating the extent to which relations have become a "full-powered, comprehensive, multilayered, deeply domestically penetrating" partnership. Nonetheless, he is right when he argues that recent summit-level forces have freed Canada and Japan from the vicissitudes of bilateralism and forced the two countries to confront each other. However complex the international influences that mould the Ottawa-Tokyo axis, one thing is certain: in this century, as in the last, Canada's relations with Japan will be shaped in large measure by the great-power rivalries that swirl around and across the Pacific.

While much is known about relations before 1945, the postwar process of bilateral rapprochement remains only incompletely understood. This volume, we hope, suggests further lines of inquiry. More detailed study of the postwar relationship, for instance, might flesh out precisely how diplomatic and political initiatives were related to changing attitudes towards nonwhite immigration and evolving trade relations. It would be particularly useful to explore relations in their multilateral setting after 1955, when Canada helped Japan join the UN, or after 1961, when both were associated in the Organization for European Co-operation and Development (OECD). Possibly, many of the recent systemic influences that Kirton detects are rooted in this earlier period.

Equally important, several of the chapters in this volume emphasize the value and importance of "soft power" and cultural influences in the contemporary Canada-Japan relationship. Part of the investigation of these contacts will undoubtedly probe the continuing fascination of Japanese girls for the Anne of Green Gables novels or the passion of Japanese teenagers for the cult-film *Cube*, by the Toronto-based screenwriter, Andre Bijelic. Others might explore the meaning behind the boom in Japanese weddings in the Rockies or the rapid expansion of sushi outlets in urban Canada. This investigation might also examine how closely and directly the new technologies of communication are connecting Canadians and Japanese in a globalized world. Virtual networks make it easier for individuals and substate institutions – NGOs, cities, or regional governments – to transcend traditional forms of state-to-state relations. Clearly, we must wonder, what does all this mean for Canada-Japan relations in the twenty-first century?

Notes

1 Mike Blanchfield, "PM takes jab at liberals for ignoring Japan," *Times-Colonist* (Victoria), 29 June 2006.

2 Robert Joseph Gowen, "Canada and the Myth of the Japan Market, 1896-1911," *Pacific Historical Review* 39 (February 1970): 71.

Suggested Reading

There is no comprehensive overview of Canada-Japan relations for the entire twentieth century. Two early efforts – A.R.M. Lower, *Canada and the Far East – 1940* (New York: IPR, 1940) and Charles J. Woodsworth, *Canada and the Orient* (Toronto: Macmillan, 1941) – deal with the pre-war period, focus only intermittently on Japan, and can most usefully be read today as historical documents. Despite its title and its author's long-standing interest in Japan and Japanese Canadians, H.F. Angus, *Canada and the Far East, 1940-1953* (Toronto: UTP, 1953) scarcely mentions Japan. Two very useful series sponsored by the Canadian Institute of International Affairs also contain material on contemporary views of the Canada-Japan relationship. The six-volume *The War* (Toronto: Oxford University Press, 1940-46) covers the period 1939-45 and overlaps with *Canada and World Affairs* (Toronto: OUP and Canadian Institute of International Affairs, 1941-80), each of whose volumes cover a period, usually about two years, from the immediate pre-war years to 1965, when the series ended.

Reflecting the growing interest in Japan that was sparked by Prime Minister Pierre Trudeau in the mid-1970s, several overviews of the relationship appeared after 1980. Sponsored by Canada's Department of External Affairs, Klaus H. Pringsheim's *Neighbors across the Pacific: The Development of Economic and Political Relations between Canada and Japan* (Westwood, CT: Greenwood, 1983) is based mainly on Canadian sources, but also draws on the records of the *Gaimushō,* Japan's Ministry of Foreign Affairs, and interviews with both Japanese and Canadian officials. More broadly based is a somewhat eclectic collection of essays edited by John Schultz and Kimitada Miwa, *Canada and Japan in the Twentieth Century* (Toronto: OUP, 1991). Both volumes are now dated, and neither thoroughly studies the relationship after 1945. A brief history of Quebec's relations with Japan may be found in Richard Leclerc's *Des Lys à l'ombre du mont Fuji: Cent ans de présence québécoise au Japan* (Quebec: Ministère des Relations Internationales, 1998).

An indispensable guide for researchers seeking primary sources on Canada-Japan relations is G. Raymond Nunn's *Canada and Asia: Guide to Archive and Manuscript Sources in Canada*, vol. 1 (London: Mansell, 1999).

Much of the early Canadian literature about Canada and Japan focused on the work of missionaries. Representative of older, detailed church-sponsored studies is a two-volume account of the first century of United Church of Canada work in Japan: Gwen Norman and W.H.H. Norman, *One Hundred Years in Japan, 1873-1973* (Toronto: Division of World Outreach, United Church of Canada, 1981). The definitive works on Canadian Protestants are A. Hamish Ion, *The Cross and the Rising Sun: The Canadian Protestant Missionary Movement in the Japanese Empire 1872-1931* (Waterloo: Wilfrid Laurier University Press, 1990) and *The Cross in the Dark Valley: The Canadian Protestant Missionary Movement in the Japanese Empire, 1931-1945* (Waterloo, ON: Wilfrid Laurier University Press, 1999). Rosemary R. Gagan has written on Canadian Methodist women missionaries in China and Japan, *A Sensitive Independence: Canadian Methodist Women Missionaries in Canada and the Orient, 1881-1925* (Montreal: McGill-Queen's University Press, 1992). An important biography of the most famous YWCA worker in early-twentieth-century Japan is Margaret Prang, *A Heart at Leisure from Itself: Caroline Macdonald of Japan* (Vancouver: UBC Press, 1995). The unpublished *Guide to Archival Resources on Canadian Missionaries in East Asia: 1890-1960* prepared by Alyvn Austin, Margo Gewurtz, and Peter Mitchell for the University of Toronto-York University Centre for Asia Pacific Studies (1988) is an essential tool for researchers in this field.

The son of one missionary couple, the historian and controversial diplomat E. Herbert Norman, is the subject of several biographies. Accused of spying for the Soviet Union in the 1950s, his foremost prosecutor since then has been the American James Barros, *No Sense of Evil: Espionage, The Case of Herbert Norman* (Toronto: Deneau, 1986). More helpfully, his main defender, also American, Roger Bowen, has published an edited collection on *E.H. Norman: His Life and Scholarship* (Toronto: University of Toronto Press, 1984) and a biography, *Innocence Is Not Enough* (Toronto: Douglas and McIntyre, 1986). Other significant contributions to the voluminous literature on Norman include Charles Taylor, *Six Journeys: A Canadian Pattern* (Toronto: Anansi Press, 1977), Greg Donaghy, ed., *Herbert Norman: A Documentary Perspective* (Ottawa: Department of Foreign Affairs, 1999), and the contributions collected in Larry Wood's sixtieth anniversary edition of Norman's *Japan's Emergence as a Modern State* (Vancouver: UBC Press, 2000). A dispassionate look at Norman's career was a report commissioned by Joe Clark, Canada's foreign minister in 1989, Peyton Lyon, "The Loyalties of E. Herbert Norman" (Ottawa: External Affairs and International Trade, 18 March 1990).

The literature on the Japanese experience in Canada is extensive. The best overall survey is still Ken Adachi, *The Enemy That Never Was* (Toronto: McClelland and Stewart, 1976). The long-standing hostility of British Columbians to Japanese (and Chinese) immigrants is analyzed in W. Peter Ward, *White Canada Forever*, 3rd ed. (Montreal and Kingston: McGill-Queen's University Press, 2002 [first edition, 1978]) and in three volumes by Patricia E. Roy, *A White Man's Province: British Columbia Politicians and Chinese and Japanese Immigrants, 1858-1914* (Vancouver: UBC Press, 1989); *The Oriental Question: Consolidating a White Man's Province, 1914-41* (Vancouver: UBC Press, 2003); and *The Triumph of Citizenship: The Japanese and Chinese in Canada, 1941-67* (Vancouver: UBC Press, 2007).

In order of publication, the major works on the wartime experiences of the Japanese in Canada are Forrest E. LaViolette, *The Canadian Japanese and World War II* (Toronto: University of Toronto Press, 1948); Ann Gomer Sunahara, *The Politics of Racism: The Uprooting of Japanese Canadians during the Second World War* (Toronto: Lorimer, 1981); and Patricia E. Roy, J.L. Granatstein, Masako Iino, and Hiroko Takamura, *Mutual Hostages: Canadians and Japanese during the Second World War* (Toronto: University of Toronto Press, 1989). As its subtitle indicates, the last includes material on Canadians who were in Japan or Japanese-occupied territory during the war.

Canadian military history remains one of the largest sectors in Canadian publishing, and its reach obviously covers operations in the Pacific War. The official history is C.P. Stacey's magisterial *Six Years of War: The Army in Canada, Britain and the Pacific* (Ottawa: Queen's Printer, 1965). A good and very readable account of Canada's overseas role in Asia is Brereton Greenhous, *"C" Force to Hong Kong: A Canadian Catastrophe* (Toronto: Dundurn Press, 1997). The home front is covered in Kenneth Coates, ed., *The Alaska Highway: Papers of the 40th Anniversary Symposium* (Vancouver: UBC Press, 1985). The Aleutian campaign is very ably treated in Galen Perras, *Stepping Stones to Nowhere: The Aleutian Islands, Alaska, and American Military Strategy, 1867-1945* (Vancouver: UBC Press, 2003).

For the experiences of Canadian POWs, in addition to *Mutual Hostages* mentioned above, readers should consult Charles G. Roland, *Long Night's Journey into Day: Prisoners of War in Hong Kong and Japan, 1941-1945* (Waterloo, ON: Wilfrid Laurier University Press, 2001). A number of former prisoners have published their memoirs. Two examples are Kenneth G. Baird, *Letters to Harvelyn* (Toronto: Harper Collins, 2002) and George S. MacDonell, *One Soldier's Story, 1939-1945* (Toronto: Dundurn, 2002). Canada's small role in the war trials is covered in Patrick Brode, *Casual Slaughters and Accidental Judgments: Canadian War Crimes Prosecutions, 1944-1948* (Toronto: University of Toronto Press, 1997). Hamish Ion is currently writing a book on this subject.

Given Canada's interest in the Japanese market and the extent of Japanese investment in Canada, it is not surprising that there is a growing library of specialized studies on particular aspects of the economic relationship. Initial trade relations are covered extensively in Robert J. Gowen, "Canada and the Myth of the Japanese Market, 1896-1911," *Pacific Historical Review* 39, 1 (1970): 63-83, and Michael G. Fry, "The Development of Canada's Relations with Japan, 1919-1947," in *Canadian Perspectives on Economic Relations with Japan*, ed. Keith Hay (Montreal: IRPP, 1980). The balance of this technical and policy-oriented collection covers narrow issues in the 1960s and 1970s. Other early studies on economic relations are cited in the notes to John Kirton's essay in this volume. Carin Holroyd and Ken Coates, *Pacific Partners* (Toronto: James Lorimer, 1996), have produced an especially good and readable overview of the contemporary picture. Michael Fry, John Kirton, and Mitsuru Kurosawa offer a more theoretical perspective in the controversial collection they edited, *The North Pacific Triangle: The United States, Japan, and Canada at Century's End* (Toronto: University of Toronto Press, 1998). The latter also includes essays on international security in the 1990s, with a limited amount of historical background. This is one of the few collections to include both Canadian and Japanese perspectives, and its notes offer a good guide to the contemporary literature in both languages. *Why Japan Matters!* is an eclectic collection of sixty-one papers presented at the 2004 Japan Studies Association of Canada conference. Edited by Joseph F. Kess and Helen Lansdowne (Victoria: Centre for Asia-Pacific Initiatives, 2005), it concentrates on Japan but has several brief essays on its contemporary relationship with Canada, comparing such diverse issues as health care and linguistic policy.

One of the most prolific Canadian scholars writing today on Canada-Japan relations is the political scientist John Kirton. His ideas have stimulated much academic debate. In addition to Holroyd's chapter in this collection, see her article, "The Costs of Falling Behind: Canada's Economic Relationship with Japan," *Canada Asia Commentary* 38 (February 2005). See also Charles McMillan, *Approaching the Millennium: Canada and Japan in the New Era* (Ottawa: Canada Japan Trade Council, 1999); Yuen Pau Woo, "The Re-emergence of the Re-emergence of Asia," *International Journal* 58 (Autumn 2003): 615-36; Yves Tiberghien, *Japan is Changing! Significant Reforms and Debates in Post-1996 Japan: Implications for Canada,* Canada in Asia Series on the Foreign Policy Dialogue (Vancouver: Asia Pacific Foundation of Canada, 2003); Anna Turinov and Yuen Pau Woo, "Canada-Japan Relations at 75: New Reasons to Revive an Old Relationship," *Canada Asia Commentary* 37 (October 2004); and Julian Dierkes and Yves Tiberghien, "Shall We Dance?" *Globe and Mail,* 18 January 2005, A19. An older but still useful survey is Wendy Dobson, "The Future of the Japan-Canada Economic Relationship" (1999) available at http://www.rotman.utoronto.ca/bicpapers/199907.pdf.

Works on Canada-Japan diplomatic relations remain thin on the ground. The documentary series produced by the Historical Section of the Department of Foreign Affairs and International Trade, *Documents on Canadian External Affairs,* contains considerable material on relations with Japan from 1908, when it begins, to the early 1960s. Additional volumes appear annually. These dry government telegrams and memoranda can be supplemented by the more lively memoirs of Canadian diplomats. An account of the early years of Canada's Tokyo legation may be found in *Memoirs of Hugh L. Keenleyside: Hammer the Golden Day* (Toronto: McClelland and Stewart, 1981). Other Canadian representatives in Japan who have produced shorter reminiscences include: K.P. Kirkwood, *The Diplomat at Table* (Metuchen: Scarecrow Press, 1974); J.P. Manion, *A Canadian Errant* (Toronto: Ryerson, 1960); and J.H. Taylor, "A New Base for Promoting Canada's Interest in Japan," in *"Special Trust and Confidence": Envoy Essays in Canadian Diplomacy,* ed. David Reece (Ottawa: Carleton University Press, 1996). Derek Burney, who served in Tokyo as a junior diplomat in the 1960s and in Ottawa as the head of the Pacific Division, devotes considerable attention to Japan in his recent volume of memoirs, *Getting It Done: A Memoir* (Montreal and Kingson: McGill-Queen's University Press, 2005). So too does Alan McGill, who was a senior officer at the Canadian embassy in Tokyo in the early 1960s. See his *My Life as I Remember It* (Abbotsford: Granville Island Publishing, 2004). Arthur Menzies, who served as head of legation in Tokyo from 1950 to 1953, is reportedly at work on his memoirs as well.

Two good pieces on key events in Canadian diplomacy during the interwar period are Michael G. Fry, "The North Atlantic Triangle and the Abrogation of the Anglo-Japanese Alliance," in his edited collection, *Illusions of Security: North Atlantic Diplomacy, 1918-22* (Toronto: University of Toronto Press, 1972), and D.C. Story, "Canada, the League of Nations and the Far East, 1931-33: The Cahan Incident," *International History Review* 3, 2 (1981): 244-45. John D. Meehan's *The Dominion and the Rising Sun: Canada Encounters Japan, 1929-41* (Vancouver: UBC Press, 2004) offers definitive coverage of the period. Sadly, there is little on postwar diplomacy.

A government of Japan website prepared by the Ministry of Foreign Affairs of Japan, "Japan-Canada Relations" (http://www.mofa.go.jp/region/n-america/canada/), contains much valuable recent information about Japan's relations with Canada. A similar page from the Canadian perspective, from Foreign Affairs and International Trade Canada, "Canada in Japan," can be found at http://geo.international.gc.ca/asia/main/japan/menu-en.asp.

This list includes only the major and readily accessible English-language sources on Canada-Japan relations. The notes accompanying the articles in this volume also provide leads for those who wish to pursue the fascinating topic of Canada-Japan relations.

Glossary

Airindan: social welfare and educational centre established in Tokyo in 1920 by Canadian Methodist missionary Percy Price.

bushidō: traditional ethical code of the samurai or warrior class.

Diet: the Japanese parliament.

Dōjinsha: a leading private school established in Tokyo by Nakamura Masanao in 1873 where the Canadian Methodist, George Cochran, taught between 1874 and 1877.

Gaimushō: Japan's Ministry of Foreign Affairs.

Issei: immigrant, or first-generation, Japanese Canadians.

kamikaze: literally "divine wind"; a Japanese pilot on a suicide mission.

Kirisutokyōdan (also known as the Kyōdan): Union Protestant Church formed in 1941 through the amalgamation of all major Protestant denominations, save for the rump of the Japan Anglican Church (the Nippon Seikōkai).

kokutai: a set of uniquely Japanese ideas that provided a political framework within which to place the system of constitutional monarchy adopted under the Meiji Constitution of 1889.

Kwansei Gakuin: boys' school and university in Nishinomiya established in 1886 by Methodist Episcopal South missionary W.R. Lambuth.

Meiji: Japanese Emperor who reigned between 1868 and 1912. Those years are known as the Meiji period.

Nihon Kirisutokyōdan: see Kirisutokyōdan.

Nipponteki Kirisutokyō: a nationalistic Japanese form of Christianity devoid of Western influence.

Nisei: second-generation Japanese Canadians, but the first born in Canada.

Shinto: an indigenous Japanese religion.

Shizuoka Eiwa Jo Gakkō: girls' school established by the Canadian Methodist missionary Mary Cunningham in Shizuoka in 1887 and opened in 1889.

Tenno: name given to Japanese Emperor.

Tennosei: term used to denote system of Emperor worship.

tōkkō kempetai: Special Military Gendarmerie responsible for stamping out dangerous thoughts.

Tokugawa: family name of the Japanese shoguns who ruled Japan from 1603 to 1868.

Tokyo Joshi Daigaku: Tokyo Woman's Christian University, a union Christian educational institution established in 1918 with Nitobe Inazō as its first president.

Tōyō Eiwa Gakkō: boys' school established in Tokyo by the Canadian Methodist missionary, George Cochran, in 1882.

Tsuda Juku Daigaku: girls' school established in Tokyo by the well-known Christian educator, Tsuda Umeko, in 1900.

Yamanshi Eiwa Jo Gakkō: girls' school established by the Canadian Methodist missionary, Agnes Wintemute, in Kofu in 1889.

zaibatsu: a business cartel or conglomerate.

Contributors

Greg Donaghy is Head of the Historical Section at Foreign Affairs and International Trade Canada.

Carin Holroyd is Senior Research Analyst at the Asia Pacific Foundation of Canada and a Senior Fellow at the Centre for International Governance Innovation (CIGI) in Waterloo, Ontario.

Masako Iino is President of Tsuda College in Kodaira, Tokyo.

Hamish A. Ion is Professor of History at the Royal Military College in Kingston, Ontario.

John Kirton is Associate Professor of Political Science at the Munk Centre for International Studies at the University of Toronto.

Gregory A. Johnson teaches at the Centre for Global and Social Analysis and in the MA Integrated Studies Program at Athabasca University.

Richard Leclerc is an independent researcher specializing in Japanese and Quebec Studies.

John D. Meehan, S.J., is Visiting Scholar at the Asian Institute, Munk Centre for International Studies at the University of Toronto.

Galen Roger Perras is Assistant Professor of History at the University of Ottawa.

John Price is Professor of History at the University of Victoria.

Bill Rawling is a historian with the Directorate of History and Heritage at the Department of National Defence, Ottawa.

Greg Robinson is Associate Professor of History at the Université du Québec à Montréal.

Patricia E. Roy is Professor Emeritus of History at the University of Victoria.

David Sulz is an independent historian based in Edmonton.

Marie-Josée Therrien is Assistant Professor of Art History at the Ontario College of Art and Design.

Index

Bold indicates illustrations.

Printed and bound in Canada by Friesens
Set in Stone by Artegraphica Design Co. Ltd.
Copy editor: Andy Carroll
Proofreader: Dianne Tiefensee
Cartographer: Eric Leinberger